STOCK TRADER'S ALMANAC 2011

Jeffrey A. Hirsch & Yale Hirsch

WILEY

John Wiley & Sons, Inc.

www.stocktradersalmanac.com

Editor in Chief	Jeffrey A. Hirsch
Editor at Large	Yale Hirsch
Director of Research	Christopher Mistal
Graphic Design	Darlene Dion Design

For general information about our other products and services, please contact our Customer Care Department within the United States at 800-762-2974, outside the United States at 317-572-3993 or fax 317-572-4002.

Wiley also publishes its books in a variety of electronic formats. Some content that appears in print may not be available in electronic books. For more information about Wiley products, visit our Web site at www.wiley.com.

ISBN 13: 978-0-470-55744-0
ISBN 10: 0-470-55744-3
10 9 8 7 6 5 4 3 2 1

Printed in China

This Forty-Fourth Edition is respectfully dedicated to:

Kenneth L. Fisher

Ken first came to our attention with, *The Wall Street Waltz*, our "Best Investment Book of 1988," still one of the best books on the market we've ever read. His latest book, *How to Smell a Rat: The Five Signs of Financial Fraud* (page 114–116), was a *New York Times* and *Wall Street Journal* bestseller. Ken's 1970s theoretical work developed the Price-to-Sales ratio, a vital component of our stock picking. Today Ken heads Fisher Investments, a highly-rated $39 billion money management firm, and for over 25 years has written the *Forbes Portfolio Strategy* column. Over three decades of amazingly accurate stock market forecasting and prescience have made Ken one of the most influential people on Wall Street. His father, legendary investor Philip A. Fisher (*Common Stocks and Uncommon Profits*), who died in 2004 at the age of 97, must have been quite proud.

INTRODUCTION TO THE FORTY-FOURTH EDITION

We are pleased and proud to introduce the Forty-Fourth Edition of the *Stock Trader's Almanac*. The *Almanac* provides you with the necessary tools to invest successfully in the twenty-first century.

J. P. Morgan's classic retort, "Stocks will fluctuate," is often quoted with a wink-of-the-eye implication that the only prediction one can make about the stock market is that it will go up, down, or sideways. Many investors agree that no one ever really knows which way the market will move. Nothing could be further from the truth.

We discovered that while stocks do indeed fluctuate, they do so in well-defined, often predictable patterns. These patterns recur too frequently to be the result of chance or coincidence. How else do we explain that since 1950 all the gains in the market were made during November through April compared to a loss May through October? (See page 48.)

The *Almanac* is a practical investment tool. It alerts you to those little-known market patterns and tendencies on which shrewd professionals enhance profit potential. You will be able to forecast market trends with accuracy and confidence when you use the *Almanac* to help you understand:

- How our presidential elections affect the economy and the stock market—just as the moon affects the tides. Many investors have made fortunes following the political cycle. You can be sure that money managers who control billions of dollars are also political cycle watchers. Astute people do not ignore a pattern that has been working effectively throughout most of our economic history.

- How the passage of the Twentieth Amendment to the Constitution fathered the January Barometer. This barometer has an outstanding record for predicting the general course of the stock market each year, with only six major errors since 1950, for a 90.0% accuracy ratio. (See page 16.)

- Why there is a significant market bias at certain times of the day, week, month, and year.

Even if you are an investor who pays scant attention to cycles, indicators, and patterns, your investment survival could hinge on your interpretation of one of the recurring patterns found within these pages. One of the most intriguing and important patterns is the symbiotic relationship between Washington and Wall Street. Aside from the potential profitability in seasonal patterns, there's the pure joy of seeing the market very often do just what you expected.

The *Stock Trader's Almanac* is also an organizer. Its wealth of information is presented on a calendar basis. The *Almanac* puts investing in a business framework and makes investing easier because it:

- Updates investment knowledge and informs you of new techniques and tools.

- Is a monthly reminder and refresher course.

- Alerts you to both seasonal opportunities and dangers.

- Furnishes a historical viewpoint by providing pertinent statistics on past market performance.

- Supplies forms necessary for portfolio planning, record keeping, and tax preparation.

 The WITCH icon signifies THIRD FRIDAY OF THE MONTH on calendar pages and alerts you to extraordinary volatility due to expiration of equity and index options and index futures contracts. Triple-witching days appear during March, June, September, and December.

 The BULL icon on calendar pages signifies favorable trading days based on the S&P 500 rising 60% or more of the time on a particular trading day during the 21-year period January 1989 to December 2009.

 A BEAR icon on calendar pages signifies unfavorable trading days based on the S&P falling 60% or more of the time for the same 21-year period.

Also, to give you even greater perspective, we have listed next to the date of every day that the market is open the Market Probability numbers for the same 21-year period for the Dow (D), S&P 500 (S), and NASDAQ (N). You will see a "D," "S," and "N" followed by a number signifying the actual Market Probability number for that trading day, based on the recent 21-year period. On pages 121–128 you will find complete Market Probability Calendars, both long-term and 21-year for the Dow, S&P, and NASDAQ, as well as for the Russell 1000 and Russell 2000 indices.

Other seasonalities near the ends, beginnings, and middles of months, plus options expirations, holiday periods, and other times are noted for *Almanac* investors' convenience on the weekly planner pages. We are not able to carry FOMC meeting dates, as they are no longer available at press time. Only the first meeting of 2011, the two-day affair on January 25–26, 2011, has been scheduled. However, the rest of the FOMC meeting dates and all other important economic releases are provided in the Strategy Calendar every month in our newsletter, *Almanac Investor*, available at our website *www.stocktradersalmanac.com*.

As a reminder to long time *Almanac* readers, the ten years of monthly Daily Dow Point Changes have moved from their respective *Almanac* pages to the Databank section toward the rear of this book. We continue to rely on the clarity of this presentation to observe market tendencies. In response to newsletter subscriber feedback, we include our well-received Monthly Vital Stats on the *Almanac* pages.

The "Notable Events" on page 6 provides a handy list of major events of the past year that can be helpful when evaluating things that may have moved the market. Over the past few years our research has been restructured to better follow the rhythm of the year. This has also allowed us more room for added data. Again, we have included historical data on the Russell 1000 and Russell 2000 indices. The Russell 2K is an excellent proxy for small and mid caps, which we have used over the years, and the Russell 1K provides a broader view of large caps. Annual highs and lows for all five indices covered in the *Almanac* appear on pages 149–151. We've tweaked the Best and Worst section, and with the Option Symbology Initiative now complete, we have "New Option Trading Codes" on page 190.

Pre-presidential election years like 2011 are the most bullish year of the 4-year cycle with no losing years since 1939 (page 32). On page 34 we show the amazing pattern of how the Dow has gained 50% on average from the midterm low to the pre-election year high. "Market Charts of Pre-Presidential Election Years" on page 28 provides a view of the last 21 pre-election years at a glance. First years have been the third worst year in the decennial cycle for 129 years, but much better when they are also pre-election years and foreign crises are at bay (pages 26 and 129). A more significant correction in 2010 increases the potential for greater gains in 2011.

Sector seasonalities have been revamped this year to include several consistent shorting opportunities, moved to pages 92–96, and expanded to three pages. In response to many reader inquiries about how and what to trade when implementing the Best Months Switching Strategies, we detail some simple techniques, including a sampling of tradable mutual funds and ETFs on page 78. Now that the worst of the global financial crisis, bear market, and the Great Recession of 2007–2009 is likely behind us, on page 36 we reveal our brand new projection for the Next Super Boom to start in 2017 and carry the Dow up 500% to 38,820 by 2025.

We are constantly searching for new insights and nuances about the stock market and welcome any suggestions from our readers.

Have a healthy and prosperous 2011!

NOTABLE EVENTS

2009

May 25	North Korea's 2nd successful nuclear test.
Jun 1	Air France Flight 447 crashes, killing all 228.
Jun 1	General Motors files for bankruptcy.
Jun 11	Swine flu deemed global pandemic, 1st in 40 years.
Jun 12	Iran presidential election protests and riots.
Jun 17	Goldman Sachs first to pay back TARP.
Jun 24	Obama signs cash-for-clunkers into law.
Jun 25	Pop icon, Michael Jackson, dies.
Jul 4	North Korea conducts ballistic missile test.
Aug 25	Senator Edward Moore "Ted" Kennedy dies of cancer.
Sep 4	Natural Gas at $2.409, last seen in 2002, crude $70.
Sep 30	2009 federal budget deficit $1.4 trillion, highest ever.
Oct 7	Australia 1st G-20 to raise rates, post-financial crisis.
Oct 15	Social Security COLA is zero, 1st in 38-year history.
Nov 6	Obama extends unemployment benefits to 99 weeks.
Nov 9	Obama extends home-buyer tax credit.
Nov 25	Dubai debt crisis.
Nov 26	U.S. unemployment 10.2%, highest in 26 years.
Dec 8	Early warning on Greece's debt levels flashed.

2010

Jan 4	World's tallest building opens in Dubai.
Jan 12	Haiti struck by 7.0 earthquake, widespread destruction.
Jan 19	Mass. elects Republican Senator, ends Dem's super majority.
Feb 22	Action Comics #1, Superman's debut, sells for record $1 mil.
Feb 27	8.8 magnitude earthquake strikes Chile.
Mar 23	Landmark healthcare bill signed into law.
Apr 3	Apple iPad released to public.
Apr 6	Toyota fined $16.4 million, largest ever.
Apr 16	SEC charges Goldman Sachs with civil fraud.
Apr 14	Icelandic volcano closes European airspace for 6 days.
Apr 20	Drilling rig explodes and sinks in Gulf of Mexico.
May 1	Times Square N.Y. evacuated, car bomb fails to explode.
May 2	1000-year flood strikes Nashville, TN.
May 5	Picasso painting sells for record $106.5 million.
May 5	Greek rioting turns deadly—three die.
May 6	Dow plunges 650 points in 5 minutes.
May 10	€750 billion bailout plan—global markets soar.
May 12	Gold trades at new all-time high $1244.45.

2011 OUTLOOK

President Obama's first 100 days were quite rocky, with the stock market posting heavy losses as the 2007–2009 bear market bottomed. Over the past year it has been an uphill battle for the new president, but the stock market rallied swiftly and powerfully, as the president pushed through many of his core agenda and policy items after some tough political battles. Much to the chagrin of his critics, the controversial liberal chief executive is gaining traction.

As with most of his predecessors, Obama will push hard to pass several other policy initiatives in 2010, including financial regulatory reform, climate change, and energy legislation. These divisive initiatives could trigger a typical midterm election year correction or bear market. Any hiccups in the one-year old economic recovery could increase the magnitude of a decline. The Democrats will likely lose some congressional seats in the midterm elections this fall. If the Democrats lose control of Congress, it could be a boon for stocks. The combination of a democratic president and a republican Congress has produced the greatest gains, averaging gains of 19.5% for the Dow since 1949.

2011 is a pre-presidential election year, and there has not been a loser among them since war-torn 1939 (page 32). The Obama political machine is well aware that they will need to begin priming the pump in 2011 if he is going to have a shot at a second term. If there is a substantial decline in 2010 and the Democrats can grease the wheels of the economy, creating millions of jobs; the prospects for a 50% gain from the midterm low to the pre-election year high (page 34)—and Obama's reelection in 2012—increase dramatically.

However, we do not expect the old all-time highs to be left behind forever just yet and expect several more years of sideways market action, as we experienced in the 1930s and 1940s, and the 1970s and 1980s, before the Next Super Boom is born and the Dow vaults 500% to 38,820 by 2025 (page 36). So, use any significant dips or bear market lows to position yourself for a big rally into 2011 and 2012, but do not get complacent as the secular bear still appears in command.

— *Jeffrey A. Hirsch, May 13, 2010*

THE 2011 STOCK TRADER'S ALMANAC

CONTENTS

DIRECTORY OF TRADING PATTERNS AND DATABANK

STRATEGY PLANNING AND RECORD SECTION

2011 STRATEGY CALENDAR

(Option expiration dates circled)

MONDAY	TUESDAY	WEDNESDAY	THURSDAY	FRIDAY	SATURDAY	SUNDAY
27	28	29	30	31	1 JANUARY New Year's Day	2
3	4	5	6	7	8	9
10	11	12	13	14	15	16
17 Martin Luther King Day	18	19	20	(21)	22	23
24	25	26	27	28	29	30
31	1 FEBRUARY	2	3	4	5	6
7	8	9	10	11	12	13
14 ♥	15	16	17	(18)	19	20
21 Presidents' Day	22	23	24	25	26	27
28	1 MARCH	2	3	4	5	6
7	8	9 Ash Wednesday	10	11	12	13 Daylight Saving Time Begins
14	15	16	17 ♣ St. Patrick's Day	(18)	19	20
21	22	23	24	25	26	27
28	29	30	31	1 APRIL	2	3
4	5	6	7	8	9	10
11	12	13	14	(15) Tax Deadline	16	17
18	19 Passover	20	21	22 Good Friday	23	24 Easter
25	26	27	28	29	30	1 MAY
2	3	4	5	6	7	8 Mother's Day
9	10	11	12	13	14	15
16	17	18	19	(20)	21	22
23	24	25	26	27	28	29
30 Memorial Day	31	1 JUNE	2	3	4	5
6	7	8	9	10	11	12
13	14	15	16	(17)	18	19 Father's Day
20	21	22	23	24	25	26

Market closed on shaded weekdays; closes early when half-shaded.

2011 STRATEGY CALENDAR
(Option expiration dates circled)

MONDAY	TUESDAY	WEDNESDAY	THURSDAY	FRIDAY	SATURDAY	SUNDAY	
27	28	29	30	1 JULY	2	3	
4 Independence Day	5	6	7	8	9	10	JULY
11	12	13	14	(15)	16	17	
18	19	20	21	22	23	24	
25	26	27	28	29	30	31	
1 AUGUST	2	3	4	5	6	7	
8	9	10	11	12	13	14	AUGUST
15	16	17	18	(19)	20	21	
22	23	24	25	26	27	28	
29	30	31	1 SEPTEMBER	2	3	4	
5 Labor Day	6	7	8	9	10	11	SEPTEMBER
12	13	14	15	(16)	17	18	
19	20	21	22	23	24	25	
26	27	28	29 Rosh Hashanah	30	1 OCTOBER	2	
3	4	5	6	7	8 Yom Kippur	9	OCTOBER
10 Columbus Day	11	12	13	14	15	16	
17	18	19	20	(21)	22	23	
24	25	26	27	28	29	30	
31 🎃	1 NOVEMBER	2	3	4	5	6 Daylight Saving Time Ends	NOVEMBER
7	8 Election Day	9	10	11 Veterans' Day	12	13	
14	15	16	17	(18)	19	20	
21	22	23	24 Thanksgiving	25	26	27	
28	29	30	1 DECEMBER	2	3	4	DECEMBER
5	6	7	8	9	10	11	
12	13	14	15	(16)	17	18	
19	20	21 Chanukah	22	23	24	25 Christmas	
26	27	28	29	30	31	1 JANUARY New Year's Day	

JANUARY ALMANAC

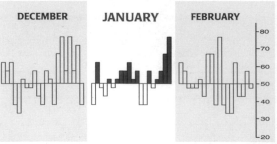

JANUARY						
S	M	T	W	T	F	S
						1
2	3	4	5	6	7	8
9	10	11	12	13	14	15
16	17	18	19	20	21	22
23	24	25	26	27	28	29
30	31					

FEBRUARY						
S	M	T	W	T	F	S
		1	2	3	4	5
6	7	8	9	10	11	12
13	14	15	16	17	18	19
20	21	22	23	24	25	26
27	28					

Market Probability Chart above is a graphic representation of the S&P 500 Recent Market Probability Calendar on page 124.

◆ January Barometer predicts year's course with .783 batting average (page 16) ◆ 14 of last 15 pre-presidential election years followed January's direction ◆ Every down January on the S&P since 1950, *without exception*, preceded a new or extended bear market, a flat market, or a 10% correction (page 42) ◆ S&P gains January's first five days preceded full-year gains 86.5% of the time; 12 of last 15 pre-presidential years followed first five day's direction (page 14) ◆ November, December, and January constitute the year's best three-month span, a 4.2% S&P gain (pages 44 and 147) ◆ January NASDAQ powerful 2.8% since 1971 (pages 54 and 148) ◆ "January Effect" now starts in mid-December and favors small-cap stocks (pages 102 and 104) ◆ 2009 has the dubious honor of the worst S&P 500 January on record.

January Vital Statistics

	DJIA		S&P 500		NASDAQ		Russell 1K		Russell 2K	
Rank	6		5		1		6		5	
Up	39		37		26		20		18	
Down	22		24		14		12		14	
Avg % Change	1.0%		1.0%		2.8%		1.0%		1.7%	
Pre-Election Year	4.3%		4.5%		7.9%		3.7%		4.5%	
Best and Worst January										
	% Change		% Change		% Change		% Change		% Change	
Best	1976	14.4	1987	13.2	1975	16.6	1987	12.7	1985	13.1
Worst	2009	−8.8	2009	−8.6	2008	−9.9	2009	−8.3	2009	−11.2
Best and Worst January Weeks										
Best	1/9/76	6.1	1/2/09	6.8	1/12/01	9.1	1/2/09	6.8	1/9/87	7.0
Worst	1/24/03	−5.3	1/28/00	−5.6	1/28/00	−8.2	1/28/00	−5.5	1/4/08	−6.5
Best and Worst January Days										
Best	1/17/91	4.6	1/3/01	5.0	1/3/01	14.2	1/3/01	5.3	1/2/09	5.3
Worst	1/8/88	−6.9	1/8/88	−6.8	1/2/01	−7.2	1/8/88	−6.1	1/20/09	−7.0
First Trading Day of Expiration Week: 1980–2010										
Record (#Up–#Down)	21–10		19–12		18–13		18–13		19–12	
Current Streak	U1		U1		U1		U1		U1	
Avg % Change	0.13		0.14		0.17		0.11		0.20	
Options Expiration Day: 1980–2010										
Record (#Up–#Down)	14–17		15–16		18–13		15–16		17–14	
Current Streak	D1		D1		D1		D1		D1	
Avg % Change	−0.17		−0.12		−0.15		−0.14		−0.13	
Options Expiration Week: 1980–2010										
Record (#Up–#Down)	15–16		13–18		17–14		13–18		16–15	
Current Streak	D3		D6		D6		D6		D6	
Avg % Change	−0.31		−0.15		0.25		−0.15		0.28	
Week After Options Expiration: 1980–2010										
Record (#Up–#Down)	17–14		19–12		17–14		19–12		20–11	
Current Streak	D2		D2		D4		D2		D2	
Avg % Change	0.01		0.22		0.06		0.17		0.12	
First Trading Day Performance										
% of Time Up	57.4		47.5		55.0		40.6		43.8	
Avg % Change	0.23		0.11		0.12		0.07		−0.05	
Last Trading Day Performance										
% of Time Up	59.0		63.9		65.0		62.5		75.0	
Avg % Change	0.24		0.27		0.31		0.36		0.27	

Dow & S&P 1950–April 2010, NASDAQ 1971–April 2010, Russell 1K & 2K 1979–April 2010.

20th Amendment made "lame ducks" disappear.
Now, "As January goes, so goes the year."

MONDAY
D 57.1
S 57.1
N 61.9
27

In nature there are no rewards or punishments; there are consequences.
— Horace Annesley Vachell (English writer, *The Face of Clay*, 1861–1955)

TUESDAY
D 85.7
S 76.2
N 76.2
28

Explosive growth of shadow banking was about the invisible hand having a party, a non-regulated drinking party, with rating agencies handing out fake IDs. — Paul McCulley (Economist, bond investor, managing director PIMCO; coined "shadow banking" in 2007, *NY Times*, 4/26/2010, b. 1957)

WEDNESDAY
D 57.1
S 57.1
N 57.1
29

Don't be scared to take big steps—you can't cross a chasm in two small jumps.
— David Lloyd George (British prime minister, 1916–1922)

THURSDAY
D 52.4
S 71.4
N 61.9
30

If you are ready to give up everything else—to study the whole history and background of the market and all the principal companies ... as carefully as a medical student studies anatomy— ... and, in addition, you have the cool nerves of a great gambler, the sixth sense of a clairvoyant, and the courage of a lion, you have a ghost of a chance. — Bernard Baruch (Financier, speculator, statesman, presidential adviser, 1870–1965)

Last Trading Day of the Year, NASDAQ Down 9 of Last 10
NASDAQ Was Up 29 Years in a Row 1971–1999

FRIDAY
D 42.9
S 38.1
N 57.1
31

Genius is the ability to put into effect what is in your mind. — F. Scott Fitzgerald (author, 1896–1940)

New Year's Day

SATURDAY
1

January Almanac Investor Seasonalities: See Pages 92, 94, and 96

SUNDAY
2

JANUARY'S FIRST FIVE DAYS: AN EARLY WARNING SYSTEM

The last 37 up First Five Days were followed by full-year gains 32 times, for an 86.5% accuracy ratio and a 14.0% average gain in all 37 years. The five exceptions include flat 1994 and four related to war. Vietnam military spending delayed start of 1966 bear market. Ceasefire imminence early in 1973 raised stocks temporarily. Saddam Hussein turned 1990 into a bear. The war on terrorism, instability in the Mideast, and corporate malfeasance shaped 2002 into one of the worst years on record. The 23 down First Five Days were followed by 12 up years and 11 down (47.8% accurate).

In pre-presidential election years this indicator has a solid record. In the last 15 pre-presidential election years 12 full years followed the direction of the First Five Days; however, 2007 was not one of these years. The full-month January Barometer (page 16) has an even better record, as 14 of the last 15 full years have followed January's direction.

THE FIRST-FIVE-DAYS-IN-JANUARY INDICATOR

	Chronological Data				Ranked by Performance		
	Previous Year's Close	January 5th Day	5-Day Change	Year Change	Rank	5-Day Change	Year Change
1950	16.76	17.09	2.0%	21.8%	1	1987	6.2%	2.0
1951	20.41	20.88	2.3	16.5	2	1976	4.9	19.1
1952	23.77	23.91	0.6	11.8	3	1999	3.7	19.5
1953	26.57	26.33	-0.9	-6.6	4	2003	3.4	26.4
1954	24.81	24.93	0.5	45.0	5	2006	3.4	13.6
1955	35.98	35.33	-1.8	26.4	6	1983	3.3	17.3
1956	45.48	44.51	-2.1	2.6	7	1967	3.1	20.1
1957	46.67	46.25	-0.9	-14.3	8	1979	2.8	12.3
1958	39.99	40.99	2.5	38.1	9	2010	2.7	??
1959	55.21	55.40	0.3	8.5	10	1963	2.6	18.9
1960	59.89	59.50	-0.7	-3.0	11	1958	2.5	38.1
1961	58.11	58.81	1.2	23.1	12	1984	2.4	1.4
1962	71.55	69.12	-3.4	-11.8	13	1951	2.3	16.5
1963	63.10	64.74	2.6	18.9	14	1975	2.2	31.5
1964	75.02	76.00	1.3	13.0	15	1950	2.0	21.8
1965	84.75	85.37	0.7	9.1	16	2004	1.8	9.0
1966	92.43	93.14	0.8	-13.1	17	1973	1.5	-17.4
1967	80.33	82.81	3.1	20.1	18	1972	1.4	15.6
1968	96.47	96.62	0.2	7.7	19	1964	1.3	13.0
1969	103.86	100.80	-2.9	-11.4	20	1961	1.2	23.1
1970	92.06	92.68	0.7	0.1	21	1989	1.2	27.3
1971	92.15	92.19	0.04	10.8	22	2002	1.1	-23.4
1972	102.09	103.47	1.4	15.6	23	1997	1.0	31.0
1973	118.05	119.85	1.5	-17.4	24	1980	0.9	25.8
1974	97.55	96.12	-1.5	-29.7	25	1966	0.8	-13.1
1975	68.56	70.04	2.2	31.5	26	1994	0.7	-1.5
1976	90.19	94.58	4.9	19.1	27	1965	0.7	9.1
1977	107.46	105.01	-2.3	-11.5	28	2009	0.7	23.5
1978	95.10	90.64	-4.7	1.1	29	1970	0.7	0.1
1979	96.11	98.80	2.8	12.3	30	1952	0.6	11.8
1980	107.94	108.95	0.9	25.8	31	1954	0.5	45.0
1981	135.76	133.06	-2.0	-9.7	32	1996	0.4	20.3
1982	122.55	119.55	-2.4	14.8	33	1959	0.3	8.5
1983	140.64	145.23	3.3	17.3	34	1995	0.3	34.1
1984	164.93	168.90	2.4	1.4	35	1992	0.2	4.5
1985	167.24	163.99	-1.9	26.3	36	1968	0.2	7.7
1986	211.28	207.97	-1.6	14.6	37	1990	0.1	-6.6
1987	242.17	257.28	6.2	2.0	38	1971	0.04	10.8
1988	247.08	243.40	-1.5	12.4	39	2007	-0.4	3.5
1989	277.72	280.98	1.2	27.3	40	1960	-0.7	-3.0
1990	353.40	353.79	0.1	-6.6	41	1957	-0.9	-14.3
1991	330.22	314.90	-4.6	26.3	42	1953	-0.9	-6.6
1992	417.09	418.10	0.2	4.5	43	1974	-1.5	-29.7
1993	435.71	429.05	-1.5	7.1	44	1998	-1.5	26.7
1994	466.45	469.90	0.7	-1.5	45	1988	-1.5	12.4
1995	459.27	460.83	0.3	34.1	46	1993	-1.5	7.1
1996	615.93	618.46	0.4	20.3	47	1986	-1.6	14.6
1997	740.74	748.41	1.0	31.0	48	2001	-1.8	-13.0
1998	970.43	956.04	-1.5	26.7	49	1955	-1.8	26.4
1999	1229.23	1275.09	3.7	19.5	50	2000	-1.9	-10.1
2000	1469.25	1441.46	-1.9	-10.1	51	1985	-1.9	26.3
2001	1320.28	1295.86	-1.8	-13.0	52	1981	-2.0	-9.7
2002	1148.08	1160.71	1.1	-23.4	53	1956	-2.1	2.6
2003	879.82	909.93	3.4	26.4	54	2005	-2.1	3.0
2004	1111.92	1131.91	1.8	9.0	55	1977	-2.3	-11.5
2005	1211.92	1186.19	-2.1	3.0	56	1982	-2.4	14.8
2006	1248.29	1290.15	3.4	13.6	57	1969	-2.9	-11.4
2007	1418.30	1412.11	-0.4	3.5	58	1962	-3.4	-11.8
2008	1468.36	1390.19	-5.3	-38.5	59	1991	-4.6	26.3
2009	903.25	909.73	0.7	23.5	60	1978	-4.7	1.1
2010	1115.10	1144.98	2.7	??	61	2008	-5.3	-38.5

Based on S&P 500

Small Caps Punished First Trading Day of Year
Russell 2000 Down 14 of Last 21, Average Loss 0.2%

MONDAY
D 61.9
S 38.1
N 57.1
3

Interviewer: How is it possible to fight an enemy willing and ready to die for his cause? Accommodate him!
— General Norman Schwartzkof (Ret. Commander of Allied Forces in 1990–1991 Gulf War, December 2001)

Second Trading Day of the Year, Dow Up 12 of Last 17
Santa Claus Rally Ends (Page 112)

TUESDAY
D 66.7
S 61.9
N 71.4
4

Today we deal with 65,000 more pieces of information each day than did our ancestors 100 years ago.
— Dr. Jean Houston (A founder of the Human Potential Movement, b. 1937)

WEDNESDAY
D 42.9
S 47.6
N 52.4
5

If the models are telling you to sell, sell, sell, but only buyers are out there, don't be a jerk. Buy!
— William Silber, Ph.D. (New York University, *Newsweek*, 1986)

January's First Five Days Act as an "Early Warning" (Page 14)

THURSDAY
D 52.4
S 42.9
N 52.4
6

Stock prices tend to discount what has been unanimously reported by the mass media.
— Louis Ehrenkrantz (Ehrenkrantz, Lyons & Ross)

FRIDAY
D 38.1
S 52.4
N 57.1
7

The only thing that saves us from the bureaucracy is its inefficiency.
— Eugene McCarthy (U.S. congressman and senator, Minnesota 1949–1971, 3-time presidential candidate, 1916–2005)

SATURDAY
8

SUNDAY
9

THE INCREDIBLE JANUARY BAROMETER (DEVISED 1972): ONLY SIX SIGNIFICANT ERRORS IN 60 YEARS

Devised by Yale Hirsch in 1972, our January Barometer states that as the S&P 500 goes in January, so goes the year. The indicator has registered **only six major errors since 1950 for a 90.0% accuracy ratio**. Vietnam affected 1966 and 1968; 1982 saw the start of a major bull market in August; two January rate cuts and 9/11 affected 2001; the anticipation of military action in Iraq held down the market in January 2003; and 2009 was the beginning of a new bull market following the second worst bear market on record. (*Almanac Investor* newsletter subscribers receive full analysis of each reading as well as its potential implications for the full year.)

Including the seven flat-year errors (less than +/– 5%) yields a 78.3% accuracy ratio. A full comparison of all monthly barometers for the Dow, S&P and NASDAQ in our newsletter archives (March 2009) at *www.stocktradersalmanac.com* details January's market forecasting prowess. Bear markets began or continued when January's suffered a loss (see page 42). Full years followed January's direction in 14 of the last 15 pre-presidential election years. The sole error was in 2003, as a new bull was beginning. *See pages 18, 20, and 24 for more January Barometer items.*

AS JANUARY GOES, SO GOES THE YEAR

Market Performance in January

	Previous Year's Close	January Close	January Change	Year Change	
1950	16.76	17.05	1.7%	21.8%	
1951	20.41	21.66	6.1	16.5	
1952	23.77	24.14	1.6	11.8	
1953	26.57	26.38	-0.7	-6.6	
1954	24.81	26.08	5.1	45.0	
1955	35.98	36.63	1.8	26.4	
1956	45.48	43.82	-3.6	2.6	flat
1957	46.67	44.72	-4.2	-14.3	
1958	39.99	41.70	4.3	38.1	
1959	55.21	55.42	0.4	8.5	
1960	59.89	55.61	-7.1	-3.0	flat
1961	58.11	61.78	6.3	23.1	
1962	71.55	68.84	-3.8	-11.8	
1963	63.10	66.20	4.9	18.9	
1964	75.02	77.04	2.7	13.0	
1965	84.75	87.56	3.3	9.1	
1966	92.43	92.88	0.5	-13.1	X
1967	80.33	86.61	7.8	20.1	
1968	96.47	92.24	-4.4	7.7	X
1969	103.86	103.01	-0.8	-11.4	
1970	92.06	85.02	-7.6	0.1	flat
1971	92.15	95.88	4.0	10.8	
1972	102.09	103.94	1.8	15.6	
1973	118.05	116.03	-1.7	-17.4	
1974	97.55	96.57	-1.0	-29.7	
1975	68.56	76.98	12.3	31.5	
1976	90.19	100.86	11.8	19.1	
1977	107.46	102.03	-5.1	-11.5	
1978	95.10	89.25	-6.2	1.1	flat
1979	96.11	99.93	4.0	12.3	
1980	107.94	114.16	5.8	25.8	
1981	135.76	129.55	-4.6	-9.7	
1982	122.55	120.40	-1.8	14.8	X
1983	140.64	145.30	3.3	17.3	
1984	164.93	163.41	-0.9	1.4	flat
1985	167.24	179.63	7.4	26.3	
1986	211.28	211.78	0.2	14.6	
1987	242.17	274.08	13.2	2.0	flat
1988	247.08	257.07	4.0	12.4	
1989	277.72	297.47	7.1	27.3	
1990	353.40	329.08	-6.9	-6.6	
1991	330.22	343.93	4.2	26.3	
1992	417.09	408.79	-2.0	4.5	flat
1993	435.71	438.78	0.7	7.1	
1994	466.45	481.61	3.3	-1.5	flat
1995	459.27	470.42	2.4	34.1	
1996	615.93	636.02	3.3	20.3	
1997	740.74	786.16	6.1	31.0	
1998	970.43	980.28	1.0	26.7	
1999	1229.23	1279.64	4.1	19.5	
2000	1469.25	1394.46	-5.1	-10.1	
2001	1320.28	1366.01	3.5	-13.0	X
2002	1148.08	1130.20	-1.6	-23.4	
2003	879.82	855.70	-2.7	26.4	X
2004	1111.92	1131.13	1.7	9.0	
2005	1211.92	1181.27	-2.5	3.0	flat
2006	1248.29	1280.08	2.5	13.6	
2007	1418.30	1438.24	1.4	3.5	flat
2008	1468.36	1378.55	-6.1	-38.5	
2009	903.25	825.88	-8.6	23.5	X
2010	1115.10	1073.87	-3.7	??	

Ranked by Performance

Rank	Year	January Change	Year Change	
1	1987	13.2%	2.0%	flat
2	1975	12.3	31.5	
3	1976	11.8	19.1	
4	1967	7.8	20.1	
5	1985	7.4	26.3	
6	1989	7.1	27.3	
7	1961	6.3	23.1	
8	1997	6.1	31.0	
9	1951	6.1	16.5	
10	1980	5.8	25.8	
11	1954	5.1	45.0	
12	1963	4.9	18.9	
13	1958	4.3	38.1	
14	1991	4.2	26.3	
15	1999	4.1	19.5	
16	1971	4.0	10.8	
17	1988	4.0	12.4	
18	1979	4.0	12.3	
19	2001	3.5	-13.0	X
20	1965	3.3	9.1	
21	1983	3.3	17.3	
22	1996	3.3	20.3	
23	1994	3.3	-1.5	flat
24	1964	2.7	13.0	
25	2006	2.5	13.6	
26	1995	2.4	34.1	
27	1972	1.8	15.6	
28	1955	1.8	26.4	
29	1950	1.7	21.8	
30	2004	1.7	9.0	
31	1952	1.6	11.8	
32	2007	1.4	3.5	flat
33	1998	1.0	26.7	
34	1993	0.7	7.1	
35	1966	0.5	-13.1	X
36	1959	0.4	8.5	
37	1986	0.2	14.6	
38	1953	-0.7	-6.6	
39	1969	-0.8	-11.4	
40	1984	-0.9	1.4	flat
41	1974	-1.0	-29.7	
42	2002	-1.6	-23.4	
43	1973	-1.7	-17.4	
44	1982	-1.8	14.8	X
45	1992	-2.0	4.5	flat
46	2005	-2.5	3.0	flat
47	2003	-2.7	26.4	X
48	1956	-3.6	2.6	flat
49	2010	-3.7	??	
50	1962	-3.8	-11.8	
51	1957	-4.2	-14.3	
52	1968	-4.4	7.7	X
53	1981	-4.6	-9.7	
54	1977	-5.1	-11.5	
55	2000	-5.1	-10.1	
56	2008	-6.1	-38.5	
57	1978	-6.2	1.1	flat
58	1990	-6.9	-6.6	
59	1960	-7.1	-3.0	flat
60	1970	-7.6	0.1	flat
61	2009	-8.6	23.5	X

X = 6 major errors   Based on S&P 500

JANUARY

MONDAY

D 47.6
S 47.6
N 61.9

10

er the last 25 years, computer processing capacity has risen more than a millionfold, while communication capacity has risen r a thousandfold. — Richard Worzel (Futurist, *Facing the Future*, b. 1950)

nuary Ends "Best Three-Month Span" (Pages 44, 54,147, and 148)

TUESDAY

D 52.4
S 52.4
N 52.4

11

hty percent of success is showing up. — Woody Allen (Filmaker, b. 1935)

WEDNESDAY

D 52.4
S 57.1
N 52.4

12

whole secret to our success is being able to con ourselves into believing that we're going to change the world n though] we are unlikely to do it. —Tom Peters (American writer, *In Search of Excellence, Fortune*, 11/13/2000, b. 1942)

THURSDAY

D 52.4
S 57.1
N 57.1

13

only gets to the top rung on the ladder by steadily climbing up one at a time, and suddenly all sorts of powers, rts of abilities, which you thought never belonged to you—suddenly become within your own possibility... 1argaret Thatcher (British prime minister, 1979–1990, b. 1925)

FRIDAY

D 57.1
S 61.9
N 52.4

14

human anywhere will blossom in a hundred unexpected talents and capacities simply by being given the opportunity to do so. oris Lessing (British novelist, born in Persia 1919)

SATURDAY

15

SUNDAY

16

JANUARY BAROMETER IN GRAPHIC FORM SINCE 1950

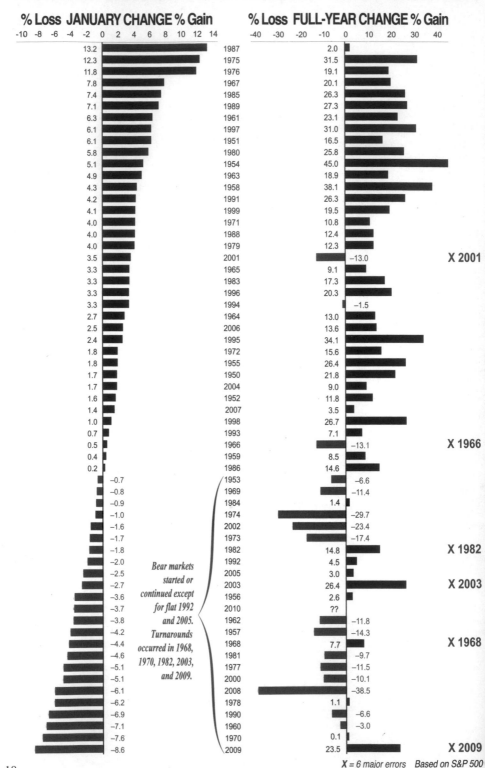

% Loss JANUARY CHANGE % Gain	Year	% Loss FULL-YEAR CHANGE % Gain	
13.2	1987	2.0	
12.3	1975	31.5	
11.8	1976	19.1	
7.8	1967	20.1	
7.4	1985	26.3	
7.1	1989	27.3	
6.3	1961	23.1	
6.1	1997	31.0	
6.1	1951	16.5	
5.8	1980	25.8	
5.1	1954	45.0	
4.9	1963	18.9	
4.3	1958	38.1	
4.2	1991	26.3	
4.1	1999	19.5	
4.0	1971	10.8	
4.0	1988	12.4	
4.0	1979	12.3	
3.5	2001	−13.0	X 2001
3.3	1965	9.1	
3.3	1983	17.3	
3.3	1996	20.3	
3.3	1994	−1.5	
2.7	1964	13.0	
2.5	2006	13.6	
2.4	1995	34.1	
1.8	1972	15.6	
1.8	1955	26.4	
1.7	1950	21.8	
1.7	2004	9.0	
1.6	1952	11.8	
1.4	2007	3.5	
1.0	1998	26.7	
0.7	1993	7.1	
0.5	1966	−13.1	X 1966
0.4	1959	8.5	
0.2	1986	14.6	
−0.7	1953	−6.6	
−0.8	1969	−11.4	
−0.9	1984	1.4	
−1.0	1974	−29.7	
−1.6	2002	−23.4	
−1.7	1973	−17.4	
−1.8	1982	14.8	X 1982
−2.0	1992	4.5	
−2.5	2005	3.0	
−2.7	2003	26.4	X 2003
−3.6	1956	2.6	
−3.7	2010	??	
−3.8	1962	−11.8	
−4.2	1957	−14.3	
−4.4	1968	7.7	X 1968
−4.6	1981	−9.7	
−5.1	1977	−11.5	
−5.1	2000	−10.1	
−6.1	2008	−38.5	
−6.2	1978	1.1	
−6.9	1990	−6.6	
−7.1	1960	−3.0	
−7.6	1970	0.1	
−8.6	2009	23.5	X 2009

Bear markets started or continued except for flat 1992 and 2005. Turnarounds occurred in 1968, 1970, 1982, 2003, and 2009.

X = 6 major errors   *Based on S&P 500*

JANUARY

artin Luther King Jr. Day (Market Closed)

MONDAY
17

---

he end, we will remember not the words of our enemies, but the silence of our friends.
Martin Luther King Jr. (Civil rights leader, 1964 Nobel Peace Prize, 1929–1968)

rst Trading Day of January Expiration Week, Dow Up 13 of Last 18
lid in 2010, Dow 1.1%, S&P 1.2%, and NASDAQ 1.4%

TUESDAY

D 52.4
S 52.4
N 61.9

18

---

e political problem of mankind is to combine three things: economic efficiency, social justice, and individual liberty.
John Maynard Keynes (British economist, 1883–1946)

nuary Expiration Week Horrible Since 1999, Dow Down Big 8 of Last 11

WEDNESDAY

D 38.1
S 57.1
N 66.7

19

---

rts not only tell what was, they tell what is; and a trend from was to is (projected linearly into the will be)
tains better percentages than clumsy guessing. — Robert A. Levy, (Chairman, Cato Institute, founder, CDA
stment Technologies, The Relative Strength Concept of Common Stock Forecasting, 1968, b. 1941)

🐻 THURSDAY

D 38.1
S 38.1
N 38.1

20

---

e did all the things we are capable of doing, we would literally astound ourselves.
Thomas Alva Edison (American inventor, 1093 patents, 1847–1931)

nuary Expiration Day, Dow Down 10 of Last 12 with Big Losses
f 2.1% in 2010, Off 2.0% in 2006 and 1.3% in 2003

 FRIDAY

D 33.3
S 38.1
N 47.6

21

---

erience is helpful, but it is judgment that matters.
eneral Colin Powell (Chairman, Joint Chiefs 1989–1993, secretary of state 2001–2005, *NY Times*, 10/22/2008, b. 1937)

SATURDAY
22

SUNDAY
23

HOT JANUARY INDUSTRIES BEAT S&P NEXT 11 MONTHS

The S&P 500 in January tends to predict the market's direction for the year. In turn, Standard & Poor's top 10 industries in January outperform the index over the next 11 months.

Our friend Sam Stovall, chief investment strategist at S&P, has crunched the numbers over the years. He calls it the "January Barometer Portfolio," or JBP. Since 1970, a portfolio of the top 10 S&P industries during January has beaten the S&P 500 itself—and performed even better in years when January was up.

The JBP went on to outperform the S&P 500 during the remaining 11 months of the year 73% of the time, 14.8% to 6.5%, on average. When the S&P 500 is up in January, a top-10 industries portfolio increases the average portfolio gain to 19.4% for the last 11 months of the year vs. 12.2% for the S&P.

For more, check Sam's Sector Watch at *businessweek.com* or our March 2009 *Almanac Investor* newsletter in the archives at *www.stocktradersalmanac.com*. Also highlighted are Sam's selected stocks from within the top 10 industries, as well as the top three sectors and related ETFs.

AS JANUARY GOES, SO GOES THE YEAR
FOR TOP-PERFORMING INDUSTRIES
January's Top 10 Industries vs. S&P 500 Next 11 Months

	11 Month % Change		S&P Jan	After S&P Up in January		After S&P Down in January	
	Portfolio	S&P	%	Portfolio	S&P	Portfolio	S&P
1970	−4.7	−0.3	−7.6			−4.7	−0.3
1971	23.5	6.1	4.0	23.5	6.1		
1972	19.7	13.7	1.8	19.7	13.7		
1973	5.2	−20.0	−1.7			5.2	−20.0
1974	−29.2	−30.2	−1.0			−29.2	−30.2
1975	57.3	22.2	12.3	57.3	22.2		
1976	16.3	8.1	11.8	16.3	8.1		
1977	−9.1	−9.6	−5.1			−9.1	−9.6
1978	7.3	6.5	−6.2			7.3	6.5
1979	21.7	8.1	4.0	21.7	8.1		
1980	38.3	20.4	5.8	38.3	20.4		
1981	5.0	−6.9	−4.6			5.0	−6.9
1982	37.2	18.8	−1.8			37.2	18.8
1983	17.2	13.9	3.3	17.2	13.9		
1984	−5.0	−1.1	−0.9			−5.0	−1.1
1985	28.2	20.8	7.4	28.2	20.8		
1986	18.1	19.4	0.2	18.1	19.4		
1987	−1.5	−8.9	13.2	−1.5	−8.9		
1988	18.4	10.4	4.0	18.4	10.4		
1989	16.1	22.1	7.1	16.1	22.1		
1990	−4.4	−3.3	−6.9			−4.4	−3.3
1991	35.7	19.4	4.2	35.7	19.4		
1992	14.6	4.7	−2.0			14.6	4.7
1993	23.7	7.2	0.7	23.7	7.2		
1994	−7.1	−4.6	3.3	−7.1	−4.6		
1995	25.6	30.9	2.4	25.6	30.9		
1996	5.4	16.5	3.3	5.4	16.5		
1997	4.7	23.4	6.1	4.7	23.4		
1998	45.2	25.4	1.0	45.2	25.4		
1999	67.9	14.8	4.1	67.9	14.8		
2000	23.6	−5.3	−5.1			23.6	−5.3
2001	−13.1	−16.0	3.5	−13.1	−16.0		
2002	−16.2	−22.2	−1.6			−16.2	−22.2
2003	69.3	29.9	−2.7			69.3	29.9
2004	9.9	7.1	1.7	9.9	7.1		
2005	20.7	5.7	−2.5			20.7	5.7
2006	−0.3	10.8	2.5	−0.3	10.8		
2007	−5.5	2.1	1.4	−5.5	2.1		
2008	−27.1	−34.5	−6.1			−27.1	−34.5
2009	38.7	35.0	−8.6			38.7	35.0
2010			−3.7				
Averages	**14.8%**	**6.5%**		**19.4%**	**12.2%**	**7.9%**	**−2.1%**

JANUARY

MONDAY
D 42.9
S 57.1
N 61.9
24

You may not have started out life in the best of circumstances. But if you can find a mission in life worth working for and believe in yourself, nothing can stop you from achieving success. — Kemmons Wilson (Holiday Inn founder, 1913–2003)

TUESDAY
D 61.9
S 47.6
N 38.1
25

Benjamin Graham was correct in suggesting that while the stock market in the short run may be a voting mechanism, in the long run it is a weighing mechanism. True value will win out in the end.
— Burton G. Malkiel (Economist, April 2003 Princeton Paper, *A Random Walk Down Wall Street*, b. 1932)

FOMC Meeting (2 Days)

WEDNESDAY
D 66.7
S 52.4
N 81.0
26

It's a lot of fun finding a country nobody knows about. The only thing better is finding a country everybody's bullish on and shorting it. — Jim Rogers (Financier, *Investment Biker*, b. 1942)

THURSDAY
D 57.1
S 57.1
N 66.7
27

A cynic is a man who knows the price of everything and the value of nothing.
— Oscar Wilde (Irish-born writer and wit, 1845–1900)

FRIDAY
D 61.9
S 66.7
N 57.1
28

A man will fight harder for his interests than his rights.
— Napoleon Bonaparte (Emperor of France 1804–1815, 1769–1821)

SATURDAY
29

February Almanac Investor Seasonalities: See Pages 92, 94, and 96

SUNDAY
30

FEBRUARY ALMANAC

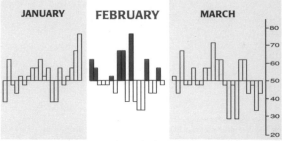

FEBRUARY	MARCH
S M T W T F S	S M T W T F S
1 2 3 4 5	1 2 3 4 5
6 7 8 9 10 11 12	6 7 8 9 10 11 12
13 14 15 16 17 18 19	13 14 15 16 17 18 19
20 21 22 23 24 25 26	20 21 22 23 24 25 26
27 28	27 28 29 30 31

Market Probability Chart above is a graphic representation of the S&P 500 Recent Market Probability Calendar on page 124.

◆ February is the weak link in "Best Six Months" (pages 44, 48, and 147)
◆ RECENT RECORD deteriorating: S&P up 4, down 8, average change –2.4%
last 12 years ◆ Sixth–ranking NASDAQ month in pre-presidential election years
average 2.3%, up 7 down 3 (page 157), #8 Dow and S&P (pages 153 and 155), both
up 9, down 6 ◆ Day before Presidents' Day weekend, S&P down 16 of 19,
11 straight 1992–2002, day after dicey, up 10 of 19 (see pages 84 and 133) ◆ Many
technicians modify market predictions based on January's market.

February Vital Statistics

	DJIA	S&P 500	NASDAQ	Russell 1K	Russell 2K
Rank	10	11	9	11	7
Up	34	32	20	18	17
Down	27	29	20	14	15
Avg % Change	–0.04%	–0.2%	0.3%	–0.1%	0.9%
Pre-Election Year	0.1%	0.1%	2.3%	0.8%	1.7%
Best and Worst February					
	% Change	% Change	% Change	% Change	% Change
Best	1986 8.8	1986 7.1	2000 19.2	1986 7.2	2000 16.4
Worst	2009 –11.7	2009 –11.0	2001 –22.4	2009 –10.7	2009 –12.3
Best and Worst February Weeks					
Best	2/1/08 4.4	2/6/09 5.2	2/4/00 9.2	2/6/09 5.3	2/1/91 6.6
Worst	2/20/09 –6.2	2/20/09 –6.9	2/9/01 –7.1	2/20/09 –6.9	2/20/09 –8.3
Best and Worst February Days					
Best	2/24/09 3.3	2/24/09 4.0	2/11/99 4.2	2/24/09 4.1	2/24/09 4.5
Worst	2/10/09 –4.6	2/10/09 –4.9	2/16/01 –5.0	2/10/09 –4.8	2/10/09 –4.7
First Trading Day of Expiration Week: 1980–2010					
Record (#Up–#Down)	19–12	21–10	16–15	21–10	17–14
Current Streak	U1	U1	U1	U1	U1
Avg % Change	0.30	0.22	–0.03	0.19	–0.01
Options Expiration Day: 1980–2010					
Record (#Up–#Down)	14–17	12–19	12–19	13–18	13–18
Current Streak	U1	U1	U1	U1	U1
Avg % Change	–0.11	–0.17	–0.31	–0.17	–0.12
Options Expiration Week: 1980–2010					
Record (#Up–#Down)	18–13	15–16	15–16	14–17	18–13
Current Streak	U1	U1	U1	U1	U1
Avg % Change	0.30	0.04	–0.13	0.04	0.02
Week After Options Expiration: 1980–2010					
Record (#Up–#Down)	13–18	14–17	17–14	14–17	17–14
Current Streak	D2	D2	D3	D2	D3
Avg % Change	–0.35	–0.25	–0.20	–0.20	–0.11
First Trading Day Performance					
% of Time Up	60.7	60.7	70.0	65.6	65.6
Avg % Change	0.12	0.13	0.31	0.15	0.30
Last Trading Day Performance					
% of Time Up	50.8	57.4	55.0	59.4	59.4
Avg % Change	0.01	–0.01	–0.04	–0.05	0.17

Dow & S&P 1950–April 2010, NASDAQ 1971–April 2010, Russell 1K & 2K 1979–April 2010.

*Either go short, or stay away
the day before Presidents' Day.*

JANUARY/FEBRUARY

MONDAY

D 71.4
S 76.2
N 66.7

31

Bill Gates' One-Minus Staffing: For every project, figure out the bare minimum of people needed to staff it.
Cut to the absolute muscle and bones, then take out one more. When you understaff, people jump on the loose ball.
You find out who the real performers are. Not so when you're overstaffed. People sit around waiting for somebody else to do it.
— Quoted by Rich Karlgaard (Publisher, Forbes Dec. 25, 2000)

First Day Trading in February, Dow and S&P Up 7 of Last 8
NASDAQ Up 6 Years in a Row

TUESDAY

D 61.9
S 61.9
N 81.0

1

The finest thought runs the risk of being irrevocably forgotten if we do not write it down.
— Arthur Schopenhauer (German philosopher, 1788–1860)

WEDNESDAY

D 47.6
S 57.1
N 66.7

2

All the features and achievements of modern civilization are, directly or indirectly, the products of the capitalist process.
— Joseph A. Schumpeter (Austrian–American economist, Theory of Economic Development, 1883–1950)

THURSDAY

D 42.9
S 47.6
N 47.6

3

The greatest safety lies in putting all your eggs in one basket and watching the basket.
— Gerald M. Loeb (E.F. Hutton, The Battle for Investment Survival, predicted 1929 Crash, 1900–1974)

FRIDAY

D 47.6
S 47.6
N 57.1

4

Your organization will never get better unless you are willing to admit that there is something wrong with it.
— General Norman Schwartzkof (Ret. commander of allied forces in 1990–1991 Gulf War)

SATURDAY

5

SUNDAY

6

1933 "LAME DUCK" AMENDMENT: REASON JANUARY BAROMETER WORKS

There would be no January Barometer without the passage in 1933 of the Twentieth "lame duck" Amendment to the Constitution. Since then, it has essentially been, "As January goes, so goes the year." January's direction has correctly forecasted the major trend for the market in most of the subsequent years.

Prior to 1934, newly elected senators and representatives did not take office until December of the following year, 13 months later (except when new presidents were inaugurated). Defeated congressmen stayed in Congress for all of the following session. They were known as "lame ducks."

Since 1934, Congress convenes in the first week of January and includes those members newly elected the previous November. Inauguration Day was also moved up from March 4 to January 20. As a result, several events have been squeezed into January, which affect our economy and our stock market and quite possibly those of many nations of the world.

The basis for January's predictive capacity comes from the fact that so many important events occur in the month: New Congresses convene; the president gives the State of the Union message, presents the annual budget, and sets national goals and priorities. Switch these events to any other month and chances are, the January Barometer would become a memory.

The table shows the January Barometer in odd years. In 1935 and 1937, the Democrats already had the most lopsided Congressional margins in history, so when these two Congresses convened it was anticlimactic.

The January Barometer in subsequent odd-numbered years had compiled a perfect record until two January interest rate cuts and the 9/11 attack affected 2001, the anticipation of military action in Iraq held the market down in January 2003, and we experienced a flat 2005. A new bull market began in 2009 when the second worst bear market on record bottomed in March.

See the January Barometer compared to prior "New Congress Barometers" at *www.stocktradersalmanac.com*.

JANUARY BAROMETER (ODD YEARS)

January % Change	12 Month % Change	Same	Opposite
−4.2%	41.2%		1935
3.8	−38.6		1937
−6.9	−5.4	1939	
−4.8	−17.9	1941	
7.2	19.4	1943	
1.4	30.7	1945	
2.4	N/C	1947	
0.1	10.3	1949	
6.1	16.5	1951	
−0.7	−6.6	1953	
1.8	26.4	1955	
−4.2	−14.3	1957	
0.4	8.5	1959	
6.3	23.1	1961	
4.9	18.9	1963	
3.3	9.1	1965	
7.8	20.1	1967	
−0.8	−11.4	1969	
4.0	10.8	1971	
−1.7	−17.4	1973	
12.3	31.5	1975	
−5.1	−11.5	1977	
4.0	12.3	1979	
−4.6	−9.7	1981	
3.3	17.3	1983	
7.4	26.3	1985	
13.2	2.0	1987	
7.1	27.3	1989	
4.1	26.3	1991	
0.7	7.1	1993	
2.4	34.1	1995	
6.1	31.0	1997	
4.1	19.5	1999	
3.5	−13.0		2001
−2.7	26.4		2003
−2.5	3.0		2005
1.4	3.5	2007	
−8.6	23.5		2009

12 months'% change includes January's % change.
Based on S&P 500.

FEBRUARY

MONDAY
7

D 52.4
S 47.6
N 52.4

It is a funny thing about life; if you refuse to accept anything but the best, you very often get it.
— W. Somerset Maugham

TUESDAY
8

D 42.9
S 52.4
N 57.1

Don't be the last bear or last bull standing, let history guide you, be contrary to the crowd, and let the tape tell you when to act.
— Jeffrey A. Hirsch (Editor, *Stock Trader's Almanac*, b. 1966)

Week Before February Expiration Week, NASDAQ Down 8 of Last 10, 2010 Up 2.0%

WEDNESDAY
9

D 52.4
S 42.9
N 42.9

If there is something you really want to do, make your plan and do it. Otherwise, you'll just regret it forever.
— Richard Rocco (PostNet franchisee, *Entrepreneur Magazine* 12/2006, b. 1946)

THURSDAY
10

D 57.1
S 66.7
N 52.4

Nothing has a stronger influence psychologically on their environment and especially on their children than the unlived life of the parent. — C. G. Jung (Swiss psychiatrist)

FRIDAY
11

D 57.1
S 66.7
N 47.6

People do not change when you tell them they should; they change when they tell themselves they must.
— Michael Mandelbaum (Johns Hopkins foreign policy specialist, *NY Times*, 6/24/2009, b. 1946)

SATURDAY
12

SUNDAY
13

THE FIRST YEAR OF DECADES

"One" years tend to be good years except when foreign crises impact the market: 1931 (Depression), 1941 (World War II), 1981 (Cold War/Mideast turmoil), 2001 (9/11 terrorist attack). With 2011 being a pre-presidential election year, prospects are brighter. Last three pre-election years ending in one were positive: 1951, 1971, and 1991. *See pages 129–130 for more.*

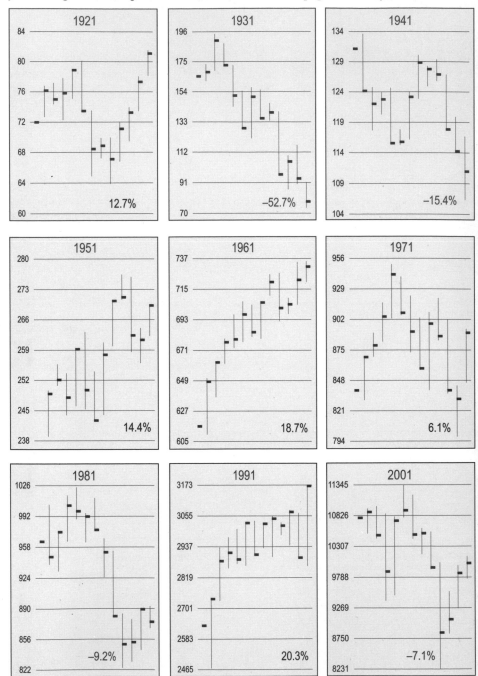

Based on Dow Jones Industrial Average monthly ranges and closing prices.

FEBRUARY

Valentine's Day ♥
First Trading Day of February Expiration Week Dow Down 4 of Last 6

🐻 **MONDAY**
D 42.9
S 38.1
N 52.4
14

Try to surround yourself with people who can give you a little happiness,
because you can only pass through this life once, Jack. You don't come back for an encore. — Elvis Presley (1935–1977)

🐻 **TUESDAY**
D 71.4
S 76.2
N 61.9
15

Most people can stay excited for two or three months. A few people can stay excited for two or three years.
But a winner will stay excited for 20 to 30 years—or as long as it takes to win. — A. L. Williams (Motivational speaker)

🐻 **WEDNESDAY**
D 42.9
S 38.1
N 33.3
16

Love your enemies, for they tell you your faults. — Benjamin Franklin (U.S. Founding Father, diplomat, inventor, 1706–1790)

🐻 **THURSDAY**
D 28.6
S 33.3
N 42.9
17

Self-discipline is a form of freedom. Freedom from laziness and lethargy, freedom from expectations and demands of others,
freedom from weakness and fear—and doubt. — Harvey A. Dorfman (Sports psychologist, The Mental ABC's of Pitching, b. 1935)

Day Before Presidents Day Weekend, S&P Down 16 of Last 19
February Expiration Day, Dow Down 7 of Last 11

🐻 🐾 **FRIDAY**
D 42.9
S 33.3
N 33.3
18

There are two kinds of people who lose money: those who know nothing and those who know everything.
— Henry Kaufman (German-American economist, b. 1927, to Robert Lenzner in Forbes 10/19/98 who added,
"With two Nobel Prize winners in the house, Long-Term Capital clearly fits the second case.")

SATURDAY
19

SUNDAY
20

MARKET CHARTS OF PRE-PRESIDENTIAL ELECTION YEARS

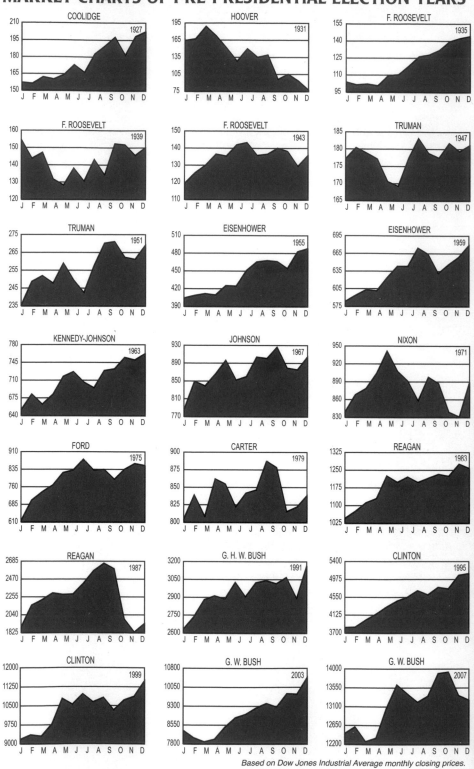

Based on Dow Jones Industrial Average monthly closing prices.

28

FEBRUARY

Presidents' Day (Market Closed)

MONDAY
21

Let us have the courage to stop borrowing to meet the continuing deficits. Stop the deficits.
— Franklin D. Roosevelt (32nd U.S. president, 1932, 1882–1945)

TUESDAY
D 52.4
S 61.9
N 61.9
22

A weakened White House creates uncertainty on Wall Street. — Robert D. Hormats (Under secretary of state for economic, energy, and agricultural affairs, 2009–, Goldman Sachs 1982–2009, CNN 10/28/2005, b.1943)

End of February Miserable in Recent Years, (Page 22 and 133)

WEDNESDAY
D 38.1
S 42.9
N 57.1
23

Fight until death over taxes? Oh, no. Women, country, God, things like that. Taxes? No.
— Daniel Patrick Moynihan (U.S. senator, New York 1977–2001, "Meet The Press", 5/23/1993, 1927–2003)

Week After February Expiration Week, Dow Down 9 of Last 12

THURSDAY
D 42.9
S 42.9
N 42.9
24

Technology has no respect for tradition.
— Peter C. Lee (Merchants' Exchange CEO, quoted in *Stocks, Futures & Options* Magazine, May 2003)

FRIDAY
D 47.6
S 57.1
N 52.4
25

The difference between life and the movies is that a script has to make sense, and life doesn't.
— Joseph L. Mankiewicz (Film director, writer, producer, 1909–1993)

SATURDAY
26

March Almanac Investor Seasonalities: See Pages 92, 94, and 96

SUNDAY
27

MARCH ALMANAC

MARCH						
S	M	T	W	T	F	S
			1	2	3	4	5
6	7	8	9	10	11	12
13	14	15	16	17	18	19
20	21	22	23	24	25	26
27	28	29	30	31		

APRIL						
S	M	T	W	T	F	S
					1	2
3	4	5	6	7	8	9
10	11	12	13	14	15	16
17	18	19	20	21	22	23
24	25	26	27	28	29	30

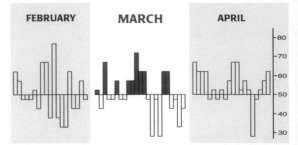

Market Probability Chart above is a graphic representation of the S&P 500 Recent Market Probability Calendar on page 124.

◆ Mid-month strength and late-month weakness are most evident above ◆ RECENT RECORD: S&P 18 up, 9 down, average gain 1.3%, fourth best ◆ Rather turbulent in recent years with wild fluctuations and large gains and losses ◆ March has been taking some mean end-of-quarter hits (page 134), down 1,469 Dow points March 9–22, 2001 ◆ Last three or four days Dow a net loser 14 out of last 19 years ◆ NASDAQ hard hit in 2001, down 14.5% after 22.4% drop in February ◆ Third best NASDAQ month during pre-presidential election years average gain 3.8%, no losers.

March Vital Statistics

	DJIA		S&P 500		NASDAQ		Russell 1K		Russell 2K	
Rank	5		4		7		5		6	
Up	39		40		26		21		23	
Down	22		21		14		11		9	
Avg % Change	1.1%		1.2%		0.8%		1.1%		1.2%	
Pre-Election Year	2.3%		2.2%		3.8%		2.7%		3.3%	
Best and Worst March										
	% Change		% Change		% Change		% Change		% Change	
Best	2000	7.8	2000	9.7	2009	10.9	2000	8.9	1979	9.7
Worst	1980	–9.0	1980	–10.2	1980	–17.1	1980	–11.5	1980	–18.5
Best and Worst March Weeks										
Best	3/13/09	9.0	3/13/09	10.7	3/13/09	10.6	3/13/09	10.7	3/13/09	12.0
Worst	3/16/01	–7.7	3/6/09	–7.0	3/16/01	–7.9	3/6/09	–7.1	3/6/09	–9.8
Best and Worst March Days										
Best	3/23/09	6.8	3/23/09	7.1	3/10/09	7.1	3/23/09	7.0	3/23/09	8.4
Worst	3/2/09	–4.2	3/2/09	–4.7	3/12/01	–6.3	3/2/09	–4.8	3/27/80	–6.0
First Trading Day of Expiration Week: 1980–2010										
Record (#Up–#Down)	20–11		20–11		14–17		19–12		16–15	
Current Streak	U1		U1		D3		D3		D3	
Avg % Change	0.15		0.02		–0.37		–0.04		–0.38	
Options Expiration Day: 1980–2010										
Record (#Up–#Down)	17–14		18–13		15–16		16–15		14–16	
Current Streak	D2		D2		D2		D2		D2	
Avg % Change	0.05		–0.01		–0.04		–0.01		–0.09	
Options Expiration Week: 1980–2010										
Record (#Up–#Down)	21–9		20–11		18–13		19–12		16–15	
Current Streak	U3		U3		U3		U3		D1	
Avg % Change	0.89		0.73		–0.04		0.66		0.08	
Week After Options Expiration: 1980–2010										
Record (#Up–#Down)	14–17		11–20		16–15		11–20		16–15	
Current Streak	U2		U2		U5		U2		U5	
Avg % Change	–0.28		–0.16		0.05		–0.16		0.04	
First Trading Day Performance										
% of Time Up	67.2		63.9		62.5		59.4		65.6	
Avg % Change	0.17		0.17		0.25		0.15		0.23	
Last Trading Day Performance										
% of Time Up	41.0		39.3		65.0		46.9		84.4	
Avg % Change	–0.11		–0.01		0.18		0.08		0.40	

Dow & S&P 1950–April 2010, NASDAQ 1971–April 2010, Russell 1K & 2K 1979–April 2010.

March has Ides and St. Patrick's Day;
Begins bullishly, then fades away.

MONDAY
D 42.9
S 47.6
N 42.9
28

There is no great mystery to satisfying your customers. Build them a quality product and treat them with respect. It's that simple.
— Lee Iacocca (American industrialist, former Chrysler CEO, b. 1924)

First Trading Day in March, Dow Down 3 of Last 4, −4.2% in 2009, 1996–2006 Up 9 of 11

TUESDAY
D 57.1
S 52.4
N 57.1
1

I tell you sure as I am sitting here, that if banking institutions are protected by the taxpayer and they are given free rein to speculate, I may not live long enough to see the crisis, but my soul is going to come back and haunt you.
— Paul A. Volcker (Fed chairman 1979–1987, chairman, Economic Recovery Advisory Board, 2/2/2010, b. 1927)

WEDNESDAY
D 52.4
S 42.9
N 38.1
2

Every great advance in natural knowledge has involved the absolute rejection of authority.
— Thomas H. Huxley (British scientist and humanist, defender of Darwinism, 1825–1895)

March Historically Strong Early in the Month (Pages 30 and 134)

THURSDAY
D 61.9
S 66.7
N 71.4
3

The biggest change we made was the move to a boundary-less company. We got rid of the corner offices, the bureaucracy, and the not-invented-here syndrome. Instead we got every mind in the game, got the best out of all our people.
— Jack Welch (retiring CEO of General Electric, *Business Week*, September 10, 2001)

FRIDAY
D 47.6
S 47.6
N 47.6
4

We may face more inflation pressure than currently shows up in formal data.
— William Poole (Economist, president Federal Reserve Bank of St. Louis 1998–2008, June 2006 speech, b. 1937)

SATURDAY
5

SUNDAY
6

PRE-PRESIDENTIAL ELECTION YEARS NO LOSERS IN 72 YEARS

Investors should feel somewhat more secure going into 2011. There hasn't been a down year in the third year of a presidential term since war-torn 1939, Dow off 2.9%. The only severe loss in a pre-presidential election year going back 100 years occurred in 1931 during the Depression.

Electing a president every four years has set in motion a 4-year political stock market cycle. Most bear markets take place in the first or second years after elections (see pages 130–131). Then, the market improves. Typically each administration does everything in its power to juice up the economy so that voters are in a positive mood at election time.

Quite an impressive record. Chances are the winning streak will continue and that the market, in pre-presidential election year 2011, will gain ground. Prospects improve considerably if the market takes a breather in 2010 following the robust bull run from the March 2009 lows.

THE RECORD SINCE 1915

Year	President	Description
1915	Wilson (D)	World War I in Europe, but Dow up 81.7%.
1919	Wilson (D)	Post-Armistice 45.5% gain through Nov. 3rd top. Dow +30.5%.
1923	Harding/Coolidge (R)	Teapot Dome scandal a depressant. Dow loses 3.3%.
1927	Coolidge (R)	Bull market rolls on, up 28.8%.
1931	Hoover (R)	Depression, stocks slashed in half. Dow –52.7%, S&P –47.1%.
1935	Roosevelt (D)	Almost straight up year, S&P 500 up 41.2%, Dow 38.5%.
1939	Roosevelt (D)	War clouds, Dow –2.9% but 23.7% Apr.–Dec. gain. S&P –5.5%.
1943	Roosevelt (D)	U.S. at war, prospects brighter, S&P +19.4%, Dow +13.8%.
1947	Truman (D)	S&P unchanged, Dow up 2.2%.
1951	Truman (D)	Dow +14.4%, S&P +16.5%.
1955	Eisenhower (R)	Dow +20.8%, S&P +26.4%.
1959	Eisenhower (R)	Dow +16.4%, S&P +8.5%.
1963	Kennedy/Johnson (D)	Dow +17.0%, S&P +18.9%.
1967	Johnson (D)	Dow +15.2%, S&P +20.1%.
1971	Nixon (R)	Dow +6.1%, S&P +10.8%, NASDAQ +27.4%.
1975	Ford (R)	Dow +38.3%, S&P +31.5%, NASDAQ +29.8%.
1979	Carter (D)	Dow +4.2%, S&P +12.3%, NASDAQ +28.1%.
1983	Reagan (R)	Dow +20.3%, S&P +17.3%, NASDAQ +19.9%.
1987	Reagan (R)	Dow +2.3%, S&P +2.0% despite Oct. meltdown. NAS –5.4%.
1991	G.H.W. Bush (R)	Dow +20.3%, S&P +26.3%, NASDAQ +56.8%.
1995	Clinton (D)	Dow +33.5%, S&P +34.1%, NASDAQ +39.9%.
1999	Clinton (D)	Millennial fever crescendo: Dow +25.2%, S&P +19.5%, NASDAQ +85.6%.
2003	G.W. Bush (R)	Straight up after fall of Saddam: Dow +25.3% S&P +26.4%, NASDAQ +50.0%.
2007	G.W. Bush (R)	Credit bubble fuels all-time market highs before bear starts & Great Recession: Dow: +6.4% S&P: +3.5% NASDAQ: 9.8%.

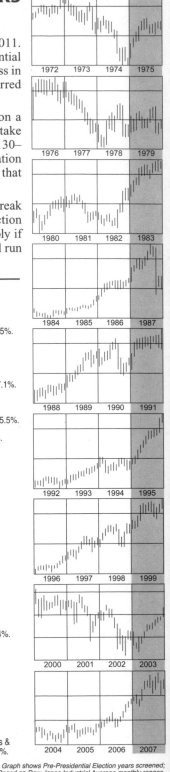

Graph shows Pre-Presidential Election years screened; Based on Dow Jones Industrial Average monthly ranges.

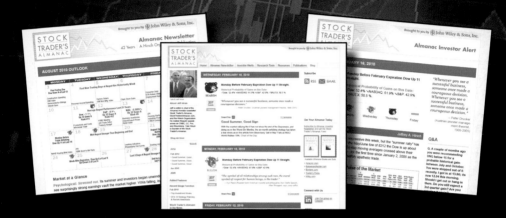

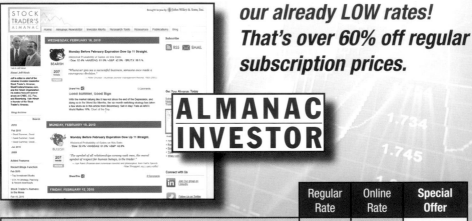

MARCH

MONDAY

D 52.4
S 47.6
N 47.6

7

To me, the "tape" is the final arbiter of any investment decision. I have a cardinal rule: Never fight the tape!
— Martin Zweig (Fund manager, *Winning on Wall Street*)

TUESDAY

D 47.6
S 57.1
N 42.9

8

Whatever method you use to pick stocks…, your ultimate success or failure will depend on your ability to ignore the worries of the world long enough to allow your investments to succeed. It isn't the head but the stomach that determines the fate of the stockpicker. — Peter Lynch (Fidelity Investments, *Beating the Street*, 1994)

Ash Wednesday

WEDNESDAY

D 57.1
S 47.6
N 47.6

9

The facts are unimportant! It's what they are perceived to be that determines the course of events.
— R. Earl Hadady (*Bullish Consensus, Contrary Opinion*)

Dow Down 1,469 Points March 9–22 in 2001

THURSDAY

D 57.1
S 47.6
N 47.6

10

The pursuit of gain is the only way in which people can serve the needs of others whom they do not know.
— Friedrich von Hayek (*Counterrevolution of Science*)

FRIDAY

D 42.9
S 57.1
N 61.9

11

Success isn't measured by the position you reach in life; it's measured by the obstacles you overcome.
— Booker T. Washington (Founder of Tuskegee Institute, 1856–1915)

SATURDAY

12

Daylight Saving Time Begins

SUNDAY

13

WHY A 50% GAIN IN THE DOW IS POSSIBLE FROM ITS 2010 LOW TO ITS 2011 HIGH

Normally, major corrections occur sometime in the first or second years following presidential elections. In the last 12 midterm election years, bear markets began or were in progress nine times—we experienced bull years in 1986 and 2006, while 1994 was flat.

The puniest midterm advance, 14.5% from the 1946 low, was during the industrial contraction after World War II. The next four smallest advances were: 1978 (OPEC-Iran) 21.0%, 1930 (economic collapse) 23.4%, 1966 (Vietnam) 26.7%, and 2006 (Iraq) 32.8%.

Since 1914, the Dow has gained 49.2% on average from its midterm election year low to its subsequent high in the following pre-election year. A swing of such magnitude is equivalent to a move from 8000 to 12000 or from 10000 to 15000.

POST-ELECTION HIGH TO MIDTERM LOW: −21.4%

Conversely, since 1913 the Dow has dropped −21.4% on average from its post-election-year high to its subsequent low in the following midterm year. The Dow's 2009 post-election year high is 10548.51. A 21.4% decline would put the Dow back at 8291.13 at the 2010 midterm bottom. Whatever the level, the rally off the 2010 midterm low could be one of the best buying opportunities of the twenty-first century.

Pretty impressive seasonality! There is no reason to think the quadrennial Presidential Election/Stock Market Cycle will not continue. Page 130 shows how effectively most presidents "managed" to have much stronger economies in the third and fourth years of their terms than in their first two.

% CHANGE IN DOW JONES INDUSTRIALS BETWEEN THE MIDTERM YEAR LOW AND THE HIGH IN THE FOLLOWING YEAR

	Midterm Year Low			Pre-Election Year High			
	Date of Low		Dow	Date of High		Dow	% Gain
1	Jul 30 1914 *		52.32	Dec 27 1915		99.21	89.6%
2	Jan 15 1918 **		73.38	Nov 3 1919		119.62	63.0
3	Jan 10 1922 **		78.59	Mar 20 1923		105.38	34.1
4	Mar 30 1926 *		135.20	Dec 31 1927		202.40	49.7
5	Dec 16 1930 *		157.51	Feb 24 1931		194.36	23.4
6	Jul 26 1934 *		85.51	Nov 19 1935		148.44	73.6
7	Mar 31 1938 *		98.95	Sep 12 1939		155.92	57.6
8	Apr 28 1942 *		92.92	Jul 14 1943		145.82	56.9
9	Oct 9 1946		163.12	Jul 24 1947		186.85	14.5
10	Jan 13 1950 **		196.81	Sep 13 1951		276.37	40.4
11	Jan 11 1954 **		279.87	Dec 30 1955		488.40	74.5
12	Feb 25 1958 **		436.89	Dec 31 1959		679.36	55.5
13	Jun 26 1962 *		535.74	Dec 18 1963		767.21	43.2
14	Oct 7 1966 *		744.32	Sep 25 1967		943.08	26.7
15	May 26 1970 *		631.16	Apr 28 1971		950.82	50.6
16	Dec 6 1974 *		577.60	Jul 16 1975		881.81	52.7
17	Feb 28 1978 *		742.12	Oct 5 1979		897.61	21.0
18	Aug 12 1982 *		776.92	Nov 29 1983		1287.20	65.7
19	Jan 22 1986		1502.29	Aug 25 1987		2722.42	81.2
20	Oct 11 1990 *		2365.10	Dec 31 1991		3168.84	34.0
21	Apr 4 1994		3593.35	Dec 13 1995		5216.47	45.2
22	Aug 31 1998 *		7539.07	Dec 31 1999		11497.12	52.5
23	Oct 9 2002 *		7286.27	Dec 31 2003		10453.92	43.5
24	Jan 20 2006		10667.39	Oct 9 2007		14164.53	32.8
	*Bear Market ended **Bear previous year					**Average**	**49.2%**

Monday Before March Triple Witching, Dow Up 17 of Last 23

MONDAY

D 61.9
S 57.1
N 52.4

14

Tell me and I'll forget; show me and I may remember; involve me and I'll understand.
— Confucius (Chinese philosopher, 551–478 B.C.)

TUESDAY

D 66.7
S 71.4
N 52.4

15

I write an email about every week to ten days... and within about 24 hours everyone will have read it.
The amazing thing is how I can change the direction of the entire company within 24 hours. Ten years ago I couldn't do that.
— Michael Marks (Former CEO Flextronics, *Forbes*, 7/7/03, b. 1951)

Bullish Cluster Highlights March's "Sweet Spot"

WEDNESDAY

D 61.9
S 61.9
N 66.7

16

The future now belongs to societies that organize themselves for learning.
What we know and can do holds the key to economic progress. — Ray Marshall (b. 1928) and Marc Tucker (b. 1939)
(*Thinking for a Living: Education and the Wealth of Nations*, 1992)

St. Patrick's Day ♣

THURSDAY

D 52.4
S 61.9
N 57.1

17

A government which robs Peter to pay Paul can always depend on the support of Paul.
— George Bernard Shaw (Irish dramatist, 1856–1950)

March Triple Witching Day Mixed Last 10 Years
Dow Down 3 of Last 4

FRIDAY

D 57.1
S 47.6
N 57.1

18

Whenever a well-known bearish analyst is interviewed [Cover story] in the financial press,
it usually coincides with an important near-term market bottom. — Clif Droke (Clifdroke.com, 11/15/04, b. 1972)

SATURDAY

19

SUNDAY

20

NEXT SUPER BOOM—DOW 38820 BY 2025

As the top chart illustrates, the market has failed to make any significant headway so long as the country is embroiled in a significant conflagration. Once the war ended, inflation caused by government spending kicked in, and the stock market made 500+% moves between all of the major wars of the twentieth century in which the U.S. was involved.

Since 2000 the markets have been in a trading range without a real advance that has left the previous highs behind for good. As government spending increased dramatically over the past two years in response to the global financial crisis and the Great Recession, it became clear to us that there is more at play than just wartime inflation.

All three previous secular bear markets associated with the three major wars of the twentieth century were also affected by crisis that required a great deal of non-war-related spending. The subsequent booms were also driven by ubiquitous enabling technologies that created major cultural paradigm shifts and sustained prosperity.

Despite continuing violence in Iraq and Afghanistan, U.S. troop withdrawals remain on schedule. Delays will likely alter the actual dates, but the trend and plan remain clear. We are working towards disengaging on those fronts. And this is a crucial component of the next super boom.

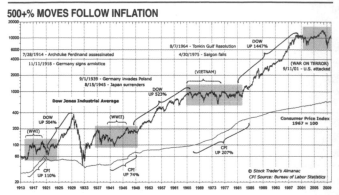

Inflation has not yet materialized, and we are still "at war" with government spending on the rise. In the bottom chart annual percentage changes in U.S. Government spending (outlays) are compared to inflation (CPI). Note the recent pop in spending. Inflation will be right behind it over the next few years.

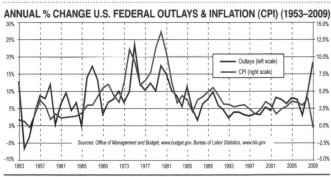

The next enabling technologies could come from energy technology and/or biotechnology. Outfitting the planet with cost-effective, innovative alternative energy and off-the-grid solutions could generate a boom. Biotech is promising because of all the health issues that exist and the potential it has to impact everyone.

From the bottom in 1974, it took eight years before the market took off in 1982 and then another eight to move up the rest of the 500%, in line with Yale Hirsch's prediction in 1976 for a 500% market move by 1990. A 500% rise in the Dow over 16 years from the intraday low of 6470 on March 6, 2009 would put the Dow at 38,820 in 2025. Next Super Boom: 2017.

A more in-depth analysis was provided to *Almanac Investor* subscribers on May 13, 2010 at *www.stocktradersalmanac.com*.

Week After Triple Witching, Dow Down 15 of Last 23,
but Rallied 4.9% in 2000, 3.1% in 2007 and 6.8% in 2009

MONDAY
D 38.1
S 28.6
N 28.6
21

Financial markets will find and exploit hidden flaws, particularly in untested new innovations—
and do so at a time that will inflict the most damage to the most people.
— Raymond F. DeVoe Jr. (Market strategist, Jesup and Lamont, The DeVoe Report, 3/30/07)

TUESDAY
D 38.1
S 47.6
N 28.6
22

Let me end my talk by abusing slightly my status as an official representative of the Federal Reserve.
I would like to say to Milton [Friedman]: regarding the Great Depression, you're right; we did it. We're very sorry.
But thanks to you, we won't do it again. — Ben Bernanke (Fed Chairman 2006–, 11/8/02 speech as Fed governor)

March Historically Weak Later in the Month (Pages 30 and 134)

WEDNESDAY
D 38.1
S 28.6
N 47.6
23

Wall Street's graveyards are filled with men who were right too soon. — William Hamilton

THURSDAY
D 38.1
S 61.9
N 61.9
24

No other country can substitute for the U.S. The U.S. is still No. 1 in military, No. 1 in economy,
No. 1 in promoting human rights, and No. 1 in idealism. Only the U.S. can lead the world. No other country can.
— Senior Korean official (to Thomas L. Friedman, NY Times Foreign Affairs columnist, 2/25/2009)

FRIDAY
D 57.1
S 61.9
N 61.9
25

Doubt is the father of invention. — Galileo Galilei (Italian physicist and astronomer, 1564–1642)

SATURDAY
26

April Almanac Investor Seasonalities: See Pages 92, 94, and 96

SUNDAY
27

APRIL ALMANAC

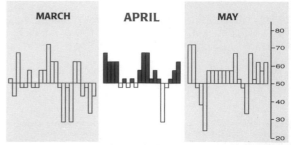

Market Probability Chart above is a graphic representation of the S&P 500 Recent Market Probability Calendar on page 124.

◆ April is still the best Dow month (average 2.0%) since 1950 (page 44) ◆ April 1999 first month ever to gain 1000 Dow points, 856 in 2001, knocked off its high horse in 2002 down 458, 2003 up 488 ◆ Up five straight, average gain 4.3% ◆ Prone to weakness after mid-month tax deadline ◆ Stocks anticipate great first quarter earnings by rising sharply before earnings are reported, rather than after ◆ Rarely a dangerous month, recent exceptions are 2002, 2004, and 2005 ◆ "Best Six Months" of the year end with April (page 48) ◆ In pre-presidential election years since 1951, average gains more than double (Dow 4.3%, S&P 3.7%, NASDAQ 3.7%) ◆ End of April NASDAQ strength (pages 125 and 126).

April Vital Statistics

	DJIA		S&P 500		NASDAQ		Russell 1K		Russell 2K	
Rank	1		3		4		2		2	
Up	39		42		26		21		21	
Down	22		19		14		11		11	
Avg % Change	2.0%		1.5%		1.5%		1.5%		1.9%	
Pre-Election Year	4.3%		3.7%		3.7%		3.0%		3.5%	
Best and Worst April										
	% Change		% Change		% Change		% Change		% Change	
Best	1978	10.6	2009	9.4	2001	15.0	2009	10.0	2009	15.3
Worst	1970	−6.3	1970	−9.0	2000	−15.6	2002	−5.8	2000	−6.1
Best and Worst April Weeks										
Best	4/11/75	5.7	4/20/00	5.8	4/12/01	14.0	4/20/00	5.9	4/3/09	6.3
Worst	4/14/00	−7.3	4/14/00	−10.5	4/14/00	−25.3	4/14/00	−11.2	4/14/00	−16.4
Best and Worst April Days										
Best	4/5/01	4.2	4/5/01	4.4	4/5/01	8.9	4/5/01	4.6	4/9/09	5.9
Worst	4/14/00	−5.7	4/14/00	−5.8	4/14/00	−9.7	4/14/00	−6.0	4/14/00	−7.3
First Trading Day of Expiration Week: 1980–2010										
Record (#Up–#Down)	19–12		19–12		18–13		18–13		13–18	
Current Streak	U1		U2		U2		U2		U1	
Avg % Change	0.24		0.20		0.22		0.19		0.09	
Options Expiration Day: 1980–2010										
Record (#Up–#Down)	21–10		20–11		18–13		20–11		19–12	
Current Streak	D1		D1		D1		D1		D1	
Avg % Change	0.23		0.19		−0.03		0.18		0.17	
Options Expiration Week: 1980–2010										
Record (#Up–#Down)	26–5		23–8		22–9		21–10		24–7	
Current Streak	U5		D1		U5		D1		U5	
Avg % Change	1.22		1.00		1.10		0.97		0.90	
Week After Options Expiration: 1980–2010										
Record (#Up–#Down)	20–11		20–11		22–9		20–11		20–11	
Current Streak	U1		U1		U4		U1		U1	
Avg % Change	0.34		0.29		0.54		0.30		0.77	
First Trading Day Performance										
% of Time Up	59.0		62.3		45.0		59.4		46.9	
Avg % Change	0.17		0.14		−0.16		0.16		−0.11	
Last Trading Day Performance										
% of Time Up	50.8		55.7		67.5		56.3		68.8	
Avg % Change	0.10		0.09		0.20		0.09		0.16	

Dow & S&P 1950–April 2010, NASDAQ 1971–April 2010, Russell 1K & 2K 1979–April 2010.

April "Best Month" for Dow since 1950;
Day-before-Good Friday gains are nifty.

MARCH/APRIL

Start Looking for the Dow and S&P MACD SELL Signal (Pages 48 and 50)
Almanac Investor Subscribers E-mailed When It Triggers (See Insert Page 96)

MONDAY
D 38.1
S 42.9
N 52.4
28

Liberties voluntarily forfeited are not easily retrieved. All the more so for those that are removed surreptitiously.
— Ted Koppel (Broadcast journalist, *Nightline* anchor 1980–2005, *NY Times,* 11/6/06, b. 1940)

TUESDAY
D 52.4
S 47.6
N 38.1
29

In an uptrend, if a higher high is made but fails to carry through, and prices dip below the previous high,
the trend is apt to reverse. The converse is true for downtrends. — Victor Sperandeo (*Trader Vic—Methods of a Wall Street Master*)

WEDNESDAY
D 47.6
S 33.3
N 42.9
30

I went to a restaurant that serves "breakfast at any time." So I ordered French toast during the Renaissance.
— Steven Wright (Comedian, b. 1955)

Last Trading Day of March, Dow Down 11 of Last 16
Russell 2000 Up 12 of Last 16

THURSDAY
D 38.1
S 42.9
N 61.9
31

Whenever you see a successful business, someone once made a courageous decision.
— Peter Drucker (Austrian-born pioneer management theorist, 1909–2005)

First Trading Day in April, Dow Up 13 of Last 16

FRIDAY
D 71.4
S 66.7
N 52.4
1

The trend is your friend ... until it ends. — Anonymous

SATURDAY
2

SUNDAY
3

THE DECEMBER LOW INDICATOR: A USEFUL PROGNOSTICATING TOOL

When the Dow closes below its December closing low in the first quarter, it is frequently an excellent warning sign. Jeffrey Saut, managing director of investment strategy at Raymond James, brought this to our attention a few years ago. The December Low Indicator was originated by Lucien Hooper, a *Forbes* columnist and Wall Street analyst back in the 1970s. Hooper dismissed the importance of January and January's first week as reliable indicators. He noted that the trend could be random or even manipulated during a holiday-shortened week. Instead, said Hooper, "Pay much more attention to the December low. If that low is violated during the first quarter of the New Year, watch out!"

Seventeen of the 31 occurrences were followed by gains for the rest of the year—and 15 full-year gains—after the low for the year was reached. For perspective we've included the January Barometer readings for the selected years. Hooper's "Watch Out" warning was absolutely correct, though. All but two of the instances since 1952 experienced further declines, as the Dow fell an additional 11.1% on average when December's low was breached in Q1.

Only three significant drops occurred (not shown) when December's low was not breached in Q1 (1974, 1981, and 1987). Both indicators were wrong only five times, and nine years ended flat. If the December low is not crossed, turn to our January Barometer for guidance. It has been virtually perfect, right nearly 100% of these times (view the complete results at *www.stocktradersalmanac.com*).

YEARS DOW FELL BELOW DECEMBER LOW IN FIRST QUARTER

Year	Previous Dec Low	Date Crossed	Crossing Price	Subseq. Low	% Change Cross-Low	Rest of Year % Change	Full Year % Change	Jan Bar
1952	262.29	2/19/52	261.37	256.35	−1.9%	11.7%	8.4%	1.6%[2]
1953	281.63	2/11/53	281.57	255.49	−9.3	−0.2	−3.8	−0.7[3]
1956	480.72	1/9/56	479.74	462.35	−3.6	4.1	2.3	−3.6[1, 2, 3]
1957	480.61	1/18/57	477.46	419.79	−12.1	−8.7	−12.8	−4.2
1960	661.29	1/12/60	660.43	566.05	−14.3	−6.7	−9.3	−7.1
1962	720.10	1/5/62	714.84	535.76	−25.1	−8.8	−10.8	−3.8
1966	939.53	3/1/66	938.19	744.32	−20.7	−16.3	−18.9	0.5[1]
1968	879.16	1/22/68	871.71	825.13	−5.3	8.3	4.3	−4.4[1, 2, 3]
1969	943.75	1/6/69	936.66	769.93	−17.8	−14.6	−15.2	−0.8
1970	769.93	1/26/70	768.88	631.16	−17.9	9.1	4.8	−7.6[2, 3]
1973	1000.00	1/29/73	996.46	788.31	−20.9	−14.6	−16.6	−1.7
1977	946.64	2/7/77	946.31	800.85	−15.4	−12.2	−17.3	−5.1
1978	806.22	1/5/78	804.92	742.12	−7.8	0.01	−3.1	−6.2[3]
1980	819.62	3/10/80	818.94	759.13	−7.3	17.7	14.9	5.8[2]
1982	868.25	1/5/82	865.30	776.92	−10.2	20.9	19.6	−1.8[1, 2]
1984	1236.79	1/25/84	1231.89	1086.57	−11.8	−1.6	−3.7	−0.9[3]
1990	2687.93	1/15/90	2669.37	2365.10	−11.4	−1.3	−4.3	−6.9[3]
1991	2565.59	1/7/91	2522.77	2470.30	−2.1	25.6	20.3	4.2[2]
1993	3255.18	1/8/93	3251.67	3241.95	−0.3	15.5	13.7	0.7[2]
1994	3697.08	3/30/94	3626.75	3593.35	−0.9	5.7	2.1	3.3[2, 3]
1996	5059.32	1/10/96	5032.94	5032.94	NC	28.1	26.0	3.3[2]
1998	7660.13	1/9/98	7580.42	7539.07	−0.5	21.1	16.1	1.0[2]
2000	10998.39	1/4/00	10997.93	9796.03	−10.9	−1.9	−6.2	−5.1
2001	10318.93	3/12/01	10208.25	8235.81	−19.3	−1.8	−7.1	3.5[1]
2002	9763.96	1/16/02	9712.27	7286.27	−25.0	−14.1	−16.8	−1.6
2003	8303.78	1/24/03	8131.01	7524.06	−7.5	28.6	25.3	−2.7[1, 2]
2005	10440.58	1/21/05	10392.99	10012.36	−3.7	3.1	−0.6	−2.5[3]
2006	10717.50	1/20/06	10667.39	10667.39	NC	16.8	16.3	2.5
2007	12194.13	3/2/07	12114.10	12050.41	−0.5	9.5	6.4	1.4[2]
2008	13167.20	1/2/08	13043.96	7552.29	−42.1	−32.7	−33.8	−6.1
2009	8149.09	1/20/09	7949.09	6547.05	−17.6	31.2	18.8	−8.6[1, 2]
2010	10285.97	1/22/10	10172.98	9908.39	−2.6	*At Press Time—not in average*		−3.7
			Average Drop		**−11.1%**			

[1] *January Barometer wrong* [2] *December Low Indicator wrong* [3] *Year Flat*

🐂 **MONDAY**

D 61.9
S 61.9
N 57.1

4

What counts more than luck, is determination and perseverance. If the talent is there, it will come through. Don't be too impatient. — Fred Astaire (The report from his first screen test stated, "Can't act. Can't sing. Balding. Can dance a little.")

April Is the Best Month for the Dow, Average 2.0% Gain Since 1950
3rd Best Month for S&P, 4th Best for NASDAQ (Since 1971)

🐂 **TUESDAY**

D 57.1
S 61.9
N 71.4

5

The common denominator: Something that matters! Something that counts! Something that defines! Something that is imbued with soul. And with life! — Tom Peters (referring to projects, *Reinventing Work*, 1999)

🐂 **WEDNESDAY**

D 66.7
S 61.9
N 52.4

6

The stock market is that creation of man which humbles him the most. — Anonymous

THURSDAY

D 42.9
S 47.6
N 38.1

7

The choice of starting a war this [pre-election] spring was made for political as well as military reasons... [The president] clearly does not want to have a war raging on the eve of his presumed reelection campaign. — Senior European diplomat (*NY Times*, 3/14/03)

FRIDAY

D 47.6
S 52.4
N 52.4

8

It was never my thinking that made the big money for me. It was always my sitting. Got that? My sitting tight! — Jesse Livermore (Early 20th century stock trader and speculator, *How to Trade in Stocks*, 1877–1940)

SATURDAY

9

SUNDAY

10

DOWN JANUARYS: A REMARKABLE RECORD

In the first third of the twentieth century, there was no correlation between January markets and the year as a whole (page 24). Then, in 1972 Yale Hirsch discovered that the 1933 "lame duck" Amendment to the Constitution changed the political calendar, and the January Barometer was born. Its record has been quite accurate (page 16).

Down Januarys are harbingers of trouble ahead, in the economic, political, or military arenas. Eisenhower's heart attack in 1955 cast doubt on whether he could run in 1956—a flat year. Two other election years with down Januarys were also flat (1984 and 1992). Twelve bear markets began and ten continued into second years with poor Januarys: 1968 started down, as we were mired in Vietnam, but Johnson's "bombing halt" changed the climate. Imminent military action in Iraq held January 2003 down before the market triple-bottomed in March. After Baghdad fell, pre-election and recovery forces fueled 2003 into a banner year. 2005 was flat, registering the narrowest Dow trading range on record. A negative reading in 2010 has yet to manifest into a 10% or worse correction, but at press time the Greek debt contagion has boiled over, increasing the probability of a substantial decline.

Unfortunately, bull and bear markets do not start conveniently at the beginnings and ends of months or years. Though some years ended higher, **every down January since 1950 was followed by a new or continuing bear market, a 10% correction or a flat year**. Excluding 1956, **down Januarys were followed by substantial declines averaging *minus* 14.3%**, providing excellent buying opportunities later in most years.

FROM DOWN JANUARY S&P CLOSES TO LOW NEXT 11 MONTHS

Year	January Close	% Change	11-Month Low	Date of Low	Jan Close to Low %	% Feb to Dec	Year % Change	
1953	26.38	−0.7%	22.71	14-Sep	−13.9%	−6.0%	−6.6%	bear
1956	43.82	−3.6	44.10	28-May	0.9	6.5	2.6	FLAT/bear
1957	44.72	−4.2	38.98	22-Oct	−12.8	−10.6	−14.3	Cont. bear
1960	55.61	−7.1	52.30	25-Oct	−6.0	4.5	−3.0	bear
1962	68.84	−3.8	52.32	26-Jun	−24.0	−8.3	−11.8	bear
1968	92.24	−4.4	87.72	5-Mar	−4.9	12.6	7.7	−10%/bear
1969	103.01	−0.8	89.20	17-Dec	−13.4	−10.6	−11.4	Cont. bear
1970	85.02	−7.6	69.20	26-May	−18.6	8.4	0.1	Cont. bear/FLAT
1973	116.03	−1.7	92.16	5-Dec	−20.6	−15.9	−17.4	bear
1974	96.57	−1.0	62.28	3-Oct	−35.5	−29.0	−29.7	Cont. bear
1977	102.03	−5.1	90.71	2-Nov	−11.1	−6.8	−11.5	bear
1978	89.25	−6.2	86.90	6-Mar	−2.6	7.7	1.1	Cont. bear/bear
1981	129.55	−4.6	112.77	25-Sep	−13.0	−5.4	−9.7	bear
1982	120.40	−1.8	102.42	12-Aug	−14.9	16.8	14.8	Cont. bear
1984	163.42	−0.9	147.82	24-Jul	−9.5	2.3	1.4	Cont. bear/FLAT
1990	329.07	−6.9	295.46	11-Oct	−10.2	0.4	−6.6	bear
1992	408.79	−2.0	394.50	8-Apr	−3.5	6.6	4.5	FLAT
2000	1394.46	−5.1	1264.74	20-Dec	−9.3	−5.3	−10.1	bear
2002	1130.20	−1.6	776.76	9-Oct	−31.3	−22.2	−23.4	bear
2003	855.70	−2.7	800.73	11-Mar	−6.4	29.9	26.4	Cont. bear
2005	1181.27	−2.5	1137.50	20-Apr	−3.7	5.7	3.0	FLAT
2008	1378.55	−6.1	752.44	20-Nov	−45.4	−34.5	−38.5	Cont. bear
2009	825.88	−8.6	676.53	9-Mar	−18.1	35.0	23.5	Cont. bear
2010	1073.87	−3.7	1056.74	8-Feb	−1.6*	—	—	—
				Totals	−327.8%	−18.2%	−109.0%	
				Average	−14.3%	−0.8%	−4.7%	

*At Press time—not in totals or average

42

APRIL

Monday Before Expiration, Dow Up 14 of Last 21, Down 4 of Last 6

MONDAY

D 47.6
S 47.6
N 47.6

11

You can't grow long-term if you can't eat short-term. Anybody can manage short. Anybody can manage long. Balancing those two things is what management is. — Jack Welch (CEO of General Electric, *Business Week*, June 8, 1998)

TUESDAY

D 66.7
S 52.4
N 61.9

12

There is a perfect inverse correlation between inflation rates and price/earnings ratios ... When inflation has been very high ... P/E has been [low]. — Liz Ann Sonders (Chief investment strategist, Charles Schwab, June 2006)

WEDNESDAY

D 57.1
S 47.6
N 47.6

13

Sell stocks whenever the market is 30% higher over a year ago. — Eugene D. Brody (Oppenheimer Capital)

*April Expiration Day, Dow Up 11 of Last 14,
2007 Up 1.2%, 2008 Up 1.8%*

THURSDAY

D 71.4
S 57.1
N 61.9

14

History shows that once the United States fully recognizes an economic problem and thereby places all its efforts on solving it, the problem is about to be solved by natural forces. — James L. Fraser (*Contrary Investor*)

Income Tax Deadline
Generally Bullish, Dow Down Only Five Times Since 1981

FRIDAY

D 76.2
S 66.7
N 42.9

15

We were fairly arrogant, until we realized the Japanese were selling quality products for what it cost us to make them.
— Paul A. Allaire (Former chairman of Xerox)

SATURDAY

16

SUNDAY

17

TOP PERFORMING MONTHS PAST 60⅓ YEARS: STANDARD & POOR'S 500 AND DOW JONES INDUSTRIALS

Monthly performance of the S&P and the Dow are ranked over the past 60⅓ years. NASDAQ monthly performance is shown on page 54.

April, November, and December still hold the top three positions in both the Dow and S&P. March has reclaimed the fourth spot on the S&P. Two disastrous Januarys in 2008 and 2009 knocked January into fifth. This, in part, led to our discovery in 1986 of the market's most consistent seasonal pattern. You can divide the year into two sections and have practically all the gains in one six-month section and very little in the other. September is the worst month on both lists. (See "Best Six Months" on page 48.)

MONTHLY % CHANGES (JANUARY 1950 TO APRIL 2010)

Standard & Poor's 500					Dow Jones Industrials				
Month	Total % Change	Avg. % Change	# Up	# Down	Month	Total % Change	Avg. % Change	# Up	# Down
Jan	62.9%	1.0%	37	24	Jan	60.3%	1.0%	39	22
Feb	−14.7	−0.2	32	29	Feb	−2.5	−0.04	34	27
Mar	71.2	1.2	40	21	Mar	65.3	1.1	39	22
Apr	93.1	1.5	42	19	Apr	120.2	2.0	39	22
May	23.7	0.4	35	25	May	10.8	0.2	31	29
Jun	2.7	0.1	32	28	Jun	−18.1	−0.3	28	32
Jul	53.0	0.9	32	28	Jul	67.2	1.1	37	23
Aug	8.0	0.1	34	26	Aug	3.9	0.1	35	25
Sep*	−37.0	−0.6	26	33	Sep	−54.8	−0.9	23	37
Oct	34.7	0.6	35	25	Oct	19.9	0.3	35	25
Nov	94.0	1.6	40	20	Nov	93.5	1.6	40	20
Dec	98.4	1.6	45	15	Dec	99.3	1.7	42	18
% Rank					**% Rank**				
Dec	98.4%	1.6%	45	15	Apr	120.2%	2.0%	39	22
Nov	94.0	1.6	40	20	Dec	99.3	1.7	42	18
Apr	93.1	1.5	42	19	Nov	93.5	1.6	40	20
Mar	71.2	1.2	40	21	Jul	67.2	1.1	37	23
Jan	62.9	1.0	37	24	Mar	65.3	1.1	39	22
Jul	53.0	0.9	32	28	Jan	60.3	1.0	39	22
Oct	34.7	0.6	35	25	Oct	19.9	0.3	35	25
May	23.7	0.4	35	25	May	10.8	0.2	31	29
Aug	8.0	0.1	34	26	Aug	3.9	0.1	35	25
Jun	2.7	0.1	32	28	Feb	−2.5	−0.04	34	27
Feb	−14.7	−0.2	32	29	Jun	−18.1	−0.3	28	32
Sep*	−37.0	−0.6	26	33	Sep	−54.8	−0.9	23	37
Totals	**490.0%**	**8.1%**			**Totals**	**465.0%**	**7.9%**		
Average		**0.68%**			**Average**		**0.66%**		

*No change 1979

Anticipators, shifts in cultural behavior, and faster information flow have altered seasonality in recent years. Here is how the months ranked over the past 15⅓ years (184 months), using total percentage gains on the S&P 500: April 38.6, November 32.4, March 28.5, May 20.7, December 18.9, October 13.8, June 1.1, July −3.1, January −4.3, September −5.5, August −9.9, February −17.0.

During the last 15⅓ years, front-runners of our Best Six Months may have helped push October into the number-six spot. May has leapfrogged into the number-four spot. January has declined in seven of the last eleven years. Sizable turnarounds in "bear killing" October were a common occurrence from 1998 to 2007. Recent big Dow losses in the period were: August 1998 (SE Asia crisis), off 15.1%; September 2001 (9/11 attack), off 11.1%; September 2002 (Iraq war drums), off 12.4%; October 2008, off 14.1% and February 2009 (financial crisis), off 11.7%.

APRIL

April Prone to Weakness After Tax Deadline (Pages 38 and 134)

MONDAY

D 61.9
S 66.7
N 57.1

18

Success is going from failure to failure without loss of enthusiasm. — Winston Churchill (British statesman, 1874–1965)

Passover

TUESDAY

D 52.4
S 52.4
N 47.6

19

A successful man is one who can lay a firm foundation with the bricks that others throw at him.
— Sidney Greenberg (Rabbi, author, 1918–2003)

WEDNESDAY

D 57.1
S 57.1
N 52.4

20

To find one man in a thousand who is your true friend from unselfish motives is to find one of the great wonders of the world.
— Leopold Mozart (Quoted by Maynard Solomon, *Mozart*)

NASDAQ Up 14 of 16 Day Before Good Friday, 10 Straight Since 2001

THURSDAY

D 57.1
S 52.4
N 52.4

21

It is totally unproductive to think the world has been unfair to you. Every tough stretch is an opportunity.
— Charlie Munger (Vice-chairman, Berkshire Hathaway, 2007 Wesco Annual Meeting, b. 1924)

Good Friday (Market Closed)

FRIDAY

22

In the realm of ideas, everything depends on enthusiasm; in the real world, all rests on perseverance.
— Johann Wolfgang von Goethe (German poet and polymath, 1749–1832)

SATURDAY

23

Easter

SUNDAY

24

MAY ALMANAC

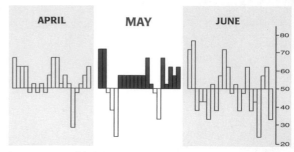

MAY							JUNE						
S	M	T	W	T	F	S	S	M	T	W	T	F	S
1	2	3	4	5	6	7				1	2	3	4
8	9	10	11	12	13	14	5	6	7	8	9	10	11
15	16	17	18	19	20	21	12	13	14	15	16	17	18
22	23	24	25	26	27	28	19	20	21	22	23	24	25
29	30	31					26	27	28	29	30		

Market Probability Chart above is a graphic representation of the S&P 500 Recent Market Probability Calendar on page 124.

◆ "May/June disaster area" between 1965 and 1984 with S&P down 15 out of 20 Mays ◆ Between 1985 and 1997 May was the best month, with 13 straight gains, gaining 3.3% per year on average, up 7, down 5 since ◆ Worst six months of the year begin with May (page 48) ◆ A $10,000 investment compounded to $527,388 for November to April in 60 years compared to a $474 loss for May to October ◆ Dow Memorial Day week record: up 12 years in a row (1984–1995), down seven of the last 14 years ◆ Since 1951, pre-presidential election year Mays rank poorly, #10 Dow & S&P and #8 NASDAQ.

May Vital Statistics

	DJIA		S&P 500		NASDAQ		Russell 1K		Russell 2K	
Rank	8		8		5		4		3	
Up	31		35		24		22		21	
Down	29		25		15		9		10	
Avg % Change	0.2%		0.4%		1.2%		1.5%		1.9%	
Pre-Election Year	0.2%		0.3%		2.2%		1.5%		3.3%	
Best and Worst May										
	% Change		% Change		% Change		% Change		% Change	
Best	1990	8.3	1990	9.2	1997	11.1	1990	8.9	1997	11.0
Worst	1962	−7.8	1962	−8.6	2000	−11.9	1984	−5.9	2000	−5.9
Best and Worst May Weeks										
Best	5/29/70	5.8	5/2/97	6.2	5/17/02	8.8	5/2/97	6.4	5/2/97	5.4
Worst	5/25/62	−6.0	5/25/62	−6.8	5/12/00	−7.5	5/15/09	−5.1	5/12/06	−7.0
Best and Worst May Days										
Best	5/27/70	5.1	5/27/70	5.0	5/30/00	7.9	5/8/02	3.7	5/30/00	4.2
Worst	5/28/62	−5.7	5/28/62	−6.7	5/23/00	−5.9	5/13/09	−2.8	5/13/09	−4.7
First Trading Day of Expiration Week: 1980–2009										
Record (#Up–#Down)	20–10		20–10		16–14		19–11		15–15	
Current Streak	D1		D1		D1		D1		D1	
Avg % Change	0.24		0.23		0.20		0.19		0.00	
Options Expiration Day: 1980–2009										
Record (#Up–#Down)	13–17		16–14		14–16		16–14		14–16	
Current Streak	D2		D1		D2		D1		D2	
Avg % Change	−0.16		−0.18		−0.17		−0.16		−0.07	
Options Expiration Week: 1980–2009										
Record (#Up–#Down)	17–13		16–14		16–14		15–15		17–13	
Current Streak	D1		D1		D1		D1		D1	
Avg % Change	0.31		0.25		0.48		0.27		0.17	
Week After Options Expiration: 1980–2009										
Record (#Up–#Down)	17–13		18–12		20–10		18–12		21–9	
Current Streak	U1		U1		U1		U1		U1	
Avg % Change	−0.04		0.06		0.03		0.08		0.12	
First Trading Day Performance										
% of Time Up	58.3		58.3		61.5		54.8		64.5	
Avg % Change	0.20		0.23		0.32		0.26		0.33	
Last Trading Day Performance										
% of Time Up	63.3		65.0		74.4		61.3		74.2	
Avg % Change	0.24		0.33		0.26		0.32		0.44	

Dow & S&P 1950–April 2010, NASDAQ 1971–April 2010, Russell 1K & 2K 1979–April 2010.

May's new pattern, a smile or a frown,
Odd years UP and even years DOWN.

Day After Easter, Worst Post-Holiday, S&P Down 16 of 20 from 1984 to 2003, But Improving Recently, Up 6 of Last 7, Including 1.5% Gain in 2008

MONDAY

D 38.1
S 28.6
N 47.6

25

I am glad that I paid so little attention to good advice; had I abided by it I might have been saved from my most valuable mistakes.
— Gene Fowler (Journalist, screenwriter, film director, biographer, 1890–1960)

April 1999 First Month Ever to Gain 1000 Dow Points

TUESDAY

D 52.4
S 47.6
N 42.9

26

Show me a good phone receptionist and I'll show you a good company. — Harvey Mackay (*Pushing the Envelope*, 1999)

WEDNESDAY

D 52.4
S 52.4
N 61.9

27

We can guarantee cash benefits as far out and at whatever size you like, but we cannot guarantee their purchasing power.
— Alan Greenspan (Fed chairman 1987–2006, on funding Social Security, to Senate Banking Committee, 2/15/05)

THURSDAY

D 61.9
S 57.1
N 66.7

28

Everything possible today was at one time impossible. Everything impossible today may at some time in the future be possible.
— Edward Lindaman (Apollo space project, president, Whitworth College, 1920–1982)

End of "Best Six Months" of the Year (Pages 44, 48, 50, and 147)

FRIDAY

D 47.6
S 61.9
N 71.4

29

We are all born originals; why is it so many die copies? — Edward Young (English poet, 1683–1765)

SATURDAY

30

May Almanac Investor Seasonalities: See Pages 92, 94, and 96

SUNDAY

1

"BEST SIX MONTHS": STILL AN EYE-POPPING STRATEGY

Our Best Six Months Switching Strategy consistently delivers. Investing in the Dow Jones Industrial Average between November 1st and April 30th each year and then switching into fixed income for the other six months has produced reliable returns with reduced risk since 1950.

The chart on page 147 shows November, December, January, March, and April to be the top months since 1950. Add February, and an excellent strategy is born! These six consecutive months gained 11703.60 Dow points in 60 years, while the remaining May through October months lost 909.32 points. The S&P gained 1153.9 points in the same best six months versus just 16.03 points in the worst six.

Percentage changes are shown, along with a compounding $10,000 investment. The November–April 527,388 gain overshadows May–October's $474 loss. (S&P results were $386,384 to $6,593.) Just three November–April losses were double-digit: April 1970 (Cambodian invasion), 1973 (OPEC oil embargo), and 2008 (financial crisis). Similarly, Iraq muted the Best Six and inflated the Worst Six in 2003. When we discovered this strategy in 1986, November–April outperformed May–October by $88,163 to minus $1,522. Results improved substantially these past 24 years, $439,225 to $1,048. A simple timing indicator triples results (page 50).

SIX-MONTH SWITCHING STRATEGY

	DJIA % Change May 1–Oct 31	Investing $10,000	DJIA % Change Nov 1–Apr 30	Investing $10,000
1950	5.0%	$10,500	15.2%	$11,520
1951	1.2	10,626	−1.8	11,313
1952	4.5	11,104	2.1	11,551
1953	0.4	11,148	15.8	13,376
1954	10.3	12,296	20.9	16,172
1955	6.9	13,144	13.5	18,355
1956	−7.0	12,224	3.0	18,906
1957	−10.8	10,904	3.4	19,549
1958	19.2	12,998	14.8	22,442
1959	3.7	13,479	−6.9	20,894
1960	−3.5	13,007	16.9	24,425
1961	3.7	13,488	−5.5	23,082
1962	−11.4	11,950	21.7	28,091
1963	5.2	12,571	7.4	30,170
1964	7.7	13,539	5.6	31,860
1965	4.2	14,108	−2.8	30,968
1966	−13.6	12,189	11.1	34,405
1967	−1.9	11,957	3.7	35,678
1968	4.4	12,483	−0.2	35,607
1969	−9.9	11,247	−14.0	30,622
1970	2.7	11,551	24.6	38,155
1971	−10.9	10,292	13.7	43,382
1972	0.1	10,302	−3.6	41,820
1973	3.8	10,693	−12.5	36,593
1974	−20.5	8,501	23.4	45,156
1975	1.8	8,654	19.2	53,826
1976	−3.2	8,377	−3.9	51,727
1977	−11.7	7,397	2.3	52,917
1978	−5.4	6,998	7.9	57,097
1979	−4.6	6,676	0.2	57,211
1980	13.1	7,551	7.9	61,731
1981	−14.6	6,449	−0.5	61,422
1982	16.9	7,539	23.6	75,918
1983	−0.1	7,531	−4.4	72,578
1984	3.1	7,764	4.2	75,626
1985	9.2	8,478	29.8	98,163
1986	5.3	8,927	21.8	119,563
1987	−12.8	7,784	1.9	121,835
1988	5.7	8,228	12.6	137,186
1989	9.4	9,001	0.4	137,735
1990	−8.1	8,272	18.2	162,803
1991	6.3	8,793	9.4	178,106
1992	−4.0	8,441	6.2	189,149
1993	7.4	9,066	0.03	189,206
1994	6.2	9,628	10.6	209,262
1995	10.0	10,591	17.1	245,046
1996	8.3	11,470	16.2	284,743
1997	6.2	12,181	21.8	346,817
1998	−5.2	11,548	25.6	435,602
1999	−0.5	11,490	0.04	435,776
2000	2.2	11,743	−2.2	426,189
2001	−15.5	9,923	9.6	467,103
2002	−15.6	8,375	1.0	471,774
2003	15.6	9,682	4.3	492,060
2004	−1.9	9,498	1.6	499,933
2005	2.4	9,726	8.9	544,427
2006	6.3	10,339	8.1	588,526
2007	6.6	11,021	−8.0	541,444
2008	−27.3	8,012	−12.4	474,305
2009	18.9	9,526	13.3	537,388
Average/Gain	**0.4%**	**($474)**	**7.4%**	**$527,388**
# Up/Down	**36/24**		**46/14**	

MAY

First Trading Day in May, Dow Up 10 of Last 12

MONDAY
D 71.4
S 71.4
N 71.4
2

"Sell in May and go away." However, no one ever said it was the beginning of the month.
— John L. Person (Professional trader, author, speaker, *Commodity Trader's Almanac*, nationalfutures.com, 6/19/2009, b. 1961)

TUESDAY
D 71.4
S 71.4
N 71.4
3

I do not rule Russia; ten thousand clerks do. — Nicholas I (1795–1855)

WEDNESDAY
D 38.1
S 47.6
N 66.7
4

Bull markets are born on pessimism, grow on skepticism, mature on optimism, and die on euphoria.
— Sir John Templeton (Founder, Templeton Funds, philanthropist, 1994)

THURSDAY
D 47.6
S 38.1
N 57.1
5

But how do we know when irrational exuberance has unduly escalated asset values,
which then become subject to unexpected and prolonged contractions as they have in Japan over the past decade?
— Alan Greenspan (Fed chairman 1987–2006, 12/5/96 speech to American Enterprise Institute, b. 1926)

Friday Before Mother's Day, Dow Up 10 of Last 15

FRIDAY
D 33.3
S 23.8
N 38.1
6

There is one thing stronger than all the armies in the world, and this is an idea whose time has come.
— Victor Hugo (French novelist, playwright, *Hunchback of Notre Dame* and *Les Misérables*, 1802–1885)

SATURDAY
7

Mother's Day

SUNDAY
8

MACD-TIMING TRIPLES "BEST SIX MONTHS" RESULTS

Using the simple MACD (Moving Average Convergence Divergence) indicator developed by our friend Gerald Appel to better time entries and exits into and out of the Best Six Months (page 48) period nearly triples the results. Several years ago, Sy Harding enhanced our Best Six Months Switching Strategy with MACD triggers, dubbing it the "best mechanical system ever." In 2006, we improved it even more, quadrupling the results with just four trades every four years (page 60).

Our *Almanac Investor Newsletter* (see insert page 96) implements this system with quite a degree of success. Starting October 1, we look to catch the market's first hint of an uptrend after the summer doldrums, and beginning April 1 we prepare to exit these seasonal positions as soon as the market falters.

In up-trending markets, MACD signals get you in earlier and keep you in longer. But if the market is trending down, entries are delayed until the market turns up and exit points can come a month earlier.

The results are astounding applying the simple MACD signals. Instead of $10,000 gaining $527,388 over the 60 recent years when invested only during the Best Six Months (page 48), the gain nearly tripled to $1,472,790. The $474 loss during the worst six months expanded to a loss of $6,542.

Impressive results for being invested during only 6.4 months of the year on average! For the rest of the year, consider money markets, bonds, puts, bear funds, covered calls, or credit call spreads. See page 78 for more executable trades employing ETFs and mutual funds.

Updated signals are e-mailed to our monthly newsletter subscribers as soon as they are triggered. Visit *www.stocktradersalmanac.com*, or see the insert at page 96 for details and a special offer for new subscribers.

SIX-MONTH SWITCHING STRATEGY+TIMING

	DJIA % Change May 1–Oct 31*	Investing $10,000	DJIA % Change Nov 1–Apr 30*	Investing $10,000
1950	7.3%	$10,730	13.3%	$11,330
1951	0.1	10,741	1.9	11,545
1952	1.4	10,891	2.1	11,787
1953	0.2	10,913	17.1	13,803
1954	13.5	12,386	16.3	16,053
1955	7.7	13,340	13.1	18,156
1956	−6.8	12,433	2.8	18,664
1957	−12.3	10,904	4.9	19,579
1958	17.3	12,790	16.7	22,849
1959	1.6	12,995	−3.1	22,141
1960	−4.9	12,358	16.9	25,883
1961	2.9	12,716	−1.5	25,495
1962	−15.3	10,770	22.4	31,206
1963	4.3	11,233	9.6	34,202
1964	6.7	11,986	6.2	36,323
1965	2.6	12,298	−2.5	35,415
1966	−16.4	10,281	14.3	40,479
1967	−2.1	10,065	5.5	42,705
1968	3.4	10,407	0.2	42,790
1969	−11.9	9,169	−6.7	39,923
1970	−1.4	9,041	20.8	48,227
1971	−11.0	8,046	15.4	55,654
1972	−0.6	7,998	−1.4	54,875
1973	−11.0	7,118	0.1	54,930
1974	−22.4	5,524	28.2	70,420
1975	0.1	5,530	18.5	83,448
1976	−3.4	5,342	−3.0	80,945
1977	−11.4	4,733	0.5	81,350
1978	−4.5	4,520	9.3	88,916
1979	−5.3	4,280	7.0	95,140
1980	9.3	4,678	4.7	99,612
1981	−14.6	3,995	0.4	100,010
1982	15.5	4,614	23.5	123,512
1983	2.5	4,729	−7.3	114,496
1984	3.3	4,885	3.9	118,961
1985	7.0	5,227	38.1	164,285
1986	−2.8	5,081	28.2	210,613
1987	−14.9	4,324	3.0	216,931
1988	6.1	4,588	11.8	242,529
1989	9.8	5,038	3.3	250,532
1990	−6.7	4,700	15.8	290,116
1991	4.8	4,926	11.3	322,899
1992	−6.2	4,621	6.6	344,210
1993	5.5	4,875	5.6	363,486
1994	3.7	5,055	13.1	411,103
1995	7.2	5,419	16.7	479,757
1996	9.2	5,918	21.9	584,824
1997	3.6	6,131	18.5	693,016
1998	−12.4	5,371	39.9	969,529
1999	−6.4	5,027	5.1	1,018,975
2000	−6.0	4,725	5.4	1,074,000
2001	−17.3	3,908	15.8	1,243,692
2002	−25.2	2,923	6.0	1,318,314
2003	16.4	3,402	7.8	1,421,142
2004	−0.9	3,371	1.8	1,446,723
2005	−0.5	3,354	7.7	1,558,121
2006	4.7	3,512	14.4	1,782,490
2007	5.6	3,709	−12.7	1,556,114
2008	−24.7	2,793	−14.0	1,338,258
2009	23.8	3,458	10.8	1,482,790
Average	**−1.2%**		**9.2%**	
# Up	**31**		**51**	
# Down	**29**		**9**	
60-Year Gain (Loss)		**($6,542)**		**$1,472,790**

*MACD generated entry and exit points (earlier or later) can lengthen or shorten six-month periods.

MAY

Monday After Mother's Day, Dow Up 12 of Last 15

MONDAY
D 66.7
S 57.1
N 71.4

9

We are nowhere near a capitulation point because it's at that point where it's despair, not hope,
that reigns supreme, and there was scant evidence of any despair at any of the meetings I gave.
— David Rosenberg (Economist, Merrill Lynch, *Barron's*, 4/21/2008)

TUESDAY
D 61.9
S 57.1
N 47.6

10

Victory goes to the player who makes the next-to-last mistake. — Savielly Grigorievitch Tartakower (Chess master, 1887–1956)

WEDNESDAY
D 66.7
S 57.1
N 42.9

11

When a company reports higher earnings for its first quarter (over its previous year's first quarter),
chances are almost five to one it will also have increased earnings in its second quarter. — Niederhoffer, Cross & Zeckhauser

THURSDAY
D 57.1
S 57.1
N 57.1

12

The test of success is not what you do when you are on top. Success is how high you bounce when you hit bottom.
— General George S. Patton Jr. (US Army field commander WWII, 1885–1945)

FRIDAY
D 61.9
S 57.1
N 52.4

13

The government would not look fondly on Caesar's Palace if it opened a table for wagering on corporate failure.
It should not give greater encouragement for Goldman Sachs [et al] to do so.
— Roger Lowenstein (Financial journalist and author, *End of Wall Street*, *NY Times* OpEd, 4/20/2010, b. 1954)

SATURDAY

14

SUNDAY

15

TAKE ADVANTAGE OF DOWN FRIDAY/ DOWN MONDAY WARNING

Fridays and Mondays are the most important days of the week. Friday is the day for squaring positions—trimming longs or covering shorts before taking off for the weekend. Traders want to limit their exposure (particularly to stocks that are not acting well) since there could be unfavorable developments before trading resumes two or more days later.

Monday is important because the market then has the chance to reflect any weekend news, plus what traders think after digesting the previous week's action and the many Monday morning research and strategy comments.

For over 30 years, a down Friday followed by down Monday has frequently corresponded with important market inflection points that exhibit a clearly negative bias, often coinciding with market tops and, on a few climactic occasions, such as in October 2002 and March 2009, near major market bottoms.

One simple way to get a quick reading on which way the market may be heading is to keep track of the performance of the Dow Jones Industrial Average on Fridays and the following Mondays. Since 1995, there have been 155 occurrences of Down Friday/Down Monday (DF/DM), with 46 falling in the bear market years of 2001, 2002, and 2008, producing an average decline of 14.1%.

To illustrate how Down Friday/Down Monday can telegraph market inflection points we created the chart below of the Dow Jones Industrials from November 2008 to April 30, 2010, with arrows

DOWN FRIDAY/DOWN MONDAYS

Year	Total Number Down Friday/ Down Monday	Subsequent Average % Dow Loss*	Average Number of Days it took
1995	8	−1.2%	18
1996	9	−3.0%	28
1997	6	−5.1%	45
1998	9	−6.4%	47
1999	9	−6.4%	39
2000	11	−6.6%	32
2001	13	−13.5%	53
2002	18	−11.9%	54
2003	9	−3.0%	17
2004	9	−3.7%	51
2005	10	−3.0%	37
2006	11	−2.0%	14
2007	8	−6.0%	33
2008	15	−17.0%	53
2009	10	−11.0%	30
2010**	0	N/A	N/A
Average	10	−6.6%	37

*Over next 3 months; **Ending April 30, 2010*

pointing to occurrences of DF/DM. Use DF/DM as a warning to examine market conditions carefully. At press time, the Dow has gone 28 weeks without a DF/DM, the longest such stretch since the NYSE discontinued Saturday trading in June 1952. The 10 instances in the past 58 years when the Dow has gone 15 weeks or more without a DF/DM occurred during extended bull markets. When more frequent DF/DM followed the end of these streaks, it was near a top.

DOW JONES INDUSTRIALS (November 2008 to April 30, 2010)

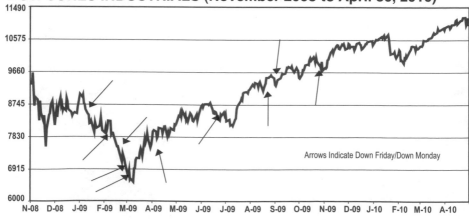

Arrows Indicate Down Friday/Down Monday

Monday Before May Expiration, Dow Up 19 of Last 22, Average Gain 0.6%

MONDAY
16
D 61.9
S 57.1
N 57.1

Innovation can't depend on trying to please the customer or the client. It is an elitist act by the inventor who acts alone and breaks rules. — Dean Kamen (Inventor, president of DEKA R&D, *Business Week*, Feb. 12, 2001)

TUESDAY
17
D 52.4
S 57.1
N 61.9

Give me a stock clerk with a goal and I will give you a man who will make history.
Give me a man without a goal, and I will give you a stock clerk. — James Cash Penney (J.C. Penney founder)

WEDNESDAY
18
D 61.9
S 66.7
N 71.4

All great truths begin as blasphemies. — George Bernard Shaw (Irish dramatist, 1856–1950)

THURSDAY
19
D 52.4
S 52.4
N 47.6

In the stock market those who expect history to repeat itself exactly are doomed to failure.
— Yale Hirsch (Creator of *Stock Trader's Almanac*, b. 1923)

May Expiration Day, Dow Down 12 of Last 20, Average Loss 0.2%

FRIDAY
20
D 47.6
S 47.6
N 52.4

Those who cannot remember the past are condemned to repeat it.
— George Santayana (American philosopher, poet, 1863–1952)

SATURDAY
21

SUNDAY
22

TOP PERFORMING NASDAQ MONTHS PAST 39⅓ YEARS

NASDAQ stocks continue to run away during three consecutive months, November, December, and January, with an average gain of 6.5% despite the slaughter of November 2000, down 22.9%, December 2000, −4.9%, December 2002, −9.7%, November 2007, −6.9%, January 2008, −9.9%, November 2008, −10.8%, and January 2009, −6.4%. Solid gains in November and December 2004 offset January 2005's 5.2% Iraq-turmoil-fueled drop.

You can see the months graphically on page 148. January by itself is impressive, up 2.8% on average. April, May, and June also shine, creating our NASDAQ Best Eight Months strategy. What appears as a Death Valley abyss occurs during NASDAQ's bleakest four months: July, August, September, and October. NASDAQ's Best Eight Months seasonal strategy using MACD timing is displayed on page 58.

MONTHLY % CHANGES (JANUARY 1971 TO APRIL 2010)

NASDAQ Composite*

Month	Total % Change	Avg. % Change	# Up	# Down
Jan	113.4%	2.8%	26	14
Feb	10.7	0.3	20	20
Mar	30.6	0.8	26	14
Apr	61.3	1.5	26	14
May	47.1	1.2	24	15
Jun	37.3	1.0	23	16
Jul	−5.5	−0.1	19	20
Aug	15.8	0.4	22	17
Sep	−33.3	−0.9	21	18
Oct	7.8	0.2	20	19
Nov	65.4	1.7	26	13
Dec	78.1	2.0	23	16

% Rank				
Jan	113.4%	2.8%	26	14
Dec	78.1	2.0	23	16
Nov	65.4	1.7	26	13
Apr	61.3	1.5	26	14
May	47.1	1.2	24	15
Jun	37.3	1.0	23	16
Mar	30.6	0.8	26	14
Aug	15.8	0.4	22	17
Feb	10.7	0.3	20	20
Oct	7.8	0.2	20	19
Jul	−5.5	−0.1	19	20
Sep	−33.3	−0.9	21	18
Totals	428.7%	10.9%		
Average		0.91%		

Dow Jones Industrials

Month	Total % Change	Avg. % Change	# Up	# Down
Jan	50.6%	1.3%	25	15
Feb	3.1	0.1	22	18
Mar	44.1	1.1	26	14
Apr	89.2	2.2	24	16
May	24.2	0.6	21	18
Jun	−0.9	−0.02	20	19
Jul	23.7	0.6	21	18
Aug	1.2	0.03	23	16
Sep	−50.9	−1.3	13	26
Oct	8.5	0.2	23	16
Nov	49.5	1.3	26	13
Dec	63.0	1.6	27	12

% Rank				
Apr	89.2%	2.2%	24	16
Dec	63.0	1.6	27	12
Jan	50.6	1.3	25	15
Nov	49.5	1.3	26	13
Mar	44.1	1.1	26	14
May	24.2	0.6	21	18
Jul	23.7	0.6	21	18
Oct	8.5	0.2	23	16
Feb	3.1	0.1	22	18
Aug	1.2	0.03	23	16
Jun	−0.9	−0.02	20	19
Sep	−50.9	−1.3	13	26
Totals	305.3%	7.7%		
Average		0.64%		

*Based on NASDAQ composite, prior to February 5, 1971, based on National Quotation Bureau indices.

For comparison, Dow figures are shown. During this period, NASDAQ averaged a 0.91% gain per month, 42 percent more than the Dow's 0.64% per month. Between January 1971 and January 1982 NASDAQ's composite index doubled in twelve years, while the Dow stayed flat. But while NASDAQ plummeted 77.9% from its 2000 highs to the 2002 bottom, the Dow only lost 37.8%. The Great Recession and bear market of 2007–2009 spread its carnage equally across Dow and NASDAQ.

MONDAY
D 33.3
S 33.3
N 42.9
23

The thing always happens that you really believe in. The belief in a thing makes it happen.
— Frank Lloyd Wright (American architect)

TUESDAY
D 57.1
S 66.7
N 61.9
24

Don't confuse brains with a bull market. — Humphrey B. Neill (Investor, analyst, author, *Neill Letters of Contrary Opinion*, 1895–1977)

WEDNESDAY
D 47.6
S 52.4
N 52.4
25

Markets are constantly in a state of uncertainty and flux, and money is made by discounting the obvious and betting on the unexpected. — George Soros (Financier, philanthropist, political activist, author, and philosopher, b. 1930)

THURSDAY
D 57.1
S 61.9
N 66.7
26

The only function of economic forecasting is to make astrology look respectable.
— John Kenneth Galbraith (Canadian/American economist and diplomat, 1908–2006)

Friday Before Memorial Day Tends to Bo Lackluster with Light Trading

FRIDAY
D 66.7
S 57.1
N 71.4
27

To know values is to know the meaning of the market. — Charles Dow (Cofounder, Dow Jones & Co, 1851–1902)

SATURDAY
28

June Almanac Investor Seasonalities: See Pages 92, 94, and 96

SUNDAY
29

JUNE ALMANAC

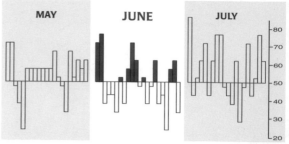

◆ The "summer rally" in most years is the weakest rally of all four seasons (page 70) ◆ Week after June Triple-Witching Day Dow down 17 of last 19 (page 76) ◆ RECENT RECORD: S&P up 10, down 5, average gain 0.1%, ranks seventh ◆ Much stronger for NASDAQ, average gain 1.2% last 15 years ◆ Watch out for end-of-quarter "portfolio pumping" on last day of June, Dow down 15 of last 21, NASDAQ down 5 straight ◆ Pre-presidential election year Junes: #5 S&P & NASDAQ, Dow weaker, ranks #7 ◆ June ends NASDAQ's Best Eight Months.

June Vital Statistics

	DJIA	S&P 500	NASDAQ	Russell 1K	Russell 2K
Rank	11	10	6	9	9
Up	28	32	23	19	20
Down	32	28	16	12	11
Avg % Change	−0.3%	0.1%	1.0%	0.4%	0.7%
Pre-Election Year	1.1%	1.6%	2.8%	1.8%	1.9%
Best and Worst June					
	% Change	% Change	% Change	% Change	% Change
Best	1955 6.2	1955 8.2	2000 16.6	1999 5.1	2000 8.6
Worst	2008 −10.2	2008 −8.6	2002 −9.4	2008 −8.5	2008 −7.8
Best and Worst June Weeks					
Best	6/7/74 6.4	6/2/00 7.2	6/2/00 19.0	6/2/00 8.0	6/2/00 12.2
Worst	6/30/50 −6.8	6/30/50 −7.6	6/15/01 −8.4	6/15/01 −4.2	6/9/06 −4.9
Best and Worst June Days					
Best	6/28/62 3.8	6/28/62 3.4	6/2/00 6.4	6/17/02 2.8	6/2/00 4.2
Worst	6/26/50 −4.7	6/26/50 −5.4	6/14/01 −3.7	6/22/09 −3.1	6/22/09 3.9
First Trading Day of Expiration Week: 1980–2009					
Record (#Up–#Down)	16–14	18–12	13–17	17–13	11–18
Current Streak	D2	D1	D1	D1	D1
Avg % Change	0.02	−0.08	−0.26	−0.09	−0.34
Options Expiration Day: 1980–2009					
Record (#Up–#Down)	17–13	18–12	17–13	18–12	16–14
Current Streak	D2	U1	U1	U1	U1
Avg % Change	−0.10	−0.01	−0.03	−0.05	−0.04
Options Expiration Week: 1980–2009					
Record (#Up–#Down)	16–14	14–16	12–18	13–17	12–18
Current Streak	D2	D2	D2	D2	D2
Avg % Change	−0.21	−0.22	−0.43	−0.28	−0.44
Week After Options Expiration: 1980–2009					
Record (#Up–#Down)	10–20	16–14	17–13	16–14	14–16
Current Streak	D11	D7	U1	D5	U1
Avg % Change	−0.37	−0.05	0.19	−0.02	−0.10
First Trading Day Performance					
% of Time Up	55.0	53.3	61.5	61.3	67.7
Avg % Change	0.22	0.21	0.29	0.26	0.42
Last Trading Day Performance					
% of Time Up	53.3	50.0	66.7	48.4	67.7
Avg % Change	0.01	0.06	0.26	−0.06	0.36

Dow & S&P 1950–April 2010, NASDAQ 1971–April 2010, Russell 1K & 2K 1979–April 2010.

Last Day of June not hot for the Dow;
Down 14 of 19, WOW!

MAY/JUNE

Memorial Day (Market Closed)

A market is the combined behavior of thousands of people responding to information, misinformation and whim.
— Kenneth Chang (NY Times journalist)

Day After Memorial Day, Dow Up 8 of Last 11

TUESDAY
D 52.4
S 61.9
N 71.4
31

War is God's way of teaching Americans geography.
— Ambrose Bierce (Writer, satirist, Civil War hero, The Devil's Dictionary, 1842–1914?)

First Trading Day in June, Dow Up 10 of Last 12, 2002 −2.2%, 2008 −1.1%

WEDNESDAY
D 81.0
S 71.4
N 71.4
1

Each day is a building block to the future. Who I am today is dependent on who I was yesterday.
— Matthew McConaughey (Actor, Parade Magazine)

Start Looking for NASDAQ MACD Sell Signal (Page 58)
Almanac Investor Subscribers Emailed When It Triggers (See Insert Page 96)

THURSDAY
D 57.1
S 76.2
N 81.0
2

There is a habitual nature to society and human activity. People's behavior and what they do with their money and time bears upon economics and the stock market. — Jeffrey A. Hirsch (Editor, Stock Trader's Almanac, b. 1966)

Memorial Day Week Dow Down 7 of Last 14, Up 12 Straight 1984–1995

FRIDAY
D 42.9
S 38.1
N 47.6
3

We're not believers that the government is bigger than the business cycle.
— David Rosenberg (Economist, Merrill Lynch, Barron's, 4/21/2008)

SATURDAY
4

SUNDAY
5

GET MORE OUT OF NASDAQ'S "BEST EIGHT MONTHS" WITH MACD TIMING

NASDAQ's amazing eight-month run from November through June is hard to miss on pages 54 and 148. A $10,000 investment in these eight months since 1971 gained $351,706, versus a loss of $4,088 during the void that is the four-month period July to October.

Using the same MACD timing indicators on the NASDAQ as is done for the Dow (page 50) has enabled us to capture much of October's improved performance, pumping up NASDAQ's results considerably. Over the 39 years since NASDAQ began, the gain on the same $10,000 more than doubles to $874,360, and the loss during the four-month void increases to $7,461. Only four sizeable losses occurred during the favorable period and the bulk of NASDAQ's bear markets were avoided, including the worst of the 2000–2002 bear. See page 78 for more executable trades employing ETFs and mutual funds.

Updated signals are e-mailed to our monthly newsletter subscribers as soon as they are triggered. Visit *www.stocktradersalmanac.com,* or see the insert at page 96 for details and a special offer for new subscribers.

BEST EIGHT MONTHS STRATEGY + TIMING

MACD Signal Date	Worst 4 Months July 1–Oct 31* NASDAQ	% Change	Investing $10,000	MACD Signal Date	Best 8 Months Nov 1–June 30* NASDAQ	% Change	Investing $10,000
22-Jul-71	109.54	−3.6	$9,640	4-Nov-71	105.56	24.1	$12,410
7-Jun-72	131.00	−1.8	9,466	23-Oct-72	128.66	−22.7	9,593
25-Jun-73	99.43	−7.2	8,784	7-Dec-73	92.32	−20.2	7,655
3-Jul-74	73.66	−23.2	6,746	7-Oct-74	56.57	47.8	11,314
11-Jun-75	83.60	−9.2	6,125	7-Oct-75	75.88	20.8	13,667
22-Jul-76	91.66	−2.4	5,978	19-Oct-76	89.45	13.2	15,471
27-Jul-77	101.25	−4.0	5,739	4-Nov-77	97.21	26.6	19,586
7-Jun-78	123.10	−6.5	5,366	6-Nov-78	115.08	19.1	23,327
3-Jul-79	137.03	−1.1	5,307	30-Nov-79	135.48	15.5	26,943
20-Jun-80	156.51	26.2	6,697	9-Oct-80	197.53	11.2	29,961
4-Jun-81	219.68	−17.6	5,518	1-Oct-81	181.09	−4.0	28,763
7-Jun-82	173.84	12.5	6,208	7-Oct-82	195.59	57.4	45,273
1-Jun-83	307.95	−10.7	5,544	3-Nov-83	274.86	−14.2	38,844
1-Jun-84	235.90	5.0	5,821	15-Oct-84	247.67	17.3	45,564
3-Jun-85	290.59	−3.0	5,646	1-Oct-85	281.77	39.4	63,516
10-Jun-86	392.83	−10.3	5,064	1-Oct-86	352.34	20.5	76,537
30-Jun-87	424.67	−22.7	3,914	2-Nov-87	328.33	20.1	91,921
8-Jul-88	394.33	−6.6	3,656	29-Nov-88	368.15	22.4	112,511
13-Jun-89	450.73	0.7	3,682	9-Nov-89	454.07	1.9	114,649
11-Jun-90	462.79	−23.0	2,835	2-Oct-90	356.39	39.3	159,706
11-Jun-91	496.62	6.4	3,016	1-Oct-91	528.51	7.4	171,524
11-Jun-92	567.68	1.5	3,061	14-Oct-92	576.22	20.5	206,686
7-Jun-93	694.61	9.9	3,364	1-Oct-93	763.23	−4.4	197,592
17-Jun-94	729.35	5.0	3,532	11-Oct-94	765.57	13.5	224,267
1-Jun-95	868.82	17.2	4,140	13-Oct-95	1018.38	21.6	272,709
3-Jun-96	1238.73	1.0	4,181	7-Oct-96	1250.87	10.3	300,798
4-Jun-97	1379.67	24.4	5,201	3-Oct-97	1715.87	1.8	306,212
1-Jun-98	1746.82	−7.8	4,795	15-Oct-98	1611.01	49.7	458,399
1-Jun-99	2412.03	18.5	5,682	6-Oct-99	2857.21	35.7	622,047
29-Jun-00	3877.23	−18.2	4,648	18-Oct-00	3171.56	−32.2	421,748
1-Jun-01	2149.44	−31.1	3,202	1-Oct-01	1480.46	5.5	444,944
3-Jun-02	1562.56	−24.0	2,434	2-Oct-02	1187.30	38.5	616,247
20-Jun-03	1644.72	15.1	2,802	6-Oct-03	1893.46	4.3	642,746
21-Jun-04	1974.38	−1.6	2,757	1-Oct-04	1942.20	6.1	681,954
8-Jun-05	2060.18	1.5	2,798	19-Oct-05	2091.76	6.1	723,553
1-Jun-06	2219.86	3.9	2,907	5-Oct-06	2306.34	9.5	792,291
7-Jun-07	2541.38	7.9	3,137	1-Oct-07	2740.99	−9.1	724,796
2-Jun-08	2491.53	−31.3	2,155	17-Oct-08	1711.29	6.1	769,000
1-May-09	1816.38	17.8	2,539	9-Oct-09	2139.28	15.0	884,360
30-Apr-10	2461.19	*As of April 30, 2010, MACD Sell Signal not triggered at press time.*					
	39-Year Loss	**($7,461)**				**39-Year Gain**	**$874,360**

MACD-generated entry and exit points (earlier or later) can lengthen or shorten eight-month periods.

JUNE

MONDAY
D 52.4
S 42.9
N 52.4
6

Buy when you are scared to death; sell when are tickled to death. — Market Maxim (*The Cabot Market Letter*, April 12, 2001)

TUESDAY
D 52.4
S 42.9
N 38.1
7

In democracies, nothing is more great or brilliant than commerce; it attracts the attention of the public and fills the imagination of the multitude; all passions of energy are directed towards it.
— Alexis de Tocqueville (Author, *Democracy in America* 1840, 1805–1859)

June Ends NASDAQ's "Best Eight Months" (Pages 54, 58, and 148)   WEDNESDAY
D 47.6
S 33.3
N 33.3
8

Don't be overly concerned about your heirs. Usually, unearned funds do them more harm than good.
— Gerald M. Loeb (E.F. Hutton, *The Battle for Investment Survival*, predicted 1929 Crash, 1900–1974)

THURSDAY
D 42.9
S 52.4
N 47.6
9

Institutions tend to dump stock in a single transaction and buy, if possible, in smaller lots, gradually accumulating a position. Therefore, many more big blocks are traded on downticks than on upticks.
—Justin Mamis (Author, *The Mamis Letter, WhenTo Sell, b. 1929*)

FRIDAY
D 47.6
S 38.1
N38.1
10

If there's anything duller than being on a board in Corporate America, I haven't found it.
— H. Ross Perot (American businessman, *NY Times*, 10/28/92, 2-time presidential candidate, 1992 and 1996, b. 1930)

SATURDAY
11

SUNDAY
12

TRIPLE RETURNS, FEWER TRADES: BEST 6 + 4-YEAR CYCLE

We first introduced this strategy to *Almanac Investor* newsletter subscribers in October 2006. Recurring seasonal stock market patterns and the four-year Presidential Election/Stock Market Cycle (page 130) have been integral to our research since the first Almanac 44 years ago. Yale Hirsch discovered the Best Six Months in 1986 (page 48) and it has been a cornerstone of our seasonal investment analysis and strategies ever since.

Most of the market's gains have occurred during the Best Six Months, and the market generally hits a low point every four years in the first (post-election) or second (midterm) year and exhibits the greatest gains in the third (pre-election) year. This strategy combines the best of these two market phenomena, the Best Six Months and the four-year cycle, timing entries and exits with MACD (pages 50 and 58).

We've gone back to 1949 to include the full four-year cycle that began with post-election year 1949. Only four trades every four years are needed to nearly triple the results of the Best Six Months. Buy and sell during the post-election and midterm years and then hold from the midterm MACD seasonal buy signal sometime after October 1 until the post-election MACD seasonal sell signal sometime after April 1, approximately 2.5 years: better returns, less effort, lower transaction fees, and fewer taxable events. See page 78 for more executable trades employing ETFs and mutual funds.

BEST SIX MONTHS+TIMING+4-YEAR CYCLE STRATEGY

	DJIA % Change May 1–Oct 31*	Investing $10,000	DJIA % Change Nov 1–Apr 30*	Investing $10,000
1949	3.0%	$10,300	17.5%	$11,750
1950	7.3	$11,052	19.7	$14,065
1951		$11,052		$14,065
1952		$11,052		$14,065
1953	0.2	$11,074	17.1	$16,470
1954	13.5	$12,569	35.7	$22,350
1955		$12,569		$22,350
1956		$12,569		$22,350
1957	−12.3	$11,023	4.9	$23,445
1958	17.3	$12,930	27.8	$29,963
1959		$12,930		$29,963
1960		$12,930		$29,963
1961	2.9	$13,305	−1.5	$29,514
1962	−15.3	$11,269	58.5	$46,780
1963		$11,269		$46,780
1964		$11,269		$46,780
1965	2.6	$11,562	−2.5	$45,611
1966	−16.4	$9,666	22.2	$55,737
1967		$9,666		$55,737
1968		$9,666		$55,737
1969	−11.9	$8,516	−6.7	$52,003
1970	−1.4	$8,397	21.5	$63,184
1971		$8,397		$63,184
1972		$8,397		$63,184
1973	−11.0	$7,473	0.1	$63,247
1974	−22.4	$5,799	42.5	$90,127
1975		$5,799		$90,127
1976		$5,799		$90,127
1977	−11.4	$5,138	0.5	$90,578
1978	−4.5	$4,907	26.8	$114,853
1979		$4,907		$114,853
1980		$4,907		$114,853
1981	−14.6	$4,191	0.4	$115,312
1982	15.5	$4,841	25.9	$145,178
1983		$4,841		$145,178
1984		$4,841		$145,178
1985	7.0	$5,180	38.1	$200,491
1986	−2.8	$5,035	33.2	$267,054
1987		$5,035		$267,054
1988		$5,035		$267,054
1989	9.8	$5,528	3.3	$275,867
1990	−6.7	$5,158	35.1	$372,696
1991		$5,158		$372,696
1992		$5,158		$372,696
1993	5.5	$5,442	5.6	$393,455
1994	3.7	$5,643	88.2	$740,482
1995		$5,643		$740,482
1996		$5,643		$740,482
1997	3.6	$5,846	18.5	$877,471
1998	−12.4	$5,121	36.3	$1,195,993
1999		$5,121		$1,195,993
2000		$5,121		$1,195,993
2001	−17.3	$4,235	15.8	$1,384,960
2002	−25.2	$3,168	34.2	$1,858,616
2003		$3,168		$1,858,616
2004		$3,168		$1,858,616
2005	−0.5	$3,152	7.7	$2,001,729
2006	4.7	$3,300	−31.7	$1,367,181
2007		$3,300		$1,367,181
2008		$3,300		$1,367,181
2009	23.8	$4,085	10.8	$1,514,738
Average	−1.1%		10.1%	
# Up	15		27	
# Down	16		4	
61-Year (Loss)		($5,915)		$1,504,738

*MACD and 2.5–year hold lengthen and shorten six–month periods. ** At press time

FOUR TRADES EVERY FOUR YEARS

Year	Worst Six Months May–Oct	Best Six Months Nov–April
Post-election	Sell	Buy
Midterm	Sell	Buy
Pre-election	Hold	Hold
Election	Hold	Hold

JUNE

Monday of Triple Witching Week, Dow Down 8 of Last 13

MONDAY
D 57.1
S 57.1
N 52.4
13

Moses Shapiro (of General Instrument) told me, "Son, this is Talmudic wisdom. Always ask the question 'If not?'
Few people have good strategies for when their assumptions are wrong." That's the best business advice I ever got.
— John Malone (CEO of cable giant TCI, *Fortune*, 2/16/98)

TUESDAY
D 71.4
S 71.4
N 57.1
14

We will have to pay more and more attention to what the funds are doing. They are the ones who have been contributing
to the activity, especially in the high-fliers. — Humphrey B. Neill (Investor, analyst, author, *NY Times*, 6/11/1966, 1895–1977)

Triple Witching Week Often Up in Bull Markets and Down in Bears (Page 76)

WEDNESDAY
D 52.4
S 61.9
N 61.9
15

It has been said that politics is the second oldest profession. I have learned that it bears a striking resemblance to the first.
— Ronald Reagan (40th U.S. president, 1911–2004)

THURSDAY
D 47.6
S 47.6
N 38.1
16

It's not that I am so smart; it's just that I stay with problems longer.
— Albert Einstein (German/American physicist, 1921 Nobel Prize, 1879–1955)

June Triple Witching Day, Dow Down 7 of Last 12,
Average Loss 0.5%

FRIDAY
D 47.6
S 52.4
N 47.6
17

The first human who hurled an insult instead of a stone was the founder of civilization.
— Sigmund Freud (Austrian neurologist, psychiatrist, "father of psychoanalysis," 1856–1939)

SATURDAY
18

Father's Day

SUNDAY
19

FIRST-TRADING-DAY-OF-THE-MONTH PHENOMENON: DOW GAINS MORE ONE DAY THAN ALL OTHER DAYS

Over the last 13 years, the Dow Jones Industrial Average has gained more points on the first trading days of all months than all other days combined. While the Dow has gained 3529.41 points between September 2, 1997 (7622.42) and May 3, 2010 (11151.83), it is incredible that 5173.23 points were gained on the first trading days of these 153 months. The remaining 3034 trading days combined lost 1643.82 points during the period. This averages out to gains of 33.81 points on first days, in contrast to a loss of 0.54 points on all others.

Note that September 1997 through October 2000 racked up a total gain of 2632.39 Dow points on the first trading days of these 38 months (winners except for seven occasions). But between November 2000 and September 2002, when the 2000–2002 bear markets did the bulk of their damage, frightened investors switched from pouring money into the market on that day to pulling it out, 14 months out of 23, netting a 404.80 Dow point loss. The 2007–2009 bear market lopped off 964.14 Dow points on first days in 17 months from November 2007–March 2009. Twelve of the last 14 first days since the March 2009 bottom produced solid gains; only September and October 2009 were losers.

First days of August have performed worst, falling 8 times out of 12. January's first day has also been weak; down 5 of the last 11, as profit taking shifts to the opening of the New Year. In rising market trends, first days perform much better, as institutions are likely anticipating strong performance at each month's outset. S&P 500 first days track the Dow's pattern closely, but NASDAQ first days are not as strong, with weakness in April, August, and October.

DOW POINTS GAINED FIRST DAY OF MONTH
SEPTEMBER 1997 TO MAY 3, 2010

	Jan	Feb	Mar	Apr	May	Jun	Jul	Aug	Sep	Oct	Nov	Dec	Totals
1997									257.36	70.24	232.31	189.98	**749.89**
1998	56.79	201.28	4.73	68.51	83.70	22.42	96.65	−96.55	288.36	−210.09	114.05	16.99	**646.84**
1999	2.84	−13.13	18.20	46.35	225.65	36.52	95.62	−9.19	108.60	−63.95	−81.35	120.58	**486.74**
2000	−139.61	100.52	9.62	300.01	77.87	129.87	112.78	84.97	23.68	49.21	−71.67	−40.95	**636.30**
2001	−140.70	96.27	−45.14	−100.85	163.37	78.47	91.32	−12.80	47.74	−10.73	188.76	−87.60	**268.11**
2002	51.90	−12.74	262.73	−41.24	113.41	−215.46	−133.47	−229.97	−355.45	346.86	120.61	−33.52	**−126.34**
2003	265.89	56.01	−53.22	77.73	−25.84	47.55	55.51	−79.83	107.45	194.14	57.34	116.59	**819.32**
2004	−44.07	11.11	94.22	15.63	88.43	14.20	−101.32	39.45	−5.46	112.38	26.92	162.20	**413.69**
2005	−53.58	62.00	63.77	−99.46	59.19	82.39	28.47	−17.76	−21.97	−33.22	−33.30	106.70	**143.23**
2006	129.91	89.09	60.12	35.62	−23.85	91.97	77.80	−59.95	83.00	−8.72	−49.71	−27.80	**397.48**
2007	11.37	51.99	−34.29	27.95	73.23	40.47	126.81	150.38	91.12	191.92	−362.14	−57.15	**311.66**
2008	−220.86	92.83	−7.49	391.47	189.87	−134.50	32.25	−51.70	−26.63	−19.59	−5.18	−679.95	**−439.48**
2009	258.30	−64.03	−299.64	152.68	44.29	221.11	57.06	114.95	−185.68	−203.00	76.71	126.74	**299.49**
2010	155.91	118.20	78.53	70.44	143.22								**566.30**
Totals	**334.09**	**789.40**	**152.14**	**944.84**	**1212.54**	**415.01**	**539.48**	**−168.00**	**412.12**	**415.45**	**213.35**	**−87.19**	**5173.23**

SUMMARY FIRST DAYS VS. OTHER DAYS OF MONTH

	# of Days	Total Points Gained	Average Daily Point Gain
First days	153	5173.23	33.81
Other days	3034	−1643.82	−0.54

MONDAY
D 38.1
S 38.1
N 38.1
20

at's the American way. If little kids don't aspire to make money like I did, what the hell good is this country?
Lee Iacocca (American industrialist, former Chrysler CEO, b. 1924)

eek After June Triple Witching, Dow Down 11 in a Row and 18 of Last 20
erage Loss Since 1990, 1.2%

TUESDAY
D 42.9
S 47.6
N 52.4
21

trepreneurs who believe they're in business to vanquish the competition are less successful than those
o believe their goal is to maximize profits or increase their company's value.
Kaihan Krippendorff (Business consultant, strategist, author, *The Art of the Advantage,* The Strategic Learning Center, b. 1971)

WEDNESDAY
D 47.6
S 61.9
N 47.6
22

n not better than the next trader, just quicker at admitting my mistakes and moving on to the next opportunity.
George Soros (Financier, philanthropist, political activist, author, and philosopher, b. 1930)

THURSDAY
D 33.3
S 38.1
N 28.6
23

you spend more than 14 minutes a year worrying about the market, you've wasted 12 minutes.
Peter Lynch (Fidelity Investments, *One Up On Wall Street,* b. 1944)

008 Second Worst June Ever, Dow −10.2%, S&P −8.6%,
nly 1930 Was Worse, NASDAQ −9.1%, June 2002 −9.4%

FRIDAY
D 42.9
S 42.9
N 42.9
24

day's Ponzi-style acute fragility and speculative dynamics dictate that he who panics first panics best.
Doug Noland (Prudent Bear Funds, *Credit Bubble Bulletin,* 10/26/07)

SATURDAY
25

ly Almanac Investor Seasonalities: See Pages 92, 94, and 96

SUNDAY
26

JULY ALMANAC

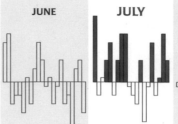

JULY							AUGUST						
S	M	T	W	T	F	S	S	M	T	W	T	F	S
					1	2		1	2	3	4	5	6
3	4	5	6	7	8	9	7	8	9	10	11	12	13
10	11	12	13	14	15	16	14	15	16	17	18	19	20
17	18	19	20	21	22	23	21	22	23	24	25	26	27
24	25	26	27	28	29	30	28	29	30	31			
31													

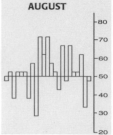

Market Probability Chart above is a graphic representation of the S&P 500 Recent Market Probability Calendar on page 124.

◆ July is the best month of the third quarter, except for NASDAQ (page 72) ◆ Start of second half brings an inflow of retirement funds ◆ First trading day Dow up 18 of last 21 ◆ Graph above shows strength in the beginning and end of July ◆ Huge gain in July usually provides better buying opportunity over next four months ◆ Start of NASDAQ's worst four months of the year (page 58) ◆ Pre-presidential election Julys are ranked #6 Dow (up 9, down 6), #7 S&P (up 9, down 6), and #10 NASDAQ (up 5, down 5).

July Vital Statistics

	DJIA	S&P 500	NASDAQ	Russell 1K	Russell 2K
Rank	4	6	11	8	10
Up	37	32	19	13	15
Down	23	28	20	18	16
Avg % Change	1.1%	0.9%	–0.1%	0.4%	–0.6%
Pre-Election Year	1.3%	1.0%	0.9%	0.7%	1.0%
Best and Worst July					
	% Change	% Change	% Change	% Change	% Change
Best	1989 9.0	1989 8.8	1997 10.5	1989 8.2	1980 11.0
Worst	1969 –6.6	2002 –7.9	2002 –9.2	2002 –7.5	2002 –15.2
Best and Worst July Weeks					
Best	7/17/09 7.3	7/17/09 7.0	7/17/09 7.4	7/17/09 7.0	7/17/09 8.0
Worst	7/19/02 –7.7	7/19/02 –8.0	7/28/00 –10.5	7/19/02 –7.4	7/27/07 –7.0
Best and Worst July Days					
Best	7/24/02 6.4	7/24/02 5.7	7/29/02 5.8	7/24/02 5.6	7/29/02 4.9
Worst	7/19/02 –4.6	7/19/02 –3.8	7/28/00 –4.7	7/19/02 –3.6	7/23/02 –4.1
First Trading Day of Expiration Week: 1980–2009					
Record (#Up–#Down)	18–12	19–11	20–10	19–11	17–13
Current Streak	U1	U1	U1	U1	U1
Avg % Change	0.12	0.07	0.07	0.04	0.0003
Options Expiration Day: 1980–2009					
Record (#Up–#Down)	14–14	15–15	13–17	15–15	11–19
Current Streak	U2	D1	U1	D1	D4
Avg % Change	–0.21	–0.27	–0.44	–0.29	–0.44
Options Expiration Week: 1980–2009					
Record (#Up–#Down)	19–11	16–14	16–14	16–14	17–13
Current Streak	U2	U2	U2	U2	U2
Avg % Change	0.51	0.16	0.06	0.11	0.03
Week After Options Expiration: 1980–2009					
Record (#Up–#Down)	14–16	13–17	11–19	13–17	10–20
Current Streak	U1	U1	U2	U1	U2
Avg % Change	–0.19	–0.41	–0.77	–0.43	–0.64
First Trading Day Performance					
% of Time Up	65.0	70.0	59.0	71.0	61.3
Avg % Change	0.25	0.23	0.04	0.27	–0.03
Last Trading Day Performance					
% of Time Up	55.0	65.0	51.3	61.3	67.7
Avg % Change	0.08	0.13	0.01	0.06	0.05

Dow & S&P 1950–April 2010, NASDAQ 1971–April 2010, Russell 1K & 2K 1979–April 2010.

When Dow and S&P in July are inferior,
NASDAQ days tend to be even drearier.

RESERVE YOUR 2012 ALMANAC TODAY!

Don't Miss This Early Bird Discount! Get Your 2012 *Stock Trader's Almanac* at **20% off** the regular price.

Order Your Copy Now – **CALL 800-356-5016** or
VISIT www.wiley.com with Promo Code STA12!

RESERVE YOUR 2012 *STOCK TRADER'S ALMANAC* BY MAIL OR CALL 800.356.5016!

☐ **PLEASE RESERVE____COPIES OF THE 2012 *STOCK TRADER'S ALMANAC*.**
Just $31.96 each (Regularly $39.95) plus shipping and handling!
Deeper discounts available for orders of 5 copies or more – call 800-356-5016 for details.
SHIPPING: US – First Item $5.00, each additional $3.00; International – First Item $10.40, each additional $7.00.
$_____ **Order Total** (Includes Book Plus Shipping Fees)

Payment Type:
☐ Check made payable to John Wiley & Sons, Inc. (US Funds only, drawn on a US Bank)
☐ Charge Credit Card (check one): ☐ Visa ☐ Mastercard ☐ AmEx

Name _____   E-mail Address _____

Address _____   Card Number _____

City _____   Expiration Date _____

State _____ Zip _____   Signature _____

RESERVE YOUR 2012 *STOCK TRADER'S ALMANAC* BY MAIL OR CALL 800.356.5016!

☐ **PLEASE RESERVE____COPIES OF THE 2012 *STOCK TRADER'S ALMANAC*.**
Just $31.96 each (Regularly $39.95) plus shipping and handling!
Deeper discounts available for orders of 5 copies or more – call 800-356-5016 for details.
SHIPPING: US – First Item $5.00, each additional $3.00; International – First Item $10.40, each additional $7.00.
$_____ **Order Total** (Includes Book Plus Shipping Fees)

Payment Type:
☐ Check made payable to John Wiley & Sons, Inc. (US Funds only, drawn on a US Bank)
☐ Charge Credit Card (check one): ☐ Visa ☐ Mastercard ☐ AmEx

Name _____   E-mail Address _____

Address _____   Card Number _____

City _____   Expiration Date _____

State _____ Zip _____   Signature _____

RESERVE YOUR 2012
STOCK TRADER'S ALMANAC
NOW AND SAVE 20%!

See front for details or **Call NOW to Learn About Bulk Pricing!**

JUNE/JULY

MONDAY
D 38.1
S 23.8
N 33.3
27

In this game, the market has to keep pitching, but you don't have to swing. You can stand there with the bat on your shoulder for six months until you get a fat pitch. — Warren Buffett (CEO Berkshire Hathaway, investor, and philanthropist, b. 1930)

TUESDAY
D 52.4
S 57.1
N 61.9
28

Intense concentration hour after hour can bring out resources in people they didn't know they had.
— Edwin Land (Polaroid inventor and founder, 1909–1991)

WEDNESDAY
D 52.4
S 61.9
N 71.4
29

If you have an important point to make, don't try to be subtle or clever. Use a pile driver. Hit the point once. Then come back and hit it again. Then hit it a third time—a tremendous whack. — Winston Churchill (British statesman, 1874–1965)

Last Day of Q2 Bearish for Dow, Down 14 of Last 19
But Bullish for NASDAQ, Up 12 of 18, Although Down 6 of last 7

THURSDAY
D 28.6
S 33.3
N 61.9
30

The authority of a thousand is not worth the humble reasoning of a single individual.
— Galileo Galilei (Italian physicist and astronomer, 1564–1642)

First Trading Day in July, Dow Up 18 of Last 21

FRIDAY
D 85.7
S 85.7
N 71.4
1

I'm not nearly so concerned about the return on my capital as I am the return of my capital.
— Will Rogers (American humorist and showman, 1879–1935)

SATURDAY
2

SUNDAY
3

2009 DAILY DOW POINT CHANGES (DOW JONES INDUSTRIAL AVERAGE)

Week #		Monday**	Tuesday	Wednesday	Thursday	Friday**	Weekly Dow Close	Net Point Change
						2008 Close	8776.39	
1					Holiday	258.30	9034.69	258.30†
2	J	−81.80	62.21	−245.40	−27.24	**−143.28**	8599.18	−435.51
3	A	**−125.21**	−25.41	−248.42	12.35	68.73	8281.22	−317.96
4	N	Holiday	−332.13	279.01	−105.30	−45.24	8077.56	−203.66
5		38.47	58.70	200.72	−226.44	**−148.15**	8000.86	−76.70
6	F	**−64.03**	141.53	−121.70	106.41	217.52	8280.59	279.73
7	E	−9.72	−381.99	50.65	−6.77	**−82.35**	7850.41	−430.18
8	B	Holiday	**−297.81**	3.03	−89.68	**−100.28**	7365.67	−484.74
9		**−250.89**	236.16	−80.05	−88.81	**−119.15**	7062.93	−302.74
10		**−299.64**	−37.27	149.82	−281.40	32.50	6626.94	−435.99
11	M	−79.89	379.44	3.91	239.66	53.92	7223.98	597.04
12	A	−7.01	178.73	90.88	−85.78	−122.42	7278.38	54.40
13	R	497.48	−115.89	89.84	174.75	**−148.38**	7776.18	497.80
14		**−254.16**	86.90	152.68	216.48	39.51	8017.59	241.41
15		−41.74	−47.55	246.27	Holiday	8083.38	65.79	
16	A	−25.57	−137.63	109.44	95.81	5.90	8131.33	47.95
17	P	−289.60	127.83	−82.99	70.49	119.23	8076.29	−55.04
18	R	−51.29	−8.05	168.78	−17.61	44.29	8212.41	136.12
19	M	214.33	−16.09	101.63	−102.43	164.80	8574.65	362.24
20	A	−155.88	50.34	−184.22	46.43	−62.68	8268.64	−306.01
21	Y	235.44	−29.23	−52.81	−129.91	−14.81	8277.32	8.68
22		Holiday	196.17	−173.47	103.78	96.53	8500.33	223.01
23		221.11	19.43	−65.59	74.96	12.89	8763.13	262.80
24	J	1.36	−1.43	−24.04	31.90	28.34	8799.26	36.13
25	U	−187.13	−107.46	−7.49	58.42	**−15.87**	8539.73	−259.53
26	N	**−200.72**	−16.10	−23.05	172.54	−34.01	8438.39	−101.34
27		90.99	−82.38	57.06	−223.32	Holiday	8280.74	−157.65
28	J	44.13	−161.27	14.81	4.76	−36.65	8146.52	−134.22
29	U	185.16	27.81	256.72	95.61	32.12	8743.94	597.42
30	L	104.21	67.79	−34.68	188.03	23.95	9093.24	349.30
31		15.27	−11.79	−26.00	83.74	17.15	9171.61	78.37
32		114.95	33.63	−39.22	−24.71	113.81	9370.07	198.46
33	A	−32.12	−96.50	120.16	36.58	**−76.79**	9321.40	−48.67
34	U	**−186.06**	82.60	61.22	70.89	155.91	9505.96	184.56
35	G	3.32	30.01	4.23	37.11	**−36.43**	9544.20	38.24
36		**−47.92**	−185.68	−29.93	63.94	96.66	9441.27	−102.93
37	S	Holiday	56.07	49.88	80.26	−22.07	9605.41	164.14
38	E	21.39	56.61	108.30	−7.79	36.28	9820.20	214.79
39	P	−41.34	51.01	−81.32	−41.11	−42.25	9665.19	−155.01
40		124.17	−47.16	−29.92	−203.00	−21.61	9487.67	−177.52
41		112.08	131.50	−5.67	61.29	78.07	9864.94	377.27
42	O	20.86	−14.74	144.80	47.08	−67.03	9995.91	130.97
43	C	96.28	−50.71	−92.12	131.95	**−109.13**	9972.18	−23.73
44	T	**−104.22**	14.21	−119.48	199.89	−249.85	9712.73	−259.45
45		76.71	−17.53	30.23	203.82	17.46	10023.42	310.69
46	N	203.52	20.03	44.29	−93.79	73.00	10270.47	247.05
47	O	136.49	30.46	−11.11	−93.87	−14.28	10318.16	47.69
48	V	132.79	−17.24	30.69	Holiday	−154.48	10309.92	−8.24
49		34.92	126.74	−18.90	−86.53	22.75	10388.90	78.98
50		1.21	−104.14	51.08	68.78	65.67	10471.50	82.60
51	D	29.55	−49.05	−10.88	−132.86	20.63	10328.89	−142.61
52	E	85.25	50.79	1.51	53.66*	Holiday	10520.10	191.21
53	C	26.98	−1.67	3.10	−120.46	Year's Close	10428.05	−92.05
TOTALS		−45.22**	161.76	617.56	932.68	−15.12**		1651.66

Bold Color: Down Friday, Down Monday   * Shortened trading day: Nov 27, Dec 24   †Partial Week

** Monday denotes first trading day of week, Friday denotes last trading day of week.

JULY

Independence Day
(Market Closed)

MONDAY
4

Nothing gives one person so much advantage over another as to remain always cool and unruffled under all circumstances.
— Thomas Jefferson (3rd U.S. president, 1743–7/4/1826)

Market Subject to Elevated Volatility After July 4th

TUESDAY
5

D 47.6
S 42.9
N 38.1

Man's mind, once stretched by a new idea, never regains its original dimensions.
— Oliver Wendell Holmes (American author, poet, and physician, 1809–1894)

July Begins NASDAQ's "Worst Four Months" (Pages 54, 58, and 148)

WEDNESDAY
6

D 47.6
S 52.4
N 38.1

Only those who will risk going too far can possibly find out how far one can go.
— T.S.Eliot (English poet, essayist, and critic, *The Wasteland*, 1888–1965)

THURSDAY
7

D 57.1
S 61.9
N 57.1

Keep me away from the wisdom which does not cry, the philosophy which does not laugh, and the greatness which does not bow before children. — Kahlil Gibran (Lebanese-born American mystic, poet, and artist, 1883–1931)

July Is the Best Performing Dow and S&P Month of the Third Quarter

FRIDAY
8

D 71.4
S 71.4
N 76.2

Three passions, simple but overwhelmingly strong, have governed my life: the longing for love, the search for knowledge, and unbearable pity for the suffering of mankind. — Bertrand Russell (British mathematician and philosopher, 1872–1970)

SATURDAY
9

SUNDAY
10

DON'T SELL STOCKS ON MONDAY OR FRIDAY

Since 1989, Monday*, Tuesday, and Wednesday have been the most consistently bullish days of the week for the Dow; Thursday and Friday* the most bearish, as traders have become reluctant to stay long going into the weekend. Since 1989, Mondays, Tuesdays, and Wednesdays gained 11658.20 Dow points, while Thursday and Friday combined for a total loss of 3402.79 points. Also broken out are the last nine and a third years to illustrate Monday's and Friday's poor performance in bear market years 2001–2002 and 2008–2009. During uncertain market times, traders often sell before the weekend and are reluctant to jump in on Monday. See pages 52, 66, and 141–144 for more.

ANNUAL DOW POINT CHANGES FOR DAYS OF THE WEEK SINCE 1953

Year	Monday*	Tuesday	Wednesday	Thursday	Friday*	Year's DJIA Closing	Year's Point Change
1953	−36.16	−7.93	19.63	5.76	7.70	280.90	−11.00
1954	15.68	3.27	24.31	33.96	46.27	404.39	123.49
1955	−48.36	26.38	46.03	−0.66	60.62	488.40	84.01
1956	−27.15	−9.36	−15.41	8.43	64.56	499.47	11.07
1957	−109.50	−7.71	64.12	3.32	−14.01	435.69	−63.78
1958	17.50	23.59	29.10	22.67	55.10	583.65	147.96
1959	−44.48	29.04	4.11	13.60	93.44	679.36	95.71
1960	−111.04	−3.75	−5.62	6.74	50.20	615.89	−63.47
1961	−23.65	10.18	87.51	−5.96	47.17	731.14	115.25
1962	−101.60	26.19	9.97	−7.70	−5.90	652.10	−79.04
1963	−8.88	47.12	16.23	22.39	33.99	762.95	110.85
1964	−0.29	−17.94	39.84	5.52	84.05	874.13	111.18
1965	−73.23	39.65	57.03	3.20	68.48	969.26	95.13
1966	−153.24	−27.73	56.13	−46.19	−12.54	785.69	−183.57
1967	−68.65	31.50	25.42	92.25	38.90	905.11	119.42
1968†	−6.41	34.94	25.16	−72.06	44.19	943.75	38.64
1969	−164.17	−36.70	18.33	23.79	15.36	800.36	−143.39
1970	−100.05	−46.09	116.07	−3.48	72.11	838.92	38.56
1971	−2.99	9.56	13.66	8.04	23.01	890.20	51.28
1972	−87.40	−1.23	65.24	8.46	144.75	1020.02	129.82
1973	−174.11	10.52	−5.94	36.67	−36.30	850.86	−169.16
1974	−149.37	47.51	−20.31	−13.70	−98.75	616.24	−234.62
1975	39.46	−109.62	56.93	124.00	125.40	852.41	236.17
1976	70.72	71.76	50.88	−33.70	−7.42	1004.65	152.24
1977	−65.15	−44.89	−79.61	−5.62	21.79	831.17	−173.48
1978	−31.29	−70.84	71.33	−64.67	69.31	805.01	−26.16
1979	−32.52	9.52	−18.84	75.18	0.39	838.74	33.73
1980	−86.51	135.13	137.67	−122.00	60.96	963.99	125.25
1981	−45.68	−49.51	−13.95	−14.67	34.82	875.00	−88.99
1982	5.71	86.20	28.37	−1.47	52.73	1046.54	171.54
1983	30.51	−30.92	149.68	61.16	1.67	1258.64	212.10
1984	−73.80	78.02	−139.24	92.79	−4.84	1211.57	−47.07
1985	80.36	52.70	51.26	46.32	104.46	1546.67	335.10
1986	−39.94	97.63	178.65	29.31	83.63	1895.95	349.28
1987	−559.15	235.83	392.03	139.73	−165.56	1938.83	42.88
1988	268.12	166.44	−60.48	−230.84	86.50	2168.57	229.74
1989	−53.31	143.33	233.25	90.25	171.11	2753.20	584.63
SubTotal	*−1937.20*	*941.79*	*1708.54*	*330.82*	*1417.35*		*2461.30*
1990	219.90	−25.22	47.96	−352.55	−9.63	2633.66	−119.54
1991	191.13	47.97	174.53	254.79	−133.25	3168.83	535.17
1992	237.80	−49.67	3.12	108.74	−167.71	3301.11	132.28
1993	322.82	−37.03	243.87	4.97	−81.65	3754.09	452.98
1994	206.41	−95.33	29.98	−168.87	108.16	3834.44	80.35
1995	262.97	210.06	357.02	140.07	312.56	5117.12	1282.68
1996	626.41	155.55	−34.24	268.52	314.91	6448.27	1331.15
1997	1136.04	1989.17	−590.17	−949.80	−125.26	7908.25	1459.98
1998	649.10	679.95	591.63	−1579.43	931.93	9181.43	1273.18
1999	980.49	−1587.23	826.68	735.94	1359.81	11497.12	2315.69
2000	2265.45	306.47	−1978.34	238.21	−1542.06	10786.85	−710.27
SubTotal	*7098.52*	*1594.69*	*−327.96*	*−1299.41*	*967.81*		*8033.65*
2001	−389.33	336.86	−396.53	976.41	−1292.76	10021.50	−765.35
2002	−1404.94	−823.76	1443.69	−428.12	−466.74	8341.63	−1679.87
2003	978.87	482.11	−425.46	566.22	510.55	10453.92	2112.29
2004	201.12	523.28	358.76	−409.72	−344.35	10783.01	329.09
2005	316.23	−305.62	27.67	−128.75	24.96	10717.50	−65.51
2006	95.74	573.98	1283.87	193.34	−401.28	12463.15	1745.65
2007	278.23	−157.93	1316.74	−766.63	131.26	13264.82	801.67
2008	−1387.20	1704.51	−3073.72	−940.88	−791.14	8776.39	−4488.43
2009	−45.22	161.76	617.56	932.68	−15.12	10428.05	1651.66
2010‡	807.39	103.60	90.69	−73.16	−347.96		
Subtotal	**−549.11**	**2598.79**	**1243.27**	**−78.61**	**−2992.58**		**−358.80**
Totals	**4612.21**	**5135.27**	**2623.85**	**−1047.20**	**−607.42**		**10136.15**

*Monday denotes first trading day of week, Friday denotes last trading day of week.
†Most Wednesdays closed last 7 months of 1968. ‡Partial year through April 30, 2010.

Monday Before July Expiration, Dow Up 6 of Last 7

MONDAY
11

D 47.6
S 42.9
N 61.9

Get inside information from the president and you will probably lose half your money.
If you get it from the chairman of the board, you will lose all your money. — Jim Rogers (Financier, b. 1942)

TUESDAY
12

D 66.7
S 61.9
N 71.4

The words "I am..." are potent words; be careful what you hitch them to.
The thing you're claiming has a way of reaching back and claiming you. — A. L.Kitselman (Author, math teacher)

WEDNESDAY
13

D 66.7
S 76.2
N 76.2

Most periodicals and trade journals are deadly dull, and indeed full of fluff provided by public relations agents.
— Jim Rogers (Financier, b. 1942)

THURSDAY
14

D 66.7
S 76.2
N 76.2

Capitalism is the legitimate racket of the ruling class. — Al Capone (American gangster, 1899–1947)

July Expiration Day, Dow Down 6 of Last 10, Off 390 Points (4.6%) in 2002

FRIDAY
15

D 52.4
• S 47.6
N 66.7

The worst mistake investors make is taking their profits too soon, and their losses too long.
— Michael Price (Mutual Shares Fund)

SATURDAY
16

SUNDAY
17

A RALLY FOR ALL SEASONS

Most years, especially when the market sells off during the first half, prospects for the perennial summer rally become the buzz on the street. Parameters for this "rally" were defined by the late Ralph Rotnem as the lowest close in the Dow Jones Industrials in May or June to the highest close in July, August, or September. Such a big deal is made of the summer rally that one might get the impression the market puts on its best performance in the summertime. Nothing could be further from the truth! Not only does the market "rally" in every season of the year, but it does so with more gusto in the winter, spring, and fall than in the summer.

Winters in 47 years averaged a 13.0% gain, as measured from the low in November or December to the first quarter closing high. Spring rose 11.6% followed by fall with 10.8%. Last and least was the average 9.2% summer rally. Even 2009's impressive 19.7% summer rally was outmatched by spring. Nevertheless, no matter how thick the gloom or grim the outlook, don't despair! There's always a rally for all seasons, statistically.

SEASONAL GAINS IN DOW JONES INDUSTRIALS

	WINTER RALLY Nov/Dec Low to Q1 High	SPRING RALLY Feb/Mar Low to Q2 High	SUMMER RALLY May/Jun Low to Q3 High	FALL RALLY Aug/Sep Low to Q4 High
1964	15.3%	6.2%	9.4%	8.3%
1965	5.7	6.6	11.6	10.3
1966	5.9	4.8	3.5	7.0
1967	11.6	8.7	11.2	4.4
1968	7.0	11.5	5.2	13.3
1969	0.9	7.7	1.9	6.7
1970	5.4	6.2	22.5	19.0
1971	21.6	9.4	5.5	7.4
1972	19.1	7.7	5.2	11.4
1973	8.6	4.8	9.7	15.9
1974	13.1	8.2	1.4	11.0
1975	36.2	24.2	8.2	8.7
1976	23.3	6.4	5.9	4.6
1977	8.2	3.1	2.8	2.1
1978	2.1	16.8	11.8	5.2
1979	11.0	8.9	8.9	6.1
1980	13.5	16.8	21.0	8.5
1981	11.8	9.9	0.4	8.3
1982	4.6	9.3	18.5	37.8
1983	15.7	17.8	6.3	10.7
1984	5.9	4.6	14.1	9.7
1985	11.7	7.1	9.5	19.7
1986	31.1	18.8	9.2	11.4
1987	30.6	13.6	22.9	5.9
1988	18.1	13.5	11.2	9.8
1989	15.1	12.9	16.1	5.7
1990	8.8	14.5	12.4	8.6
1991	21.8	11.2	6.6	9.3
1992	14.9	6.4	3.7	3.3
1993	8.9	7.7	6.3	7.3
1994	9.7	5.2	9.1	5.0
1995	13.6	19.3	11.3	13.9
1996	19.2	7.5	8.7	17.3
1997	17.7	18.4	18.4	7.3
1998	20.3	13.6	8.2	24.3
1999	15.1	21.6	8.2	12.6
2000	10.8	15.2	9.8	3.5
2001	6.4	20.8	1.7	23.1
2002	14.8	7.9	2.8	17.6
2003	6.5	23.9	14.3	15.7
2004	11.6	5.2	4.4	10.6
2005	9.0	2.1	5.6	5.3
2006	8.8	8.3	9.5	13.0
2007	6.7	13.5	6.6	10.3
2008	2.5	11.2	3.8	4.5
2009	19.6	34.4	19.7	15.5
2010	11.6			
Totals	**611.4%**	**533.4%**	**425.0%**	**496.9%**
Average	**13.0%**	**11.6%**	**9.2%**	**10.8%**

MONDAY

D 52.4
S 42.9
N 47.6

18

Unless you've interpreted changes before they've occurred, you'll be decimated trying to follow them.
— Robert J. Nurock (Market strategist, *Investor's Analysis*, *Bob Nurock's Advisory*, *Wall Street Week* panelist 1970–1989)

Week After July Expiration, Dow Down 7 of Last 12, 2007 – 4.2%, 2008 – 4.3%, But Up 4.0% in 2009

TUESDAY

D 42.9
S 38.1
N 42.9

19

Being uneducated is sometimes beneficial. Then you don't know what can't be done. — Michael Ott (Venture capitalist)

WEDNESDAY

D 61.9
S 61.9
N 57.1

20

I'm very big on having clarified principles. I don't believe in being reactive. You can't do that in the markets effectively. I can't. I need perspective. I need a game plan.
— Ray Dalio (Money manager, founder, Bridgewater Associates, *Fortune,* 3/16/2009, b. 1949)

THURSDAY

D 33.3
S 28.6
N 33.3

21

The principles of successful stock speculation are based on the supposition that people will continue in the future to make the mistakes that they have made in the past.
— Thomas F. Woodlock (*Wall Street Journal* editor and columnist, quoted in *Reminiscences of a Stock Operator*, 1866–1945)

FRIDAY

D 52.4
S 47.6
N 42.9

22

I've learned that only through focus can you do world-class things, no matter how capable you are.
— William H. Gates (Microsoft founder, *Fortune*, July 8, 2002)

SATURDAY

23

SUNDAY

24

FIRST MONTH OF QUARTERS IS THE MOST BULLISH

We have observed over the years that the investment calendar reflects the annual, semiannual, and quarterly operations of institutions during January, April, and July. The opening month of the first three quarters produces the greatest gains in the Dow Jones Industrials and the S&P 500. NASDAQ's record differs slightly.

The fourth quarter had behaved quite differently, since it is affected by year-end portfolio adjustments and presidential and congressional elections in even-numbered years. Since 1991, major turnarounds have helped October join the ranks of bullish first months of quarters. October transformed into a bear-killing-turnaround month, posting some mighty gains in seven of the last 12 years, 2008 sharply reversed this trend. (See pages 152–160.)

After experiencing the most powerful bull market of all time during the 1990s, followed by the ferocious bear market early in the millennium, we divided the monthly average percentage changes into two groups: before 1991 and after. Comparing the month-by-month quarterly behavior of the three major U.S. averages in the table, you'll see that first months of the first three quarters perform best overall. Nasty sell-offs in April 2000, 2002, 2004, and 2005 and July 2000–2002 and 2004, hit the NASDAQ hardest. The bear market of October 2007–March 2009, which more than cut the markets in half, took a toll on every first month except April. October 2008 was the worst month in a decade. January has also been a difficult month the past three years: 2008, 2009, and 2010. (See pages 152–160.)

Between 1950 and 1990, the S&P 500 gained 1.3% (Dow, 1.4%) on average in first months of the first three quarters. Second months barely eked out any gain, while third months, thanks to March, moved up 0.23% (Dow, 0.07%) on average. NASDAQ's first month of the first three quarters averages 1.67% from 1971–1990, with July being a negative drag.

DOW JONES INDUSTRIALS, S&P 500 AND NASDAQ
AVERAGE MONTHLY % CHANGES BY QUARTER

	DJIA 1950–1990			S&P 500 1950–1990			NASDAQ 1971–1990		
	1st Mo	2nd Mo	3rd Mo	1st Mo	2nd Mo	3rd Mo	1st Mo	2nd Mo	3rd Mo
1Q	1.5%	−0.01%	1.0%	1.5%	−0.1%	1.1%	3.8%	1.2%	0.9%
2Q	1.6	−0.4	0.1	1.3	−0.1	0.3	1.7	0.8	1.1
3Q	1.1	0.3	−0.9	1.1	0.3	−0.7	−0.5	0.1	−1.6
Tot	4.2%	−0.1%	0.2%	3.9%	0.1%	0.7%	5.0%	2.1%	0.4%
Avg	1.40%	−0.04%	0.07%	1.30%	0.03%	0.23%	1.67%	0.70%	0.13%
4Q	−0.1%	1.4%	1.7%	0.4%	1.7%	1.6%	−1.4%	1.6%	1.4%
	DJIA 1991–April 2010			S&P 500 1991–April 2010			NASDAQ 1991–April 2010		
1Q	0.004%	−0.1%	1.1%	0.1%	−0.6%	1.3%	1.9%	−0.7%	0.6%
2Q	2.6	1.5	−1.1	2.0	1.5	−0.4	1.4	1.6	0.9
3Q	1.2	−0.4	−1.0	0.4	−0.2	−0.5	0.3	0.7	−0.1
Tot	3.8%	1.0%	−1.0%	2.5%	0.7%	0.4%	3.6%	1.6%	1.4%
Avg	1.27%	0.33%	−0.33%	0.83%	0.23%	0.13%	1.20%	0.53%	0.47%
4Q	1.3%	1.8%	1.6%	1.0%	1.4%	1.8%	1.8%	1.8%	2.6%
	DJIA 1950–April 2010			S&P 500 1950–April 2010			NASDAQ 1971–April 2010		
1Q	1.0%	−0.04%	1.1%	1.0%	−0.2%	1.2%	2.8%	0.3%	0.8%
2Q	2.0	0.2	−0.3	1.5	0.4	0.1	1.5	1.2	1.0
3Q	1.1	0.1	−0.9	0.9	0.1	−0.6	−0.1	0.4	0.9
Tot	4.1%	0.26%	−0.1%	3.4%	0.3%	0.7%	4.2%	1.9%	0.9%
Avg	1.37%	0.09%	−0.03%	1.13%	0.10%	0.22%	1.40%	0.64%	0.30%
4Q	0.3%	1.6%	1.7%	0.6%	1.6%	1.6%	0.2%	1.7%	2.0%

MONDAY
D 66.7
S 71.4
N 76.2
25

Today's generation of young people holds more power than any generation before it to make a positive impact on the world.
— William J. Clinton (42nd U.S. president, Clinton Global Initiative, b. 1946)

TUESDAY
D 38.1
S 42.9
N 57.1
26

People become attached to their burdens sometimes more than the burdens are attached to them.
— George Bernard Shaw (Irish dramatist, 1856–1950)

Beware the "Summer Rally" Hype
Historically the Weakest Rally of All Seasons (Page 70)

WEDNESDAY
D 47.6
S 52.4
N 52.4
27

Anyone who believes that exponential growth can go on forever in a finite world is either a madman or an economist.
— Kenneth Ewart Boulding (Economist, activist, poet, scientist, philosopher, cofounder, General Systems Theory, 1910–1993)

THURSDAY
D 66.7
S 76.2
N 71.4
28

I always keep these seasonal patterns in the back of my mind. My antennae start to purr at certain times of the year.
— Kenneth Ward (VP Hayden Stone, *General Technical Survey*, 1899–1976)

Last Trading Day in July, NASDAQ Down 5 Years Straight

FRIDAY
D 52.4
S 61.9
N 47.6
29

All a parent can give a child is roots and wings. — Chinese proverb

SATURDAY
30

August Almanac Investor Seasonalities: See Pages 92, 94, and 96

SUNDAY
31

AUGUST ALMANAC

AUGUST						
S	M	T	W	T	F	S
	1	2	3	4	5	6
7	8	9	10	11	12	13
14	15	16	17	18	19	20
21	22	23	24	25	26	27
28	29	30	31			

SEPTEMBER						
S	M	T	W	T	F	S
				1	2	3
4	5	6	7	8	9	10
11	12	13	14	15	16	17
18	19	20	21	22	23	24
25	26	27	28	29	30	

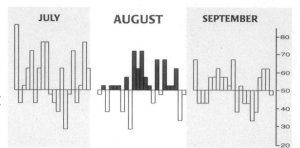

Market Probability Chart above is a graphic representation of the S&P 500 Recent Market Probability Calendar on page 124.

◆ Harvesting made August the best stock market month 1901–1951 ◆ Now about 2% farm, August is the second-worst Dow and S&P month since 1987, and fifth-worst NASDAQ month (2000 up 11.7%, 2001 down 10.9%); up across the board last 4 years ◆ Shortest bear in history (45 days), caused by turmoil in Russia, currency crisis, and hedge fund debacle, ended here in 1998, 1344.22-point drop in the Dow, second worst behind October 2008, off 15.1% ◆ Saddam Hussein triggered a 10.0% slide in 1990 ◆ Best Dow gains: 1982 (11.5%) and 1984 (9.8%), as bear markets ended ◆ Next to last day, S&P was up only twice in last 14 years ◆ Pre-presidential election year boosts Augusts' rankings: #5 Dow, #6 S&P, and #7 NASDAQ.

August Vital Statistics

	DJIA	S&P 500	NASDAQ	Russell 1K	Russell 2K
Rank	9	9	8	7	8
Up	35	34	22	21	19
Down	25	26	17	10	12
Avg % Change	0.1%	0.1%	0.4%	0.7%	0.8%
Pre-Election Year	−2.0%	−1.8%	−1.9%	−2.0%	−0.9%
Best and Worst August					
	% Change	% Change	% Change	% Change	% Change
Best	1982 11.5	1982 11.6	2000 11.7	1982 11.3	1984 11.5
Worst	1998 −15.1	1998 −14.6	1998 −19.9	1998 −15.1	1998 −19.5
Best and Worst August Weeks					
Best	8/20/82 10.3	8/20/82 8.8	8/3/84 7.4	8/20/82 8.5	8/3/84 7.0
Worst	8/23/74 −6.1	8/16/74 −6.4	8/28/98 −8.8	8/28/98 −5.4	8/28/98 −9.4
Best and Worst August Days					
Best	8/17/82 4.9	8/17/82 4.8	8/14/02 5.1	8/17/82 4.4	8/6/02 3.7
Worst	8/31/98 −6.4	8/31/98 −6.8	8/31/98 −8.6	8/31/98 −6.7	8/31/98 −5.7
First Trading Day of Expiration Week: 1980–2009					
Record (#Up–#Down)	20–10	22–8	21–9	22–8	18–12
Current Streak	D1	D1	D1	D1	D1
Avg % Change	0.26	0.25	0.25	0.21	0.13
Options Expiration Day: 1980–2009					
Record (#Up–#Down)	17–13	18–12	17–13	18–12	20–10
Current Streak	U7	U7	U1	U7	U1
Avg % Change	0.01	0.07	−0.04	0.07	0.17
Options Expiration Week: 1980–2009					
Record (#Up–#Down)	16–14	19–11	17–13	19–11	19–11
Current Streak	U1	U2	U2	U2	U2
Avg % Change	0.43	0.63	0.81	0.66	0.89
Week After Options Expiration: 1980–2009					
Record (#Up–#Down)	19–11	20–10	19–11	20–10	18–12
Current Streak	U1	U1	U1	U1	D2
Avg % Change	0.19	0.20	0.32	0.18	−0.19
First Trading Day Performance					
% of Time Up	48.3	51.7	53.8	48.4	51.6
Avg % Change	−0.001	0.02	−0.11	0.06	0.003
Last Trading Day Performance					
% of Time Up	60.0	63.3	69.2	58.1	74.2
Avg % Change	0.13	0.13	0.06	−0.06	0.09

Dow & S&P 1950–April 2010, NASDAQ 1971–April 2010, Russell 1K & 2K 1979–April 2010.

August's a good month to go on vacation;
Trading stocks will likely lead to frustration.

irst Trading Day in August Weak, Dow Down 9 of Last 13,
o 1.1% in 2007 and 1.3% in 2009

D 38.1
S 47.6
N 52.4

he machine can do the work of fifty ordinary men. No machine can do the work of one extraordinary man.
— Elbert Hubbard (American author, *A Message to Garcia*, 1856–1915)

D 57.1
S 52.4
N 47.6

nce 1950, the S&P 500 has enjoyed total returns averaging 33.18% annually during periods when the S&P 500 price/peak
rnings ratio was below 15 and both 3-month T-bill yields and 10-year Treasury yields were below their levels of 6 months earlier.
— John P. Hussman, Ph.D. (Hussman Funds, 5/22/06)

D 38.1
S 38.1
N 33.3

vill never knowingly buy any company that has a real time quote of their stock price in the building lobby.
— Robert Mahan (A trader commenting on Enron)

irst Nine Trading Days of August Are Historically Weak (Pages 72 and 124)

D 47.6
S 52.4
N 57.1

hings may come to those who wait, but only the things left by those who hustle.
— Abraham Lincoln (16th U.S. president, 1809–1865)

D 52.4
S 52.4
N 52.4

you don't keep [your employees] happy, they're not going to keep the [customers] happy.
— David Longest (Red Lobster VP, *NY Times*, 4/23/89)

AURA OF THE TRIPLE WITCH—4TH QUARTER MOST BULLISH: DOWN WEEKS TRIGGER MORE WEAKNESS WEEK AFTER

Options expire the third Friday of every month, but in March, June, September, and December, a powerful coven gathers. Since the S&P index futures began trading on April 21, 1982, stock options, index options, as well as index futures all expire at the same time four times each year—known as Triple Witching. Traders have long sought to understand and master the magic of this quarterly phenomenon.

The market for single-stock and ETF futures (1936 at this writing) continues to grow. However, their impact on the market has thus far been subdued. As their availability continues to expand, trading volumes and market influence are also likely to broaden. Until such time, we do not believe the term "quadruple witching" is applicable just yet.

We have analyzed what the market does prior, during, and following Triple Witching expirations in search of consistent trading patterns. Here are some of our findings of how the Dow Jones Industrials perform around Triple-Witching Week (TWW).

- TWWs became more bullish since 1990, except in the second quarter.
- Following weeks became more bearish. Since Q1 2000, only 13 of 40 were up, and 6 occurred in December, 5 in March, 2 in September, none in June.
- TWWs have tended to be down in flat periods and dramatically so during bear markets.
- DOWN WEEKS TEND TO FOLLOW DOWN TWWs is a most interesting pattern. Since 1991, of 27 down TWWs, 21 following weeks were also down. This is surprising, inasmuch as the previous decade had an exactly opposite pattern: There were 13 down TWWs then, but 12 up weeks followed them.
- TWWs in the second and third quarter (Worst Six Months May through October) are much weaker and the weeks following, horrendous. But in the first and fourth quarter (Best Six Months period November through April) only the week after Q1 expiration is negative.

Throughout the *Almanac* you will also see notations on the performance of Mondays and Fridays of TWW, as we place considerable significance on the beginnings and ends of weeks (pages 52, 66, 68, and 141–144).

TRIPLE WITCHING WEEK AND WEEK AFTER DOW POINT CHANGES

	Expiration Week Q1	Week After	Expiration Week Q2	Week After	Expiration Week Q3	Week After	Expiration Week Q4	Week After
1991	−6.93	−89.36	−34.98	−58.81	33.54	−13.19	20.12	167.04
1992	40.48	−44.95	−69.01	−2.94	21.35	−76.73	9.19	12.97
1993	43.76	−31.60	−10.24	−3.88	−8.38	−70.14	10.90	6.15
1994	32.95	−120.92	3.33	−139.84	58.54	−101.60	116.08	26.24
1995	38.04	65.02	86.80	75.05	96.85	−33.42	19.87	−78.76
1996	114.52	51.67	55.78	−50.60	49.94	−15.54	179.53	76.51
1997	−130.67	−64.20	14.47	−108.79	174.30	4.91	−82.01	−76.98
1998	303.91	−110.35	−122.07	231.67	100.16	133.11	81.87	314.36
1999	27.20	−81.31	365.05	−303.00	−224.80	−524.30	32.73	148.33
2000	666.41	517.49	−164.76	−44.55	−293.65	−79.63	−277.95	200.60
2001	−821.21	−318.63	−353.36	−19.05	−1369.70	611.75	224.19	101.65
2002	34.74	−179.56	−220.42	−10.53	−326.67	−284.57	77.61	−207.54
2003	662.26	−376.20	83.63	−211.70	173.27	−331.74	236.06	46.45
2004	−53.48	26.37	6.31	−44.57	−28.61	−237.22	106.70	177.20
2005	−144.69	−186.80	110.44	−325.23	−36.62	−222.35	97.01	7.68
2006	203.31	0.32	122.63	−25.46	168.66	−52.67	138.03	−102.30
2007	−165.91	370.60	215.09	−279.22	377.67	75.44	110.80	−84.78
2008	410.23	−144.92	−464.66	−496.18	−33.55	−245.31	−50.57	−63.56
2009	54.40	497.80	−259.53	−101.34	214.79	−155.01	−142.61	191.21
2010	117.29	108.38						
Up	14	8	10	2	11	4	15	13
Down	6	12	9	17	8	15	4	6

AUGUST

August Worst Dow and S&P Month 1988–2005 — Up Last 4 Years, 3rd Best
Harvesting Made August Best Dow Month 1901–1951

MONDAY
D 47.6
S 52.4
N 42.9
8

What investors really get paid for is holding dogs. Small stocks tend to have higher average returns than big stocks, and value stocks tend to have higher average returns than growth stocks. — Kenneth R. French (Economist, Dartmouth, NBER, b. 1954)

TUESDAY
D 42.9
S 38.1
N 38.1
9

If I have seen further, it is by standing upon the shoulders of giants
— Sir Isaac Newton (English physicist, mathematician, Laws of Gravity, letter to Robert Hooke 2/15/1676, 1643–1727)

WEDNESDAY
D 57.1
S 57.1
N 52.4
10

Cannot people realize how large an income is thrift? — Marcus Tullius Cicero (Great Roman orator, politician, 106–43 B.C.)

THURSDAY
D 28.6
S 28.6
N 42.9
11

The average man is always waiting for something to happen to him instead of setting to work to make things happen.
For one person who dreams of making 50,000 pounds, a hundred people dream of being left 50,000 pounds.
— A. A. Milne (British author, *Winnie-the-Pooh*, 1882–1956)

Mid-August Stronger Than Beginning and End

FRIDAY
D 66.7
S 71.4
N 71.4
12

To succeed in the markets, it is essential to make your own decisions. Numerous traders cited listening to others as their worst blunder.
— Jack D. Schwager (Investment manager, author, *Stock Market Wizards: Interviews with America's Top Stock Traders*, b. 1948)

SATURDAY
13

SUNDAY
14

WHAT TO TRADE DURING BEST AND WORST MONTHS

Our Best Months Switching Strategies found on pages 48, 50, 58, and 62 are simple and reliable with a proven 60-year track record. Thus far we have failed to find a similar trading strategy that even comes close over the past six decades. And to top it off, the strategy has only been improving, since we first discovered it in 1986.

Exogenous factors and cultural shifts must be considered. "Backward" tests that go back to 1925 or even 1896 and conclude that the pattern does not work are best ignored. They do not take into account these factors. Farming made August the best month from 1900–1951. Since 1987 it is the second worst month of the year for Dow and S&P. Panic caused by financial crisis in 2007–2008 caused every asset class aside from U.S. Treasuries to decline substantially. But the bulk of the major decline in equities in the worst months of 2008 was sidestepped using these strategies.

Our Best Months Switching Strategy will not make you an instant millionaire, as other strategies claim they can do. What it will do is steadily build wealth over time with half the risk (or less) of a "buy and hold" approach.

A sampling of tradable funds for the Best and Worst Months appears in the table below. These are just a starting point and only skim the surface of possible trading vehicles available to take advantage of these strategies. Your specific situation and risk tolerance will dictate a suitable choice. If you are trading in a tax-advantaged account, such as a company sponsored 401(k) or Individual Retirement Account (IRA), your investment options may be limited to what has been selected by your employer or IRA administrator. But if you are a self-directed trader with a brokerage account, then you likely have unlimited choices (perhaps too many).

TRADABLE BEST AND WORST MONTHS SWITCHING STRATEGY FUNDS

Best Months		Worst Months	
Exchange Traded Funds (ETF)		**Exchange Traded Funds (ETF)**	
Symbol	Name	Symbol	Name
DIA	SPDR Dow Jones Industrial Average	SHY	iShares 1–3 Year Treasury Bond
SPY	SPDR S&P 500	IEI	iShares 3–7 Year Treasury Bond
QQQQ	PowerShares QQQ	IEF	iShares 7–10 Year Treasury Bond
IWM	iShares Russell 2000	TLT	iShares 20+ Year Treasury Bond
Mutual Funds		**Mutual Funds**	
Symbol	Name	Symbol	Name
VWNDX	Vanguard Windsor Fund	VFSTX	Vanguard Short-Term Investment-Grade Bond Fund
FMAGX	Fidelity Magellan Fund	FBNDX	Fidelity Investment Grade Bond Fund
AMCPX	American Funds AMCAP Fund	ABNDX	American Funds Bond Fund of America
FKCGX	Franklin Flex Cap Growth Fund	FKUSX	Franklin U.S. Government Securities Fund
SECEX	Rydex Large Cap Core Fund	SIUSX	Rydex U.S. Intermediate Bond Fund

Generally speaking, during the Best Months you want to be invested in equities that offer similar exposure to the companies that constitute Dow, S&P 500, and NASDAQ indices. These would typically be large-cap growth and value stocks as well as technology concerns. Reviewing the holdings of a particular ETF or mutual fund and comparing them to the index members is an excellent way to correlate.

During the Worst Months, switch into Treasury bonds, money market funds, or a bear/short fund. **Federated Prudent Bear** (BEARX) and **Grizzly Short** (GRZZX) worked quite well during the bear market of 2007–2009. Money market funds will be the safest, but are likely to offer the smallest return, while bear/short funds offer potentially greater returns, but more risk. If the market moves sideways or higher during the Worst Months, a bear/short fund is likely to lose money. Treasuries offer a combination of decent returns with limited risk. In the *2011 Commodity Trader's Almanac*, a detailed study of 30-year Treasury bonds covers their seasonal tendency to advance during summer months as well as a correlating ETF trade.

Additional Worst Month possibilities include precious metals and the companies that mine them. **SPDR Gold Shares** (GLD), **Market Vectors Gold Miners** (GDX), and **ETF Securities Physical Swiss Gold** (SGOL) are a few well recognized names available from the ETF universe. Gold's seasonal price tendencies are also covered in the *2011 Commodity Trader's Almanac*.

Become an *Almanac Investor*

Trading and investing do not need to be difficult, complicated, or time consuming. Since July 2001, we have been providing subscribers to *Almanac Investor* specific buy and sell recommendations, based upon the Best Months Switching Strategies, online and via email. Sector Index Seasonalities, found on page 92, are also put into action throughout the year with ETF recommendations. Buy limits, stop losses, and auto-sell price points for the majority of seasonal trades are delivered directly to your inbox. Visit *www.stocktradersalmanac.com*, or see the insert at page 96 for details and a special offer for new subscribers. Then, sit back and relax during the often turbulent summer months, knowing that your personal savings or portfolio is well-positioned and that you will still manage to capture the bulk of market gains during the Best Months.

AUGUST

Monday Before August Expiration, Dow Up 11 of Last 15, Average Gain 0.3%

MONDAY
D 52.4
S 61.9
N 61.9
15

Those who are of the opinion that money will do everything may very well be suspected to do everything for money.
— Sir George Savile (British statesman and author, 1633–1695)

TUESDAY
D 61.9
S 71.4
N 61.9
16

The four most expensive words in the English language, "This time it's different."
— Sir John Templeton (Founder, Templeton Funds, philanthropist, b. 1912)

WEDNESDAY
D 52.4
S 57.1
N 61.9
17

From very early on, I understood that you can touch a piece of paper once... if you touch it twice, you're dead. Therefore, paper only touches my hand once. After that, it's either thrown away, acted on, or given to somebody else.
— Manuel Fernandez (Businessman, *Investor's Business Daily*)

THURSDAY
D 57.1
S 52.4
N 47.6
18

Never doubt that a small group of thoughtful, committed citizens can change the world: indeed it's the only thing that ever has.
— Margaret Mead (American anthropologist)

August Expiration Day Bullish Lately, Dow Up 7 in a Row 2003–2009
Up 156 Points (1.7%) in 2009

FRIDAY
D 38.1
S 42.9
N 33.3
19

I have but one lamp by which my feet (or "investments") are guided, and that is the lamp of experience. I know of no way of judging the future but by the past. — Patrick Henry (U.S. Founding Father, twice governor of VA, 1736–1799, March 23, 1775 speech)

SATURDAY
20

SUNDAY
21

A CORRECTION FOR ALL SEASONS

While there's a rally for every season (page 70), almost always there's a decline or correction, too. Fortunately, corrections tend to be smaller than rallies, and that's what gives the stock market its long-term upward bias. In each season the average bounce outdoes the average setback. On average, the net gain between the rally and the correction is smallest in summer and fall.

The summer setback tends to be slightly outdone by the average correction in the fall. Tax selling and portfolio cleaning are the usual explanations—individuals sell to register a tax loss and institutions like to get rid of their losers before preparing year-end statements. The October jinx also plays a major part. Since 1964, there have been 17 fall declines of over 10%, and in 10 of them (1966, 1974, 1978, 1979, 1987, 1990, 1997, 2000, 2002, and 2008) much damage was done in October, where so many bear markets end. Recent October lows were also seen in 1998, 1999, 2004, and 2005. Most often, it has paid to buy after fourth quarter or late third quarter "waterfall declines" for a rally that may continue into January or even beyond. War in Iraq affected the pattern in 2003. Anticipation of our invasion put the market down in the Q1. Quick success rallied stocks through summer. Financial crisis affected the pattern in 2008–2009, producing the worst winter decline since 1932.

SEASONAL CORRECTIONS IN DOW JONES INDUSTRIALS

	WINTER SLUMP Nov/Dec High to Q1 Low	SPRING SLUMP Feb/Mar High to Q2 Low	SUMMER SLUMP May/Jun High to Q3 Low	FALL SLUMP Aug/Sep High to Q4 Low
1964	−0.1%	−2.4%	−1.0%	−2.1%
1965	−2.5	−7.3	−8.3	−0.9
1966	−6.0	−13.2	−17.7	−12.7
1967	−4.2	−3.9	−5.5	−9.9
1968	−8.8	−0.3	−5.5	+0.4
1969	−8.7	−8.7	−17.2	−8.1
1970	−13.8	−20.2	−8.8	−2.5
1971	−1.4	−4.8	−10.7	−13.4
1972	−0.5	−2.6	−6.3	−5.3
1973	−11.0	−12.8	−10.9	−17.3
1974	−15.3	−10.8	−29.8	−27.6
1975	−6.3	−5.5	−9.9	−6.7
1976	−0.2	−5.1	−4.7	−8.9
1977	−8.5	−7.2	−11.5	−10.2
1978	−12.3	−4.0	−7.0	−13.5
1979	−2.5	−5.8	−3.7	−10.9
1980	−10.0	−16.0	−1.7	−6.8
1981	−6.9	−5.1	−18.6	−12.9
1982	−10.9	−7.5	−10.6	−3.3
1983	−4.1	−2.8	−6.8	−3.6
1984	−11.9	−10.5	−8.4	−6.2
1985	−4.8	−4.4	−2.8	−2.3
1986	−3.3	−4.7	−7.3	−7.6
1987	−1.4	−6.6	−1.7	−36.1
1988	−6.7	−7.0	−7.6	−4.5
1989	−1.7	−2.4	−3.1	−6.6
1990	−7.9	−4.0	−17.3	−18.4
1991	−6.3	−3.6	−4.5	−6.3
1992	+0.1	−3.3	−5.4	−7.6
1993	−2.7	−3.1	−3.0	−2.0
1994	−4.4	−9.6	−4.4	−7.1
1995	−0.8	−0.1	−0.2	−2.0
1996	−3.5	−4.6	−7.5	+0.2
1997	−1.8	−9.8	−2.2	−13.3
1998	−7.0	−3.1	−18.2	−13.1
1999	−2.7	−1.7	−8.0	−11.5
2000	−14.8	−7.4	−4.1	−11.8
2001	−14.5	−13.6	−27.4	−16.2
2002	−5.1	−14.2	−26.7	−19.5
2003	−15.8	−5.3	−3.1	−2.1
2004	−3.9	−7.7	−6.3	−5.7
2005	−4.5	−8.5	−3.3	−4.5
2006	−2.4	−5.4	−7.8	−0.4
2007	−3.7	−3.2	−6.1	−8.4
2008	−14.5	−11.0	−20.6	−35.9
2009	−32.0	−6.3	−7.4	−3.5
2010	−6.1			
Totals	**−318.1%**	**−307.1%**	**−410.6%**	**−428.5%**
Average	**−6.8%**	**−6.7%**	**−8.9%**	**−9.3%**

End of August Stronger Last 7 Years

MONDAY
D 66.7
S 66.7
N 81.0
22

Half the people alive today are already living in what we would consider intolerable conditions. One-sixth don't have access to clean drinking water; one-fifth live on less than a dollar a day; half the women in the world don't have equal rights with men; the forests are shrinking; the temperature's rising, and the oceans are rising because of the melting of the ice cap.
— Ted Turner (Billionaire, *New Yorker Magazine*, April 23, 2001)

TUESDAY
D 47.6
S 47.6
N 52.4
23

There's no trick to being a humorist when you have the whole government working for you.
— Will Rogers (American humorist and showman, 1879–1935)

WEDNESDAY
D 61.9
S 66.7
N 52.4
24

When everybody thinks alike, everyone is likely to be wrong.
— Humphrey B. Neill (Investor, analyst, author, *Art of Contrary Thinking* 1954, 1895–1977)

THURSDAY
D 52.4
S 52.4
N 57.1
25

If investing is entertaining, if you're having fun, you're probably not making any money. Good investing is boring.
— George Soros (Financier, philanthropist, political activist, author, and philosopher, b. 1930)

FRIDAY
D 47.6
S 52.4
N 47.6
26

A "tired businessman" is one whose business is usually not a successful one.
— Joseph R. Grundy (U.S. senator, Pennsylvania 1929–1930, businessman, 1863–1961)

SATURDAY
27

September Almanac Investor Seasonalities: See Pages 92, 94, and 96

SUNDAY
28

SEPTEMBER ALMANAC

SEPTEMBER						
S	M	T	W	T	F	S
				1	2	3
4	5	6	7	8	9	10
11	12	13	14	15	16	17
18	19	20	21	22	23	24
25	26	27	28	29	30	

OCTOBER						
S	M	T	W	T	F	S
						1
2	3	4	5	6	7	8
9	10	11	12	13	14	15
16	17	18	19	20	21	22
23	24	25	26	27	28	29
30	31					

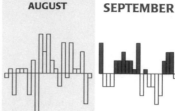
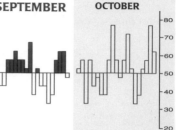

Market Probability Chart above is a graphic representation of the S&P 500 Recent Market Probability Calendar on page 124.

◆ Start of business year, end of vacations, and back to school made September a leading barometer month in first 60 years of 20th century; now portfolio managers back after Labor Day tend to clean house ◆ Biggest % loser on the S&P, Dow, and NASDAQ (pages 44 and 54) ◆ Streak of four great Dow Septembers averaging 4.2% gains ended in 1999 with six losers in a row averaging –5.9% (see page 152), up three straight 2005–2007, down 6% in 2008 ◆ Day after Labor Day, Dow up 13 of last 16 ◆ S&P opened strong 11 of last 15 years but tends to close weak due to end-of-quarter mutual fund portfolio restructuring; last trading day, S&P down 11 of past 17 ◆ September Triple-Witching Week can be dangerous, week after is pitiful (see page 76).

September Vital Statistics

	DJIA	S&P 500	NASDAQ	Russell 1K	Russell 2K
Rank	12	12	12	12	11
Up	23	26	21	15	17
Down	37	33	18	16	14
Avg % Change	–0.9%	–0.6%	–0.9%	–0.9%	–0.6%
Pre-Election Year	–0.6%	–0.4%	–0.1%	0.1%	0.1%
Best and Worst September					
	% Change	% Change	% Change	% Change	% Change
Best	1954 7.3	1954 8.3	1998 13.0	1998 6.5	1998 7.6
Worst	2002 –12.4	1974 –11.9	2001 –17.0	2002 –10.9	2001 –13.6
Best and Worst September Weeks					
Best	9/28/01 7.4	9/28/01 7.8	9/20/74 5.7	9/28/01 7.6	9/28/01 6.9
Worst	9/21/01 –14.3	9/21/01 –11.6	9/21/01 –16.1	9/21/01 –11.7	9/21/01 –14.0
Best and Worst September Days					
Best	9/8/98 5.0	9/30/08 5.4	9/8/98 6.0	9/30/08 5.3	9/18/08 7.0
Worst	9/17/01 –7.1	9/29/08 –8.8	9/29/08 –9.1	9/29/08 –8.7	9/29/08 –6.7
First Trading Day of Expiration Week: 1980–2009					
Record (#Up–#Down)	19–11	16–14	11–19	16–14	11–19
Current Streak	U1	U1	U1	U1	U1
Avg % Change	–0.16	–0.21	–0.46	–0.23	–0.34
Options Expiration Day: 1980–2009					
Record (#Up–#Down)	15–15	17–13	20–10	17–13	20–10
Current Streak	U6	U6	U6	U6	U5
Avg % Change	0.03	0.17	0.16	0.15	0.20
Options Expiration Week: 1980–2009					
Record (#Up–#Down)	15–15	17–13	16–14	17–13	15–15
Current Streak	U1	U4	U4	U4	U4
Avg % Change	–0.52	–0.26	–0.32	–0.26	–0.14
Week After Options Expiration: 1980–2009					
Record (#Up–#Down)	11–19	9–21	13–17	9–20	10–20
Current Streak	D2	D2	D2	D2	D8
Avg % Change	–0.63	–0.65	–0.83	–0.65	–1.25
First Trading Day Performance					
% of Time Up	61.7	63.3	53.8	51.6	48.4
Avg % Change	0.02	–0.01	–0.06	–0.08	–0.04
Last Trading Day Performance					
% of Time Up	40.0	43.3	51.3	51.6	67.7
Avg % Change	–0.10	–0.03	0.04	0.10	0.41

Dow & S&P 1950–April 2010, NASDAQ 1971–April 2010, Russell 1K & 2K 1979–April 2010.

September is when leaves and stocks tend to fall;
On Wall Street it's the worst month of all.

82

MONDAY
D 61.9
S 61.9
N 66.7
29

All there is to investing is picking good stocks at good times and staying with them as long as they remain good companies.
— Warren Buffett (CEO Berkshire Hathaway, investor, and philanthropist, b. 1930)

August's Next-to-Last Trading Day, S&P Up Only Twice in Last 14 Years

TUESDAY
D 33.3
S 33.3
N 61.9
30

Selling a soybean contract short is worth two years at the Harvard Business School.
— Robert Stovall (Managing director, Wood Asset Management)

WEDNESDAY
D 47.6
S 47.6
N 57.1
31

When someone told me "We're going with you guys because no one ever got fired for buying Cisco (products)."
That's what they used to say in IBM's golden age. — Mark Dickey (Former Cisco sales exec, then at SmartPipes, *Fortune* 5/15/00)

First Trading Day in September, S&P Up 11 of Last 15
Back-to-Back Huge Gains 1997 and 1998, Up 3.1% and 3.9%

THURSDAY
D 57.1
S 66.7
N 61.9
1

There are three principal means of acquiring knowledge... observation of nature, reflection, and experimentation.
Observation collects facts; reflection combines them; experimentation verifies the result of that combination.
— Denis Diderot (French philosopher, edited first modern Encyclopedia in 1745, 1713–1784)

FRIDAY
D 57.1
S 42.9
N 61.9
2

No profession requires more hard work, intelligence, patience, and mental discipline than successful speculation.
— Robert Rhea (Economist, trader, *The Dow Theory*, 1887–1952)

SATURDAY
3

SUNDAY
4

MARKET BEHAVIOR THREE DAYS BEFORE AND THREE DAYS AFTER HOLIDAYS

The *Stock Trader's Almanac* has tracked holiday seasonality annually since the first edition in 1968. Stocks used to rise on the day before holidays and sell off the day after, but nowadays, each holiday moves to its own rhythm. Eight holidays are separated into seven groups. Average percentage changes for the Dow, S&P 500, NASDAQ, and Russell 2000 are shown.

The Dow and S&P consist of blue chips and the largest cap stocks, whereas NASDAQ and the Russell 2000 would be more representative of smaller-cap stocks. This is evident on the last day of the year with NASDAQ and the Russell 2000 having a field day, while their larger brethren in the Dow and S&P are showing losses on average.

Thanks to the Santa Claus Rally, the three days before and after New Year's Day and Christmas are best. NASDAQ and the Russell 2000 average gains of 1.6% to 1.7% over the six-day spans. However, trading around the first day of the year has been mixed. Traders have been selling more the first trading day of the year recently, pushing gains and losses into the New Year.

Bullishness before Labor Day and after Memorial Day is affected by strength the first day of September and June. The second worst day after a holiday is the day after Easter. Surprisingly, the following day is one of the best second days after a holiday, right up there with the second day after New Year's Day.

Presidents' Day is the least bullish of all the holidays, bearish the day before and three days after. NASDAQ has dropped 17 of the last 21 days before Presidents' Day (Dow, 16 of 21; S&P, 17 of 21; Russell 2000, 12 of 21).

HOLIDAYS: 3 DAYS BEFORE, 3 DAYS AFTER (Average % Change 1980 to April 2010)

	-3	-2	-1	Mixed	+1	+2	+3
S&P 500	0.06	0.28	-0.13	New Year's	0.12	0.40	0.03
DJIA	0.02	0.22	-0.21	Day	0.28	0.38	0.18
NASDAQ	0.15	0.33	0.21	1/1/11	0.10	0.75	0.18
Russell 2K	0.15	0.45	0.52		-0.07	0.33	0.10
S&P 500	0.39	-0.03	-0.28	Negative Before and After	-0.21	-0.005	-0.15
DJIA	0.40	-0.01	-0.22	Presidents' Day	-0.12	-0.06	-0.17
NASDAQ	0.59	0.23	-0.42	2/21/11	-0.58	0.03	-0.11
Russell 2K	0.45	0.08	-0.13		-0.42	-0.05	-0.12
S&P 500	0.19	-0.07	0.41	Positive Before and	-0.21	0.36	0.11
DJIA	0.17	-0.11	0.32	Negative After	-0.13	0.34	0.09
NASDAQ	0.47	0.23	0.52	Good Friday	-0.35	0.38	0.21
Russell 2K	0.25	0.09	0.56	4/22/11	-0.29	0.26	0.13
S&P 500	0.05	-0.06	0.02	Positive After	0.36	0.18	0.27
DJIA	0.02	-0.09	-0.03	Memorial	0.42	0.19	0.19
NASDAQ	0.11	0.12	0.03	Day	0.25	-0.01	0.51
Russell 2K	-0.11	0.15	0.11	5/30/11	0.29	0.12	0.42
S&P 500	0.05	0.06	0.01	Negative After	-0.18	-0.03	-0.003
DJIA	0.02	0.06	0.01	Independence	-0.11	0.003	-0.02
NASDAQ	0.19	0.07	-0.01	Day	-0.20	-0.17	0.16
Russell 2K	0.18	-0.03	-0.10	7/4/11	-0.21	-0.11	-0.07
S&P 500	0.07	-0.22	0.23	Positive Day	0.11	-0.02	-0.14
DJIA	0.05	-0.27	0.21	Before	0.17	0.07	-0.24
NASDAQ	0.31	0.03	0.24	Labor Day	-0.03	-0.18	0.02
Russell 2K	0.45	0.11	0.21	9/5/11	0.09	-0.002	0.04
S&P 500	0.16	0.07	0.31	Positive Before	0.22	-0.56	0.36
DJIA	0.19	0.08	0.32	and After	0.18	-0.47	0.38
NASDAQ	0.04	-0.22	0.45	Thanksgiving	0.51	-0.58	0.18
Russell 2K	0.14	-0.08	0.42	11/24/11	0.41	-0.66	0.33
S&P 500	0.14	0.19	0.24	Christmas	0.16	0.03	0.35
DJIA	0.24	0.24	0.28	12/25/11 (Closed 12/26)	0.21	0.03	0.30
NASDAQ	-0.12	0.46	0.46		0.13	0.10	0.41
Russell 2K	0.15	0.39	0.41		0.21	0.15	0.54

SEPTEMBER

Labor Day (Market Closed)

The only title in our democracy superior to that of president is the title of citizen.
— Louis D. Brandeis (U.S. Supreme Court justice 1916–1939, 1856–1941)

Day After Labor Day, Dow Up 13 of Last 16, 1997 Up 3.4%, 1998 Up 5.0%

TUESDAY

D 47.6
S 42.9
N 47.6

6

Make sure you have a jester because people in high places are seldom told the truth.
— Radio caller to President Ronald Reagan

WEDNESDAY

D 38.1
S 42.9
N 57.1

7

Executives owe it to the organization and to their fellow workers not to tolerate nonperforming individuals in important jobs.
— Peter Drucker (Austria-born pioneer management theorist, 1909–2005)

THURSDAY

D 61.9
S 57.1
N 66.7

8

Liberals have practiced tax and tax, spend and spend, elect and elect but conservatives have perfected borrow and borrow, spend and spend, elect and elect. — George Will (*Newsweek*, 1989)

FRIDAY

D 47.6
S 57.1
N 57.1

9

Our philosophy here is identifying change, anticipating change. Change is what drives earnings growth,
and if you identify the underlying change, you recognize the growth before the market, and the deceleration of that growth.
— Peter Vermilye (Baring America Asset Management, 1987)

SATURDAY

10

 SUNDAY

"In Memory" 11

FOURTH QUARTER MARKET MAGIC

Examining market performance on a quarterly basis reveals several intriguing and helpful patterns. Fourth-quarter market gains have been magical, providing the greatest and most consistent gains over the years. First-quarter performance runs a respectable second. This should not be surprising, as cash inflows, trading volume, and buying bias are generally elevated during these two quarters.

Positive market psychology hits a fever pitch as the holiday season approaches and does not begin to wane until spring. Professionals drive the market higher, as they make portfolio adjustments to maximize year-end numbers. Bonuses are paid and invested around the turn of the year.

The market's sweet spot of the four-year cycle begins in the fourth quarter of the midterm year. The best two-quarter span runs from the fourth quarter of the midterm year through the first quarter of the pre-election year, averaging 14.4% for the Dow, 15.0% for the S&P 500, and an amazing 24.0% for NASDAQ.

Quarterly strength fades in the latter half of the pre-election year, but stays impressively positive through the election year. Losses dominate the first and third quarter of post-election years and the first and second quarters of midterm years. Once again, the global financial crisis trumped seasonality, hammering the fourth quarter of 2008 onto the list of 10 worst quarters of all time (see page 168).

QUARTERLY % CHANGES

	Q1	Q2	Q3	Q4	Year	Q2–Q3	Q4–Q1
Dow Jones Industrials (1949 to March 2010)							
Average	2.0%	1.8%	0.5%	3.7%	8.2%	2.3%	5.9%
Post-Election	−1.1%	1.6%	0.2%	3.4%	4.4%	1.8%	5.2%
Midterm	1.5%	−1.2%	−1.2%	7.3%	6.4%	−2.1%	14.4%
Pre-Election	7.6%	5.6%	2.5%	1.6%	17.7%	7.5%	1.9%
Election	0.3%	1.2%	0.4%	2.3%	4.6%	1.6%	1.2%
S&P 500 (1949 to March 2010)							
Average	1.9%	1.9%	0.6%	3.9%	8.7%	2.6%	6.1%
Post-Election	−1.2%	2.2%	0.4%	3.1%	4.8%	2.7%	4.3%
Midterm	1.0%	−2.2%	−0.6%	7.9%	6.0%	−2.5%	15.0%
Pre-Election	7.6%	5.6%	2.1%	2.5%	18.3%	7.2%	3.1%
Election	0.7%	2.1%	0.6%	2.1%	6.1%	2.6%	1.0%
NASDAQ Composite (1971 to March 2010)							
Average	4.0%	3.8%	−0.4%	4.2%	12.2%	3.7%	8.4%
Post-Election	−3.3%	6.8%	1.3%	4.2%	8.4%	8.1%	6.3%
Midterm	2.1%	−2.5%	−7.1%	8.5%	0.0002%	−8.9%	24.0%
Pre-Election	14.7%	8.9%	3.1%	4.9%	34.2%	12.1%	7.8%
Election	2.5%	1.3%	0.6%	−0.6%	4.8%	2.4%	−3.1%

SEPTEMBER

Markets Mugged Monday Before September Triple Witching 2008
Dow Lost 504 Points (−4.4%), S&P −4.7%, NASDAQ −3.6%

MONDAY
D 61.9
S 61.9
N 57.1
12

Banking establishments are more dangerous than standing armies; and that the principle of spending money
to be paid by posterity, under the name of funding, is but swindling futurity on a large scale.
— Thomas Jefferson (3rd U.S. president, 1743–7/4/1826, 1816 letter to *John Taylor of Caroline*)

2001 4-Day Market Closing, Longest Since
9-Day Banking Moratorium in March 1933

TUESDAY
D 61.9
S 57.1
N 61.9
13

Vietnam, the original domino in the Cold War, now faces the prospect of becoming, in the words
of political scientist Sunai Phasuk of Chulalongkorn University in Bangkok, one of the new "dominos of democracy."
— Quoted by Seth Mydans (*NY Times*, Jan. 6, 2001)

Expiration Week 2001, Dow Lost 1370 Points (14.3%)
2nd Worst Weekly Point Loss Ever, 5th Worst Week Overall

WEDNESDAY
D 47.6
S 57.1
N 66.7
14

Knowledge born from actual experience is the answer to why one profits; lack of it is the reason one loses.
— Gerald M. Loeb (E.F. Hutton, *The Battle for Investment Survival*, predicted 1929 Crash, 1900–1974)

THURSDAY
D 52.4
S 52.4
N 28.6
15

Cooperation is essential to address 21st-century challenges; you can't fire cruise missiles at the global financial crisis.
— Nicholas D. Kristof (*NY Times* columnist, 10/23/2008)

September Triple Witching, Dow Up 6 Straight and 7 of Last 8

FRIDAY
D 52.4
S 66.7
N 57.1
16

There are one-story intellects, two-story intellects, and three-story intellects with skylights. All fact collectors with no aim
beyond their facts are one-story men. Two-story men compare, reason and generalize, using labors of the fact collectors as well
as their own. Three-story men idealize, imagine, and predict. Their best illuminations come from above through the skylight.
— Oliver Wendell Holmes (American author, poet, and physician, 1809–1894)

SATURDAY
17

SUNDAY
18

MARKET GAINS MORE ON SUPER-8 DAYS EACH MONTH THAN ON ALL 13 REMAINING DAYS COMBINED

For many years, the last day plus the first four days were the best days of the month. The market currently exhibits greater bullish bias from the last three trading days of the previous month through the first two days of the current month, and now shows significant bullishness during the middle three trading days, 9 to 11, due to 401(k) cash inflows (see pages 145 and 146). This pattern was not as pronounced during the boom years of the 1990s, with market strength all month long. It returned in 2000 with monthly bullishness at the ends, beginnings and middles of months versus weakness during the rest of the month. From late 2007 to early 2009, the "Super 8" were mauled by the bear. The second half of 2009 was not much kinder, but thus far 2010 is seeing a revival in the pattern.

SUPER-8 DAYS* DOW % CHANGES VS. REST OF MONTH

	Super-8 Days	Rest of Month	Super-8 Days	Rest of Month	Super-8 Days	Rest of Month
	2002		**2003**		**2004**	
Jan	−1.92%	−0.24%	1.00%	−4.86%	3.79%	−1.02%
Feb	−1.41	4.27	2.71	−4.82	−1.20	0.83
Mar	4.11	−2.64	5.22	−0.90	−1.64	−1.69
Apr	−2.46	0.08	2.87	−1.91	3.20	−0.60
May	3.62	−4.07	3.17	2.46	−2.92	−0.51
Jun	−2.22	−6.51	3.09	−0.38	1.15	1.36
Jul	−5.04	−4.75	1.18	1.64	−1.91	−0.88
Aug	2.08	4.59	−0.74	1.55	0.51	0.40
Sep	−6.58	−5.00	3.58	−3.47	0.47	−2.26
Oct	8.48	−1.50	2.87	1.41	0.85	−1.82
Nov	4.74	0.99	−0.47	0.48	3.08	3.20
Dec	−0.76	−4.02	2.10	3.70	2.03	1.13
Totals	**2.64%**	**−18.80%**	**26.58%**	**−5.10%**	**7.41%**	**−1.86%**
Average	**0.22%**	**−1.57%**	**2.22%**	**−0.43%**	**0.62%**	**−0.16%**
	2005		**2006**		**2007**	
Jan	−1.96%	−1.35%	−0.03%	0.34%	0.68%	−0.04%
Feb	1.76	−0.07	1.67	0.71	3.02	−1.72
Mar	0.31	−2.05	0.81	−0.03	−5.51	3.64
Apr	−4.62	1.46	1.69	−0.53	2.66	2.82
May	0.57	2.43	−0.66	0.08	2.21	0.95
Jun	1.43	−3.00	2.39	−4.87	3.84	−5.00
Jul	0.96	1.83	1.65	0.07	2.50	−1.47
Aug	1.36	−3.07	1.83	0.41	−2.94	−0.26
Sep	0.90	−0.31	1.13	1.64	4.36	1.18
Oct	1.14	−2.18	1.58	2.59	1.28	−1.05
Nov	1.67	3.89	−0.01	−0.31	−0.59	−5.63
Dec	0.57	−1.96	2.40	−0.05	−0.04	4.62
Totals	**4.09%**	**−4.37%**	**14.45%**	**0.04%**	**11.56%**	**−1.96%**
Average	**0.34%**	**−0.36%**	**1.20%**	**0.003%**	**0.96%**	**−0.16%**
	2008		**2009**		**2010**	
Jan	−4.76%	−4.11%	3.16%	−6.92%	0.66%	−3.92%
Feb	1.83	0.65	−6.05	−4.39	3.31	−2.38
Mar	−4.85	2.92	−4.37	12.84	1.91	3.51
Apr	−0.27	4.09	1.52	−0.24	1.13	0.18
May	2.19	−4.81	2.64	2.98		
Jun	0.37	−6.30	1.71	−1.64		
Jul	−3.80	−1.99	2.30	5.03		
Aug	1.53	1.06	0.04	4.91		
Sep	−2.23	−1.19	−0.81	2.21		
Oct	−3.39	−13.70	−0.05	2.40		
Nov	6.07	−11.90	0.00	5.57		
Dec	−2.54	3.49	0.62	0.46		
Totals	**−9.85%**	**−31.79%**	**0.71%**	**23.21%**	**7.01%**	**−2.61%**
Average	**−0.82%**	**−2.65%**	**0.06%**	**1.93%**	**1.75%**	**−0.65%**

	Super-8 Days*		Rest of Month (13 Days)	
100 Month Totals	Net % Changes	64.60%	Net % Changes	−43.23%
	Average Period	0.65%	Average Period	−0.43%
	Average Day	0.08%	Average Day	−0.03%

Super-8 Days = Last 3 + First 2 + Middle 3

SEPTEMBER

🐻 **MONDAY**
D 28.6
S 38.1
N 52.4
19

Capitalism without bankruptcy is like Christianity without hell. — Frank Borman (CEO Eastern Airlines, April 1986)

TUESDAY
D 47.6
S 52.4
N 61.9
20

It is better to be out wishing you were in, than in wishing you were out.
— Albert W. Thomas (Trader, investor, *Over My Shoulder*, mutualfundmagic.com, *If It Doesn't Go Up, Don't Buy It!*, b. 1927)

WEDNESDAY
D 38.1
S 42.9
N 47.6
21

In my experience, selling a put is much safer than buying a stock. — Kyle Rosen (Boston Capital Mgmt., *Barron's*, 8/23/04)

THURSDAY
D 33.3
S 42.9
N 47.6
22

It's better to have your enemies inside the tent pissing out than outside pissing in.
— Lyndon B. Johnson (36th U.S. president, 1908–1973)

🐻 **FRIDAY**
D 28.6
S 33.3
N 38.1
23

I have a simple philosophy. Fill what's empty. Empty what's full. And scratch where it itches.
— Alice Roosevelt Longworth (Theodore Roosevelt's eldest child, 1884–1980)

SATURDAY
24

SUNDAY
25

OCTOBER ALMANAC

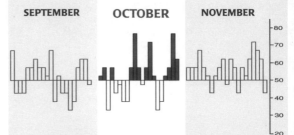

OCTOBER							NOVEMBER					
S	M	T	W	T	F	S	S	M	T	W	T	F	S
						1		1	2	3	4	5
2	3	4	5	6	7	8	6	7	8	9	10	11	12
9	10	11	12	13	14	15	13	14	15	16	17	18	19
16	17	18	19	20	21	22	20	21	22	23	24	25	26
23	24	25	26	27	28	29	27	28	29	30		
30	31											

Market Probability Chart above is a graphic representation of the S&P 500 Recent Market Probability Calendar on page 124.

◆ Known as the jinx month because of crashes in 1929, 1987, the 554-point drop on October 27, 1997, back-to-back massacres in 1978 and 1979, Friday the 13th in 1989, and the meltdown in 2008 ◆ Yet October is a "bear killer" and turned the tide in 11 post-WWII bear markets: 1946, 1957, 1960, 1962, 1966, 1974, 1987, 1990, 1998, 2001, and 2002 ◆ First October Dow top in 2007, 20-year 1987 crash anniversary –2.6% ◆ Worst six months of the year ends with October (page 48) ◆ No longer worst month (pages 44 and 56) ◆ Best Dow, S&P, and NASDAQ month from 1993 to 2007 ◆ Pre-presidential election year Octobers since 1951, rank last across the board; excluding 1987 still near the bottom ◆ October is a great time to buy ◆ Big October gains five years 1999–2003 after atrocious Septembers ◆ Can get into Best Six Months earlier using MACD (page 50).

October Vital Statistics

	DJIA	S&P 500	NASDAQ	Russell 1K	Russell 2K
Rank	7	7	10	10	12
Up	35	35	20	19	16
Down	25	25	19	12	15
Avg % Change	0.3%	0.6%	0.2%	0.4%	–1.2%
Pre-Election Year	–1.7%	–1.1%	–2.0%	–2.1%	–5.0%
Best and Worst October					
	% Change	% Change	% Change	% Change	% Change
Best	1982　10.7	1974　16.3	1974　17.2	1982　11.3	1982　14.1
Worst	1987　–23.2	1987　–21.8	1987　–27.2	1987　–21.9	1987　–30.8
Best and Worst October Weeks					
Best	10/11/74　12.6	10/11/74　14.1	10/31/08　10.9	10/31/08　10.8	10/31/08　14.1
Worst	10/10/08　–18.2	10/10/08　–18.2	10/23/87　–19.2	10/10/08　–18.2	10/23/87　–20.4
Best and Worst October Days					
Best	10/13/08　11.1	10/13/08　11.6	10/13/08　11.8	10/13/08　11.7	10/13/08　9.3
Worst	10/19/87　–22.6	10/19/87　–20.5	10/19/87　–11.4	10/19/87　–19.0	10/19/87　–12.5
First Trading Day of Expiration Week: 1980–2009					
Record (#Up–#Down)	25–5	23–7	21–9	24–6	24–6
Current Streak	U2	U2	D1	U2	D1
Avg % Change	0.95	0.91	0.73	0.89	0.57
Options Expiration Day: 1980–2009					
Record (#Up–#Down)	13–17	14–16	15–15	14–16	13–17
Current Streak	D5	D3	D3	D3	D4
Avg % Change	–0.27	–0.35	–0.24	–0.34	–0.25
Options Expiration Week: 1980–2009					
Record (#Up–#Down)	20–10	20–10	17–13	20–10	18–12
Current Streak	U2	U2	U2	U2	U2
Avg % Change	0.63	0.64	0.70	0.62	0.28
Week After Options Expiration: 1980–2009					
Record (#Up–#Down)	12–18	11–19	14–16	11–19	12–18
Current Streak	D2	D2	D2	D2	D2
Avg % Change	–0.66	–0.70	–0.78	–0.73	–1.00
First Trading Day Performance					
% of Time Up	48.3	48.3	48.7	51.6	48.4
Avg % Change	0.11	0.10	–0.08	0.35	–0.14
Last Trading Day Performance					
% of Time Up	55.0	56.7	69.2	64.5	74.2
Avg % Change	0.11	0.20	0.61	0.47	0.75

Dow & S&P 1950–April 2010, NASDAQ 1971–April 2010, Russell 1K & 2K 1979–April 2010.

October has killed many a bear;
Buy tech stocks and soon wear a grin ear to ear.

SEPTEMBER/OCTOBER

End of September Prone to Weakness
From End-of-Q3 Institutional Portfolio Restructuring

MONDAY
D 42.9
S 38.1
N 38.1
26

In order to be great writer (or "investor") a person must have a built-in, shockproof crap detector.
— Ernest Hemingway (American writer, 1954 Nobel Prize, 1899–1961)

TUESDAY
D 61.9
S 57.1
N 57.1
27

Change is the law of life. And those who look only to the past or present are certain to miss the future.
— John F. Kennedy (35th U.S. president, 1917–1963)

WEDNESDAY
D 57.1
S 61.9
N 38.1
28

Inflation is the modern way that governments default on their debt. — Mike Epstein (MTA, MIT/Sloan Lab for Financial Engineering)

Rosh Hashanah

THURSDAY
D 57.1
S 61.9
N 52.4
29

There is no one who can replace America. Without American leadership, there is no leadership.
That puts a tremendous burden on the American people to do something positive. You can't be tempted by the usual nationalism.
— Lee Hong-koo (South Korean prime minister 1994–1995 and ambassador to U.S. 1998–2000, NY Times, 2/25/2009)

Last Day of Q3, Dow Down 9 of Last 13, Massive 4.7% Rally in 2008

FRIDAY
D 42.9
S 47.6
N 47.6
30

When you're one step ahead of the crowd, you're a genius. When you're two steps ahead, you're a crackpot.
— Shlomo Riskin (Rabbi, author, b. 1940)

SATURDAY
1

October Almanac Investor Seasonalities: See Pages 92, 94, and 96

SUNDAY
2

SECTOR SEASONALITY: SELECTED PERCENTAGE PLAYS

Sector seasonality was featured in the first 1968 *Almanac*. A Merrill Lynch study showed that buying seven sectors around September or October and selling in the first few months of 1954–1964 tripled the gains of holding them for 10 years. Over the years we have honed this strategy significantly and now devote a large portion of our time and resources to investing and trading during positive and negative seasonal periods for different sectors with Exchange Traded Funds (ETFs).

Updated seasonalities appear in the table below. We specify whether the seasonality starts or finishes in the beginning third (B), middle third (M), or last third (E) of the month. These selected percentage plays are geared to take advantage of the bulk of seasonal sector strength or weakness.

By design, entry points are in advance of the major seasonal moves, providing traders ample opportunity to accumulate positions at favorable prices. Conversely, exit points have been selected to capture the majority of the move.

From the major seasonalities in the table below, we created the Sector Index Seasonality Strategy Calendar on pages 94 and 96. Note the concentration of bullish sector seasonalities during the Best Six Months, November to April and bearish sector seasonalities during the Worst Six Months, May to October.

Almanac Investor newsletter subscribers receive specific entry and exit points for highly correlated ETFs and detailed analysis in our monthly ETF Lab. Visit *www.stocktradersalmanac.com,* or see the insert at page 96 for additional details and a special offer for new subscribers. Top 300 ETFs appear on pages 188–189.

SECTOR INDEX SEASONALITY TABLE

Ticker	Sector Index	Type	Start		Finish		15-Year	10-Year	5-Year
					Seasonality		**Average % Return[†]**		
XCI	Computer Tech	Short	January	B	March	B	−7.9	−12.2	−11.6
IIX	Internet	Short	January	B	February	E	−12.2	−12.7	−6.8
XNG	Natural Gas	Long	February	E	June	B	18.7[1]	21.6	13.3
RXP	Healthcare Prod	Long	March	M	June	M	7.5[1]	8.7	6.8
RXH	Healthcare Prov	Long	March	M	June	M	16.8[1]	19.3	22.2
MSH	High-Tech	Long	March	M	July	B	13.2[1]	10.0	13.2
XCI	Computer Tech	Long	April	M	July	M	15.6	8.4	9.4
IIX	Internet	Long	April	M	July	B	14.0[1]	9.0	7.6
CYC	Cyclical	Short	May	M	October	E	−7.6	−7.6	−7.0
XAU	Gold and Silver	Short	May	M	June	E	−8.6	−7.3	−7.3
S5MATR*	Materials	Short	May	M	October	M	−9.9	−10.2	−10.5
BKX	Banking	Short	June	B	July	B	−5.4	−8.1	−9.1
XNG	Natural Gas	Short	June	M	July	E	−9.0	−10.7	−6.8
XAU	Gold and Silver	Long	July	E	December	E	12.0	18.0	13.8
DJT	Transports	Short	July	M	October	M	−7.9	−8.0	−6.2
UTY	Utilities	Long	July	E	January	B	9.8	10.2	3.6
BTK	Biotech	Long	August	B	March	B	31.5	8.3	8.6
RXP	Healthcare Prod	Long	August	B	February	B	11.2[1]	7.8	3.6
MSH	High-Tech	Long	August	M	January	M	16.1	8.2	2.9
IIX	Internet	Long	August	B	January	B	27.9[1]	13.1	8.8
SOX	Semiconductor	Short	August	M	October	E	−13.6	−15.0	−13.2
CMR	Consumer	Long	September	E	June	B	12.9	8.0	3.6
RXH	Healthcare Prov	Short	September	M	November	B	−6.8[1]	−5.2	−9.9
XOI	Oil	Short	September	B	November	E	−4.5	−7.0	−9.2
BKX	Banking	Long	October	B	June	B	13.7	6.9	−6.1
XBD	Broker/Dealer	Long	October	B	June	E	34.6	15.5	9.8
XCI	Computer Tech	Long	October	B	January	B	17.5	13.7	8.3
CYC	Cyclical	Long	October	B	May	M	18.1	15.9	10.3
RXH	Healthcare Prov	Long	October	E	January	M	10.9[1]	8.9	5.9
S5MATR*	Materials	Long	October	M	May	M	17.1	17.9	17.1
DRG	Pharmaceutical	Long	October	M	January	B	8.2	6.7	7.1
RMZ	Real Estate	Long	October	E	July	B	13.4[1]	13.9	4.6
SOX	Semiconductor	Long	October	E	December	B	17.1	13.9	7.2
XTC	Telecom	Long	October	M	December	E	12.1	8.5	5.3
DJT	Transports	Long	October	B	May	B	18.7	14.6	13.5
XOI	Oil	Long	December	M	July	B	14.7	14.0	15.7

[†]*Average % Return based on full seasonality completion through April 2010.*
* *S5MATR Available @ bloomberg.com.* [1] *Since Index Inception.*

OCTOBER

rst Trading Day in October, Dow Down 4 of Last 5
ff 2.1% in 2009

MONDAY
D 57.1
S 52.4
N 47.6
3

fe is what happens, while you're busy making other plans. — John Lennon (Beatle, 1940–1980)

TUESDAY
D 47.6
S 57.1
N 57.1
4

*e investor who concentrated on the 50 stocks in the S&P 500 that are followed by the
west Wall Street analysts wound up with a rousing 24.6% gain in [2006 versus] 13.6% [for] the S&P 500.*
Rich Bernstein (Chief Investment Strategist, Merrill Lynch, *Barron's*, 1/8/07)

*tart Looking for MACD BUY Signals (Pages 50 and 58)
manac Investor Subscribers E-mailed When It Triggers (See Insert Page 96)*

WEDNESDAY
D 38.1
S 33.3
N 42.9
5

*u have to keep digging, keep asking questions, because otherwise you'll be seduced or brainwashed into the idea
t it's somehow a great privilege, an honor, to report the lies they've been feeding you.*
David Halberstam (American writer, war reporter, 1964 Pulitzer Prize, 1934–2007)

THURSDAY
D 61.9
S 57.1
N 61.9
6

x words that spell business success: create concept, communicate concept, sustain momentum.
Yale Hirsch (Creator of *Stock Trader's Almanac*, b. 1923)

*ow Lost 1874 Points (18.2%) on the Week Ending 10/10/08;
/orst Dow Week in the History of Wall Street*

FRIDAY
D 38.1
S 42.9
N 47.6
7

u know you're right when the other side starts to shout. — I. A. O'Shaughnessy (American oilman, 1885–1973)

om Kippur

SATURDAY
8

SUNDAY
9

Sector Index Seasonality Strategy Calendar*

* Graphic representation of the Sector Index Seasonality Percentage Plays on page 92.
L = Long Trade, S = Short Trade, ➞ = Start of Trade

OCTOBER

Columbus Day (Bond Market Closed)

MONDAY
D 47.6
S 47.6
N 61.9
10

The commodity futures game is a money game—not a game involving the supply–demand of the actual commodity as commonly depicted. — R. Earl Hadady (*Bullish Consensus, Contrary Opinion*)

TUESDAY
D 42.9
S 38.1
N 47.6
11

Even being right 3 or 4 times out of 10 should yield a person a fortune, if he has the sense to cut his losses quickly on the ventures where he has been wrong. — Bernard Baruch (Financier, speculator, statesman, presidential adviser, 1870–1965)

October Ends Dow and S&P "Worst Six Months" (Pages 44, 48, 50, and 147) and NASDAQ "Worst Four Months" (Pages 54, 58, and 148)

WEDNESDAY
D 33.3
S 38.1
N 52.4
12

... the most successful positions I've taken have been those about which I've been most nervous (and ignored that emotion anyway). Courage is not about being fearless; courage is about acting appropriately even when you are fearful. — Daniel Turov (*Turov on Timing*)

THURSDAY
D 57.1
S 57.1
N 71.4
13

[Look for companies] where the executives have a good ownership position—not only options, but outright ownership— so that they will ride up and down with the shareholder. — George Roche (Chairman, T. Rowe Price, *Barron's*, 12/18/06)

FRIDAY
D 76.2
S 76.2
N 71.4
14

A senior European diplomat said he was convinced that the choice of starting a war this spring was made for political as well as military reasons. [The President] clearly does not want to have a war raging on the eve of his presumed reelection campaign. — Reported by Steven R. Weisman (*NY Times*, 3/14/03)

SATURDAY
15

SUNDAY
16

Sector Index Seasonality Strategy Calendar*

* Graphic representation of the Sector Index Seasonality Percentage Plays on page 92.
L = Long Trade, S = Short Trade, → = Start of Trade

Monday Before October Expiration, Dow Up 25 of 30

MONDAY
D 61.9
S 57.1
N 52.4
17

Nothing is more uncertain than the favor of the crowd. — Marcus Tullius Cicero (Great Roman orator, politician, 106–43 B.C.)

TUESDAY
D 42.9
S 47.6
N 38.1
18

Always grab the reader by the throat in the first paragraph, sink your thumbs into his windpipe in the second, and hold him against the wall until the tag line. — Paul O'Neil (Marketer, *Writing Changes Everything*)

Crash of October 19, 1987, Dow Down 22.6% in One Day

WEDNESDAY
D 52.4
S 57.1
N 47.6
19

The CROWD is always wrong at market turning points but often times right once a trend sets in.
The reason many market fighters go broke is they believe the CROWD is always wrong. There is nothing further from the truth.
Unless volatility is extremely low or very high, one should think twice before betting against the CROWD.
— Shawn Andrew (Trader, Ricecar Fund /SA, 12/21/01)

THURSDAY
D 66.7
S 71.4
N 76.2
20

Drawing on my fine command of language, I said nothing. — Robert Benchley (American writer, actor, and humorist, 1889–1945)

October Expiration Day, Dow Down 5 Straight and 6 of Last 7
Eked Out a Modest 0.4% Gain in 2004

FRIDAY
D 47.6
S 52.4
N 47.6
21

History must repeat itself because we pay such little attention to it the first time. — Blackie Sherrod (Sportswriter, b. 1919)

SATURDAY
22

SUNDAY
23

TRADING THE THANKSGIVING MARKET

For 35 years, the "holiday spirit" gave Wednesday before Thanksgiving and Friday after a great track record, except for two occasions. Publishing it in the 1987 *Almanac* was the "kiss of death." Wednesday, Friday, and Monday were all crushed, down 6.6% over the three days in 1987. Since 1988, Wednesday–Friday, gained 13 of 22 times, with a total Dow point-gain of 657.51 versus Monday's total Dow point-loss of 870.79, down five straight 2004–2009. The best strategy appears to be coming into the week long and exiting into strength Friday. Dubai's debt crisis cancelled Black Friday on Wall Street in 2009.

DOW JONES INDUSTRIALS BEFORE AND AFTER THANKSGIVING

	Tuesday Before	Wednesday Before		Friday After	Total Gain Dow Points	Dow Close	Next Monday
1952	−0.18	1.54		1.22	2.76	283.66	0.04
1953	1.71	0.65		2.45	3.10	280.23	1.14
1954	3.27	1.89		3.16	5.05	387.79	0.72
1955	4.61	0.71		0.26	0.97	482.88	−1.92
1956	−4.49	−2.16		4.65	2.49	472.56	−2.27
1957	−9.04	10.69		3.84	14.53	449.87	−2.96
1958	−4.37	8.63		8.31	16.94	557.46	2.61
1959	2.94	1.41		1.42	2.83	652.52	6.66
1960	−3.44	1.37		4.00	5.37	606.47	−1.04
1961	−0.77	1.10		2.18	3.28	732.60	−0.61
1962	6.73	4.31	T	7.62	11.93	644.87	−2.81
1963	32.03	−2.52		9.52	7.00	750.52	1.39
1964	−1.68	−5.21	H	−0.28	−5.49	882.12	−6.69
1965	2.56	N/C		−0.78	−0.78	948.16	−1.23
1966	−3.18	1.84	A	6.52	8.36	803.34	−2.18
1967	13.17	3.07		3.58	6.65	877.60	4.51
1968	8.14	−3.17	N	8.76	5.59	985.08	−1.74
1969	−5.61	3.23		1.78	5.01	812.30	−7.26
1970	5.21	1.98	K	6.64	8.62	781.35	12.74
1971	−5.18	0.66		17.96	18.62	816.59	13.14
1972	8.21	7.29	S	4.67	11.96	1025.21	−7.4
1973	−17.76	10.08		−0.98	9.10	854.00	−29.05
1974	5.32	2.03	G	−0.63	1.40	618.66	−15.64
1975	9.76	3.15		2.12	5.27	860.67	−4.33
1976	−6.57	1.66	I	5.66	7.32	956.62	−6.57
1977	6.41	0.78		1.12	1.90	844.42	−4.85
1978	−1.56	2.95	V	3.12	6.07	810.12	3.72
1979	−6.05	−1.80		4.35	2.55	811.77	16.98
1980	3.93	7.00	I	3.66	10.66	993.34	−23.89
1981	18.45	7.90		7.80	15.70	885.94	3.04
1982	−9.01	9.01	N	7.36	16.37	1007.36	−4.51
1983	7.01	−0.20		1.83	1.63	1277.44	−7.62
1984	9.83	6.40	G	18.78	25.18	1220.30	−7.95
1985	0.12	18.92		−3.56	15.36	1472.13	−14.22
1986	6.05	4.64		−2.53	2.11	1914.23	−1.55
1987	40.45	−16.58		−36.47	−53.05	1910.48	−76.93
1988	11.73	14.58	D	−17.60	−3.02	2074.68	6.76
1989	7.25	17.49		18.77	36.26	2675.55	19.42
1990	−35.15	9.16	A	−12.13	−2.97	2527.23	5.94
1991	14.08	−16.10		−5.36	−21.46	2894.68	40.70
1992	25.66	17.56	Y	15.94	33.50	3282.20	22.96
1993	3.92	13.41		−3.63	9.78	3683.95	−6.15
1994	−91.52	−3.36		33.64	30.28	3708.27	31.29
1995	40.46	18.06		7.23*	25.29	5048.84	22.04
1996	−19.38	−29.07		22.36*	−6.71	6521.70	N/C
1997	41.03	−14.17		28.35*	14.18	7823.13	189.98
1998	−73.12	13.13		18.80*	31.93	9333.08	−216.53
1999	−93.89	12.54		−19.26*	−6.72	10988.91	−40.99
2000	31.85	−95.18		70.91*	−24.27	10470.23	75.84
2001	−75.08	−66.70		125.03*	58.33	9959.71	23.04
2002	−172.98	255.26		−35.59*	219.67	8896.09	−33.52
2003	16.15	15.63		2.89*	18.52	9782.46	116.59
2004	3.18	27.71		1.92*	29.63	10522.23	−46.33
2005	51.15	44.66		15.53*	60.19	10931.62	−40.90
2006	5.05	5.36		−46.78*	−41.42	12280.17	−158.46
2007	51.70	−211.10		181.84*	−29.26	12980.88	−237.44
2008	36.08	247.14		102.43*	349.57	8829.04	−679.95
2009	−17.24	30.69		−154.48*	−123.79	10309.92	34.92

*Shortened trading day

OCTOBER

🐻 MONDAY
D 42.9
S 33.3
N 28.6
24

All free governments are managed by the combined wisdom and folly of the people.
— James A. Garfield (20th U.S. president, 1831–1881)

🐻 TUESDAY
D 33.3
S 38.1
N 33.3
25

Civility is not a sign of weakness, and sincerity is always subject to proof. Let us never negotiate out of fear.
But let us never fear to negotiate. — John F. Kennedy (35th U.S. president, Inaugural Address 1/20/1961, 1917–1963)

Late October is Time to Buy Depressed Stocks, Especially Techs and Small Caps

WEDNESDAY
D 47.6
S 52.4
N 42.9
26

People with a sense of fulfillment think the world is good, while the frustrated blame the world for their failure.
— Eric Hoffer (*The True Believer*, 1951)

THURSDAY
D 61.9
S 57.1
N 52.4
27

Never tell people how to do things. Tell them what to do and they will surprise you with their ingenuity.
— General George S. Patton, Jr. (US Army field commander WWII, 1885–1945)

82nd Anniversary of 1929 Crash, Dow Down 23.0% in Two Days, October 28 and 29

🐂 FRIDAY
D 71.4
S 76.2
N 66.7
28

How a minority, reaching majority, seizing authority, hates a minority. — Leonard H. Robbins

SATURDAY
29

SUNDAY
30

NOVEMBER ALMANAC

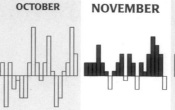

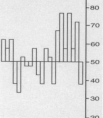

NOVEMBER							DECEMBER						
S	M	T	W	T	F	S	S	M	T	W	T	F	S
		1	2	3	4	5				1	2	3
6	7	8	9	10	11	12	4	5	6	7	8	9	10
13	14	15	16	17	18	19	11	12	13	14	15	16	17
20	21	22	23	24	25	26	18	19	20	21	22	23	24
27	28	29	30				25	26	27	28	29	30	31

Market Probability Chart above is a graphic representation of the S&P 500 Recent Market Probability Calendar on page 124.

◆ #2 S&P month and #3 on Dow since 1950, #3 on NASDAQ since 1971 (pages 44 and 54) ◆ Start of the "Best Six Months" of the year (page 48), NASDAQ's Best Eight Months and Best Three (pages 147 and 148) ◆ Simple timing indicator almost triples "Best Six Months" strategy (page 50), doubles NASDAQ's Best Eight (page 58) ◆ Day before and after Thanksgiving Day combined, only 12 losses in 58 years (page 98) ◆ Week before Thanksgiving, Dow up 14 of last 17 ◆ Pre-presidential election year Novembers rank #9 Dow, S&P, and NASDAQ.

November Vital Statistics

	DJIA		S&P 500		NASDAQ		Russell 1K		Russell 2K	
Rank	3		2		3		1		4	
Up	40		40		26		22		20	
Down	20		20		13		9		11	
Avg % Change	1.6%		1.6%		1.7%		1.8%		1.8%	
Pre-Election Year	0.3%		0.3%		1.2%		−0.2%		1.2%	
Best and Worst November										
	% Change		% Change		% Change		% Change		% Change	
Best	1962	10.1	1980	10.2	2001	14.2	1980	10.1	2002	8.8
Worst	1973	−14.0	1973	−11.4	2000	−22.9	2000	−9.3	2008	−12.0
Best and Worst November Weeks										
Best	11/28/08	9.7	11/28/08	12.0	11/28/08	10.9	11/28/08	12.5	11/28/08	16.4
Worst	11/21/08	−5.3	11/21/08	−8.4	11/10/00	−12.2	11/21/08	−8.8	11/21/08	−11.0
Best and Worst November Days										
Best	11/13/08	6.7	11/13/08	6.9	11/13/08	6.5	11/13/08	7.0	11/13/08	8.5
Worst	11/20/08	−5.6	11/20/08	−6.7	11/19/08	−6.5	11/20/08	−6.9	11/19/08	−7.9
First Trading Day of Expiration Week: 1980–2009										
Record (#Up–#Down)	15–15		13–17		12–18		14–16		13–17	
Current Streak	U1		U1		U1		U1		U1	
Avg % Change	−0.04		−0.06		−0.14		−0.08		−0.06	
Options Expiration Day: 1980–2009										
Record (#Up–#Down)	18–12		17–13		15–15		17–13		13–16	
Current Streak	D1		D1		D1		D1		D1	
Avg % Change	0.22		0.15		0.01		0.14		0.07	
Options Expiration Week: 1980–2009										
Record (#Up–#Down)	20–10		18–12		16–14		17–13		15–15	
Current Streak	U1		D2		D2		D2		D3	
Avg % Change	0.39		0.11		0.07		0.08		−0.24	
Week After Options Expiration: 1980–2009										
Record (#Up–#Down)	18–12		19–11		19–11		19–11		17–13	
Current Streak	D1		U2		D1		D1		D1	
Avg % Change	0.87		0.83		0.88		0.83		0.94	
First Trading Day Performance										
% of Time Up	63.3		63.3		66.7		71.0		67.7	
Avg % Change	0.31		0.34		0.35		0.48		0.33	
Last Trading Day Performance										
% of Time Up	55.0		55.0		66.7		48.4		74.2	
Avg % Change	0.05		0.09		−0.17		−0.08		0.07	

Dow & S&P 1950–April 2010, NASDAQ 1971–April 2010, Russell 1K & 2K 1979–April 2010.

Astute investors always smile and remember,
When stocks seasonally start soaring, and salute November.

Halloween

MONDAY
D 52.4
S 61.9
N 76.2
31

When a country lives on borrowed time, borrowed money, and borrowed energy, it is just begging the markets to discipline it in their own way at their own time. Usually the markets do it in an orderly way—except when they don't.
— Thomas L. Friedman (*NY Times* Foreign Affairs columnist, 2/24/05)

First Trading Day in November, Dow Down 4 of Last 5
2009 Up 0.8%

TUESDAY
D 57.1
S 57.1
N 71.4
1

When Paris sneezes, Europe catches cold. — Prince Klemens Metternich (Austrian statesman, 1773–1859)

WEDNESDAY
D 47.6
S 57.1
N 57.1
2

To achieve satisfactory investment results is easier than most people realize.
The typical individual investor has a great advantage over the large institutions.
— Benjamin Graham (Economist, investor, *Securities Analysis* 1934, *The Intelligent Investor* 1949, 1894–1976)

November Begins Dow and S&P "Best Six Months" (Pages 44, 48, 50, 147)
And NASDAQ "Best Eight Months" (Pages 54, 58, and 148)

THURSDAY
D 57.1
S 57.1
N 71.4
3

My best shorts come from research reports where there are recommendations to buy stocks on weakness; also, where a brokerage firm changes its recommendation from a buy to a hold. — Marc Howard (Hedge fund manager, *New York* magazine, 1976, b. 1941)

FRIDAY
D 66.7
S 66.7
N 61.9
4

The more feted by the media, the worse a pundit's accuracy.
— Sharon Begley (Senior editor, *Newsweek*, 2/23/2009, referencing Philip E. Tetlock's 2005 *Expert Political Judgment*)

SATURDAY
5

Daylight Saving Time Ends

SUNDAY
6

MOST OF THE SO-CALLED "JANUARY EFFECT" TAKES PLACE IN THE LAST HALF OF DECEMBER

Over the years we reported annually on the fascinating January Effect, showing that small-cap stocks handily outperformed large-cap stocks during January 40 out of 43 years between 1953 and 1995. Readers saw that "Cats and Dogs" on average quadrupled the returns of blue chips in this period. Then, the January Effect disappeared over the next four years.

Looking at the graph on page 104, comparing the Russell 1000 index of large-capitalization stocks to the Russell 2000 smaller-capitalization stocks, shows small-cap stocks beginning to outperform the blue chips in mid-December. Narrowing the comparison down to half-month segments was an inspiration and proved to be quite revealing, as you can see in the table below.

23-YEAR AVERAGE RATES OF RETURN (DEC 1987 TO FEB 2010)

| From | Russell 1000 | | Russell 2000 | |
mid-Dec*	Change	Annualized	Change	Annualized
12/15–12/31	1.8%	50.5%	3.5%	119.9%
12/15–01/15	1.8	22.7	3.7	51.6
12/15–01/31	2.1	18.4	4.0	37.6
12/15–02/15	2.7	17.3	5.3	36.3
12/15–02/28	1.8	9.4	5.0	27.9
end-Dec*				
12/31–01/15	0.1	2.1	0.2	4.3
12/31–01/31	0.3	3.7	0.5	6.2
12/31–02/15	0.9	7.3	1.7	14.2
12/31–02/28	0.1	0.6	1.4	9.2

31-YEAR AVERAGE RATES OF RETURN (DEC 1979 TO FEB 2010)

| From | Russell 1000 | | Russell 2000 | |
mid-Dec*	Change	Annualized	Change	Annualized
12/15–12/31	1.6%	43.9%	3.1%	101.3%
12/15–01/15	2.1	26.9	4.2	60.2
12/15–01/31	2.5	22.2	4.6	44.1
12/15–02/15	3.0	19.4	5.9	41.1
12/15–02/28	2.5	13.3	5.7	32.2
end-Dec*				
12/31–01/15	0.6	13.4	1.1	25.8
12/31–01/31	0.9	11.4	1.5	19.6
12/31–02/15	1.5	12.4	2.8	24.3
12/31–02/28	0.9	5.7	2.6	17.1

* Mid-month dates are the 11th trading day of the month; month end dates are monthly closes.

Small-cap strength in the last half of December became even more magnified after the 1987 market crash. Note the dramatic shift in gains in the last half of December during the 23-year period starting in 1987, versus the 31 years from 1979 to 2010. With all the beaten-down small stocks being dumped for tax loss purposes, it generally pays to get a head start on the January Effect in mid-December. You don't have to wait until December either; the small-cap sector often begins to turn around toward the end of October and November.

MONDAY
7

D 57.1
S 57.1
N 61.9

A person's greatest virtue is his ability to correct his mistakes and continually make a new person of himself.
— Yang-Ming Wang (Chinese philosopher, 1472–1529)

Election Day

TUESDAY
8

D 57.1
S 52.4
N 57.1

Politics ought to be the part-time profession of every citizen who would protect the rights and privileges of free people and who would preserve what is good and fruitful in our national heritage. — Dwight D. Eisenhower (34th U.S. president, 1890–1969)

WEDNESDAY
9

D 38.1
S 42.9
N 52.4

Regret for the things we did can be tempered by time; it is regret for the things we did not do that is inconsolable.
— Sydney J. Harris (American journalist and author, 1917–1986)

THURSDAY
10

D 57.1
S 52.4
N 57.1

Learn from the mistakes of others; you can't live long enough to make them all yourself.
— Eleanor Roosevelt (First Lady, 1884–1962)

Veterans' Day

FRIDAY
11

D 61.9
S 57.1
N 61.9

[A contrarian's opportunity] If everybody is thinking alike, then somebody isn't thinking.
— General George S. Patton Jr. (U.S. Army field commander WWII, 1885–1945)

SATURDAY
12

SUNDAY
13

JANUARY EFFECT NOW STARTS IN MID-DECEMBER

Small-cap stocks tend to outperform big caps in January. Known as the "January Effect," the tendency is clearly revealed by the graph below. Thirty-two years of daily data for the Russell 2000 index of smaller companies are divided by the Russell 1000 index of largest companies, and then compressed into a single year to show an idealized yearly pattern. When the graph is descending, big blue chips are outperforming smaller companies; when the graph is rising, smaller companies are moving up faster than their larger brethren.

In a typical year, the smaller fry stay on the sidelines while the big boys are on the field. Then, around late October, small stocks begin to wake up, and in mid-December, they take off. Anticipated year-end dividends, payouts, and bonuses could be a factor. Other major moves are quite evident just before Labor Day—possibly because individual investors are back from vacations—and off the low points in late October and November. Small caps hold the lead through the beginning of June.

RUSSELL 2000/RUSSELL 1000 ONE-YEAR SEASONAL PATTERN

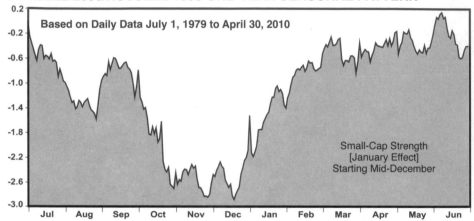

The bottom graph shows the actual ratio of the Russell 2000 divided by the Russell 1000 from 1979. Smaller companies had the upper hand for five years into 1983 as the last major bear trend wound to a close and the nascent bull market logged its first year. After falling behind for about eight years, they came back after the Persian Gulf War bottom in 1990, moving up until 1994, when big caps ruled the latter stages of the millennial bull. For six years the picture was bleak for small fry, as the blue chips and tech stocks moved to stratospheric PE ratios. Small caps spiked in late 1999 and early 2000 and reached a peak in early 2006, as the four-year-old bull entered its final year. Note how the small-cap advantage has waned during major bull moves and intensified during weak market times. Look for a clear move lower to confirm a major bull move is in place.

RUSSELL 2000/RUSSELL 1000 (1979 TO APRIL 2010)

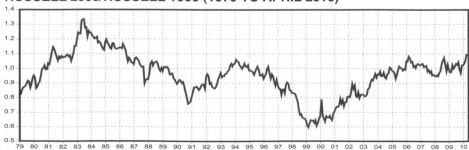

NOVEMBER

Monday Before November Expiration, Dow Down 7 of Last 11;
Dow Hit Big in 2008, Down 224 Points (2.6%)

MONDAY
14

D 66.7
S 61.9
N 61.9

Welch's genius was the capacity to energize and inspire hundreds of thousands of people across a range of
businesses and countries. — Warren G. Bennis (USC business professor, Business Week, September 10, 2001,
referring to retiring CEO Jack Welch of General Electric)

TUESDAY
15

D 52.4
S 47.6
N 42.9

When I have to depend upon hope in a trade, I get out of it.
— Jesse Livermore (Early 20th century stock trader and speculator, How to Trade in Stocks, 1877–1940)

Week Before Thanksgiving, Dow Up 14 of Last 17,
2003 –1.4%, 2004 –0.8%, 2008 –5.3%

WEDNESDAY
16

D 52.4
S 61.9
N 47.6

There are ways for the individual investor to make money in the securities markets. Buying value and holding long term while
collecting dividends has been proven over and over again. — Robert M. Sharp (Author, The Lore and Legends of Wall Street)

THURSDAY
17

D 57.1
S 57.1
N 52.4

When a falling stock becomes a screaming buy because it cannot conceivably drop further, try to buy it 30 percent lower.
— Al Rizzo (1986)

November Expiration Day, Dow Up 6 of Last 8
Dow Surged in 2008, Up 494 Points (6.5%)

FRIDAY
18

D 42.9
S 42.9
N 52.4

Based on my own personal experience—both as an investor in recent years and an expert witness in years past—rarely do more than
three or four variables really count. Everything else is noise. — Martin J. Whitman (Founder, Third Avenue Funds, b. 1924)

SATURDAY
19

SUNDAY
20

WALL STREET'S ONLY "FREE LUNCH" SERVED BEFORE CHRISTMAS

Investors tend to get rid of their losers near year-end for tax purposes, often hammering these stocks down to bargain levels. Over the years, the *Almanac* has shown that NYSE stocks selling at their lows on December 15 will usually outperform the market by February 15 in the following year. Preferred stocks, closed-end funds, splits, and new issues are eliminated. When there are a huge number of new lows, stocks down the most are selected, even though there are usually good reasons why some stocks have been battered.

BARGAIN STOCKS VS. THE MARKET*

Short Span* Late Dec–Jan/Feb	New Lows Late Dec	% Change Jan/Feb	% Change NYSE Composite	Bargain Stocks Advantage
1974–75	112	48.9%	22.1%	26.8%
1975–76	21	34.9	14.9	20.0
1976–77	2	1.3	−3.3	4.6
1977–78	15	2.8	−4.5	7.3
1978–79	43	11.8	3.9	7.9
1979–80	5	9.3	6.1	3.2
1980–81	14	7.1	−2.0	9.1
1981–82	21	−2.6	−7.4	4.8
1982–83	4	33.0	9.7	23.3
1983–84	13	−3.2	−3.8	0.6
1984–85	32	19.0	12.1	6.9
1985–86	4	−22.5	3.9	−26.4
1986–87	22	9.3	12.5	−3.2
1987–88	23	13.2	6.8	6.4
1988–89	14	30.0	6.4	23.6
1989–90	25	−3.1	−4.8	1.7
1990–91	18	18.8	12.6	6.2
1991–92	23	51.1	7.7	43.4
1992–93	9	8.7	0.6	8.1
1993–94	10	−1.4	2.0	−3.4
1994–95	25	14.6	5.7	8.9
1995–96	5	−11.3	4.5	−15.8
1996–97	16	13.9	11.2	2.7
1997–98	29	9.9	5.7	4.2
1998–99	40	−2.8	4.3	−7.1
1999–00	26	8.9	−5.4	14.3
2000–01	51	44.4	0.1	44.3
2001–02	12	31.4	−2.3	33.7
2002–03	33	28.7	3.9	24.8
2003–04	15	16.7	2.3	14.4
2004–05	36	6.8	−2.8	9.6
2005–06	71	12.0	2.6	9.4
2006–07	43	5.1	−0.5	5.6
2007–08	71	−3.2	−9.4	6.2
2008–09	88	11.4	−2.4	13.8
2009–10	25	1.8	−3.0	4.8
36-Year Totals		**454.7%**	**110.0%**	**344.7%**
Average		**12.6%**	**3.1%**	**9.6%**

Dec 15 to Feb 15 (1974–1999), Dec 1999–2009 based on actual newsletter advice.

In response to changing market conditions we tweaked the strategy the last 11 years, adding selections from NASDAQ, AMEX, and the OTC Bulletin Board and selling in mid-January some years. We e-mail the list of stocks to our *Almanac Investor* newsletter subscribers. Visit *www.stocktradersalmanac.com,* or see the insert at page 96 for additional details and a special offer for new subscribers.

We have come to the conclusion that the most prudent course of action is to compile our list from the stocks making new lows on Triple-Witching Friday before Christmas, capitalizing on the Santa Claus Rally (page 110). This also gives us the weekend to evaluate the issues in greater depth and weed out any glaringly problematic stocks. Subscribers will receive the list of stocks selected from the new lows made on December 17, 2010 via e-mail.

This "Free Lunch" strategy is only an extremely short-term strategy reserved for the nimblest traders. It has performed better after market corrections and when there are more new lows to choose from. The object is to buy bargain stocks near their 52-week lows and sell any quick, generous gains, as these issues can often be real dogs.

Trading Thanksgiving Market: Long into Weakness Prior,
Exit into Strength After (Page 98)

MONDAY
D 61.9
S 57.1
N 52.4
21

If you can buy more of your best idea, why put [the money] into your 10th-best idea or your 20th-best idea?
The more positions you have, the more average you are. — Bruce Berkowitz (Fairholme Fund, *Barron's*, 3/17/08)

TUESDAY
D 61.9
S 52.4
N 61.9
22

History is replete with episodes in which the real patriots were the ones who defied their governments.
— Jim Rogers (Financier, *Adventure Capitalist*, b. 1942)

WEDNESDAY
D 66.7
S 61.9
N 57.1
23

The job of central banks: To take away the punch bowl just as the party is getting going.
— William McChesney Martin (Federal Reserve chairman 1951–1970, 1906–1998)

Thanksgiving (Market Closed)

THURSDAY
24

At a time of war, we need you to work for peace. At a time of inequality, we need you to work for opportunity.
At a time of so much cynicism and so much doubt, we need you to make us believe again.
— Barack H. Obama (44th U.S. president, Commencement Wesleyan University, 5/28/2008, b. 1961)

(Shortened Trading Day)

FRIDAY
D 71.4
S 71.4
N 57.1
25

Those that forget the past are condemned to repeat its mistakes, and those that mis-state the past should be condemned.
— Eugene D. Cohen (Letter to the Editor, *Financial Times*, 10/30/06)

SATURDAY
26

December Almanac Investor Seasonalities: See Pages 92, 94, and 96

SUNDAY
27

DECEMBER ALMANAC

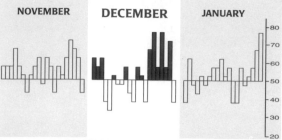

DECEMBER						
S	M	T	W	T	F	S
				1	2	3
4	5	6	7	8	9	10
11	12	13	14	15	16	17
18	19	20	21	22	23	24
25	26	27	28	29	30	31

JANUARY						
S	M	T	W	T	F	S
1	2	3	4	5	6	7
8	9	10	11	12	13	14
15	16	17	18	19	20	21
22	23	24	25	26	27	28
29	30	31				

Market Probability Chart above is a graphic representation of the S&P 500 Recent Market Probability Calendar on page 124.

◆ #1 S&P (+1.6%) and #2 Dow (+1.7%) month since 1950 (page 44), #2 NASDAQ (2.0%) since 1971 ◆ 2002 worst December since 1931, down over 6% Dow and S&P, –9.7% on NASDAQ (pages 152, 155, and 157)◆"Free lunch" served on Wall Street before Christmas (page 106) ◆ Small caps start to outperform larger caps near middle of month (pages 102 and 104)◆"Santa Claus Rally" visible in graph above and on page 110 ◆ In 1998 was part of best fourth quarter since 1928 (page 167) ◆ Fourth-quarter expiration week most bullish triple witching week, Dow up 15 of last 19 (page 76) ◆ In pre-presidential election years, Decembers rankings slip: #3 S&P and Dow, still #2 NASDAQ month.

December Vital Statistics

	DJIA	S&P 500	NASDAQ	Russell 1K	Russell 2K
Rank	2	1	2	3	1
Up	42	45	23	24	24
Down	18	15	16	7	7
Avg % Change	1.7%	1.6%	2.0%	1.6%	2.7%
Pre-Election Year	3.1%	3.3%	5.4%	3.8%	4.4%

		Best and Worst December							
		% Change		% Change		% Change		% Change		% Change

	% Change		% Change		% Change		% Change		% Change	
Best	1991	9.5	1991	11.2	1999	22.0	1991	11.2	1999	11.2
Worst	2002	–6.2	2002	–6.0	2002	–9.7	2002	–5.8	2002	–5.7

	Best and Worst December Weeks									
Best	12/18/87	5.8	12/18/87	5.9	12/8/00	10.3	12/18/87	6.0	12/18/87	7.7
Worst	12/4/87	–7.5	12/6/74	–7.1	12/15/00	–9.1	12/4/87	–7.0	12/12/80	–6.5

	Best and Worst December Days									
Best	12/16/08	4.2	12/16/08	5.1	12/5/00	10.5	12/16/08	5.2	12/16/08	6.7
Worst	12/1/08	–7.7	12/1/08	–8.9	12/1/08	–9.0	12/1/08	–9.1	12/1/08	–11.9

	First Trading Day of Expiration Week: 1980–2009				
Record (#Up–#Down)	17–13	18–12	13–17	19–11	14–16
Current Streak	U1	U1	U1	U1	U1
Avg % Change	0.20	0.16	–0.05	0.13	–0.15

	Options Expiration Day: 1980–2009				
Record (#Up–#Down)	21–9	22–8	21–9	22–8	19–11
Current Streak	U1	U4	U4	U4	U3
Avg % Change	0.40	0.44	0.39	0.42	0.43

	Options Expiration Week: 1980–2009				
Record (#Up–#Down)	23–7	22–8	17–13	21–9	15–15
Current Streak	D2	D1	U4	D1	U4
Avg % Change	0.76	0.79	0.23	0.73	0.57

	Week After Options Expiration: 1980–2009				
Record (#Up–#Down)	20–9	17–13	18–12	17–13	20–10
Current Streak	U1	U1	U1	U1	U1
Avg % Change	0.70	0.39	0.64	0.42	0.76

	First Trading Day Performance				
% of Time Up	48.3	51.7	61.5	54.8	54.8
Avg % Change	–0.09	–0.06	0.12	–0.09	–0.13

	Last Trading Day Performance				
% of Time Up	53.3	63.3	76.9	54.8	74.2
Avg % Change	0.08	0.11	0.37	–0.08	0.52

Dow & S&P 1950–April 2010, NASDAQ 1971–April 2010, Russell 1K & 2K 1979–April 2010.

If Santa Claus should fail to call,
Bears may come to Broad and Wall.

NOVEMBER/DECEMBER

MONDAY
D 61.9
S 66.7
N 61.9
28

The usual bull market successfully weathers a number of tests until it is considered invulnerable, whereupon it is ripe for a bust.
— George Soros (Financier, philanthropist, political activist, author, and philosopher, b. 1930)

TUESDAY
D 47.6
S 61.9
N 71.4
29

Anytime there is change there is opportunity. So it is paramount that an organization get energized rather than paralyzed.
— Jack Welch (GE CEO, *Fortune*)

WEDNESDAY
D 57.1
S 42.9
N 57.1
30

100% I did. 90% I will. 80% I can. 70% I think I can. 60% I might. 50% I think I might.
40% What is it? 30% I wish I could. 20% I don't know how. 10% I can't. 0% I won't. — (Ladder of Achievement)

First Trading Day in December, NASDAQ Up 17 of 23
Down Three Straight 2006–2008

THURSDAY
D 57.1
S 61.9
N 71.4
1

Oil has fostered massive corruption in almost every country that has been "blessed" with it, and the expectation that oil wealth will transform economies has lead to disastrous policy choices. — Ted Tyson (Chief investment officer, Mastholm Asset Management)

FRIDAY
D 52.4
S 57.1
N 66.7
2

When America sneezes, the rest of the word catches cold. — Anonymous (circa 1929)

SATURDAY
3

SUNDAY
4

IF SANTA CLAUS SHOULD FAIL TO CALL, BEARS MAY COME TO BROAD AND WALL

Santa Claus tends to come to Wall Street nearly every year, bringing a short, sweet, respectable rally within the last five days of the year and the first two in January. This has been good for an average 1.6% gain since 1969 (1.5% since 1950). Santa's failure to show tends to precede bear markets, or times stocks could be purchased later in the year at much lower prices. We discovered this phenomenon in 1972.

DAILY % CHANGE IN S&P 500 AT YEAR END

	Trading Days Before Year End						First Days in January			Rally % Change
	6	5	4	3	2	1	1	2	3	
1969	−0.4	1.1	0.8	−0.7	0.4	0.5	1.0	0.5	−0.7	3.6
1970	0.1	0.6	0.5	1.1	0.2	−0.1	−1.1	0.7	0.6	1.9
1971	−0.4	0.2	1.0	0.3	−0.4	0.3	−0.4	0.4	1.0	1.3
1972	−0.3	−0.7	0.6	0.4	0.5	1.0	0.9	0.4	−0.1	3.1
1973	−1.1	−0.7	3.1	2.1	−0.2	0.01	0.1	2.2	−0.9	6.7
1974	−1.4	1.4	0.8	−0.4	0.03	2.1	2.4	0.7	0.5	7.2
1975	0.7	0.8	0.9	−0.1	−0.4	0.5	0.8	1.8	1.0	4.3
1976	0.1	1.2	0.7	−0.4	0.5	0.5	−0.4	−1.2	−0.9	0.8
1977	0.8	0.9	N/C	0.1	0.2	0.2	−1.3	−0.3	−0.8	−0.3
1978	0.03	1.7	1.3	−0.9	−0.4	−0.2	0.6	1.1	0.8	3.3
1979	−0.6	0.1	0.1	0.2	−0.1	0.1	−2.0	0.5	1.2	−2.2
1980	−0.4	0.4	0.5	−1.1	0.2	0.3	0.4	1.2	0.1	2.0
1981	−0.5	0.2	−0.2	−0.5	0.5	0.2	0.2	−2.2	−0.7	−1.8
1982	0.6	1.8	−1.0	0.3	−0.7	0.2	−1.6	2.2	0.4	1.2
1983	−0.2	−0.03	0.9	0.3	−0.2	0.05	−0.5	1.7	1.2	2.1
1984	−0.5	0.8	−0.2	−0.4	0.3	0.6	−1.1	−0.5	−0.5	−0.6
1985	−1.1	−0.7	0.2	0.9	0.5	0.3	−0.8	0.6	−0.1	1.1
1986	−1.0	0.2	0.1	−0.9	−0.5	−0.5	1.8	2.3	0.2	2.4
1987	1.3	−0.5	−2.6	−0.4	1.3	−0.3	3.6	1.1	0.1	2.2
1988	−0.2	0.3	−0.4	0.1	0.8	−0.6	−0.9	1.5	0.2	0.9
1989	0.6	0.8	−0.2	0.6	0.5	0.8	1.8	−0.3	−0.9	4.1
1990	0.5	−0.6	0.3	−0.8	0.1	0.5	−1.1	−1.4	−0.3	−3.0
1991	2.5	0.6	1.4	0.4	2.1	0.5	0.04	0.5	−0.3	5.7
1992	−0.3	0.2	−0.1	−0.3	0.2	−0.7	−0.1	−0.2	0.04	−1.1
1993	0.01	0.7	0.1	−0.1	−0.4	−0.5	−0.2	0.3	0.1	−0.1
1994	0.01	0.2	0.4	−0.3	0.1	−0.4	−0.03	0.3	−0.1	0.2
1995	0.8	0.2	0.4	0.04	−0.1	0.3	0.8	0.1	−0.6	1.8
1996	−0.3	0.5	0.6	0.1	−0.4	−1.7	−0.5	1.5	−0.1	0.1
1997	−1.5	−0.7	0.4	1.8	1.8	−0.04	0.5	0.2	−1.1	4.0
1998	2.1	−0.2	−0.1	1.3	−0.8	−0.2	−0.1	1.4	2.2	1.3
1999	1.6	−0.1	0.04	0.4	0.1	0.3	−1.0	−3.8	0.2	−4.0
2000	0.8	2.4	0.7	1.0	0.4	−1.0	−2.8	5.0	−1.1	5.7
2001	0.4	−0.02	0.4	0.7	0.3	−1.1	0.6	0.9	0.6	1.8
2002	0.2	−0.5	−0.3	−1.6	0.5	0.05	3.3	−0.05	2.2	1.2
2003	0.3	−0.2	0.2	1.2	0.01	0.2	−0.3	1.2	0.1	2.4
2004	0.1	−0.4	0.7	−0.01	0.01	−0.1	−0.8	−1.2	−0.4	−1.8
2005	0.4	0.04	−1.0	0.1	−0.3	−0.5	1.6	0.4	0.002	0.4
2006	−0.4	−0.5	0.4	0.7	v.1	−0.5	−0.1	0.1	−0.6	0.003
2007	1.7	0.8	0.1	−1.4	0.1	−0.7	−1.4	N/C	−2.5	−2.5
2008	−1.0	0.6	0.5	−0.4	2.4	1.4	3.2	−0.5	0.8	7.4
2009	0.2	0.5	0.1	−0.1	0.02	−1.0	1.6	0.3	0.05	1.4
Avg	0.10	0.33	0.30	0.08	0.22	0.02	0.16	0.45	0.02	1.6

The couplet above was certainly on the mark in 1999, as the period suffered a horrendous 4.0% loss. On January 14, 2000, the Dow started its 33-month 37.8% slide to the October 2002 midterm election year bottom. NASDAQ cracked eight weeks later, falling 37.3% in 10 weeks, eventually dropping 77.9% by October 2002. Saddam Hussein cancelled Christmas by invading Kuwait in 1990. Energy prices and Middle East terror woes may have grounded Santa in 2004. In 2007, the third worst reading since 1950 was recorded, as subprime mortgages and their derivatives led to a full-blown financial crisis and the second worst bear market in history.

MONDAY

D 57.1
S 61.9
N 66.7

5

Statements by high officials are practically always misleading when they are designed to bolster a falling market.
— Gerald M. Loeb (E.F. Hutton, *The Battle for Investment Survival*, predicted 1929 Crash, 1900–1974)

TUESDAY

D 52.4
S 38.1
N 52.4

6

There is nothing as invigorating as the ego boost that comes from having others sign on when your company is just a dream. What they are saying when they agree to service customers, suppliers, employers or distributors is that they believe in you.
— Joshua Hyatt (*Inc.* magazine, *Mapping the Entrepreneurial Mind*, August 1991)

Small Cap Strength Starts in Mid-December (Page 102)

WEDNESDAY

D 38.1
S 33.3
N 33.3

7

The incestuous relationship between government and big business thrives in the dark.
— Jack Anderson (Washington journalist and author, *Peace, War, and Politics*, 1922–2005)

THURSDAY

D 52.4
S 52.4
N 47.6

8

Government is like fire—useful when used legitimately, but dangerous when not.
— David Brooks (*NY Times columnist*, 10/5/07)

FRIDAY

D 52.4
S 47.6
N 42.9

9

A weak currency is the sign of a weak economy, and a weak economy leads to a weak nation.
— H. Ross Perot (American businessman, *The Dollar Crisis*, 2-time 3rd-party presidential candidate, 1992 and 1996, b. 1930)

SATURDAY

10

SUNDAY

11

BEST INVESTMENT BOOK OF THE YEAR

Far From Random: Using Investor Behavior and Trend Analysis to Forecast Market Movement
By Richard Lehman

For 44 years the *Stock Trader's Almanac* has uncovered many patterns that astute investors could take advantage of: the Best Consecutive Six Months of the year, the January Barometer, the enormous superiority of the market in the last two years of the Four-Year Presidential Cycle over the first two years, and so on. Burton Malkiel's book, *A Random Walk Down Wall Street* (Norton, 1st edition 1973), espouses that no one can predict the market at any time. Professor Malkiel is a renowned and influential economist whom we quote on page 21 on January 25. But we beg to differ. Quite to the contrary are the myriad proven patterns in these pages.

The financial world has for decades swallowed whole the idea that market movement is chaotic, random, and entirely unpredictable. In his new book, *Far From Random*, Richard Lehman takes on these stalwarts of finance and easily disproves the widely accepted investment principle "that stock market movement cannot be predicted." With his new take on trend channel analysis, Lehman shows that market trends exist, are discernible before they are wholly formed, and can be employed to boost investment returns. Lehman unequivocally proves that the market moves in well-defined, often predictable patterns.

Far From Random demonstrates Lehman's new, simple way to really beat the market. He convincingly agues that the, "stock market is not entirely random" and its patterns, cycles, and trends "can be explained within certain parameters." His unique charting technique provides perspective at any point in time over almost any time period. *Far From Random* delivers a methodology for determining precisely when market trends change, explains seemingly chaotic or extreme market moves, helps you time investment decisions, and gives you the tools to develop a robust trading strategy to beat the market under any conditions.

If anyone out there still believes in the "random walk" theory, have them explain how it was possible for first days of the month in the last 153 months, starting September 1997, to gain a total 5173.23 Dow points for an average point gain of +33.81; while all the other 3034 trading days of these months lost 1643.82 Dow points for an average daily loss of half a Dow point (−0.54) (page 62).

Wall Street practitioners, academics, and so many market commentators have encouraged the notion that we are not able to forecast the markets and therefore should not try. From the front flap: "Lehman's trend channel analysis allows investors to: identify a bull or bear market, discern between a rally and a true trend, find and take advantage of market tops and bottoms, spot a sideways market, and stay on the sideline."

As market pro Robert R. Prechter Jr. says on the front cover, "Lehman's persistent wisdom puts investors on the right path to understanding how markets do and do not behave." As we have said many times in the past, "Random Walkers, eat your heart out!"

Monday Before December Triple Witching, S&P Up 7 of Last 10

MONDAY

D 57.1
S 47.6
N 42.9

12

As for it being different this time, it is different every time. The question is in what way, and to what extent.
— Tom McClellan (*The McClellan Market Report*)

TUESDAY

D 52.4
S 57.1
N 57.1

13

If you torture the data long enough, it will confess to anything. — Darrell Huff (*How to Lie With Statistics*, 1954)

December Triple Witching Week, S&P Up 21 of Last 26;
2009 Broke 8-Year Bull Run

WEDNESDAY

D 47.6
S 42.9
N 38.1

14

If the market does not rally, as it should during bullish seasonal periods, it is a sign that other forces are stronger and that when the seasonal period ends those forces will really have their say.
— Edson Gould (Stock market analyst, *Findings & Forecasts*, 1902–1987)

THURSDAY

D 42.9
S 38.1
N 42.9

15

I'd be a bum on the street with a tin cup, if the markets were always efficient.
— Warren Buffett (CEO Berkshire Hathaway, investor, and philanthropist, b. 1930)

December Triple Witching, S&P Up 20 of 28
Average Gain 0.4%

FRIDAY

D 57.1
S 57.1
N 47.6

16

An economist is someone who sees something happen, and then wonders if it would work in theory.
— Ronald Reagan (40th U.S. president, 1911–2004)

SATURDAY

17

SUNDAY

18

YEAR'S TOP INVESTMENT BOOKS

Far From Random: Using Investor Behavior and Trend Analysis to Forecast Market Movement, Richard Lehman, Bloomberg, $39.95. 2011 Best Investment Book of the Year.

The Capitalist Spirit: How Each and Every One of Us Can Make a Giant Difference in Our Fast-Changing World, Yale Hirsch, Wiley, $19.95. Ken Fisher says, "This mind boggling wonderful compilation is not only phenomenal overall but has dozens of snippets that by themselves are worth many times the book's price."

Buy—Don't Hold: Investing With ETFs Using Relative Strength to Increase Returns With Less Risk, Leslie N. Masonson, FT Press, $26.99. Shows investors and traders how to buy and sell the right ETFs at the right time with proven strategies, tools, and indicators.

Super Sectors: How to Outsmart the Market Using Sector Rotation and ETFs, John Nyaradi, Wiley, $49.95. Identifies 5 "super sectors" that will likely advance far faster and higher than the general indexes due to several economic and social "megatrends" on the horizon.

Higher Returns From Safe Investments: Using Bonds, Stocks, and Options to Generate Lifetime Income, Marvin Appel, FT Press, $24.99. Money manager and Systems and Forecasts editor reveals no-nonsense, simple strategies for increasing retirement returns with little risk.

The Small-Cap Investor: Secrets to Winning Big with Small-Cap Stocks, Ian Wyatt, Wiley, $27.95. A field manual for big profits. Shows you how to find them, analyze them, and ride them for all they are worth.

Spread Trading: An Introduction to Trading Options in Nine Simple Steps, Greg Jensen, Wiley, $49.95. All you need to know to safely earn remarkable profits in today's market.

The Swing Trader's Bible: Strategies to Profit from Market Volatility, Matthew McCall & Mark Whistler, Wiley, $70.00. A straightforward approach to trading that allows you to make sense of today's markets and profit from volatility.

Wisdom on Value Investing: How to Profit on Fallen Angels: Gabriel Wisdom, Wiley, $27.95. How the smart investor stays calm and waits patiently for the incredible deals—the Fallen Angels—that are certain to come along.

Market Indicators: The Best-Kept Secret to More Effective Trading and Investing, Richard Sipley, Bloomberg Press, $39.95. Introduces the many key indicators used by professional traders and investors every day.

A Gift to My Children: A Father's Lessons for Life and Investing, Jim Rogers, Random House, $16.00. A legendary investor reveals how to learn from his triumphs and mistakes in order to achieve a prosperous, well-lived life. A great book to give to your children.

How to Smell a Rat: The Five Signs of Financial Fraud, Ken Fisher with Lara Hoffmans, Wiley, $24.95. Highlights various features of potential frauds and provides an insider's view on how to spot financial disasters before you become part of them.

The Making of a Market Guru: Forbes Presents 25 Years of Ken Fisher, Aaron Anderson, Editor, Wiley, $29.95. How Fisher called three of the last four bear markets. Perhaps you can learn how to become your own market guru.

No One Would Listen: A True Financial Thriller, Harry Markopolos, Wiley, $27.95. The story of how Harry uncovered the biggest Ponzi scheme in history years before Bernie Madoff confessed and wound up in prison. Harry was fearful as some whistle blowers get murdered.

The Genius of the Beast: A Radical Re-Vision of Capitalism, Howard Bloom, Prometheus, $29.00. The key to next-generation capitalism lies in a big-picture view with which we can ignite the world, get a new handle on our lives, and help transform society.

Stephen Roach on the Next Asia: Opportunities and Challenges for a New Globalization, Stephen Roach, Wiley, $39.95. Chairman of Morgan Stanley Asia says that "the next Asia" will be a rebalanced Asia, providing enormous opportunities for the world's largest population mass, as well as for the rest of us, in an increasingly globalized world.

This Time Is Different: Eight Centuries of Financial Folly, Carmen M. Reinhart and Kenneth S. Rogoff, Princeton, $35.00. They show us what happened in over 250 historical crises in 66 countries and offer clear ideas on how our current crisis might play out.

(continued on page 116)

The Only FREE LUNCH on Wall Street is Served (Page 106),
Almanac Investors E-mailed Alert Before the Open (See Insert Page 96)

MONDAY
D 47.6
S 52.4
N 42.9
19

The "canonical" market bottom typically features below-average valuations, falling interest rates,
new lows in some major indices on diminished trading volume ... and finally, a quick high-volume reversal in breadth ...
— John P. Hussman, Ph.D. (Hussman Funds, 5/22/06)

TUESDAY
D 47.6
S 38.1
N 52.4
20

Laws are like sausages. It's better not to see them being made.
— Otto von Bismarck (German-Prussian politician, First chancellor of Germany, 1815–1898)

Chanukah

WEDNESDAY
D 71.4
S 66.7
N 61.9
21

Almost any insider purchase is worth investigating for a possible lead to a superior speculation.
But very few insider sales justify concern. — William Chidester (*Scientific Investing*)

THURSDAY
D 71.4
S 76.2
N 81.0
22

You have powers you never dreamed of. You can do things you never thought you could do. There are no limitations
in what you can do except the limitations in your own mind. — Darwin P. Kingsley (President, New York Life, 1857–1932)

Last Trading Day Before Christmas, Dow Up Last 3 Years;
Watch for the Santa Claus Rally (Page 110)

FRIDAY
D 57.1
S 57.1
N 61.9
23

Towering genius disdains a beaten path. It scorns to tread in the footsteps of any predecessor, however illustrious.
It thirsts for distinction. — Abraham Lincoln (16th U.S. president, 1809–1865)

SATURDAY
24

Christmas Day

SUNDAY
25

YEAR'S TOP INVESTMENT BOOKS

(continued from page 114)

The Great Reflation: How Investors Can Profit from the New World of Money, J. Anthony Boeckh, Wiley, $34.95. Book is endorsed by some impressive names: Henry Kaufman, John Maudlin, Marc Faber, etc. Boeckh is the former head of Bank Credit Analyst.

Denial: Why Business Leaders Fail to Look Facts in the Face—and What to Do About It, Richard S. Tedlow, Portfolio, $26.95. Details about major companies that did or didn't defeat denial, including Sears, A&P, Goodyear, DuPont, and Intel.

The 10 Laws of Enduring Success, Maria Bartiromo, Crown Business, $26.00. Many of the tools for success are not external but entirely within us. Maria explores what Joe Torre, Bill Gates, Goldie Hawn, Mary Hart, Garry Kasparov, and Jack Welch have in common.

How Capitalism Will Save Us: Why Free People and Free Markets Are the Best Answer in Today's Economy, Steve Forbes and Elizabeth Ames, Crown Business, $25.00. Despite some criticisms, capitalism has produced the world's highest standard of living by promoting the moral values of cooperation, democracy, and free choice.

Nerds On Wall Street: Math, Machines and Wired Markets, David J. Leinweber, Wiley, $39.95. The profound impact of technology on Wall Street over 200 years, its role in the multi-faceted crises of today, and its dominance of the markets of tomorrow.

Too Big to Fail: The Inside Story of How Wall Street and Washington Fought to Save the Financial System—and Themselves, Andrew Ross Sorkin, Viking, $32.95. Takes readers into corner offices at Lehman, secret meetings in South Korea, and Washington's corridors of power.

FREEFALL: America, Free Markets, and the Sinking of the World Economy, Joseph E. Stiglitz, Norton, $27.95. Nobelist Stiglitz gives us an incisive look at the global economic crisis, our flawed response, and the implications for the world's future prosperity.

On the Brink: Inside the Race to Stop the Collapse of the Global Financial System, Henry Paulson Jr., Business Plus, $28.99. Former CEO of Goldman Sachs and U.S. Treasury Secretary tells his side of the story.

For Crying Out Loud: From Open Outcry to the Electronic Screen, Leo Melamed, Wiley, $39.95. The chairman of the Chicago Mercantile Exchange tells how the CME became the global powerhouse of futures and options.

Diary of a Hedge Fund Manager: From the Top to the Bottom and Back Again, Keith McCullough with Rich Blake, Wiley, $29.95. A fascinating account of life on the Street. Reminds us all that the giants of the hedge fund world are mere mortals.

Reminiscences of a Stock Operator: With a New Commentary and Insights in the Life and Times of Jesse Livermore, Edwin Lefevre, Wiley, $34.95. Jon D. Markman has enhanced the new version of one of the best market books of all time.

Confidence Game: How a Hedge Fund Manager Called Wall Street's Bluff, Christine Richard, Wiley, $27.95. Bill Ackman's six-year campaign of how he warned that the $2.5 trillion bond insurance business was a catastrophe waiting to happen.

It's Not as Bad as You Think: Why Capitalism Trumps Fear and the Economy Will Thrive, Brian S. Wesbury, Wiley, $24.95. Debunks the pouting pundits of pessimism to show you how to prosper now and in the future.

Invest in Europe Now!: Why Europe's Markets Will Outperform the US in the Coming Years, David R. Kotok, Vincenzo Sciarretta, and Kathleen Stephensen, Wiley, $29.95. Outlines the best ways to take advantage of the rapidly shifting global financial environment.

The End of Wall Street, Roger Lowenstein, Penguin, $27.95. A blow-by-blow account of America's biggest financial collapse since the Great Depression.

The Big Short: Inside the Doomsday Machine, Michael Lewis, Norton, $27.95. One of our leading financial writers looks at the recent financial meltdown

The Greatest Trade Ever: The Behind-the-Scenes Story of How John Paulson Defied Wall Street and Made Financial History, Gregory Zuckerman, Broadway Books, $26.00. He made $15 billion in 2007 shorting the housing bubble.

DECEMBER/JANUARY 2012

(Market Closed)

MONDAY
26

Take care of your employees and they'll take care of your customers.
— John W. Marriott (Founder, Marriott International, 1900–1985)

TUESDAY
D 85.7
S 76.2
N 76.2
27

Companies already dominant in a field rarely produce the breakthroughs that transform it. — George Gilder

WEDNESDAY
D 57.1
S 57.1
N 57.1
28

The market can stay irrational longer than you can stay solvent. — John Maynard Keynes (British economist, 1883–1946)

THURSDAY
D 52.4
S 71.4
N 61.9
29

A small debt produces a debtor; a large one, an enemy. — Publilius Syrus (Syrian-born Roman mime and former slave, 83–43 B.C.)

Last Trading Day of the Year, NASDAQ Down 9 of last 10
NASDAQ Was Up 29 Years in a Row 1971–1999

FRIDAY
D 42.9
S 38.1
N 57.1
30

Our firm conviction is that, sooner or later, capitalism will give way to socialism ... We will bury you.
— Nikita Khrushchev (Soviet leader 1953–1964, 1894–1971)

SATURDAY
31

New Year's Day

SUNDAY
1

2012 STRATEGY CALENDAR
(Option expiration dates circled)

	MONDAY	TUESDAY	WEDNESDAY	THURSDAY	FRIDAY	SATURDAY	SUNDAY
JANUARY	26	27	28	29	30	31	1 JANUARY New Year's Day
	2	3	4	5	6	7	8
	9	10	11	12	13	14	15
	16 Martin Luther King Day	17	18	19	⃝20	21	22
	23	24	25	26	27	28	29
FEBRUARY	30	31	1 FEBRUARY	2	3	4	5
	6	7	8	9	10	11	12
	13	14 ♥	15	16	⃝17	18	19
	20 Presidents' Day	21	22 Ash Wednesday	23	24	25	26
MARCH	27	28	29	1 MARCH	2	3	4
	5	6	7	8	9	10	11 Daylight Saving Time Begins
	12	13	14	15	⃝16	17 ♣ St. Patrick's Day	18
	19	20	21	22	23	24	25
APRIL	26	27	28	29	30	31	1 APRIL
	2	3	4	5	6 Good Friday	7 Passover	8 Easter
	9	10	11	12	13	14	15
	16 Tax Deadline	17	18	19	⃝20	21	22
	23	24	25	26	27	28	29
MAY	30	1 MAY	2	3	4	5	6
	7	8	9	10	11	12	13 Mother's Day
	14	15	16	17	⃝18	19	20
	21	22	23	24	25	26	27
JUNE	28 Memorial Day	29	30	31	1 JUNE	2	3
	4	5	6	7	8	9	10
	11	12	13	14	⃝15	16	17 Father's Day
	18	19	20	21	22	23	24
	25	26	27	28	29	30	1 JULY

Market closed on shaded weekdays; closes early when half-shaded.

2012 STRATEGY CALENDAR
(Option expiration dates circled)

MONDAY	TUESDAY	WEDNESDAY	THURSDAY	FRIDAY	SATURDAY	SUNDAY	
2	3	4 Independence Day	5	6	7	8	JULY
9	10	11	12	13	14	15	
16	17	18	19	(20)	21	22	
23	24	25	26	27	28	29	
30	31	1 AUGUST	2	3	4	5	AUGUST
6	7	8	9	10	11	12	
13	14	15	16	(17)	18	19	
20	21	22	23	24	25	26	
27	28	29	30	31	1 SEPTEMBER	2	SEPTEMBER
3 Labor Day	4	5	6	7	8	9	
10	11	12	13	14	15	16	
17 Rosh Hashanah	18	19	20	(21)	22	23	
24	25	26 Yom Kippur	27	28	29	30	
1 OCTOBER	2	3	4	5	6	7	OCTOBER
8 Columbus Day	9	10	11	12	13	14	
15	16	17	18	(19)	20	21	
22	23	24	25	26	27	28	
29	30	31	1 NOVEMBER	2	3	4 Daylight Saving Time Ends	NOVEMBER
5	6 Election Day	7	8	9	10	11 Veterans' Day	
12	13	14	15	(16)	17	18	
19	20	21	22 Thanksgiving	23	24	25	
26	27	28	29	30	1 DECEMBER	2	DECEMBER
3	4	5	6	7	8	9 Chanukah	
10	11	12	13	14	15	16	
17	18	19	20	(21)	22	23	
24	25 Christmas	26	27	28	29	30	
31	1 JANUARY New Year's Day	2	3	4	5	6	

DIRECTORY OF TRADING PATTERNS AND DATABANK

CONTENTS

DOW JONES INDUSTRIALS MARKET PROBABILITY CALENDAR 2011

THE % CHANCE OF THE MARKET RISING ON ANY TRADING DAY OF THE YEAR*

(Based on the number of times the DJIA rose on a particular trading day during **January 1953 to December 2009.**)

Date	Jan	Feb	Mar	Apr	May	Jun	Jul	Aug	Sep	Oct	Nov	Dec
1	S	57.9	64.9	59.6	S	57.9	64.9	45.6	59.6	S	61.4	45.6
2	S	54.4	63.2	S	57.9	54.4	S	47.4	57.9	S	50.9	54.4
3	56.1	36.8	59.6	S	66.7	50.9	S	47.4	S	47.4	66.7	S
4	73.7	54.4	49.1	57.9	50.9	S	H	52.6	S	59.6	57.9	S
5	47.4	S	S	56.1	50.9	S	61.4	54.4	H	49.1	S	63.2
6	56.1	S	S	59.6	43.9	57.9	59.6	S	57.9	59.6	S	57.9
7	45.6	45.6	45.6	54.4	S	52.6	56.1	S	45.6	47.4	45.6	45.6
8	S	40.4	54.4	57.9	S	43.9	64.9	43.9	49.1	S	59.6	43.9
9	S	43.9	59.6	S	50.9	36.8	S	47.4	43.9	S	52.6	54.4
10	47.4	63.2	54.4	S	50.9	56.1	S	50.9	S	50.9	59.6	S
11	47.4	43.9	52.6	59.6	50.9	S	56.1	45.6	S	43.9	47.4	S
12	47.4	S	S	63.2	45.6	S	50.9	63.2	54.4	36.8	S	57.9
13	57.9	S	S	54.4	56.1	59.6	38.6	S	57.9	54.4	S	45.6
14	56.1	49.1	52.6	70.2	S	59.6	63.2	S	45.6	59.6	50.9	52.6
15	S	54.4	59.6	64.9	S	49.1	49.1	57.9	52.6	S	56.1	45.6
16	S	36.8	63.2	S	54.4	45.6	S	50.9	52.6	S	50.9	57.9
17	H	47.4	56.1	S	45.6	49.1	S	45.6	S	54.4	50.9	S
18	57.9	49.1	50.9	56.1	52.6	S	47.4	57.9	S	49.1	49.1	S
19	38.6	S	S	56.1	45.6	S	49.1	43.9	38.6	43.9	S	49.1
20	36.8	S	S	52.6	43.9	43.9	50.9	S	47.4	59.6	S	54.4
21	40.4	H	45.6	50.9	S	50.9	42.1	S	45.6	42.1	59.6	56.1
22	S	36.8	38.6	H	S	49.1	47.4	61.4	43.9	S	66.7	49.1
23	S	47.4	49.1	S	33.3	40.4	S	49.1	40.4	S	59.6	61.4
24	47.4	59.6	38.6	S	50.9	38.6	S	52.6	S	47.4	H	S
25	56.1	45.6	45.6	52.6	43.9	S	59.6	49.1	S	26.3	64.9	S
26	59.6	S	S	57.9	45.6	S	50.9	45.6	50.9	52.6	S	H
27	50.9	S	S	52.6	54.4	47.4	47.4	S	56.1	54.4	S	71.9
28	61.4	50.9	45.6	47.4	S	45.6	64.9	S	52.6	61.4	59.6	49.1
29	S		54.4	50.9	S	54.4	54.4	56.1	49.1	S	52.6	57.9
30	S		40.4	S	H	52.6	S	42.1	40.4	S	52.6	54.4
31	61.4		42.1		61.4		S	59.6		54.4		S

*See new trends developing on pages 68, 88, 141–146.

RECENT DOW JONES INDUSTRIALS MARKET PROBABILITY CALENDAR 2011

THE % CHANCE OF THE MARKET RISING ON ANY TRADING DAY OF THE YEAR*

(Based on the number of times the DJIA rose on a particular trading day during **January 1989 to December 2009.****)

Date	Jan	Feb	Mar	Apr	May	Jun	Jul	Aug	Sep	Oct	Nov	Dec
1	S	61.9	57.1	71.4	S	81.0	85.7	38.1	57.1	S	57.1	57.1
2	S	47.6	52.4	S	71.4	57.1	S	57.1	57.1	S	47.6	52.4
3	61.9	42.9	61.9	S	71.4	42.9	S	38.1	S	57.1	57.1	S
4	66.7	47.6	47.6	61.9	38.1	S	H	47.6	S	47.6	66.7	S
5	42.9	S	S	57.1	47.6	S	47.6	52.4	H	38.1	S	57.1
6	52.4	S	S	66.7	33.3	52.4	47.6	S	47.6	61.9	S	52.4
7	38.1	52.4	52.4	42.9	S	52.4	57.1	S	38.1	38.1	57.1	38.1
8	S	42.9	47.6	47.6	S	47.6	71.4	47.6	61.9	S	57.1	52.4
9	S	52.4	57.1	S	66.7	42.9	S	42.9	47.6	S	38.1	52.4
10	47.6	57.1	57.1	S	61.9	47.6	S	57.1	S	47.6	57.1	S
11	52.4	57.1	42.9	47.6	66.7	S	47.6	28.6	S	42.9	61.9	S
12	52.4	S	S	66.7	57.1	S	66.7	66.7	61.9	33.3	S	57.1
13	52.4	S	S	57.1	61.9	57.1	66.7	S	61.9	57.1	S	52.4
14	57.1	42.9	61.9	71.4	S	71.4	66.7	S	47.6	76.2	66.7	47.6
15	S	71.4	66.7	76.2	S	52.4	52.4	52.4	52.4	S	52.4	42.9
16	S	42.9	61.9	S	61.9	47.6	S	61.9	52.4	S	52.4	57.1
17	H	28.6	52.4	S	52.4	47.6	S	52.4	S	61.9	57.1	S
18	52.4	42.9	57.1	61.9	61.9	S	52.4	57.1	S	42.9	42.9	S
19	38.1	S	S	52.4	52.4	S	42.9	38.1	28.6	52.4	S	47.6
20	38.1	S	S	57.1	47.6	38.1	61.9	S	47.6	66.7	S	47.6
21	33.3	H	38.1	57.1	S	42.9	33.3	S	38.1	47.6	61.9	71.4
22	S	52.4	38.1	H	S	47.6	52.4	66.7	33.3	S	61.9	71.4
23	S	38.1	38.1	S	33.3	33.3	S	47.6	28.6	S	66.7	57.1
24	42.9	42.9	38.1	S	57.1	42.9	S	61.9	S	42.9	H	S
25	61.9	47.6	57.1	38.1	47.6	S	66.7	52.4	S	33.3	71.4	S
26	66.7	S	S	52.4	57.1	S	38.1	47.6	42.9	47.6	S	H
27	57.1	S	S	52.4	66.7	38.1	47.6	S	61.9	61.9	S	85.7
28	61.9	42.9	38.1	61.9	S	52.4	66.7	S	57.1	71.4	61.9	57.1
29	S		52.4	47.6	S	52.4	52.4	61.9	57.1	S	47.6	52.4
30	S		47.6	S	H	28.6	S	33.3	42.9	S	57.1	42.9
31	71.4		38.1		52.4		S	47.6		52.4		S

*See new trends developing on pages 68, 88, 141–146. ** Based on most recent 21-year period.

S&P 500 MARKET PROBABILITY CALENDAR 2011

THE % CHANCE OF THE MARKET RISING ON ANY TRADING DAY OF THE YEAR*

(Based on the number of times the S&P 500 rose on a particular trading day during **January 1953 to December 2009**.)

Date	Jan	Feb	Mar	Apr	May	Jun	Jul	Aug	Sep	Oct	Nov	Dec
1	S	59.6	61.4	63.2	S	56.1	70.2	49.1	63.2	S	61.4	49.1
2	S	57.9	57.9	S	57.9	63.2	S	45.6	54.4	S	56.1	54.4
3	45.6	45.6	61.4	S	71.9	50.9	S	47.4	S	47.4	68.4	S
4	71.9	49.1	47.4	57.9	57.9	S	H	52.6	S	66.7	54.4	S
5	50.9	S	S	56.1	45.6	S	57.9	56.1	H	50.9	S	61.4
6	50.9	S	S	56.1	40.4	56.1	54.4	S	57.9	61.4	S	57.9
7	43.9	49.1	47.4	56.1	S	47.4	59.6	S	45.6	50.9	47.4	38.6
8	S	42.1	56.1	59.6	S	42.1	63.2	43.9	50.9	S	57.9	49.1
9	S	38.6	59.6	S	50.9	42.1	S	52.6	52.6	S	59.6	54.4
10	49.1	64.9	50.9	S	49.1	56.1	S	49.1	S	49.1	57.9	S
11	50.9	50.9	61.4	61.4	50.9	S	54.4	45.6	S	40.4	47.4	S
12	54.4	S	S	54.4	43.9	S	50.9	64.9	54.4	42.1	S	49.1
13	61.4	S	S	49.1	52.6	63.2	47.4	S	61.4	52.6	S	49.1
14	63.2	43.9	49.1	61.4	S	59.6	70.2	S	50.9	54.4	50.9	45.6
15	S	54.4	61.4	63.2	S	56.1	52.6	61.4	52.6	S	49.1	45.6
16	S	33.3	63.2	S	54.4	43.9	S	54.4	56.1	S	52.6	57.9
17	H	50.9	56.1	S	50.9	54.4	S	52.6	S	52.6	54.4	S
18	52.6	42.1	49.1	59.6	54.4	S	43.9	52.6	S	52.6	52.6	S
19	50.9	S	S	52.6	42.1	S	43.9	45.6	45.6	42.1	S	43.9
20	45.6	S	S	54.4	50.9	38.6	50.9	S	52.6	66.7	S	45.6
21	43.9	H	45.6	43.9	S	50.9	40.4	S	50.9	42.1	57.9	52.6
22	S	42.1	43.9	H	S	54.4	43.9	61.4	50.9	S	64.9	47.4
23	S	40.4	42.1	S	42.1	43.9	S	47.4	38.6	S	59.6	61.4
24	61.4	56.1	54.4	S	52.6	38.6	S	50.9	S	40.4	H	S
25	50.9	50.9	42.1	47.4	47.4	S	57.9	47.4	S	31.6	68.4	S
26	54.4	S	S	57.9	47.4	S	52.6	45.6	49.1	57.9	S	H
27	47.4	S	S	47.4	54.4	38.6	50.9	S	52.6	57.9	S	71.9
28	64.9	57.9	47.4	43.9	S	50.9	66.7	S	59.6	61.4	61.4	52.6
29	S		54.4	57.9	S	57.9	64.9	56.1	50.9	S	57.9	66.7
30	S		35.1	S	H	49.1	S	43.9	43.9	S	52.6	64.9
31	66.7		40.4		63.2		S	63.2		56.1		S

*See new trends developing on pages 68, 88, 141–146.

RECENT S&P 500 MARKET PROBABILITY CALENDAR 2011

THE % CHANCE OF THE MARKET RISING ON ANY TRADING DAY OF THE YEAR*

(Based on the number of times the S&P 500 rose on a particular trading day during **January 1989 to December 2009.****)

Date	Jan	Feb	Mar	Apr	May	Jun	Jul	Aug	Sep	Oct	Nov	Dec
1	S	61.9	52.4	66.7	S	71.4	85.7	47.6	66.7	S	57.1	61.9
2	S	57.1	42.9	S	71.4	76.2	S	52.4	42.9	S	57.1	57.1
3	38.1	47.6	66.7	S	71.4	38.1	S	38.1	S	52.4	57.1	S
4	61.9	47.6	47.6	61.9	47.6	S	H	52.4	S	57.1	66.7	S
5	47.6	S	S	61.9	38.1	S	42.9	52.4	H	33.3	S	61.9
6	42.9	S	S	61.9	23.8	42.9	52.4	S	42.9	57.1	S	38.1
7	52.4	47.6	47.6	47.6	S	42.9	61.9	S	42.9	42.9	57.1	33.3
8	S	52.4	57.1	52.4	S	33.3	71.4	52.4	57.1	S	52.4	52.4
9	S	42.9	47.6	S	57.1	52.4	S	38.1	57.1	S	42.9	47.6
10	47.6	66.7	47.6	S	57.1	38.1	S	57.1	S	47.6	52.4	S
11	52.4	66.7	57.1	47.6	57.1	S	42.9	28.6	S	38.1	57.1	S
12	57.1	S	S	52.4	57.1	S	61.9	71.4	61.9	38.1	S	47.6
13	57.1	S	S	47.6	57.1	57.1	76.2	S	57.1	57.1	S	57.1
14	61.9	38.1	57.1	57.1	S	71.4	76.2	S	57.1	76.2	61.9	42.9
15	S	76.2	71.4	66.7	S	61.9	47.6	61.9	52.4	S	47.6	38.1
16	S	38.1	61.9	S	57.1	47.6	S	71.4	66.7	S	61.9	57.1
17	H	33.3	61.9	S	57.1	52.4	S	57.1	S	57.1	57.1	S
18	52.4	33.3	47.6	66.7	66.7	S	42.9	52.4	S	47.6	42.9	S
19	57.1	S	S	52.4	52.4	S	38.1	42.9	38.1	57.1	S	52.4
20	38.1	S	S	57.1	47.6	38.1	61.9	S	52.4	71.4	S	38.1
21	38.1	H	28.6	52.4	S	47.6	28.6	S	42.9	52.4	57.1	66.7
22	S	61.9	47.6	H	S	61.9	47.6	66.7	42.9	S	52.4	76.2
23	S	42.9	28.6	S	33.3	38.1	S	47.6	33.3	S	61.9	57.1
24	57.1	42.9	61.9	S	66.7	42.9	S	66.7	S	33.3	H	S
25	47.6	57.1	61.9	28.6	52.4	S	71.4	52.4	S	38.1	71.4	S
26	52.4	S	S	47.6	61.9	S	42.9	52.4	38.1	52.4	S	H
27	57.1	S	S	52.4	57.1	23.8	52.4	S	57.1	57.1	S	76.2
28	66.7	47.6	42.9	57.1	S	57.1	76.2	S	61.9	76.2	66.7	57.1
29	S		47.6	61.9	S	61.9	61.9	61.9	61.9	S	61.9	71.4
30	S		33.3	S	H	33.3	S	33.3	47.6	S	42.9	38.1
31	76.2		42.9		61.9		S	47.6		61.9		S

*See new trends developing on pages 68, 88, 141–146. ** Based on most recent 21-year period.

NASDAQ COMPOSITE MARKET PROBABILITY CALENDAR 2011
THE % CHANCE OF THE MARKET RISING ON ANY TRADING DAY OF THE YEAR*
(Based on the number of times the NASDAQ rose on a particular trading day during **January 1971 to December 2009.**)

Date	Jan	Feb	Mar	Apr	May	Jun	Jul	Aug	Sep	Oct	Nov	Dec
1	S	69.2	61.5	43.6	S	61.5	59.0	53.8	53.8	S	66.7	61.5
2	S	69.2	53.8	S	61.5	74.4	S	43.6	61.5	S	53.8	64.1
3	53.8	53.8	69.2	S	74.4	56.4	S	46.2	S	48.7	69.2	S
4	71.8	66.7	53.8	64.1	61.5	S	H	59.0	S	61.5	59.0	S
5	59.0	S	S	66.7	56.4	S	48.7	59.0	H	53.8	S	64.1
6	64.1	S	S	53.8	51.3	61.5	41.0	S	59.0	64.1	S	59.0
7	53.8	53.8	51.3	48.7	S	51.3	51.3	S	56.4	61.5	48.7	41.0
8	S	51.3	53.8	61.5	S	43.6	64.1	38.5	56.4	S	51.3	53.8
9	S	46.2	56.4	S	61.5	43.6	S	51.3	48.7	S	59.0	46.2
10	61.5	64.1	51.3	S	53.8	53.8	S	51.3	S	59.0	61.5	S
11	56.4	56.4	69.2	61.5	41.0	S	64.1	53.8	S	48.7	53.8	S
12	59.0	S	S	61.5	56.4	S	61.5	61.5	48.7	48.7	S	46.2
13	64.1	S	S	51.3	59.0	64.1	69.2	S	59.0	74.4	S	46.2
14	66.7	59.0	53.8	61.5	S	64.1	71.8	S	59.0	64.1	56.4	41.0
15	S	61.5	53.8	53.8	S	56.4	66.7	56.4	35.9	S	41.0	43.6
16	S	43.6	64.1	S	56.4	43.6	S	51.3	48.7	S	48.7	56.4
17	H	53.8	56.4	S	56.4	51.3	S	59.0	S	51.3	51.3	S
18	66.7	35.9	61.5	64.1	51.3	S	48.7	53.8	S	46.2	53.8	S
19	61.5	S	S	53.8	43.6	S	51.3	35.9	51.3	38.5	S	48.7
20	43.6	S	S	53.8	51.3	43.6	56.4	S	64.1	71.8	S	51.3
21	48.7	H	38.5	53.8	S	61.5	41.0	S	53.8	46.2	51.3	59.0
22	S	48.7	38.5	H	S	48.7	51.3	69.2	53.8	S	66.7	66.7
23	S	56.4	56.4	S	48.7	46.2	S	53.8	46.2	S	59.0	66.7
24	59.0	59.0	56.4	S	56.4	48.7	S	51.3	S	38.5	H	S
25	43.6	53.8	46.2	51.3	53.8	S	59.0	53.8	S	30.8	59.0	S
26	69.2	S	S	46.2	61.5	S	48.7	53.8	51.3	43.6	S	H
27	61.5	S	S	69.2	56.4	43.6	46.2	S	46.2	53.8	S	74.4
28	56.4	53.8	48.7	61.5	S	59.0	56.4	S	48.7	61.5	66.7	51.3
29	S		51.3	69.2	S	69.2	51.3	61.5	51.3	S	66.7	69.2
30	S		51.3	S	H	66.7	S	61.5	51.3	S	66.7	76.9
31	66.7		66.7		74.4		S	69.2		69.2		S

* See new trends developing on pages 68, 88, 141–146.
Based on NASDAQ composite, prior to February 5, 1971, based on National Quotation Bureau indices.

RECENT NASDAQ COMPOSITE MARKET PROBABILITY CALENDAR 2011

THE % CHANCE OF THE MARKET RISING ON ANY TRADING DAY OF THE YEAR*

(Based on the number of times the NASDAQ rose on a particular trading day during **January 1989 to December 2009.**)

Date	Jan	Feb	Mar	Apr	May	Jun	Jul	Aug	Sep	Oct	Nov	Dec
1	S	81.0	57.1	52.4	S	71.4	71.4	52.4	61.9	S	71.4	71.4
2	S	66.7	38.1	S	71.4	81.0	S	47.6	61.9	S	57.1	66.7
3	57.1	47.6	71.4	S	71.4	47.6	S	33.3	S	47.6	71.4	S
4	71.4	57.1	47.6	57.1	66.7	S	H	57.1	S	57.1	61.9	S
5	52.4	S	S	71.4	57.1	S	38.1	52.4	H	42.9	S	66.7
6	52.4	S	S	52.4	38.1	52.4	38.1	S	47.6	61.9	S	52.4
7	57.1	52.4	47.6	38.1	S	38.1	57.1	S	57.1	47.6	61.9	33.3
8	S	57.1	42.9	52.4	S	33.3	76.2	42.9	66.7	S	57.1	47.6
9	S	42.9	47.6	S	71.4	47.6	S	38.1	57.1	S	52.4	42.9
10	61.9	52.4	47.6	S	47.6	38.1	S	52.4	S	61.9	57.1	S
11	52.4	47.6	61.9	47.6	42.9	S	61.9	42.9	S	47.6	61.9	S
12	52.4	S	S	61.9	57.1	S	71.4	71.4	57.1	52.4	S	42.9
13	57.1	S	S	47.6	52.4	52.4	76.2	S	61.9	71.4	S	57.1
14	52.4	52.4	52.4	61.9	S	57.1	76.2	S	66.7	71.4	61.9	38.1
15	S	61.9	52.4	42.9	S	61.9	66.7	61.9	28.6	S	42.9	42.9
16	S	33.3	66.7	S	57.1	38.1	S	61.9	57.1	S	47.6	47.6
17	H	42.9	57.1	S	61.9	47.6	S	61.9	S	52.4	52.4	S
18	61.9	33.3	57.1	57.1	71.4	S	47.6	47.6	S	38.1	52.4	S
19	66.7	S	S	47.6	47.6	S	42.9	33.3	52.4	47.6	S	42.9
20	38.1	S	S	52.4	52.4	38.1	57.1	S	61.9	76.2	S	52.4
21	47.6	H	28.6	52.4	S	52.4	33.3	S	47.6	47.6	52.4	61.9
22	S	61.9	28.6	H	S	47.6	42.9	81.0	47.6	S	61.9	81.0
23	S	57.1	47.6	S	42.9	28.6	S	52.4	38.1	S	57.1	61.9
24	61.9	42.9	61.9	S	61.9	42.9	S	52.4	S	28.6	H	S
25	38.1	52.4	61.9	47.6	52.4	S	76.2	57.1	S	33.3	57.1	S
26	81.0	S	S	42.9	66.7	S	57.1	47.6	38.1	42.9	S	H
27	66.7	S	S	61.9	71.4	33.3	52.4	S	57.1	52.4	S	76.2
28	57.1	42.9	52.4	66.7	S	61.9	71.4	S	38.1	66.7	61.9	57.1
29	S		38.1	71.4	S	71.4	47.6	66.7	52.4	S	71.4	61.9
30	S		42.9	S	H	61.9	S	61.9	47.6	S	57.1	57.1
31	66.7		61.9		71.4		S	57.1		76.2		S

*See new trends developing on page 68, 88, 141–146. ** Based on most recent 21-year period.*

RUSSELL 1000 INDEX MARKET PROBABILITY CALENDAR 2011

THE % CHANCE OF THE MARKET RISING ON ANY TRADING DAY OF THE YEAR*

(Based on the number of times the Russell 1000 rose on a particular trading day during **January 1979 to December 2009**.)

Date	Jan	Feb	Mar	Apr	May	Jun	Jul	Aug	Sep	Oct	Nov	Dec
1	S	64.5	58.1	58.1	S	61.3	71.0	48.4	51.6	S	71.0	54.8
2	S	58.1	45.2	S	54.8	64.5	S	45.2	48.4	S	54.8	54.8
3	38.7	54.8	61.3	S	71.0	48.4	S	45.2	S	51.6	58.1	S
4	64.5	51.6	38.7	61.3	58.1	S	H	51.6	S	58.1	58.1	S
5	58.1	S	S	54.8	41.9	S	45.2	58.1	H	48.4	S	61.3
6	54.8	S	S	58.1	35.5	58.1	41.9	S	51.6	61.3	S	41.9
7	48.4	58.1	41.9	48.4	S	35.5	58.1	S	38.7	48.4	45.2	35.5
8	S	48.4	54.8	64.5	S	38.7	61.3	54.8	51.6	S	54.8	48.4
9	S	38.7	54.8	S	54.8	45.2	S	45.2	54.8	S	48.4	51.6
10	61.3	71.0	48.4	S	61.3	51.6	S	51.6	S	51.6	58.1	S
11	51.6	61.3	58.1	54.8	48.4	S	48.4	41.9	S	35.5	58.1	S
12	54.8	S	S	51.6	58.1	S	61.3	64.5	58.1	35.5	S	45.2
13	61.3	S	S	41.9	54.8	58.1	64.5	S	64.5	64.5	S	51.6
14	71.0	41.9	45.2	54.8	S	61.3	80.6	S	61.3	67.7	58.1	45.2
15	S	64.5	61.3	67.7	S	61.3	48.4	61.3	48.4	S	48.4	51.6
16	S	29.0	61.3	S	58.1	45.2	S	61.3	48.4	S	48.4	58.1
17	H	41.9	58.1	S	61.3	61.3	S	64.5	S	58.1	64.5	S
18	64.5	35.5	48.4	61.3	58.1	S	51.6	67.7	S	45.2	48.4	S
19	41.9	S	S	45.2	51.6	S	41.9	51.6	41.9	41.9	S	48.4
20	32.3	S	S	54.8	51.6	35.5	58.1	S	51.6	74.2	S	41.9
21	41.9	H	41.9	54.8	S	51.6	38.7	S	41.9	45.2	54.8	67.7
22	S	45.2	45.2	H	S	58.1	38.7	74.2	51.6	S	64.5	58.1
23	S	45.2	45.2	S	38.7	41.9	S	48.4	35.5	S	64.5	61.3
24	51.6	54.8	48.4	S	64.5	38.7	S	58.1	S	32.3	H	S
25	48.4	54.8	51.6	45.2	61.3	S	77.4	45.2	S	32.3	67.7	S
26	67.7	S	S	54.8	58.1	S	54.8	54.8	38.7	54.8	S	H
27	58.1	S	S	51.6	51.6	32.3	48.4	S	51.6	54.8	S	71.0
28	61.3	58.1	38.7	48.4	S	51.6	71.0	S	67.7	67.7	74.2	61.3
29	S		45.2	58.1	S	61.3	61.3	51.6	58.1	S	64.5	71.0
30	S		38.7	S	H	48.4	S	48.4	51.6	S	48.4	54.8
31	64.5		48.4		61.3		S	58.1		64.5		S

See new trends developing on pages 68, 88, 141–146.

RUSSELL 2000 INDEX MARKET PROBABILITY CALENDAR 2011

THE % CHANCE OF THE MARKET RISING ON ANY TRADING DAY OF THE YEAR*

(Based on the number of times the Russell 2000 rose on a particular trading day during **January 1979 to December 2009**.)

Date	Jan	Feb	Mar	Apr	May	Jun	Jul	Aug	Sep	Oct	Nov	Dec
1	S	64.5	64.5	45.2	S	67.7	61.3	51.6	48.4	S	67.7	54.8
2	S	64.5	58.1	S	64.5	74.2	S	51.6	61.3	S	71.0	61.3
3	41.9	51.6	64.5	S	67.7	51.6	S	45.2	S	48.4	64.5	S
4	71.0	67.7	54.8	61.3	67.7	S	H	51.6	S	48.4	58.1	S
5	61.3	S	S	48.4	61.3	S	51.6	51.6	H	48.4	S	67.7
6	64.5	S	S	54.8	48.4	58.1	41.9	S	54.8	71.0	S	61.3
7	58.1	64.5	61.3	45.2	S	54.8	51.6	S	64.5	48.4	54.8	41.9
8	S	61.3	48.4	58.1	S	35.5	54.8	45.2	54.8	S	51.6	61.3
9	S	45.2	54.8	S	51.6	48.4	S	58.1	58.1	S	51.6	45.2
10	64.5	71.0	41.9	S	61.3	54.8	S	54.8	S	45.2	71.0	S
11	51.6	58.1	58.1	61.3	45.2	S	58.1	48.4	S	48.4	51.6	S
12	67.7	S	S	61.3	61.3	S	54.8	77.4	58.1	51.6	S	51.6
13	67.7	S	S	48.4	51.6	61.3	61.3	S	64.5	71.0	S	41.9
14	67.7	61.3	58.1	51.6	S	64.5	64.5	S	58.1	64.5	58.1	48.4
15	S	58.1	51.6	61.3	S	58.1	58.1	61.3	29.0	S	45.2	35.5
16	S	48.4	61.3	S	48.4	45.2	S	61.3	48.4	S	19.4	54.8
17	H	41.9	67.7	S	61.3	41.9	S	61.3	S	61.3	61.3	S
18	71.0	32.3	54.8	61.3	54.8	S	51.6	54.8	S	35.5	41.9	S
19	74.2	S	S	45.2	54.8	S	45.2	51.6	41.9	48.4	S	58.1
20	32.3	S	S	58.1	51.6	38.7	51.6	S	45.2	71.0	S	58.1
21	51.6	H	51.6	51.6	S	54.8	38.7	S	51.6	48.4	32.3	61.3
22	S	48.4	48.4	H	S	48.4	48.4	77.4	58.1	S	61.3	67.7
23	S	61.3	61.3	S	51.6	45.2	S	48.4	41.9	S	61.3	77.4
24	54.8	54.8	51.6	S	61.3	45.2	S	58.1	S	38.7	H	S
25	41.9	61.3	51.6	54.8	54.8	S	64.5	54.8	S	35.5	64.5	S
26	71.0	S	S	61.3	67.7	S	67.7	58.1	41.9	41.9	S	H
27	58.1	S	S	61.3	64.5	41.9	48.4	S	32.3	54.8	S	71.0
28	58.1	61.3	48.4	54.8	S	58.1	61.3	S	54.8	64.5	64.5	58.1
29	S		48.4	71.0	S	74.2	67.7	61.3	58.1	S	71.0	67.7
30	S		48.4	S	H	67.7	S	64.5	67.7	S	74.2	74.2
31	77.4		87.1		74.2		S	74.2		74.2		S

* See new trends developing on pages 68, 88, 141–146.

DECENNIAL CYCLE: A MARKET PHENOMENON

By arranging each year's market gain or loss so the first and succeeding years of each decade fall into the same column, certain interesting patterns emerge—strong fifth and eighth years; weak first, seventh, and zero years.

This fascinating phenomenon was first presented by Edgar Lawrence Smith in *Common Stocks and Business Cycles* (William-Frederick Press, 1959). Anthony Gaubis co-pioneered the decennial pattern with Smith.

When Smith first cut graphs of market prices into 10-year segments and placed them above one another, he observed that each decade tended to have three bull market cycles and that the longest and strongest bull markets seem to favor the middle years of a decade.

Don't place too much emphasis on the decennial cycle nowadays, other than the extraordinary fifth and zero years, as the stock market is more influenced by the quadrennial presidential election cycle, shown on page 130. Also, the last half-century, which has been the most prosperous in U.S. history, has distributed the returns among most years of the decade. Interestingly, NASDAQ suffered its worst bear market ever in a zero year.

First years have the third worst record within the Decennial Cycle. However, 2011 is a pre-presidential election year, which has the best record of the 4-year presidential election cycle. The last three pre-presidential election years since the Depression that were also first years have produced an average gain of 13.6%. As historical patterns reassert themselves, the probability for a positive 2011 is increasing (see pages 26, 28, 32, 34, and 130).

THE 10-YEAR STOCK MARKET CYCLE
Annual % Change in Dow Jones Industrial Average
Year of Decade

DECADES	1st	2nd	3rd	4th	5th	6th	7th	8th	9th	10th
1881–1890	3.0%	−2.9%	−8.5%	−18.8%	20.1%	12.4%	−8.4%	4.8%	5.5%	−14.1%
1891–1900	17.6	−6.6	−24.6	−0.6	2.3	−1.7	21.3	22.5	9.2	7.0
1901–1910	−8.7	−0.4	−23.6	41.7	38.2	−1.9	−37.7	46.6	15.0	−17.9
1911–1920	0.4	7.6	−10.3	−5.4	81.7	−4.2	−21.7	10.5	30.5	−32.9
1921–1930	12.7	21.7	−3.3	26.2	30.0	0.3	28.8	48.2	−17.2	−33.8
1931–1940	−52.7	−23.1	66.7	4.1	38.5	24.8	−32.8	28.1	−2.9	−12.7
1941–1950	−15.4	7.6	13.8	12.1	26.6	−8.1	2.2	−2.1	12.9	17.6
1951–1960	14.4	8.4	−3.8	44.0	20.8	2.3	−12.8	34.0	16.4	−9.3
1961–1970	18.7	−10.8	17.0	14.6	10.9	−18.9	15.2	4.3	−15.2	4.8
1971–1980	6.1	14.6	−16.6	−27.6	38.3	17.9	−17.3	−3.1	4.2	14.9
1981–1990	−9.2	19.6	20.3	−3.7	27.7	22.6	2.3	11.8	27.0	−4.3
1991–2000	20.3	4.2	13.7	2.1	33.5	26.0	22.6	16.1	25.2	−6.2
2001–2010	−7.1	−16.8	25.3	3.1	−0.6	16.3	6.4	−33.8	18.8	
Total % Change	0.1%	23.1%	66.1%	91.8%	368.0%	87.3%	−31.9%	187.9%	129.4%	−86.9%
Avg % Change	0.01%	1.8%	5.1%	7.1%	28.3%	6.8%	−2.5%	14.5%	10.0%	−7.2%
Up Years	8	7	6	8	12	8	7	10	10	4
Down Years	5	6	7	5	1	5	6	3	3	8

Based on annual close; Cowles indices 1881–1885; 12 Mixed Stocks, 10 Rails, 2 Inds 1886–1889;
20 Mixed Stocks, 18 Rails, 2 Inds 1890–1896; Railroad average 1897 (First industrial average published May 26, 1896).

PRESIDENTIAL ELECTION/STOCK MARKET CYCLE: THE 177-YEAR SAGA CONTINUES

It is no mere coincidence that the last two years (pre-election year and election year) of the 44 administrations since 1833 produced a total net market gain of 718.5%, dwarfing the 262.1% gain of the first two years of these administrations.

Presidential elections every four years have a profound impact on the economy and the stock market. Wars, recessions, and bear markets tend to start or occur in the first half of the term; prosperous times and bull markets, in the latter half. After nine straight annual Dow gains during the millennial bull, the four-year election cycle reasserted its overarching domination of market behavior the last ten years. 2007 continued the streak of 17 up pre-elections in the last 68 years.

STOCK MARKET ACTION SINCE 1833
Annual % Change In Dow Jones Industrial Average[1]

4-Year Cycle Beginning	Elected President	Post-Election Year	Mid-Term Year	Pre-Election Year	Election Year
1833	Jackson (D)	−0.9	13.0	3.1	−11.7
1837	Van Buren (D)	−11.5	1.6	−12.3	5.5
1841*	W.H. Harrison (W)**	−13.3	−18.1	45.0	15.5
1845*	Polk (D)	8.1	−14.5	1.2	−3.6
1849*	Taylor (W)	N/C	18.7	−3.2	19.6
1853*	Pierce (D)	−12.7	−30.2	1.5	4.4
1857	Buchanan (D)	−31.0	14.3	−10.7	14.0
1861*	Lincoln (R)	−1.8	55.4	38.0	6.4
1865	Lincoln (R)**	−8.5	3.6	1.6	10.8
1869	Grant (R)	1.7	5.6	7.3	6.8
1873	Grant (R)	−12.7	2.8	−4.1	−17.9
1877	Hayes (R)	−9.4	6.1	43.0	18.7
1881	Garfield (R)**	3.0	−2.9	−8.5	−18.8
1885*	Cleveland (D)	20.1	12.4	−8.4	4.8
1889*	B. Harrison (R)	5.5	−14.1	17.6	−6.6
1893*	Cleveland (D)	−24.6	−0.6	2.3	−1.7
1897*	McKinley (R)	21.3	22.5	9.2	7.0
1901	McKinley (R)**	−8.7	−0.4	−23.6	41.7
1905	T. Roosevelt (R)	38.2	−1.9	−37.7	46.6
1909	Taft (R)	15.0	−17.9	0.4	7.6
1913*	Wilson (D)	−10.3	−5.4	81.7	−4.2
1917	Wilson (D)	−21.7	10.5	30.5	−32.9
1921*	Harding (R)**	12.7	21.7	−3.3	26.2
1925	Coolidge (R)	30.0	0.3	28.8	48.2
1929	Hoover (R)	−17.2	−33.8	−52.7	−23.1
1933*	F. Roosevelt (D)	66.7	4.1	38.5	24.8
1937	F. Roosevelt (D)	−32.8	28.1	−2.9	−12.7
1941	F. Roosevelt (D)	−15.4	7.6	13.8	12.1
1945	F. Roosevelt (D)**	26.6	−8.1	2.2	−2.1
1949	Truman (D)	12.9	17.6	14.4	8.4
1953*	Eisenhower (R)	−3.8	44.0	20.8	2.3
1957	Eisenhower (R)	−12.8	34.0	16.4	−9.3
1961*	Kennedy (D)**	18.7	−10.8	17.0	14.6
1965	Johnson (D)	10.9	−18.9	15.2	4.3
1969*	Nixon (R)	−15.2	4.8	6.1	14.6
1973	Nixon (R)***	−16.6	−27.6	38.3	17.9
1977*	Carter (D)	−17.3	−3.1	4.2	14.9
1981*	Reagan (R)	−9.2	19.6	20.3	−3.7
1985	Reagan (R)	27.7	22.6	2.3	11.8
1989	G. H. W. Bush (R)	27.0	−4.3	20.3	4.2
1993*	Clinton (D)	13.7	2.1	33.5	26.0
1997	Clinton (D)	22.6	16.1	25.2	−6.2
2001*	G. W. Bush (R)	−7.1	−16.8	25.3	3.1
2005	G. W. Bush (R)	−0.6	16.3	6.4	−33.8
2009*	Obama (D)	18.8			
Total % Gain		**86.1%**	**176.0%**	**464.0%**	**254.5%**
Average % Gain		**2.0%**	**4.0%**	**10.5%**	**5.8%**
# Up		20	26	33	29
# Down		24	18	11	15

*Party in power ousted   **Death in office   ***Resigned   **D**–Democrat, **W**–Whig, **R**–Republican
[1] Based on annual close; Prior to 1886 based on Cowles and other indices; 12 Mixed Stocks, 10 Rails, 2 Inds 1886–1889; 20 Mixed Stocks, 18 Rails, 2 Inds 1890–1896; Railroad average 1897 (First industrial average published May 26, 1896).

DOW JONES INDUSTRIALS BULL AND BEAR MARKETS SINCE 1900

Bear markets begin at the end of one bull market and end at the start of the next bull market (7/17/90 to 10/11/90 as an example). The high at Dow 3978.36 on 1/31/94, was followed by a 9.7 percent correction. A 10.3 percent correction occurred between the 5/22/96, closing high of 5778 and the intraday low on 7/16/96. The longest bull market on record ended on 7/17/98, and the shortest bear market on record ended on 8/31/98, when the new bull market began. The greatest bull super cycle in history that began 8/12/82 ended in 2000 after the Dow gained 1409% and NASDAQ climbed 3072%. The Dow gained only 497% in the eight-year super bull from 1921 to the top in 1929. NASDAQ suffered its worst loss ever from the 2000 top to the 2002 bottom, down 77.9%, nearly as much as the 89.2% drop in the Dow from the 1929 top to the 1932 bottom. The third longest Dow bull since 1900 that began 10/9/02 ended on its fifth anniversary. The ensuing bear market was the second worst bear market since 1900, slashing the Dow 53.8%. At press time, the current bull market was under pressure, as Greek debt contagion fears were escalating, threatening to end this bull well before the average lifespan. (See page 132 for S&P 500 and NASDAQ bulls and bears.)

DOW JONES INDUSTRIALS BULL AND BEAR MARKETS SINCE 1900

— Beginning —		— Ending —		Bull		Bear	
Date	DJIA	Date	DJIA	% Gain	Days	% Change	Days
9/24/00	38.80	6/17/01	57.33	47.8%	266	−46.1%	875
11/9/03	30.88	1/19/06	75.45	144.3	802	−48.5	665
11/15/07	38.83	11/19/09	73.64	89.6	735	−27.4	675
9/25/11	53.43	9/30/12	68.97	29.1	371	−24.1	668
7/30/14	52.32	11/21/16	110.15	110.5	845	−40.1	393
12/19/17	65.95	11/3/19	119.62	81.4	684	−46.6	660
8/24/21	63.90	3/20/23	105.38	64.9	573	−18.6	221
10/27/23	85.76	9/3/29	381.17	344.5	2138	−47.9	71
11/13/29	198.69	4/17/30	294.07	48.0	155	−86.0	813
7/8/32	41.22	9/7/32	79.93	93.9	61	−37.2	173
2/27/33	50.16	2/5/34	110.74	120.8	343	−22.8	171
7/26/34	85.51	3/10/37	194.40	127.3	958	−49.1	386
3/31/38	98.95	11/12/38	158.41	60.1	226	−23.3	147
4/8/39	121.44	9/12/39	155.92	28.4	157	−40.4	959
4/28/42	92.92	5/29/46	212.50	128.7	1492	−23.2	353
5/17/47	163.21	6/15/48	193.16	18.4	395	−16.3	363
6/13/49	161.60	1/5/53	293.79	81.8	1302	−13.0	252
9/14/53	255.49	4/6/56	521.05	103.9	935	−19.4	564
10/22/57	419.79	1/5/60	685.47	63.3	805	−17.4	294
10/25/60	566.05	12/13/61	734.91	29.8	414	−27.1	195
6/26/62	535.76	2/9/66	995.15	85.7	1324	−25.2	240
10/7/66	744.32	12/3/68	985.21	32.4	788	−35.9	539
5/26/70	631.16	4/28/71	950.82	50.6	337	−16.1	209
11/23/71	797.97	1/11/73	1051.70	31.8	415	−45.1	694
12/6/74	577.60	9/21/76	1014.79	75.7	655	−26.9	525
2/28/78	742.12	9/8/78	907.74	22.3	192	−16.4	591
4/21/80	759.13	4/27/81	1024.05	34.9	371	−24.1	472
8/12/82	776.92	11/29/83	1287.20	65.7	474	−15.6	238
7/24/84	1086.57	8/25/87	2722.42	150.6	1127	−36.1	55
10/19/87	1738.74	7/17/90	2999.75	72.5	1002	−21.2	86
10/11/90	2365.10	7/17/98	9337.97	294.8	2836	−19.3	45
8/31/98	7539.07	1/14/00	11722.98	55.5	501	−29.7	616
9/21/01	8235.81	3/19/02	10635.25	29.1	179	−31.5	204
10/9/02	7286.27	10/9/07	14164.53	94.4	1826	−53.8	517
3/9/09	6547.05	4/26/10	11205.03	71.1*	413*	*At Press Time–not in averages	
		Average		**85.7%**	**755**	**−31.5%**	**410**

Based on Dow Jones industrial average.
The NYSE was closed from 7/31/1914 to 12/11/1914 due to World War I.
DJIA figures were then adjusted back to reflect the composition change from 12 to 20 stocks in September 1916.

1900–2000 Data: Ned Davis Research

STANDARD & POOR'S 500 BULL & BEAR MARKETS SINCE 1929 NASDAQ COMPOSITE SINCE 1971

A constant debate of the definition and timing of bull and bear markets permeates Wall Street like the bell that signals the open and close of every trading day. We have relied on the Ned Davis Research parameters for years to track bulls and bears on the Dow (see page 131). Standard & Poor's 500 index has been a stalwart indicator for decades and at times marched to a different beat than the Dow. With the increasing prominence of NASDAQ as a benchmark, we felt the time had come to add bull and bear data on the other two main stock averages to the *Almanac*. We conferred with Sam Stovall, chief investment strategist at Standard & Poor's, and correlated the moves of the S&P 500 and NASDAQ to the bull and bear dates on page 131 to compile the data below on bull and bear markets for the S&P 500 and NASDAQ. Many dates line up for the three indices, but you will notice quite a lag or lead on several occasions, including NASDAQ's independent cadence from 1975 to 1980.

STANDARD & POOR'S 500 BULL AND BEAR MARKETS

— Beginning —		— Ending —		Bull		Bear	
Date	S&P 500	Date	S&P 500	% Gain	Days	% Change	Days
11/13/29	17.66	4/10/30	25.92	46.8%	148	−83.0%	783
6/1/32	4.40	9/7/32	9.31	111.6	98	−40.6	173
2/27/33	5.53	2/6/34	11.82	113.7	344	−31.8	401
3/14/35	8.06	3/6/37	16.68	106.9	723	−49.0	390
3/31/38	8.50	11/9/38	13.79	62.2	223	−26.2	150
4/8/39	10.18	10/25/39	13.21	29.8	200	−43.5	916
4/28/42	7.47	5/29/46	19.25	157.7	1492	−28.8	353
5/17/47	13.71	6/15/48	17.06	24.4	395	−20.6	363
6/13/49	13.55	1/5/53	26.66	96.8	1302	−14.8	252
9/14/53	22.71	8/2/56	49.74	119.0	1053	−21.6	446
10/22/57	38.98	8/3/59	60.71	55.7	650	−13.9	449
10/25/60	52.30	12/12/61	72.64	38.9	413	−28.0	196
6/26/62	52.32	2/9/66	94.06	79.8	1324	−22.2	240
10/7/66	73.20	11/29/68	108.37	48.0	784	−36.1	543
5/26/70	69.29	4/28/71	104.77	51.2	337	−13.9	209
11/23/71	90.16	1/11/73	120.24	33.4	415	−48.2	630
10/3/74	62.28	9/21/76	107.83	73.1	719	−19.4	531
3/6/78	86.90	9/12/78	106.99	23.1	190	−8.2	562
3/27/80	98.22	11/28/80	140.52	43.1	246	−27.1	622
8/12/82	102.42	10/10/83	172.65	68.6	424	−14.4	288
7/24/84	147.82	8/25/87	336.77	127.8	1127	−33.5	101
12/4/87	223.92	7/16/90	368.95	64.8	955	−19.9	87
10/11/90	295.46	7/17/98	1186.75	301.7	2836	−19.3	45
8/31/98	957.28	3/24/00	1527.46	59.6	571	−36.8	546
9/21/01	965.80	1/4/02	1172.51	21.4	105	−33.8	278
10/9/02	776.76	10/9/07	1565.15	101.5	1826	−56.8	517
3/9/09	676.53	4/23/10	1217.28	79.9*	410*	*At Press Time–not in averages	
		Average		**79.3%**	**727**	**−30.4%**	**387**

NASDAQ COMPOSITE BULL AND BEAR MARKETS

— Beginning —		— Ending —		Bull		Bear	
Date	NASDAQ	Date	NASDAQ	% Gain	Days	% Change	Days
11/23/71	100.31	1/11/73	136.84	36.4%	415	−59.9%	630
10/3/74	54.87	7/15/75	88.00	60.4	285	−16.2	63
9/16/75	73.78	9/13/78	139.25	88.7	1093	−20.4	62
11/14/78	110.88	2/8/80	165.25	49.0	451	−24.9	48
3/27/80	124.09	5/29/81	223.47	80.1	428	−28.8	441
8/13/82	159.14	6/24/83	328.91	106.7	315	−31.5	397
7/25/84	225.30	8/26/87	455.26	102.1	1127	−35.9	63
10/28/87	291.88	10/9/89	485.73	66.4	712	−33.0	372
10/16/90	325.44	7/20/98	2014.25	518.9	2834	−29.5	80
10/8/98	1419.12	3/10/00	5048.62	255.8	519	−71.8	560
9/21/01	1423.19	1/4/02	2059.38	44.7	105	−45.9	278
10/9/02	1114.11	10/31/07	2859.12	156.6	1848	−55.6	495
3/9/09	1268.64	4/23/10	2530.15	99.4*	410*	*At Press Time– not in averages	
		Average		**130.5%**	**844**	**−37.8%**	**291**

JANUARY DAILY POINT CHANGES DOW JONES INDUSTRIALS

Previous Month Close	2001	2002	2003	2004	2005	2006	2007	2008	2009	2010
	10786.85	10021.50	8341.63	10453.92	10783.01	10717.50	12463.15	13264.82	8776.39	10428.05
1	H	H	H	H	S	S	H	H	H	H
2	−140.70	51.90	265.89	−44.07	S	H	H*	−220.86	258.30	S
3	299.60	98.74	−5.83	S	−53.58	129.91	11.37	12.76	S	S
4	−33.34	87.60	S	S	−98.65	32.74	6.17	−256.54	S	155.91
5	−250.40	S	S	134.22	−32.95	2.00	−82.68	S	−81.80	−11.94
6	S	S	171.88	−5.41	25.05	77.16	S	S	62.21	1.66
7	S	−62.69	−32.98	−9.63	−18.92	S	S	27.31	−245.40	33.18
8	−40.66	−46.50	−145.28	63.41	S	S	25.48	−238.42	−27.24	11.33
9	−48.80	−56.46	180.87	−133.55	S	52.59	−6.89	146.24	−143.28	S
10	31.72	−26.23	8.71	S	17.07	−0.32	25.56	117.78	S	S
11	5.28	−80.33	S	S	−64.81	31.86	72.82	−246.79	S	45.80
12	−84.17	S	S	26.29	61.56	−81.08	41.10	S	−125.21	−36.73
13	S	S	1.09	−58.00	−111.95	−2.49	S	S	−25.41	53.51
14	S	−96.11	56.64	111.19	52.17	S	S	171.85	−248.42	29.78
15	H	32.73	−119.44	15.48	S	S	H	−277.04	12.35	−100.90
16	127.28	−211.88	−25.31	46.66	S	S	26.51	−34.95	68.73	S
17	−68.32	137.77	−111.13	S	H	−63.55	−5.44	−306.95	S	S
18	93.94	−78.19	S	S	70.79	−41.46	−9.22	−59.91	S	H
19	−90.69	S	S	H	−88.82	25.85	−2.40	S	H	115.78
20	S	S	H	−71.85	−68.50	−213.32	S	S	−332.13	−122.28
21	S	H	−143.84	94.96	−78.48	S	S	H	279.01	−213.27
22	−9.35	−58.05	−124.17	−0.44	S	S	−88.37	−128.11	−105.30	−216.90
23	71.57	17.16	50.74	−54.89	S	21.38	56.64	298.98	−45.24	S
24	−2.84	65.11	−238.46	S	−24.38	23.45	87.97	108.44	S	S
25	82.55	44.01	S	S	92.95	−2.48	−119.21	−171.44	S	23.88
26	−69.54	S	S	134.22	37.03	99.73	−15.54	S	38.47	−2.57
27	S	S	−141.45	−92.59	−31.19	97.74	S	S	58.70	41.87
28	S	25.67	99.28	−141.55	−40.20	S	S	176.72	200.72	−115.70
29	42.21	−247.51	21.87	41.92	S	S	3.76	96.41	−226.44	−53.13
30	179.01	144.62	−165.58	−22.22	S	−7.29	32.53	−37.47	−148.15	S
31	6.16	157.14	108.68	S	62.74	−35.06	98.38	207.53	S	S
Close	10887.36	9920.00	8053.81	10488.07	10489.94	10864.86	12621.69	12650.36	8000.86	10067.33
Change	100.51	−101.50	−287.82	34.15	−293.07	147.36	158.54	−614.46	−775.53	−360.72

Ford funeral

FEBRUARY DAILY POINT CHANGES DOW JONES INDUSTRIALS

Previous Month Close	2001	2002	2003	2004	2005	2006	2007	2008	2009	2010
	10887.36	9920.00	8053.81	10488.07	10489.94	10864.86	12621.69	12650.36	8000.86	10067.33
1	96.27	−12.74	S	S	62.00	89.09	51.99	92.83	S	118.20
2	−119.53	S	S	11.11	44.85	−101.97	−20.19	S	−64.03	111.32
3	S	S	56.01	6.00	−3.69	−58.36	S	−108.03	141.53	−26.30
4	S	−220.17	−96.53	−34.44	123.03	S	S	−108.03	−121.70	−268.37
5	101.75	−1.66	−28.11	24.81	S	S	8.25	−370.03	106.41	10.05
6	−8.43	−32.04	−55.88	97.48	S	4.65	4.57	−65.03	217.52	S
7	−10.70	−27.95	−65.07	S	−0.37	−48.51	0.56	46.90	S	S
8	−66.17	118.80	S	S	8.87	108.86	−29.24	−64.87	S	−103.84
9	−99.10	S	S	−14.00	−60.52	24.73	−56.80	S	−9.72	150.25
10	S	S	55.88	34.82	85.50	35.70	S	S	−381.99	−20.26
11	S	140.54	−77.00	123.85	46.40	S	S	57.88	50.65	105.81
12	165.32	−21.04	−84.94	−43.63	S	S	−28.28	133.40	−6.77	−45.05
13	−43.45	125.93	−8.30	−66.22	S	−26.73	102.30	178.83	−82.35	S
14	−107.91	12.32	158.93	S	−4.88	136.07	87.01	−175.26	S	S
15	95.61	−98.95	S	S	46.19	30.58	23.15	−28.77	S	H
16	−91.20	S	S	H	−2.44	61.71	2.56	S	S	169.67
17	S	S	H	87.03	−80.62	−5.36	S	S	−297.81	40.43
18	S	H	132.35	−42.89	30.96	S	S	H	3.03	83.66
19	H	−157.90	−40.55	−7.26	S	S	H	−10.99	−89.68	9.45
20	−68.94	196.03	−85.64	−45.70	S	H	19.07	90.04	−100.28	S
21	−204.30	−106.49	103.15	S	H	−46.26	−48.23	−142.96	S	S
22	0.23	133.47	S	S	−174.02	68.11	−52.39	96.72	S	−18.97
23	−84.91	S	S	−9.41	62.59	−67.95	−38.54	S	−250.89	−100.97
24	S	S	−159.87	−43.25	75.00	−7.37	S	S	236.16	91.75
25	S	177.56	51.26	35.25	92.81	S	S	189.20	−80.05	−53.13
26	200.63	−30.45	−102.52	−21.48	S	S	−15.22	114.70	−88.81	4.23
27	−5.65	12.32	78.01	3.78	S	S	35.70	−416.02	−119.15	S
28	−141.60	−21.45	6.09	S	−75.37	−104.14	52.39	−112.10	S	S
29	—	—	—	—	—	—	—	−315.79	—	—
Close	10495.28	10106.13	7891.08	10583.92	10766.23	10993.41	12268.63	12266.39	7062.93	10325.26
Change	−392.08	186.13	−162.73	95.85	276.29	128.55	−353.06	−383.97	−937.93	257.93

MARCH DAILY POINT CHANGES DOW JONES INDUSTRIALS

Previous Month Close	2001	2002	2003	2004	2005	2006	2007	2008	2009	2010
	10495.28	10106.13	7891.08	10583.92	10766.23	10993.41	12268.63	12266.39	7062.93	10325.26
1	−45.14	262.73	S	S	94.22	63.77	60.12	−34.29	S	78.53
2	16.17	S	S	−86.66	−18.03	−28.02	−120.24	S	−299.64	2.19
3	S	S	−53.22	1.63	21.06	−3.92	S	−7.49	−37.27	−9.22
4	S	217.96	−132.99	−5.11	107.52	S	S	−45.10	149.82	47.38
5	95.99	−153.41	70.73	7.55	S	S	−63.69	41.19	−281.40	122.06
6	28.92	140.88	−101.61	S	S	−63.00	157.18	−214.60	32.50	S
7	138.38	−48.92	66.04	S	−3.69	22.10	−15.14	−146.70	S	S
8	128.65	47.12	S	−66.07	−24.24	25.05	68.25	S	S	−13.68
9	−213.63	S	S	−72.52	−107.00	−33.46	15.62	S	−79.89	11.86
10	S		−171.85	−160.07	45.89	104.06	S	−153.54	379.44	2.95
11	·S	38.75	−44.12	−168.51	−77.15	S		416.66	3.91	44.51
12	−436.37	21.11	28.01	111.70	S	S	42.30	−46.57	239.66	12.85
13	82.55	−130.50	269.68	S	S	−0.32	−242.66	35.50	53.92	S
14	−317.34	15.29	37.96	S	30.15	75.32	57.44	−194.65	S	S
15	57.82	90.09	S	−137.19	−59.41	58.43	26.28	S	S	17.46
16	−207.87	S	S	81.78	−112.03	43.47	−49.27	S	−7.01	43.83
17	S	S	282.21	115.63	−6.72	26.41	S	21.16	178.73	47.69
18	S	−29.48	52.31	−4.52	3.32	S	S	420.41	90.88	45.50
19	135.70	57.50	71.22	−109.18	S	S	115.76	−293.00	−85.78	−37.19
20	−238.35	−133.68	21.15	S	S	−5.12	61.93	261.66	−122.42	S
21	−233.76	−21.73	235.37	S	−64.28	−39.06	159.42	H	S	S
22	−97.52	−52.17	S	−121.85	−94.88	81.96	13.62	S	S	43.91
23	115.30	S	S	−1.11	−14.49	−47.14	19.87	S	497.48	102.94
24	S	S	−307.29	−15.41	−13.15	9.68	S	187.32	−115.89	−52.68
25	S	−146.00	65.55	170.59	H	S	S	−16.04	89.84	5.06
26	182.75	71.69	−50.35	−5.85	S	S	−11.94	−109.74	174.75	9.15
27	260.01	73.55	−28.43	S	S	−29.86	−71.78	−120.40	−148.38	S
28	−162.19	−22.97	−55.68	S	42.78	−95.57	−96.93	−86.06	S	S
29	13.71	H	S	116.66	−79.95	61.16	48.39	S	S	45.50
30	79.72	S	S	52.07	135.23	−65.00	5.60	S	−254.16	11.56
31	S	S	−153.64	−24.00	−37.17	−41.38	S	46.49	86.90	−50.79
Close	9878.78	10403.94	7992.13	10357.70	10503.76	11109.32	12354.35	12262.89	7608.92	10856.63
Change	−616.50	297.81	101.05	−226.22	−262.47	115.91	85.72	−3.50	545.99	531.37

APRIL DAILY POINT CHANGES DOW JONES INDUSTRIALS

Previous Month Close	2001	2002	2003	2004	2005	2006	2007	2008	2009	2010
	9878.78	10403.94	7992.13	10357.70	10503.76	11109.32	12354.35	12262.89	7608.92	10856.63
1	S	−41.24	77.73	15.63	−99.46	S	S	391.47	152.68	70.44
2	−100.85	−48.99	215.20	97.26	S	S	27.95	−48.53	216.48	H
3	−292.22	−115.42	−44.68	S	S	35.62	128.00	20.20	39.51	S
4	29.71	36.88	36.77	S	16.84	58.91	19.75	−16.61	S	S
5	402.63	36.47	S	87.78	37.32	35.70	30.15	S	S	46.48
6	−126.96	S	S	12.44	27.56	−23.05	H	S	−41.74	−3.56
7	S	S	23.26	−90.66	60.30	−96.46	S	3.01	−186.29	−72.47
8	S	−22.56	−1.49	−38.12	−84.98	S	S	−35.99	47.55	29.55
9	54.06	−40.41	−100.98	H	S	S	8.94	−49.18	246.27	70.28
10	257.59	173.06	23.39	S	S	21.29	4.71	54.72	H	S
11	−89.27	−205.65	−17.92	S	−12.78	−51.70	−89.23	−256.56	S	S
12	113.47	14.74	S	73.53	59.41	40.34	68.34	S	S	8.62
13	H	S		−134.28	−104.04	7.68	59.17	S	−25.57	13.45
14	S	S	147.69	−3.33	−125.18	H	S	−23.36	−137.63	103.69
15	S	−97.15	51.26	19.51	−191.24	S	S	60.41	109.44	21.46
16	31.62	207.65	−144.75	54.51	S	S	108.33	256.80	95.81	−125.91
17	58.17	−80.54	80.04	S	S	−63.87	52.58	1.22	5.90	S
18	399.10	−15.50	H	S	−16.26	194.99	30.80	228.87	S	S
19	77.88	51.83	S	−14.12	56.16	10.00	4.79	S	S	73.39
20	−113.86	S	S	−123.35	−115.05	64.12	153.35	S	−289.60	25.01
21	S	S	−8.75	2.77	206.24	4.56	S	S	127.83	7.86
22	S	−120.68	156.09	143.93	−60.89	S	S	−104.79	−82.99	9.37
23	−47.62	−47.19	30.67	11.64	S	S	−42.58	42.99	70.49	69.99
24	−77.89	−58.81	−75.62	−133.69	S	−11.13	34.54	85.73	119.23	S
25	170.86	4.63	−133.69	S	84.76	−53.07	135.95	42.91	S	S
26	67.15	−124.34	S	−28.11	−91.34	71.24	15.61	S	S	0.75
27	117.70	S	S	33.43	47.67	28.02	15.44	S	−51.29	−213.04
28	S	S	165.26	−135.56	−128.43	−15.37	S	−20.11	−8.05	53.28
29	S	−90.85	31.38	−70.33	122.14	S	S	−39.81	168.78	122.05
30	−75.08	126.35	−22.90	−46.70	S	S	−58.03	−11.81	−17.61	−158.71
Close	10734.97	9946.22	8480.09	10225.57	10192.51	11367.14	13062.91	12820.13	8168.12	11008.61
Change	856.19	−457.72	487.96	−132.13	−311.25	257.82	708.56	557.24	559.20	151.98

MAY DAILY POINT CHANGES DOW JONES INDUSTRIALS

	2000	2001	2002	2003	2004	2005	2006	2007	2008	2009
Previous Month Close	10733.91	10734.97	9946.22	8480.09	10225.57	10192.51	11367.14	13062.91	12820.13	8168.12
1	77.87	163.37	113.41	−25.84	S	S	−23.85	73.23	189.87	44.29
2	−80.66	−21.66	32.24	128.43	S	59.19	73.16	75.74	48.20	S
3	−250.99	−80.03	−85.24	S	88.43	5.25	−16.17	29.50	S	S
4	−67.64	154.59	S	S	3.20	127.69	38.58	23.24	S	214.33
5	165.37	S	S	−51.11	−6.25	−44.26	138.88	S	−88.66	−16.09
6	S	S	−198.59	56.79	−69.69	5.02	S	S	51.29	101.63
7	S	−16.07	28.51	−27.73	−123.92	S	S	48.35	−206.48	−102.43
8	25.77	−51.66	305.28	−69.41	S	S	6.80	−3.90	52.43	164.80
9	−66.88	−16.53	−104.41	113.38	S	38.94	55.23	53.80	−120.90	S
10	−168.97	43.46	−97.50	S	−127.32	−103.23	2.88	−147.74	S	S
11	178.19	−89.13	S	S	29.45	19.14	−141.92	111.09	S	−155.88
12	63.40	S	S	122.13	25.69	−110.77	−119.74	S	130.43	50.34
13	S	S	169.74	−47.48	−34.42	−49.36	S	S	−44.13	−184.22
14	S	56.02	188.48	−31.43	2.13	S	S	20.56	66.20	46.43
15	198.41	−4.36	−54.46	65.32	S	S	47.78	37.06	94.28	−62.68
16	126.79	342.95	45.53	−34.17	S	112.17	−8.88	103.69	−5.86	S
17	−164.83	32.66	63.87	S	−105.96	79.59	−214.28	−10.81	S	S
18	7.54	53.16	S	S	61.60	132.57	−77.32	79.81	S	235.44
19	−150.43	S	S	−185.58	−30.80	28.74	15.77	S	41.36	−29.23
20	S	S	−123.58	−2.03	−0.07	−21.28	S	S	−199.48	−52.81
21	S	36.18	−123.79	25.07	29.10	S	S	−13.65	−227.49	−129.91
22	−84.30	−80.68	52.17	77.59	S	S	−18.73	−2.93	24.43	−14.81
23	−120.28	−151.73	58.20	7.36	S	51.65	−26.98	−14.30	−145.99	S
24	113.08	16.91	−111.82	S	−8.31	−19.88	18.97	−84.52	S	S
25	−211.43	−117.05	S	S	159.19	−45.88	93.73	66.15	S	H
26	−24.68	S	S	H	−7.73	79.80	67.56	S	H	196.17
27	S	S	H	179.97	95.31	4.95	S	S	68.72	−173.47
28	S	H	−122.68	11.77	−16.75	S	S	H	45.68	103.78
29	H	33.77	−58.54	−81.94	S	S	H	14.06	52.19	96.53
30	227.89	−166.50	−11.35	139.08	S	H	−184.18	111.74	−7.90	S
31	−4.80	39.30	13.56	S	H	−75.07	73.88	−5.44	S	S
Close	10522.33	10911.94	9925.25	8850.26	10188.45	10467.48	11168.31	13627.64	12638.32	8500.33
Change	−211.58	176.97	−20.97	370.17	−37.12	274.97	−198.83	564.73	−181.81	332.21

JUNE DAILY POINT CHANGES DOW JONES INDUSTRIALS

	2000	2001	2002	2003	2004	2005	2006	2007	2008	2009
Previous Month Close	10522.33	10911.94	9925.25	8850.26	10188.45	10467.48	11168.31	13627.64	12638.32	8500.33
1	129.87	78.47	S	S	14.20	82.39	91.97	40.47	S	221.11
2	142.56	S	S	47.55	60.32	3.62	−12.41	S	−134.50	19.43
3	S	S	−215.46	25.14	−67.06	−92.52	S	S	−100.97	−65.59
4	S	71.11	−21.95	116.03	46.91	S	S	8.21	−12.37	74.96
5	20.54	114.32	108.96	2.32	S	S	−199.15	−80.86	213.97	12.89
6	−79.73	−105.60	−172.16	21.49	S	6.06	−46.58	−129.79	−394.64	S
7	77.29	20.50	−34.97	S	148.26	16.04	−71.24	−198.94	S	S
8	−144.14	−113.74	S	S	41.44	−6.21	7.92	157.66	S	1.36
9	−54.66	S	S	−82.79	−64.08	26.16	−46.90	S	70.51	−1.43
10	S	S	55.73	74.89	41.66	9.61	S	S	9.44	−24.04
11	S	−54.91	−128.14	128.33	H*	S	S	0.57	−205.99	31.90
12	−49.85	26.29	100.45	13.33	S	S	−99.34	−129.95	57.81	28.34
13	57.63	−76.76	−114.91	−79.43	S	9.93	−86.44	187.34	165.77	S
14	66.11	−181.49	−28.59	S	−75.37	25.01	110.78	71.37	S	S
15	26.87	−66.49	S	S	45.70	18.80	198.27	85.76	S	−187.13
16	−265.52	S	S	201.84	−0.85	12.28	−0.64	S	−38.27	−107.46
17	S	S	213.21	4.06	−2.06	44.42	S	S	−108.78	−7.49
18	S	21.74	18.70	−29.22	38.89	S	S	−26.50	−131.24	58.42
19	108.54	−48.71	−144.55	−114.27	S	S	−72.44	22.44	34.03	−15.87
20	−122.68	50.66	−129.80	21.22	S	−13.96	32.73	−146.00	−220.40	S
21	62.58	68.10	−177.98	S	−44.94	−9.44	104.62	56.42	S	S
22	−121.62	−110.84	S	S	23.60	−11.74	−60.35	−185.58	S	−200.72
23	28.63	S	S	−127.80	84.50	−166.49	−30.02	S	−0.33	−16.10
24	S	S	28.03	36.90	−35.76	−123.60	S	S	−34.93	−23.05
25	S	−100.37	−155.00	−98.32	−71.97	S	S	−8.21	4.40	172.54
26	138.24	−31.74	−6.71	67.51	S	S	56.19	−14.39	−358.41	−34.01
27	−38.53	−37.64	149.81	−89.99	S	−7.06	−120.54	90.07	−106.91	S
28	23.33	131.37	−26.66	S	−14.75	114.85	48.82	−5.45	S	S
29	−129.75	−63.81	S	S	56.34	−31.15	217.24	−13.66	S	90.99
30	49.85	S	S	−3.61	22.05	−99.51	−40.58	S	3.50	−82.38
Close	10447.89	10502.40	9243.26	8985.44	10435.48	10274.97	11150.22	13408.62	11350.01	8447.00
Change	−74.44	−409.54	−681.99	135.18	247.03	−192.51	−18.09	−219.02	−1288.31	−53.33

Reagan funeral

JULY DAILY POINT CHANGES DOW JONES INDUSTRIALS

Previous Month Close	2000	2001	2002	2003	2004	2005	2006	2007	2008	2009
	10447.89	10502.40	9243.26	8985.44	10435.48	10274.97	11150.22	13408.62	11350.01	8447.00
1	S	S	−133.47	55.51	−101.32	28.47	S	S	32.25	57.06
2	S	91.32	−102.04	101.89	−51.33	S	S	126.81	−166.75	−223.32
3	112.78*	−22.61*	47.22	−72.63*	S	S	77.80*	41.87*	73.03*	H
4	H	H	H	H	S	H	H	H	H	S
5	−77.07	−91.25	324.53*	S	H	68.36	−76.20	−11.46	S	S
6	−2.13	−227.18	S	S	−63.49	−101.12	73.48	45.84	S	44.13
7	154.51	S	S	146.58	20.95	31.61	−134.63	S	−56.58	−161.27
8	S	S	−104.60	6.30	−68.73	146.85	S	S	152.25	14.81
9	S	46.72	−178.81	−66.88	41.66	S	S	38.29	−236.77	4.76
10	10.60	−123.76	−282.59	−120.17	S	S	12.88	−148.27	81.58	−36.65
11	80.61	65.38	−11.97	83.55	S	70.58	31.22	76.17	−128.48	S
12	56.22	237.97	−117.00	S	25.00	−5.83	−121.59	283.86	S	S
13	5.30	60.07	S	S	9.37	43.50	−166.89	45.52	S	185.16
14	24.04	S	S	57.56	−38.79	71.50	−106.94	S	−45.35	27.81
15	S	−66.94	−45.34	−48.18	−45.64	11.94	S	S	−92.65	256.72
16	S	−66.94 ...								
16	S	−66.94	−166.08	−34.38	−23.38	S	S	43.73	276.74	95.61
17	−8.48	134.27	69.37	−43.77	S	S	8.01	20.57	207.38	32.12
18	−64.35	−36.56	−132.99	137.33	S	−65.84	51.87	−53.33	49.91	S
19	−43.84	40.17	−390.23	S	−45.72	71.57	212.19	82.19	S	S
20	147.79	−33.35	S	S	55.01	42.59	−83.32	−149.33	S	104.21
21	−110.31	S	S	−91.46	−102.94	−61.38	−59.72	S	−29.23	67.79
22	S	S	−234.68	61.76	4.20	23.41	S	S	135.16	−34.68
23	S	−152.23	−82.24	35.79	−88.11	S	S	92.34	29.88	188.03
24	−48.44	−183.30	488.95	−81.73	S	S	182.67	−226.47	−283.10	23.95
25	14.85	164.55	−4.98	172.06	S	−54.70	52.66	68.12	21.41	S
26	−183.49	49.96	78.08	S	−0.30	−16.71	−1.20	−311.50	S	S
27	69.65	−38.96	S	S	123.22	57.32	−2.08	−208.10	S	15.27
28	−74.96	S	S	−18.06	31.93	68.46	119.27	S	−239.61	−11.79
9	S	S	447.49	−62.05	12.17	−64.64	S	S	266.48	−26.00
30	S	−[[14.95	−31.85	−4.41	10.47	S	S	92.84	186.13	83.74
31	10.81	121.09	56.56	33.75	S	S	−34.02	−146.32	−205.67	17.15
Close	10521.98	10522.81	8736.59	9233.80	10139.71	10640.91	11185.68	13211.99	11378.02	9171.61
Change	74.09	20.41	−506.67	248.36	−295.77	365.94	35.46	−196.63	28.01	724.61

* Shortened trading day

AUGUST DAILY POINT CHANGES DOW JONES INDUSTRIALS

Previous Month Close	2000	2001	2002	2003	2004	2005	2006	2007	2008	2009
	10521.98	10522.81	8736.59	9233.80	10139.71	10640.91	11185.68	13211.99	11378.02	9171.61
1	84.97	−12.80	−229.97	−79.83	S	−17.76	−59.95	150.38	−51.70	S
2	80.58	41.17	−193.49	S	39.45	60.59	74.20	100.96	S	S
3	19.05	−38.40	S	S	−58.92	13.85	42.66	281.42	S	114.95
4	61.17	S	S	32.07	6.27	−87.49	−2.24	S	−42.17	33.63
5	S	S	−269.50	−149.72	−163.48	−52.07	S	S	331.62	−39.22
6	S	−111.47	230.46	25.42	−147.70	S	S	286.87	40.30	−24.71
7	99.26	57.43	182.06	64.71	S	S	−20.97	35.52	−224.64	113.81
8	109.88	−165.24	255.87	64.64	S	−21.10	−45.79	153.56	302.89	S
9	−71.06	5.06	33.43	S	−0.67	78.74	−97.41	−387.18	S	S
10	2.93	117.69	S	S	130.01	−21.26	48.19	−31.14	S	−32.12
11	119.04	S	S	26.26	−6.35	91.48	−36.34	S	48.03	−96.50
12	S	S	−56.56	92.71	−123.73	−85.58	S	S	−139.88	120.16
13	S	−0.34	−206.50	−38.30	10.76	S	S	−3.01	−109.51	36.58
14	148.34	−3.74	260.92	38.80	S	S	9.84	−207.61	82.97	−76.79
15	−109.14	−66.22	74.83	11.13	S	34.07	132.39	−167.45	43.97	S
16	−58.61	46.57	−40.08	S	129.20	−120.93	96.86	−15.69	S	S
17	47.25	−151.74	S	S	18.28	37.26	7.84	233.30	S	−186.06
18	−9.16	S	S	90.76	110.32	4.22	46.51	S	−180.51	82.60
19	S	S	212.73	16.45	−42.33	4.30	S	S	−130.84	61.22
20	S	79.29	−118.72	−31.39	69.32	S	S	42.27	68.88	70.89
21	33.33	−145.93	85.16	26.17	S	S	−36.42	−30.49	12.78	155.91
22	59.34	102.76	96.41	−74.81	S	10.66	−5.21	145.27	197.85	S
23	5.50	−47.75	−180.68	S	−37.09	−50.31	−41.94	−0.25	S	S
24	38.09	194.02	S	S	25.58	−84.71	6.56	142.99	S	3.32
25	9.89	S	S	−31.23	83.11	15.76	−20.41	S	−241.81	30.01
26	S	S	46.05	22.81	−8.33	−53.34	S	S	26.62	4.23
27	S	−40.82	−94.60	−6.66	21.60	S	S	−56.74	89.64	37.11
28	60.21	−160.32	−130.32	40.42	S	S	67.96	−280.28	212.67	−36.43
29	−37.74	−131.13	−23.10	41.61	S	65.76	17.93	247.44	−171.63	S
30	−112.09	−171.32	−7.49	S	−72.49	−50.23	12.97	−50.56	S	S
31	112.09	30.17	S	S	51.40	68.78	−1.76	119.01	S	−47.92
Close	11215.10	9949.75	8663.50	9415.82	10173.92	10481.60	11381.15	13357.74	11543.55	9496.28
Change	693.12	−573.06	−73.09	182.02	34.21	−159.31	195.47	145.75	165.53	324.67

SEPTEMBER DAILY POINT CHANGES DOW JONES INDUSTRIALS

Previous Month	2000	2001	2002	2003	2004	2005	2006	2007	2008	2009
Close	11215.10	9949.75	8663.50	9415.82	10173.92	10481.60	11381.15	13357.74	11543.55	9496.28
1	23.68	S	S	H	−5.46	−21.97	83.00	S	H	−185.68
2	S	S	H	107.45	121.82	−12.26	S	S	−26.63	−29.93
3	S	H	−355.45	45.19	−30.08	S	S	H	15.96	63.94
4	H	47.74	117.07	19.44	S	S	H	91.12	−344.65	96.66
5	21.83	35.78	−141.42	−84.56	S	H	5.13	−143.39	32.73	S
6	50.03	−192.43	143.50	S	H	141.87	−63.08	57.88	S	S
7	−50.77	−234.99	S	S	82.59	44.26	−74.76	−249.97	S	H
8	−39.22	S	S	82.95	−29.43	−37.57	60.67	S	289.78	56.07
9	S	S	92.18	−79.09	−24.26	82.63	S	S	−280.01	49.88
10	S	−0.34	83.23	−86.74	23.97	S	S	14.47	38.19	80.26
11	−25.16	Closed*	−21.44	39.30	S	S	4.73	180.54	164.79	−22.07
12	37.74	Closed*	−201.76	11.79	S	4.38	101.25	−16.74	−11.72	S
13	−51.05	Closed*	−66.72	S	1.69	−85.50	45.23	133.23	S	S
14	−94.71	Closed*	S	S	3.40	−52.54	−15.93	17.64	S	21.39
15	−160.47	S	S	−22.74	−86.80	13.85	33.38	S	−504.48	56.61
16	S	S	67.49	118.53	13.13	83.19	S	S	141.51	108.30
17	S	−684.81	−172.63	−21.69	39.97	S	S	−39.10	−449.36	−7.79
18	−118.48	−17.30	−35.10	113.48	S	S	−5.77	335.97	410.03	36.28
19	−19.23	−144.27	−230.06	−14.31	S	−84.31	−14.09	76.17	368.75	S
20	−101.37	−382.92	43.63	S	−79.57	−76.11	72.28	−48.86	S	S
21	77.60	−140.40	S	S	40.04	−103.49	−79.96	53.49	S	−41.34
22	81.85	S	S	−109.41	−135.75	44.02	−25.13	S	−372.75	51.01
23	S	S	−113.87	40.63	−70.28	−2.46	S	S	−161.52	−81.32
24	S	368.05	−189.02	−150.53	8.34	S	S	−61.13	−29.00	−41.11
25	−39.22	56.11	158.69	−81.55	S	S	67.71	19.59	196.89	−42.25
26	−176.83	−92.58	155.30	−30.88	S	24.04	93.58	99.50	121.07	S
27	−2.96	114.03	−295.67	S	−58.70	12.58	19.85	34.79	S	S
28	195.70	166.14	S	S	88.86	16.88	29.21	−17.31	S	124.17
29	−173.14	S	S	67.16	58.84	79.69	−39.38	S	−777.68	−47.16
30	S	S	−109.52	−105.18	−55.97	15.92	S	S	485.21	−29.92
Close	10650.92	8847.56	7591.93	9275.06	10080.27	10568.70	11679.07	13895.63	10850.66	9712.28
Change	−564.18	−1102.19	−1071.57	−140.76	−93.65	87.10	297.92	537.89	−692.89	216.00

Market closed for four days following 9/11 terrorist attacks

OCTOBER DAILY POINT CHANGES DOW JONES INDUSTRIALS

Previous Month	2000	2001	2002	2003	2004	2005	2006	2007	2008	2009
Close	10650.92	8847.56	7591.93	9275.06	10080.27	10568.70	11679.07	13895.63	10850.66	9712.28
1	S	−10.73	346.86	194.14	112.38	S	S	191.92	−19.59	−203.00
2	49.21	113.76	−183.18	18.60	S	S	−8.72	−40.24	−348.22	−21.61
3	19.61	173.19	−38.42	84.51	S	−33.22	56.99	−79.26	−157.47	S
4	64.74	−62.90	−188.79	S	23.89	−94.37	123.27	6.26	S	S
5	−59.56	58.89	S	S	−38.66	−123.75	16.08	91.70	S	112.08
6	−128.38	S	S	22.67	62.24	−30.26	−16.48	S	−369.88	131.50
7	S	S	−105.56	59.63	−114.52	5.21	S	S	−508.39	−5.67
8	S	−51.83	78.65	−23.71	−70.20	S	S	−22.28	−189.01	61.29
9	−28.11	−15.50	−215.22	49.11	S	S	7.60	120.80	−678.91	78.07
10	−44.03	188.42	247.68	−5.33	S	−53.55	9.36	−85.84	−128.00	S
11	−110.61	169.59	316.34	S	26.77	14.41	−15.04	−63.57	S	S
12	−379.21	−66.29	S	89.70	−4.79	−36.26	95.57	77.96	S	20.86
13	157.60	S	S	89.70	−74.85	−0.32	12.81	S	936.42	−14.74
14	S	S	27.11	48.60	−107.88	70.75	S	S	−76.62	144.80
15	S	3.46	378.28	−9.93	38.93	S	S	−108.28	−733.08	47.08
16	46.62	36.61	−219.65	−11.33	S	S	20.09	−71.86	401.35	−67.03
17	−149.09	−151.26	239.01	−69.93	S	60.76	−30.58	−20.40	−127.04	S
18	−114.69	−69.75	47.36	S	22.94	−62.84	42.66	−3.58	S	S
19	167.96	40.89	S	S	−58.70	128.87	19.05	−366.94	S	96.28
20	83.61	S	S	56.15	−10.69	−133.03	−9.36	S	413.21	−50.71
21	S	S	215.84	−30.30	−21.17	−65.88	S	S	−231.77	−92.12
22	S	172.92	−88.08	−149.40	−107.95	S	S	44.95	−514.45	131.95
23	45.13	−36.95	44.11	14.89	S	S	114.54	109.26	172.04	−109.13
24	121.35	5.54	−176.93	−30.67	S	169.78	10.97	−0.98	−312.30	S
25	−66.59	117.28	126.65	S	−7.82	−7.13	6.80	−3.33	S	S
26	53.64	82.27	S	S	138.49	−32.89	28.98	134.78	S	−104.22
27	210.50	S	S	25.70	113.55	−115.03	−73.40	S	−203.18	14.21
28	S	S	−75.95	140.15	2.51	172.82	S	S	889.35	−119.48
29	S	−275.67	0.90	26.22	22.93	S	S	63.56	−74.16	199.89
30	245.15	−147.52	58.47	12.08	S	S	−3.76	−77.79	189.73	−249.85
31	135.37	−46.84	−30.38	14.51	S	37.30	−5.77	137.54	144.32	S
Close	10971.14	9075.14	8397.03	9801.12	10027.47	10440.07	12080.73	13930.01	9325.01	9712.73
Change	320.22	227.58	805.10	526.06	−52.80	−128.63	401.66	34.38	−1525.65	0.45

NOVEMBER DAILY POINT CHANGES DOW JONES INDUSTRIALS

Previous Month Close	2000	2001	2002	2003	2004	2005	2006	2007	2008	2009
	10971.14	9075.14	8397.03	9801.12	10027.47	10440.07	12080.73	13930.01	9325.01	9712.73
1	-71.67	188.76	120.61	S	26.92	-33.30	-49.71	-362.14	S	S
2	-18.96	59.64	S	S	-18.66	65.96	-12.48	27.23	S	76.71
3	-62.56	S	S	57.34	101.32	49.86	-32.50	S	-5.18	-17.53
4	S	S	53.96	-19.63	177.71	8.17	S	S	305.45	30.23
5	S	117.49	106.67	-18.00	72.78	S	S	-51.70	-486.01	203.82
6	159.26	150.09	92.74	36.14	S	S	119.51	117.54	-443.48	17.46
7	-25.03	-36.75	-184.77	-47.18	S	55.47	51.22	-360.92	248.02	S
8	-45.12	33.15	-49.11	S	3.77	-46.51	19.77	-33.73	S	S
9	-72.81	20.48	S	S	-4.94	6.49	-73.24	-223.55	S	203.52
10	-231.30	S	S	-53.26	-0.89	93.89	5.13	S	-73.27	20.03
11	S	S	-178.18	-18.74	84.36	45.94	S	S	-176.58	44.29
12	S	-53.63	27.05	111.04	69.17	S	S	-55.19	-411.30	-93.79
13	-85.70	196.58	12.49	-10.89	S	S	23.45	319.54	552.59	73.00
14	163.81	72.66	143.64	-69.26	S	11.13	86.13	-76.08	-337.94	S
15	26.54	48.78	36.96	S	11.23	-10.73	33.70	-120.96	S	S
16	-51.57	-5.40	S	S	-62.59	-11.68	54.11	66.74	S	136.49
17	-26.16	S	S	-57.85	61.92	45.46	36.74	S	-223.73	30.46
18	S	S	-92.52	-86.67	22.98	46.11	S	S	151.17	-11.11
19	S	109.47	-11.79	66.30	-115.64	S	S	-218.35	-427.47	-93.87
20	-167.22	-75.08	148.23	-71.04	S	S	-26.02	51.70	-444.99	-14.28
21	31.85	-66.70	222.14	9.11	S	53.95	5.05	-211.10	494.13	S
22	-95.18	H	-40.31	S	32.51	51.15	5.36	H	S	S
23	H	125.03*	S	S	3.18	44.66	H	181.84*	S	132.79
24	70.91*	S	S	119.26	27.71	H	-46.78*	S	396.97	-17.24
25	S	S	44.56	16.15	H	15.53*	S	S	36.08	30.69
26	S	23.04	-172.98	15.63	1.92*	S	S	-237.44	247.14	H
27	75.84	-110.15	255.26	H	S	S	-158.46	215.00	H	-154.48*
28	-38.49	-160.74	H	2.89*	S	-40.90	14.74	331.01	102.43*	S
29	121.53	117.56	-35.59*	S	-46.33	-2.56	90.28	22.28	S	S
30	-214.62	22.14	S	S	-47.88	-82.29	-4.80	59.99	S	34.92
Close	10414.49	9851.56	8896.09	9782.46	10428.02	10805.87	12221.93	13371.72	8829.04	10344.84
Change	-556.65	776.42	499.06	-18.66	400.55	365.80	141.20	-558.29	-495.97	632.11

* Shortened trading day

DECEMBER DAILY POINT CHANGES DOW JONES INDUSTRIALS

Previous Month Close	2000	2001	2002	2003	2004	2005	2006	2007	2008	2009
	10414.49	9851.56	8896.09	9782.46	10428.02	10805.87	12221.93	13371.72	8829.04	10344.84
1	-40.95	S	S	116.59	162.20	106.70	-27.80	S	-679.95	126.74
2	S	S	-33.52	-45.41	-5.10	-35.06	S	S	270.00	-18.90
3	S	-87.60	-119.64	19.78	7.09	S	S	-57.15	172.60	-86.53
4	186.56	129.88	-5.08	57.40	S	S	89.72	-65.84	-215.45	22.75
5	338.62	220.45	-114.57	-68.14	S	-42.50	47.75	196.23	259.18	S
6	-234.34	-15.15	22.49	S	-45.15	21.85	-22.35	174.93	S	S
7	-47.02	-49.68	S	S	-106.48	-45.95	-30.84	5.69	S	1.21
8	95.55	S	S	102.59	53.65	-55.79	29.08	S	298.76	-104.14
9	S	S	-172.36	-41.85	58.59	23.46	S	S	-242.85	51.08
10	S	-128.01	100.85	-1.56	-9.60	S	S	101.45	70.09	68.78
11	12.89	-33.08	14.88	86.30	S	S	20.99	-294.26	-196.33	65.67
12	42.47	6.44	-50.74	34.00	S	-10.81	-12.90	41.13	64.59	S
13	26.17	-128.36	-104.69	S	95.10	55.95	1.92	44.06	S	S
14	-119.45	44.70	S	S	38.13	59.79	99.26	-178.11	S	29.55
15	-240.03	S	S	-19.34	15.00	-1.84	28.76	S	-65.15	-49.05
16	S	S	193.69	106.74	14.19	-6.08	S	S	359.61	-10.88
17	S	80.82	-92.01	15.70	-55.72	S	S	-172.65	-99.80	-132.86
18	210.46	106.42	-88.04	102.82	S	S	-4.25	65.27	-219.35	20.63
19	-61.05	72.10	-82.55	30.14	S	-39.06	30.05	-25.20	-25.88	S
20	-265.44	-85.31	146.52	S	11.68	-30.98	-7.45	38.37	S	S
21	168.36	50.16	S	S	97.83	28.18	-42.62	205.01	S	85.25
22	148.27	S	S	59.78	56.46	55.71	-78.03	S	-59.34	50.79
23	S	S	-18.03	3.26	11.23	-6.17	S	S	-100.28	1.51
24	S	N/C*	-45.18*	-36.07*	H	S	S	98.68*	48.99*	53.66*
25	H	H	H	H	S	S	H	H	H	H
26	56.88	52.80	-15.50	19.48*	S	H	64.41	2.36	47.07	S
27	110.72	43.17	-128.83	S	-50.99	-105.50	102.94	-192.08	S	S
28	65.60	5.68	S	S	78.41	18.49	-9.05	6.26	S	26.98
29	-81.91	S	S	125.33	-25.35	-11.44	-38.37	S	-31.62	-1.67
30	S	S	29.07	-24.96	-28.89	-67.32	S	S	184.46	3.10
31	S	-115.49	8.78	28.88	-17.29	S	S	-101.05	108.00	-120.46
Close	10786.85	10021.50	8341.63	10453.92	10783.01	10717.50	12463.15	13264.82	8776.39	10428.05
Change	372.36	169.94	-554.46	671.46	354.99	-88.37	241.22	-106.90	-52.65	83.21

* Shortened trading day

A TYPICAL DAY IN THE MARKET

Half-hourly data became available for the Dow Jones Industrial Average starting in January 1987. The NYSE switched 10:00 a.m. openings to 9:30 a.m. in October 1985. Below is the comparison between half-hourly performance 1987 to April 1, 2010, and hourly November 1963 to June 1985. Stronger openings and closings in a more bullish climate are evident. Morning and afternoon weaknesses appear an hour earlier.

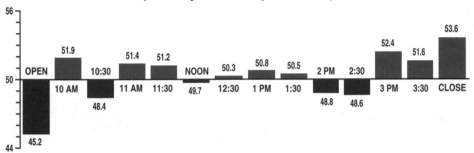

**MARKET % PERFORMANCE EACH HALF-HOUR OF THE DAY
(January 1987 to April 1, 2010)**

Based on the number of times the Dow Jones Industrial Average increased over previous half-hour.

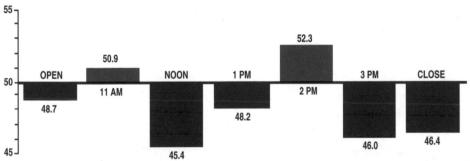

**MARKET % PERFORMANCE EACH HOUR OF THE DAY
(November 1963 to June 1985)**

Based on the number of times the Dow Jones Industrial Average increased over previous hour.

On the next page, half-hourly movements since January 1987 are separated by day of the week. From 1953 to 1989, Monday was the worst day of the week, especially during long bear markets, but times changed. Monday reversed positions and became the best day of the week and on the plus side eleven years in a row from 1990 to 2000.

During the last ten years (2001 to April 30, 2010) Monday, Thursday and Friday are net losers, Friday the worst. Only Tuesday and Wednesday are solid gainers, Tuesday the best (page 68). On all days, stocks do tend to firm up near the close with weakness early morning and from 2 to 2:30 frequently.

THROUGH THE WEEK ON A HALF-HOURLY BASIS

From the chart showing the percentage of times the Dow Jones Industrial Average rose over the preceding half-hour (January 1987 to April 1, 2010*), the typical week unfolds.

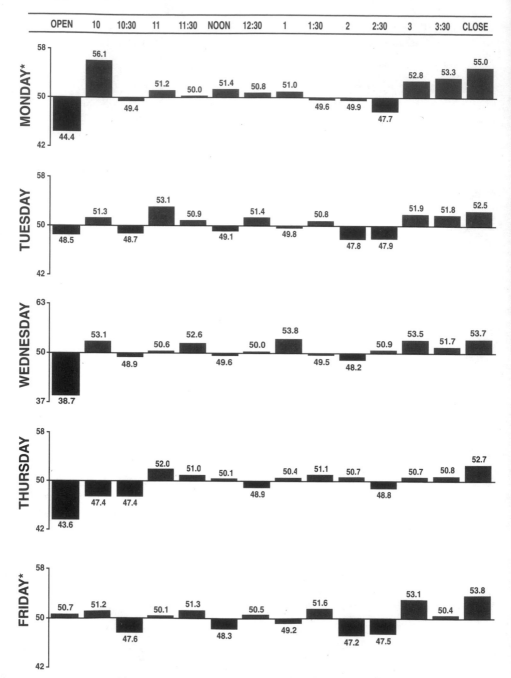

*Monday denotes first trading day of the week, Friday denotes last trading day of the week.

TUESDAY MOST PROFITABLE DAY OF WEEK

Between 1952 and 1989, Monday was the worst trading day of the week. The first trading day of the week (including Tuesday, when Monday is a holiday) rose only 44.3% of the time, while the other trading days closed higher 54.8% of the time. (NYSE Saturday trading discontinued June 1952.)

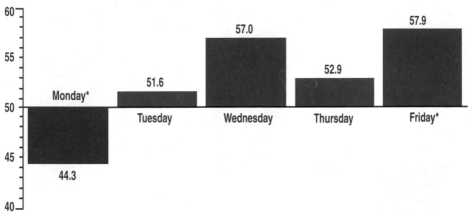

MARKET % PERFORMANCE EACH DAY OF THE WEEK
(June 1952 to December 1989)

A dramatic reversal occurred in 1990—Monday became the most powerful day of the week. However, during the last nine and a third years, Tuesday has produced the most gains. Since the top in 2000, traders have not been inclined to stay long over the weekend nor buy up equities at the outset of the week. This is not uncommon during uncertain market times. Monday was the worst day during the 2007–2009 bear, and only Tuesday was a net gainer. Since the March 2009 bottom, Monday is best. See pages 68 and 143.

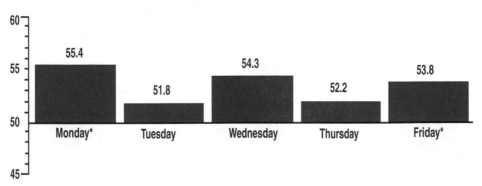

MARKET % PERFORMANCE EACH DAY OF THE WEEK
(January 1990 to April 23, 2010)

Charts based on the number of times S&P 500 index closed higher than previous day.
*Monday denotes first trading day of the week, Friday denotes last trading day of the week.

NASDAQ STRONGEST LAST 3 DAYS OF WEEK

Despite 20 years less data, daily trading patterns on NASDAQ through 1989 appear to be fairly similar to the S&P on page 141, except for more bullishness on Thursdays. During the mostly flat markets of the 1970s and early 1980s, it would appear that apprehensive investors decided to throw in the towel over weekends and sell on Mondays and Tuesdays.

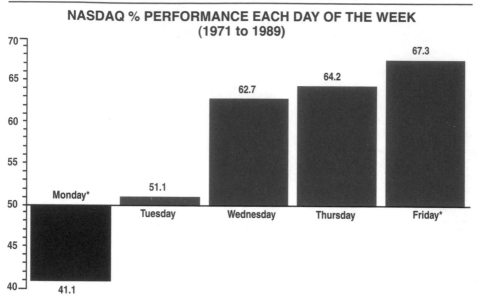

NASDAQ % PERFORMANCE EACH DAY OF THE WEEK (1971 to 1989)

Notice the vast difference in the daily trading pattern between NASDAQ and S&P from January 1, 1990, to recent times. The reason for so much more bullishness is that NASDAQ moved up 1010%, over three times as much during the 1990 to 2000 period. The gain for the S&P was 332% and for the Dow Jones industrials, 326%. NASDAQ's weekly patterns are beginning to move in step with the rest of the market. Notice the similarities to the S&P since 2001 on pages 143 and 144—Monday and Friday weakness, midweek strength.

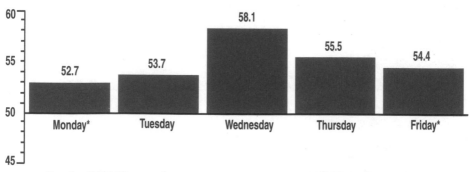

NASDAQ % PERFORMANCE EACH DAY OF THE WEEK (1990 to APRIL 23, 2010)

Based on NASDAQ composite, prior to February 5, 1971, based on National Quotation Bureau indices.
*Monday denotes first trading day of the week, Friday denotes last trading day of the week.

S&P DAILY PERFORMANCE EACH YEAR SINCE 1952

To determine if market trend alters performance of different days of the week, we separated 21 bear years—1953, '56, '57, '60, '62, '66, '69, '70, '73, '74, '77, '78, '81, '84, '87, '90, '94, 2000, '01, '02, and '08—from 37 bull market years. While Tuesday and Thursday did not vary much between bull and bear years, Mondays and Fridays were sharply affected. There was a swing of 10.6 percentage points in Monday's and 9.9 in Friday's performance. Tuesday is developing a reputation as the best day of the week based upon total points gained. See page 68.

PERCENTAGE OF TIMES MARKET CLOSED HIGHER THAN PREVIOUS DAY
(June 1952 to April 23, 2010)

	Monday*	Tuesday	Wednesday	Thursday	Friday*
1952	48.4%	55.6%	58.1%	51.9%	66.7%
1953	32.7	50.0	54.9	57.5	56.6
1954	50.0	57.5	63.5	59.2	73.1
1955	50.0	45.7	63.5	60.0	78.9
1956	36.5	39.6	46.9	50.0	59.6
1957	25.0	54.0	66.7	48.9	44.2
1958	59.6	52.0	59.6	68.1	72.6
1959	42.3	53.1	55.8	48.9	69.8
1960	34.6	50.0	44.2	54.0	59.6
1961	52.9	54.4	64.7	56.0	67.3
1962	28.3	52.1	54.0	51.0	50.0
1963	46.2	63.3	51.0	57.5	69.2
1964	40.4	48.0	61.5	58.7	77.4
1965	44.2	57.5	55.8	51.0	71.2
1966	36.5	47.8	53.9	42.0	57.7
1967	38.5	50.0	60.8	64.0	69.2
1968†	49.1	57.5	64.3	42.6	54.9
1969	30.8	45.8	50.0	67.4	50.0
1970	38.5	46.0	63.5	48.9	52.8
1971	44.2	64.6	57.7	55.1	51.9
1972	38.5	60.9	57.7	51.0	67.3
1973	32.1	51.1	52.9	44.9	44.2
1974	32.7	57.1	51.0	36.7	30.8
1975	53.9	38.8	61.5	56.3	55.8
1976	55.8	55.3	55.8	40.8	58.5
1977	40.4	40.4	46.2	53.1	53.9
1978	51.9	43.5	59.6	54.0	48.1
1979	54.7	53.2	58.8	66.0	44.2
1980	55.8	54.2	71.7	35.4	59.6
1981	44.2	38.8	55.8	53.2	47.2
1982	46.2	39.6	44.2	44.9	50.0
1983	55.8	46.8	61.5	52.0	55.8
1984	39.6	63.8	31.4	46.0	44.2
1985	44.2	61.2	54.9	56.3	53.9
1986	51.9	44.9	67.3	58.3	55.8
1987	51.9	57.1	63.5	61.7	49.1
1988	51.9	61.7	51.9	48.0	59.6
1989	51.9	47.8	69.2	58.0	69.2
1990	67.9	53.2	52.9	40.0	51.9
1991	44.2	46.9	52.9	49.0	51.9
1992	51.9	49.0	53.9	56.3	45.3
1993	65.4	41.7	55.8	44.9	48.1
1994	55.8	46.8	52.9	48.0	59.6
1995	63.5	56.5	63.5	62.0	63.5
1996	54.7	44.9	51.0	57.1	63.5
1997	67.3	67.4	42.3	41.7	57.7
1998	57.7	62.5	57.7	38.3	60.4
1999	46.2	29.8	67.3	53.1	57.7
2000	51.9	43.5	40.4	56.0	46.2
2001	45.3	51.1	44.0	59.2	43.1
2002	40.4	37.5	56.9	38.8	48.1
2003	59.6	62.5	42.3	58.3	50.0
2004	51.9	61.7	59.6	52.1	52.8
2005	59.6	47.8	59.6	56.0	55.8
2006	55.8	55.6	67.3	52.0	48.1
2007	47.2	50.0	64.0	50.0	61.5
2008	42.3	50.0	41.5	60.4	55.8
2009	53.9	50.0	57.7	63.8	52.8
2010 ‡	81.3	78.6	56.3	60.0	56.3
Average	**47.7%**	**51.2%**	**56.0%**	**52.5%**	**56.4%**
36 Bull Years	**51.5%**	**52.7%**	**58.5%**	**53.4%**	**60.0%**
21 Bear Years	**40.9%**	**48.5%**	**51.6%**	**51.0%**	**50.1%**

Based on S&P 500

† Most Wednesdays closed last 7 months of 1968. ‡ Through 4/23/2010 only, not included in averages.
*Monday denotes first trading day of the week, Friday denotes last trading day of the week.

NASDAQ DAILY PERFORMANCE EACH YEAR SINCE 1971

After dropping a hefty 77.9% from its 2000 high (versus −37.8% on the Dow and −49.1% on the S&P 500), NASDAQ tech stocks still outpace the blue chips and big caps—but not by nearly as much as they did. From January 1, 1971, through April 23, 2010, NASDAQ moved up an impressive 2724%. The Dow (up 1236%) and the S&P (up 1221%) gained just over half as much.

Monday's performance on NASDAQ was lackluster during the three-year bear market of 2000–2002. As NASDAQ rebounded (up 50% in 2003), strength returned to Monday during 2003–2006. During the bear market from late 2007 to early 2009, weakness was most consistent on Monday and Friday.

PERCENTAGE OF TIMES NASDAQ CLOSED HIGHER THAN PREVIOUS DAY
(1971 to April 23, 2010)

	Monday*	Tuesday	Wednesday	Thursday	Friday*
1971	51.9%	52.1%	59.6%	65.3%	71.2%
1972	30.8	60.9	63.5	57.1	78.9
1973	34.0	48.9	52.9	53.1	48.1
1974	30.8	44.9	52.9	51.0	42.3
1975	44.2	42.9	63.5	64.6	63.5
1976	50.0	63.8	67.3	59.2	58.5
1977	51.9	40.4	53.9	63.3	73.1
1978	48.1	47.8	73.1	72.0	84.6
1979	45.3	53.2	64.7	86.0	82.7
1980	46.2	64.6	84.9	52.1	73.1
1981	42.3	32.7	67.3	76.6	69.8
1982	34.6	47.9	59.6	51.0	63.5
1983	42.3	44.7	67.3	68.0	73.1
1984	22.6	53.2	35.3	52.0	51.9
1985	36.5	59.2	62.8	68.8	66.0
1986	38.5	55.1	65.4	72.9	75.0
1987	42.3	49.0	65.4	68.1	66.0
1988	50.0	55.3	61.5	66.0	63.5
1989	38.5	54.4	71.2	72.0	75.0
1990	54.7	42.6	60.8	46.0	55.8
1991	51.9	59.2	66.7	65.3	51.9
1992	44.2	53.1	59.6	60.4	45.3
1993	55.8	56.3	69.2	57.1	67.3
1994	51.9	46.8	54.9	52.0	55.8
1995	50.0	52.2	63.5	64.0	63.5
1996	50.9	57.1	64.7	61.2	63.5
1997	65.4	59.2	53.9	52.1	55.8
1998	59.6	58.3	65.4	44.7	58.5
1999	61.5	40.4	63.5	57.1	65.4
2000	40.4	41.3	42.3	60.0	57.7
2001	41.5	57.8	52.0	55.1	47.1
2002	44.2	37.5	56.9	46.9	46.2
2003	57.7	60.4	40.4	60.4	46.2
2004	57.7	59.6	53.9	50.0	50.9
2005	61.5	47.8	51.9	48.0	59.6
2006	55.8	51.1	65.4	50.0	44.2
2007	47.2	63.0	66.0	56.0	57.7
2008	34.6	52.1	49.1	54.2	42.3
2009	51.9	54.2	63.5	63.8	50.9
2010†	68.8	78.6	56.3	60.0	56.3
Average	**46.6%**	**51.8%**	**60.4%**	**59.6%**	**60.6%**
27 Bull Years	**49.3%**	**54.1%**	**63.1%**	**61.0%**	**63.6%**
10 Bear Years	**39.9%**	**46.1%**	**53.6%**	**55.9%**	**53.0%**

Based on NASDAQ composite; prior to February 5, 1971, based on National Quotation Bureau indices.
† Through 4/23/2010 only, not included in averages.
*Monday denotes first trading day of the week, Friday denotes last trading day of the week.

MONTHLY CASH INFLOWS INTO S&P STOCKS

For many years, the last trading day of the month, plus the first four of the following month, were the best market days of the month. This pattern is quite clear in the first chart, showing these five consecutive trading days towering above the other 16 trading days of the average month in the 1953–1981 period. The rationale was that individuals and institutions tended to operate similarly, causing a massive flow of cash into stocks near beginnings of months.

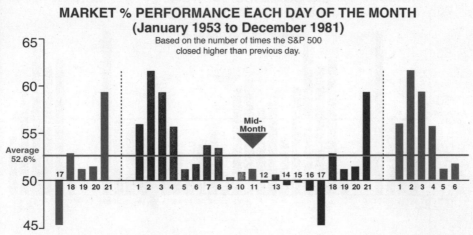

MARKET % PERFORMANCE EACH DAY OF THE MONTH
(January 1953 to December 1981)

Based on the number of times the S&P 500 closed higher than previous day.

Clearly "front-running" traders took advantage of this phenomenon, drastically altering the previous pattern. The second chart from 1982 onward shows the trading shift caused by these "anticipators" to the last three trading days of the month, plus the first two. Another astonishing development shows the ninth, tenth, and eleventh trading days rising strongly as well. Perhaps the enormous growth of 401(k) retirement plans (participants' salaries are usually paid twice monthly) is responsible for this mid-month bulge. First trading days of the month have produced the greatest gains in recent years (see page 62).

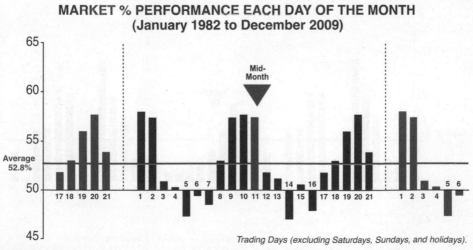

MARKET % PERFORMANCE EACH DAY OF THE MONTH
(January 1982 to December 2009)

Trading Days (excluding Saturdays, Sundays, and holidays).

MONTHLY CASH INFLOWS INTO NASDAQ STOCKS

NASDAQ stocks moved up 58.1% of the time through 1981 compared to 52.6% for the S&P on page 145. Ends and beginnings of the month are fairly similar, specifically the last plus the first four trading days. But notice how investors piled into NASDAQ stocks until mid-month. NASDAQ rose 118.6% from January 1, 1971, to December 31, 1981, compared to 33.0% for the S&P.

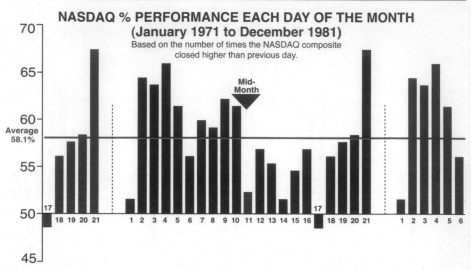

NASDAQ % PERFORMANCE EACH DAY OF THE MONTH
(January 1971 to December 1981)
Based on the number of times the NASDAQ composite closed higher than previous day.

After the air was let out of the tech market 2000–2002, S&P's 810% gain over the last 28 years is more evenly matched with NASDAQ's 1059% gain. Last three, first four, and middle ninth and tenth days rose the most. Where the S&P has five days of the month that go down more often than up, NASDAQ has none. NASDAQ exhibits the most strength on the last trading day of the month; however, over the past 13 years, last days have weakened considerably, down more often then not.

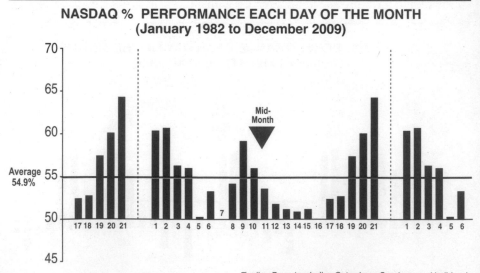

NASDAQ % PERFORMANCE EACH DAY OF THE MONTH
(January 1982 to December 2009)

Trading Days (excluding Saturdays, Sundays, and holidays).
Based on NASDAQ composite, prior to February 5, 1971, based on National Quotation Bureau indices.

NOVEMBER, DECEMBER, AND JANUARY: YEAR'S BEST THREE-MONTH SPAN

The most important observation to be made from a chart showing the average monthly percent change in market prices since 1950 is that institutions (mutual funds, pension funds, banks, etc.) determine the trading patterns in today's market.

The "investment calendar" reflects the annual, semi-annual and quarterly operations of institutions during January, April and July. October, besides being the last campaign month before elections, is also the time when most bear markets seem to end, as in 1946, 1957, 1960, 1966, 1974, 1987, 1990, 1998 and 2002. (August and September tend to combine to make the worst consecutive two-month period.)

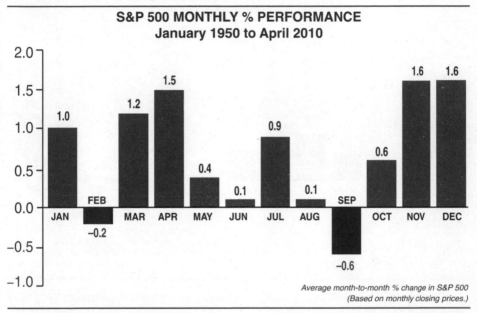

S&P 500 MONTHLY % PERFORMANCE
January 1950 to April 2010

Average month-to-month % change in S&P 500
(Based on monthly closing prices.)

Unusual year-end strength comes from corporate and private pension funds, producing a 4.2% gain on average between November 1 and January 31. In 2007–2008, these three months were all down for the fourth time since 1930; previously in 1931–1932, 1940–1941 and 1969–1970, also bear markets. September's dismal performance makes it the worst month of the year. However, in the last 15 years it has been up nine times—down five in a row 1999–2003.

In pre-presidential election years since 1950, the best three months are January +4.5% (14–1), April +3.7% (14–1), and December +3.3% (11–4). February, March, May, June, July, August, and November are gainers while September and October are losers. October is worst, –1.1% (7–8).

See page 44 for monthly performance tables for the S&P 500 and the Dow Jones industrials. See pages 48, 50, and 60 for unique switching strategies.

On page 72, you can see how the first month of the first three quarters far outperforms the second and the third months since 1950, and note the improvement in May's and October's performance since 1991.

NOVEMBER THROUGH JUNE: NASDAQ'S EIGHT-MONTH RUN

The two-and-a-half-year plunge of 77.9% in NASDAQ stocks, between March 10, 2000, and October 9, 2002, brought several horrendous monthly losses (the two greatest were November 2000, –22.9%, and February 2001, –22.4%), which trimmed average monthly performance over the 39⅓-year period. Ample Octobers in 8 of the last 12 years, including two huge turnarounds in 2001 (+12.8%) and 2002 (+13.5%), have put bear-killing October in the number two spot since 1998. January's 2.8% average gain is still awesome, and twice S&P's 1.2% January average since 1971.

NASDAQ MONTHLY PERFORMANCE
January 1971 to April 2010

Average month-to-month % change in NASDAQ composite, prior to February 5, 1971, based on National Quotation Bureau indices. (Based on monthly closing prices.)

Bear in mind, when comparing NASDAQ to the S&P on page 147, that there are 22 fewer years of data here. During this 39⅓-year (1971–April 2010) period, NASDAQ gained 2647%, while the S&P and the Dow rose only 1188% and 1212%, respectively. On page 54 is a statistical monthly comparison between NASDAQ and the Dow, and on page 58, NASDAQ's eight-month switching strategy.

Year-end strength is even more pronounced in NASDAQ, producing a 6.5% gain on average between November 1 and January 31—1.5 times greater than that of the S&P 500 on page 147. September is the worst month of the year for the over-the-counter index as well, posting a deeper average loss of –0.9%. These extremes underscore NASDAQ's higher volatility and potential for moves of greater magnitude.

In pre-presidential election years since 1971, the best three months are January +7.9% (9–1), December +5.4% (6–4), and March +3.8% (10–0). February, April, May, June, July, August, and November are also solid performers. October is the worst, –2.0% (5–5), and September is also slightly negative, –0.1% (6–4).

DOW JONES INDUSTRIALS ANNUAL HIGHS, LOWS, & CLOSES SINCE 1901

YEAR	HIGH DATE	HIGH CLOSE	LOW DATE	LOW CLOSE	YEAR CLOSE
1901	6/17	57.33	12/24	45.07	47.29
1902	4/24	50.14	12/15	43.64	47.10
1903	2/16	49.59	11/9	30.88	35.98
1904	12/5	53.65	3/12	34.00	50.99
1905	12/29	70.74	1/25	50.37	70.47
1906	1/19	75.45	7/13	62.40	69.12
1907	1/7	70.60	11/15	38.83	43.04
1908	11/13	64.74	2/13	42.94	63.11
1909	11/19	73.64	2/23	58.54	72.56
1910	1/3	72.04	7/26	53.93	59.60
1911	6/19	63.78	9/25	53.43	59.84
1912	9/30	68.97	2/10	58.72	64.37
1913	1/9	64.88	6/11	52.83	57.71
1914	3/20	61.12	7/30	52.32	54.58
1915	12/27	99.21	2/24	54.22	99.15
1916	11/21	110.15	4/22	84.96	95.00
1917	1/3	99.18	12/19	65.95	74.38
1918	10/18	89.07	1/15	73.38	82.20
1919	11/3	119.62	2/8	79.15	107.23
1920	1/3	109.88	12/21	66.75	71.95
1921	12/15	81.50	8/24	63.90	81.10
1922	10/14	103.43	1/10	78.59	98.73
1923	3/20	105.38	10/27	85.76	95.52
1924	12/31	120.51	5/20	88.33	120.51
1925	11/6	159.39	3/30	115.00	156.66
1926	8/14	166.64	3/30	135.20	157.20
1927	12/31	202.40	1/25	152.73	202.40
1928	12/31	300.00	2/20	191.33	300.00
1929	9/3	381.17	11/13	198.69	248.48
1930	4/17	294.07	12/16	157.51	164.58
1931	2/24	194.36	12/17	73.79	77.90
1932	3/8	88.78	7/8	41.22	59.93
1933	7/18	108.67	2/27	50.16	99.90
1934	2/5	110.74	7/26	85.51	104.04
1935	11/19	148.44	3/14	96.71	144.13
1936	11/17	184.90	1/6	143.11	179.90
1937	3/10	194.40	11/24	113.64	120.85
1938	11/12	150.41	3/31	98.95	154.76
1939	9/12	155.92	4/8	121.44	150.24
1940	1/3	152.80	6/10	111.84	131.13
1941	1/10	133.59	12/23	106.34	110.96
1942	12/26	119.71	4/28	92.92	119.40
1943	7/14	145.82	1/8	119.26	135.89
1944	12/16	152.53	2/7	134.22	152.32
1945	12/11	195.82	1/24	151.35	192.91
1946	5/29	212.50	10/9	163.12	177.20
1947	7/24	186.85	5/17	163.21	181.16
1948	6/15	193.16	3/16	165.39	177.30
1949	12/30	200.52	6/13	161.60	200.13
1950	11/24	235.47	1/13	196.81	235.41
1951	9/13	276.37	1/3	238.99	269.23
1952	12/30	292.00	5/1	256.35	291.90
1953	1/5	293.79	9/14	255.49	280.90
1954	12/31	404.39	1/11	279.87	404.39
1955	12/30	488.40	1/17	388.20	488.40
1956	4/6	521.05	1/23	462.35	499.47
1957	7/12	520.77	10/22	419.79	435.69
1958	12/31	583.65	2/25	436.89	583.65
1959	12/31	679.36	2/9	574.46	679.36
1960	1/5	685.47	10/25	566.05	615.89
1961	12/13	734.91	1/3	610.25	731.14
1962	1/3	726.01	6/26	535.76	652.10
1963	12/18	767.21	1/2	646.79	762.95
1964	11/18	891.71	1/2	766.08	874.13
1965	12/31	969.26	6/28	840.59	969.26
1966	2/9	995.15	10/7	744.32	785.69
1967	9/25	943.08	1/3	786.41	905.11
1968	12/3	985.21	3/21	825.13	943.75
1969	5/14	968.85	12/17	769.93	800.36
1970	12/29	842.00	5/26	631.16	838.92
1971	4/28	950.82	11/23	797.97	890.20
1972	12/11	1036.27	1/26	889.15	1020.02
1973	1/11	1051.70	12/5	788.31	850.86
1974	3/13	891.66	12/6	577.60	616.24
1975	7/15	881.81	1/2	632.04	852.41
1976	9/21	1014.79	1/2	858.71	1004.65
1977	1/3	999.75	11/2	800.85	831.17
1978	9/8	907.74	2/28	742.12	805.01
1979	10/5	897.61	11/7	796.67	838.74
1980	11/20	1000.17	4/21	759.13	963.99
1981	4/27	1024.05	9/25	824.01	875.00
1982	12/27	1070.55	8/12	776.92	1046.54
1983	11/29	1287.20	1/3	1027.04	1258.64
1984	1/6	1286.64	7/24	1086.57	1211.57
1985	12/16	1553.10	1/4	1184.96	1546.67
1986	12/2	1955.57	1/22	1502.29	1895.95
1987	8/25	2722.42	10/19	1738.74	1938.83
1988	10/21	2183.50	1/20	1879.14	2168.57
1989	10/9	2791.41	1/3	2144.64	2753.20
1990	7/17	2999.75	10/11	2365.10	2633.66
1991	12/31	3168.83	1/9	2470.30	3168.83
1992	6/1	3413.21	10/9	3136.58	3301.11
1993	12/29	3794.33	1/20	3241.95	3754.09
1994	1/31	3978.36	4/4	3593.35	3834.44
1995	12/13	5216.47	1/30	3832.08	5117.12
1996	12/27	6560.91	1/10	5032.94	6448.27
1997	8/6	8259.31	4/11	6391.69	7908.25
1998	11/23	9374.27	8/31	7539.07	9181.43
1999	12/31	11497.12	1/22	9120.67	11497.12
2000	1/14	11722.98	3/7	9796.03	10786.85
2001	5/21	11337.92	9/21	8235.81	10021.50
2002	3/19	10635.25	10/9	7286.27	8341.63
2003	12/31	10453.92	3/11	7524.06	10453.92
2004	12/28	10854.54	10/25	9749.99	10783.01
2005	3/4	10940.55	4/20	10012.36	10717.50
2006	12/27	12510.57	1/20	10667.39	12463.15
2007	10/9	14164.53	3/5	12050.41	13264.82
2008	5/2	13058.20	11/20	7552.29	8776.39
2009	12/30	10548.51	3/9	6547.05	10428.05
2010*	4/26	11205.03	2/8	9908.39	At Press Time

*Through April 30, 2010

S&P 500 ANNUAL HIGHS, LOWS, & CLOSES SINCE 1930

YEAR	HIGH DATE	HIGH CLOSE	LOW DATE	LOW CLOSE	YEAR CLOSE	YEAR	HIGH DATE	HIGH CLOSE	LOW DATE	LOW CLOSE	YEAR CLOSE
1930	4/10	25.92	12/16	14.44	15.34	1971	4/28	104.77	11/23	90.16	102.09
1931	2/24	18.17	12/17	7.72	8.12	1972	12/11	119.12	1/3	101.67	118.05
1932	9/7	9.31	6/1	4.40	6.89	1973	1/11	120.24	12/5	92.16	97.55
1933	7/18	12.20	2/27	5.53	10.10	1974	1/3	99.80	10/3	62.28	68.56
1934	2/6	11.82	7/26	8.36	9.50	1975	7/15	95.61	1/8	70.04	90.19
1935	11/19	13.46	3/14	8.06	13.43	1976	9/21	107.83	1/2	90.90	107.46
1936	11/9	17.69	1/2	13.40	17.18	1977	1/3	107.00	11/2	90.71	95.10
1937	3/6	18.68	11/24	10.17	10.55	1978	9/12	106.99	3/6	86.90	96.11
1938	11/9	13.79	3/31	8.50	13.21	1979	10/5	111.27	2/27	96.13	107.94
1939	1/4	13.23	4/8	10.18	12.49	1980	11/28	140.52	3/27	98.22	135.76
1940	1/3	12.77	6/10	8.99	10.58	1981	1/6	138.12	9/25	112.77	122.55
1941	1/10	10.86	12/29	8.37	8.69	1982	11/9	143.02	8/12	102.42	140.64
1942	12/31	9.77	4/28	7.47	9.77	1983	10/10	172.65	1/3	138.34	164.93
1943	7/14	12.64	1/2	9.84	11.67	1984	11/6	170.41	7/24	147.82	167.24
1944	12/16	13.29	2/7	11.56	13.28	1985	12/16	212.02	1/4	163.68	211.28
1945	12/10	17.68	1/23	13.21	17.36	1986	12/2	254.00	1/22	203.49	242.17
1946	5/29	19.25	10/9	14.12	15.30	1987	8/25	336.77	12/4	223.92	247.08
1947	2/8	16.20	5/17	13.71	15.30	1988	10/21	283.66	1/20	242.63	277.72
1948	6/15	17.06	2/14	13.84	15.20	1989	10/9	359.80	1/3	275.31	353.40
1949	12/30	16.79	6/13	13.55	16.76	1990	7/16	368.95	10/11	295.46	330.22
1950	12/29	20.43	1/14	16.65	20.41	1991	12/31	417.09	1/9	311.49	417.09
1951	10/15	23.85	1/3	20.69	23.77	1992	12/18	441.28	4/8	394.50	435.71
1952	12/30	26.59	2/20	23.09	26.57	1993	12/28	470.94	1/8	429.05	466.45
1953	1/5	26.66	9/14	22.71	24.81	1994	2/2	482.00	4/4	438.92	459.27
1954	12/31	35.98	1/11	24.80	35.98	1995	12/13	621.69	1/3	459.11	615.93
1955	11/14	46.41	1/17	34.58	45.48	1996	11/25	757.03	1/10	598.48	740.74
1956	8/2	49.74	1/23	43.11	46.67	1997	12/5	983.79	1/2	737.01	970.43
1957	7/15	49.13	10/22	38.98	39.99	1998	12/29	1241.81	1/9	927.69	1229.23
1958	12/31	55.21	1/2	40.33	55.21	1999	12/31	1469.25	1/14	1212.19	1469.25
1959	8/3	60.71	2/9	53.58	59.89	2000	3/24	1527.46	12/20	1264.74	1320.28
1960	1/5	60.39	10/25	52.30	58.11	2001	2/1	1373.47	9/21	965.80	1148.08
1961	12/12	72.64	1/3	57.57	71.55	2002	1/4	1172.51	10/9	776.76	879.82
1962	1/3	71.13	6/26	52.32	63.10	2003	12/31	1111.92	3/11	800.73	1111.92
1963	12/31	75.02	1/2	62.69	75.02	2004	12/30	1213.55	8/12	1063.23	1211.92
1964	11/20	86.28	1/2	75.43	84.75	2005	12/14	1272.74	4/20	1137.50	1248.29
1965	11/15	92.63	6/28	81.60	92.43	2006	12/15	1427.09	6/13	1223.69	1418.30
1966	2/9	94.06	10/7	73.20	80.33	2007	10/9	1565.15	3/5	1374.12	1468.36
1967	9/25	97.59	1/3	80.38	96.47	2008	1/2	1447.16	11/20	752.44	903.25
1968	11/29	108.37	3/5	87.72	103.86	2009	12/28	1127.78	3/9	676.53	1115.10
1969	5/14	106.16	12/17	89.20	92.06	2010*	4/23	1217.28	2/8	1056.74	*At Press Time*
1970	1/5	93.46	5/26	69.29	92.15						

*Through April 30, 2010

150

NASDAQ ANNUAL HIGHS, LOWS, & CLOSES SINCE 1971

YEAR	HIGH DATE	HIGH CLOSE	LOW DATE	LOW CLOSE	YEAR CLOSE	YEAR	HIGH DATE	HIGH CLOSE	LOW DATE	LOW CLOSE	YEAR CLOSE
1971	12/31	114.12	1/5	89.06	114.12	1991	12/31	586.34	1/14	355.75	586.34
1972	12/8	135.15	1/3	113.65	133.73	1992	12/31	676.95	6/26	547.84	676.95
1973	1/11	136.84	12/24	88.67	92.19	1993	10/15	787.42	4/26	645.87	776.80
1974	3/15	96.53	10/3	54.87	59.82	1994	3/18	803.93	6/24	693.79	751.96
1975	7/15	88.00	1/2	60.70	77.62	1995	12/4	1069.79	1/3	743.58	1052.13
1976	12/31	97.88	1/2	78.06	97.88	1996	12/9	1316.27	1/15	988.57	1291.03
1977	12/30	105.05	4/5	93.66	105.05	1997	10/9	1745.85	4/2	1201.00	1570.35
1978	9/13	139.25	1/11	99.09	117.98	1998	12/31	2192.69	10/8	1419.12	2192.69
1979	10/5	152.29	1/2	117.84	151.14	1999	12/31	4069.31	1/4	2208.05	4069.31
1980	11/28	208.15	3/27	124.09	202.34	2000	3/10	5048.62	12/20	2332.78	2470.52
1981	5/29	223.47	9/28	175.03	195.84	2001	1/24	2859.15	9/21	1423.19	1950.40
1982	12/8	240.70	8/13	159.14	232.41	2002	1/4	2059.38	10/9	1114.11	1335.51
1983	6/24	328.91	1/3	230.59	278.60	2003	12/30	2009.88	3/11	1271.47	2003.37
1984	1/6	287.90	7/25	225.30	247.35	2004	12/30	2178.34	8/12	1752.49	2175.44
1985	12/16	325.16	1/2	245.91	324.93	2005	12/2	2273.37	4/28	1904.18	2205.32
1986	7/3	411.16	1/9	323.01	349.33	2006	11/22	2465.98	7/21	2020.39	2415.29
1987	8/26	455.26	10/28	291.88	330.47	2007	10/31	2859.12	3/5	2340.68	2652.28
1988	7/5	396.11	1/12	331.97	381.38	2008	1/2	2609.63	11/20	1316.12	1577.03
1989	10/9	485.73	1/3	378.56	454.82	2009	12/30	2291.28	3/9	1268.64	2269.15
1990	7/16	469.60	10/16	325.44	373.84	2010*	4/23	2530.15	2/4	2125.43	At Press-time

RUSSELL 1000 ANNUAL HIGHS, LOWS, & CLOSES SINCE 1979

YEAR	HIGH DATE	HIGH CLOSE	LOW DATE	LOW CLOSE	YEAR CLOSE	YEAR	HIGH DATE	HIGH CLOSE	LOW DATE	LOW CLOSE	YEAR CLOSE
1979	10/5	61.18	2/27	51.83	59.87	1995	12/13	331.18	1/3	244.41	328.89
1980	11/28	78.26	3/27	53.68	75.20	1996	12/2	401.21	1/10	318.24	393.75
1981	1/6	76.34	9/25	62.03	67.93	1997	12/5	519.72	4/11	389.03	513.79
1982	11/9	78.47	8/12	55.98	77.24	1998	12/29	645.36	1/9	490.26	642.87
1983	10/10	95.07	1/3	76.04	90.38	1999	12/31	767.97	2/9	632.53	767.97
1984	1/6	92.80	7/24	79.49	90.31	2000	9/1	813.71	12/20	668.75	700.09
1985	12/16	114.97	1/4	88.61	114.39	2001	1/30	727.35	9/21	507.98	604.94
1986	7/2	137.87	1/22	111.14	130.00	2002	3/19	618.74	10/9	410.52	466.18
1987	8/25	176.22	12/4	117.65	130.02	2003	12/31	594.56	3/11	425.31	594.56
1988	10/21	149.94	1/20	128.35	146.99	2004	12/30	651.76	8/13	566.06	650.99
1989	10/9	189.93	1/3	145.78	185.11	2005	12/14	692.09	4/20	613.37	679.42
1990	7/16	191.56	10/11	152.36	171.22	2006	12/15	775.08	6/13	665.81	770.08
1991	12/31	220.61	1/9	161.94	220.61	2007	10/9	852.32	3/5	749.85	799.82
1992	12/18	235.06	4/8	208.87	233.59	2008	1/2	788.62	11/20	402.91	487.77
1993	10/15	252.77	1/8	229.91	250.71	2009	12/28	619.22	3/9	367.55	612.01
1994	2/1	258.31	4/4	235.38	244.65	2010*	4/23	672.14	2/8	580.17	At Press-time

RUSSELL 2000 ANNUAL HIGHS, LOWS, & CLOSES SINCE 1979

YEAR	HIGH DATE	HIGH CLOSE	LOW DATE	LOW CLOSE	YEAR CLOSE	YEAR	HIGH DATE	HIGH CLOSE	LOW DATE	LOW CLOSE	YEAR CLOSE
1979	12/31	55.91	1/2	40.81	55.91	1995	9/14	316.12	1/30	246.56	315.97
1980	11/28	77.70	3/27	45.36	74.80	1996	5/22	364.61	1/16	301.75	362.61
1981	6/15	85.16	9/25	65.37	73.67	1997	10/13	465.21	4/25	335.85	437.02
1982	12/8	91.01	8/12	60.33	88.90	1998	4/21	491.41	10/8	310.28	421.96
1983	6/24	126.99	1/3	88.29	112.27	1999	12/31	504.75	3/23	383.37	504.75
1984	1/12	116.69	7/25	93.95	101.49	2000	3/9	606.05	12/20	443.80	483.53
1985	12/31	129.87	1/2	101.21	129.87	2001	5/22	517.23	9/21	378.89	488.50
1986	7/3	155.30	1/9	128.23	135.00	2002	4/16	522.95	10/9	327.04	383.09
1987	8/25	174.44	10/28	106.08	120.42	2003	12/30	565.47	3/12	345.94	556.91
1988	7/15	151.42	1/12	121.23	147.37	2004	12/28	654.57	8/12	517.10	651.57
1989	10/9	180.78	1/3	146.79	168.30	2005	12/2	690.57	4/28	575.02	673.22
1990	6/15	170.90	10/30	118.82	132.16	2006	12/27	797.73	7/21	671.94	787.66
1991	12/31	189.94	1/15	125.25	189.94	2007	7/13	855.77	11/26	735.07	766.03
1992	12/31	221.01	7/8	185.81	221.01	2008	6/5	763.27	11/20	385.31	499.45
1993	11/2	260.17	2/23	217.55	258.59	2009	12/24	634.07	3/9	343.26	625.39
1994	3/18	271.08	12/9	235.16	250.36	2010*	4/23	741.92	2/8	586.49	At Press-time

*Through April 30, 2010

DOW JONES INDUSTRIALS MONTHLY PERCENT CHANGE SINCE 1950

	Jan	Feb	Mar	Apr	May	Jun	Jul	Aug	Sep	Oct	Nov	Dec	Year's Change
1950	0.8	0.8	1.3	4.0	4.2	-6.4	0.1	3.6	4.4	-0.6	1.2	3.4	17.6
1951	5.7	1.3	-1.6	4.5	-3.7	-2.8	6.3	4.8	0.3	-3.2	-0.4	3.0	14.4
1952	0.5	-3.9	3.6	-4.4	2.1	4.3	1.9	-1.6	-1.6	-0.5	5.4	2.9	8.4
1953	-0.7	-1.9	-1.5	-1.8	-0.9	-1.5	2.7	-5.1	1.1	4.5	2.0	-0.2	-3.8
1954	4.1	0.7	3.0	5.2	2.6	1.8	4.3	-3.5	7.3	-2.3	9.8	4.6	44.0
1955	1.1	0.7	-0.5	3.9	-0.2	6.2	3.2	0.5	-0.3	-2.5	6.2	1.1	20.8
1956	-3.6	2.7	5.8	0.8	-7.4	3.1	5.1	-3.0	-5.3	1.0	-1.5	5.6	2.3
1957	-4.1	-3.0	2.2	4.1	2.1	-0.3	1.0	-4.8	-5.8	-3.3	2.0	-3.2	-12.8
1958	3.3	-2.2	1.6	2.0	1.5	3.3	5.2	1.1	4.6	2.1	2.6	4.7	34.0
1959	1.8	1.6	-0.3	3.7	3.2	-0.03	4.9	-1.6	-4.9	2.4	1.9	3.1	16.4
1960	-8.4	1.2	-2.1	-2.4	4.0	2.4	-3.7	1.5	-7.3	0.04	2.9	3.1	-9.3
1961	5.2	2.1	2.2	0.3	2.7	-1.8	3.1	2.1	-2.6	0.4	2.5	1.3	18.7
1962	-4.3	1.1	-0.2	-5.9	-7.8	-8.5	6.5	1.9	-5.0	1.9	10.1	0.4	-10.8
1963	4.7	-2.9	3.0	5.2	1.3	-2.8	-1.6	4.9	0.5	3.1	-0.6	1.7	17.0
1964	2.9	1.9	1.6	-0.3	1.2	1.3	1.2	-0.3	4.4	-0.3	0.3	-0.1	14.6
1965	3.3	0.1	-1.6	3.7	-0.5	-5.4	1.6	1.3	4.2	3.2	-1.5	2.4	10.9
1966	1.5	-3.2	-2.8	1.0	-5.3	-1.6	-2.6	-7.0	-1.8	4.2	-1.9	-0.7	-18.9
1967	8.2	-1.2	3.2	3.6	-5.0	0.9	5.1	-0.3	2.8	-5.1	-0.4	3.3	15.2
1968	-5.5	-1.7	0.02	8.5	-1.4	-0.1	-1.6	1.5	4.4	1.8	3.4	-4.2	4.3
1969	0.2	-4.3	3.3	1.6	-1.3	-6.9	-6.6	2.6	-2.8	5.3	-5.1	-1.5	-15.2
1970	-7.0	4.5	1.0	-6.3	-4.8	-2.4	7.4	4.1	-0.5	-0.7	5.1	5.6	4.8
1971	3.5	1.2	2.9	4.1	-3.6	-1.8	-3.7	4.6	-1.2	-5.4	-0.9	7.1	6.1
1972	1.3	2.9	1.4	1.4	0.7	-3.3	-0.5	4.2	-1.1	0.2	6.6	0.2	14.6
1973	-2.1	-4.4	-0.4	-3.1	-2.2	-1.1	3.9	-4.2	6.7	1.0	-14.0	3.5	-16.6
1974	0.6	0.6	-1.6	-1.2	-4.1	0.03	-5.6	-10.4	-10.4	9.5	-7.0	-0.4	-27.6
1975	14.2	5.0	3.9	6.9	1.3	5.6	-5.4	0.5	-5.0	5.3	2.9	-1.0	38.3
1976	14.4	-0.3	2.8	-0.3	-2.2	2.8	-1.8	-1.1	1.7	-2.6	-1.8	6.1	17.9
1977	-5.0	-1.9	-1.8	0.8	-3.0	2.0	-2.9	-3.2	-1.7	-3.4	1.4	0.2	-17.3
1978	-7.4	-3.6	2.1	10.6	0.4	-2.6	5.3	1.7	-1.3	-8.5	0.8	0.7	-3.1
1979	4.2	-3.6	6.6	-0.8	-3.8	2.4	0.5	4.9	-1.0	-7.2	0.8	2.0	4.2
1980	4.4	-1.5	-9.0	4.0	4.1	2.0	7.8	-0.3	-0.02	-0.9	7.4	-3.0	14.9
1981	-1.7	2.9	3.0	-0.6	-0.6	-1.5	-2.5	-7.4	-3.6	0.3	4.3	-1.6	-9.2
1982	-0.4	-5.4	-0.2	3.1	-3.4	-0.9	-0.4	11.5	-0.6	10.7	4.8	0.7	19.6
1983	2.8	3.4	1.6	8.5	-2.1	1.8	-1.9	1.4	1.4	-0.6	4.1	-1.4	20.3
1984	-3.0	-5.4	0.9	0.5	-5.6	2.5	-1.5	9.8	-1.4	0.1	-1.5	1.9	-3.7
1985	6.2	-0.2	-1.3	-0.7	4.6	1.5	0.9	-1.0	-0.4	3.4	7.1	5.1	27.7
1986	1.6	8.8	6.4	-1.9	5.2	0.9	-6.2	6.9	-6.9	6.2	1.9	-1.0	22.6
1987	13.8	3.1	3.6	-0.8	0.2	5.5	6.3	3.5	-2.5	-23.2	-8.0	5.7	2.3
1988	1.0	5.8	-4.0	2.2	-0.1	5.4	-0.6	-4.6	4.0	1.7	-1.6	2.6	11.8
1989	8.0	-3.6	1.6	5.5	2.5	-1.6	9.0	2.9	-1.6	-1.8	2.3	1.7	27.0
1990	-5.9	1.4	3.0	-1.9	8.3	0.1	0.9	-10.0	-6.2	-0.4	4.8	2.9	-4.3
1991	3.9	5.3	1.1	-0.9	4.8	-4.0	4.1	0.6	-0.9	1.7	-5.7	9.5	20.3
1992	1.7	1.4	-1.0	3.8	1.1	-2.3	2.3	-4.0	0.4	-1.4	2.4	-0.1	4.2
1993	0.3	1.8	1.9	-0.2	2.9	-0.3	0.7	3.2	-2.6	3.5	0.1	1.9	13.7
1994	6.0	-3.7	-5.1	1.3	2.1	-3.5	3.8	4.0	-1.8	1.7	-4.3	2.5	2.1
1995	0.2	4.3	3.7	3.9	3.3	2.0	3.3	-2.1	3.9	-0.7	6.7	0.8	33.5
1996	5.4	1.7	1.9	-0.3	1.3	0.2	-2.2	1.6	4.7	2.5	8.2	-1.1	26.0
1997	5.7	0.9	-4.3	6.5	4.6	4.7	7.2	-7.3	4.2	-6.3	5.1	1.1	22.6
1998	-0.02	8.1	3.0	3.0	-1.8	0.6	-0.8	-15.1	4.0	9.6	6.1	0.7	16.1
1999	1.9	-0.6	5.2	10.2	-2.1	3.9	-2.9	1.6	-4.5	3.8	1.4	5.7	25.2
2000	-4.8	-7.4	7.8	-1.7	-2.0	-0.7	0.7	6.6	-5.0	3.0	-5.1	3.6	-6.2
2001	0.9	-3.6	-5.9	8.7	1.6	-3.8	0.2	-5.4	-11.1	2.6	8.6	1.7	-7.1
2002	-1.0	1.9	2.9	-4.4	-0.2	-6.9	-5.5	-0.8	-12.4	10.6	5.9	-6.2	-16.8
2003	-3.5	-2.0	1.3	6.1	4.4	1.5	2.8	2.0	-1.5	5.7	-0.2	6.9	25.3
2004	0.3	0.9	-2.1	-1.3	-0.4	2.4	-2.8	0.3	-0.9	-0.5	4.0	3.4	3.1
2005	-2.7	2.6	-2.4	-3.0	2.7	-1.8	3.6	-1.5	0.8	-1.2	3.5	-0.8	-0.6
2006	1.4	1.2	1.1	2.3	-1.7	-0.2	0.3	1.7	2.6	3.4	1.2	2.0	16.3
2007	1.3	-2.8	0.7	5.7	4.3	-1.6	-1.5	1.1	4.0	0.2	-4.0	-0.8	6.4
2008	-4.6	-3.0	-0.03	4.5	-1.4	-10.2	0.2	1.5	-6.0	-14.1	-5.3	-0.6	-33.8
2009	-8.8	-11.7	7.7	7.3	4.1	-0.6	8.6	3.5	2.3	0.005	6.5	0.8	18.8
2010	-3.5	2.6	5.1	1.4									
TOTALS	60.3	-2.5	65.3	120.2	10.8	-18.1	67.2	3.9	-54.8	19.9	93.5	99.3	
AVG.	1.0	-0.04	1.1	2.0	0.2	-0.3	1.1	0.1	-0.9	0.3	1.6	1.7	
# Up	39	34	39	39	31	28	37	35	23	35	40	42	
# Down	22	27	22	22	29	32	23	25	37	25	20	18	

	Jan	Feb	Mar	Apr	May	Jun	Jul	Aug	Sep	Oct	Nov	Dec	Year's Close
1950	1.66	1.65	2.61	8.28	9.09	− 14.31	0.29	7.47	9.49	− 1.35	2.59	7.81	235.41
1951	13.42	3.22	− 4.11	11.19	− 9.48	− 7.01	15.22	12.39	0.91	− 8.81	− 1.08	7.96	269.23
1952	1.46	− 10.61	9.38	− 11.83	5.31	11.32	5.30	− 4.52	− 4.43	− 1.38	14.43	8.24	291.90
1953	− 2.13	− 5.50	− 4.40	− 5.12	− 2.47	− 4.02	7.12	− 14.16	2.82	11.77	5.56	− 0.47	280.90
1954	11.49	2.15	8.97	15.82	8.16	6.04	14.39	− 12.12	24.66	− 8.32	34.63	17.62	404.39
1955	4.44	3.04	− 2.17	15.95	− 0.79	26.52	14.47	2.33	− 1.56	− 11.75	28.39	5.14	488.40
1956	− 17.66	12.91	28.14	4.33	− 38.07	14.73	25.03	− 15.77	−26.79	4.60	− 7.07	26.69	499.47
1957	− 20.31	− 14.54	10.19	19.55	10.57	− 1.64	5.23	− 24.17	−28.05	− 15.26	8.83	− 14.18	435.69
1958	14.33	− 10.10	6.84	9.10	6.84	15.48	24.81	5.64	23.46	11.13	14.24	26.19	583.65
1959	10.31	9.54	− 1.79	22.04	20.04	− 0.19	31.28	− 10.47	−32.73	14.92	12.58	20.18	679.36
1960	− 56.74	7.50	− 13.53	− 14.89	23.80	15.12	− 23.89	9.26	− 45.85	0.22	16.86	18.67	615.89
1961	32.31	13.88	14.55	2.08	18.01	− 12.76	21.41	14.57	− 18.73	2.71	17.68	9.54	731.14
1962	− 31.14	8.05	− 1.10	− 41.62	− 51.97	− 52.08	36.65	11.25	− 30.20	10.79	59.53	2.80	652.10
1963	30.75	− 19.91	19.58	35.18	9.26	− 20.08	− 11.45	33.89	3.47	22.44	− 4.71	12.43	762.95
1964	22.39	14.80	13.15	− 2.52	9.79	10.94	9.60	− 2.62	36.89	− 2.29	2.35	− 1.30	874.13
1965	28.73	0.62	− 14.43	33.26	− 4.27	− 50.01	13.71	11.36	37.48	30.24	− 14.11	22.55	969.26
1966	14.25	− 31.62	− 27.12	8.91	− 49.61	− 13.97	− 22.72	− 58.97	− 14.19	32.85	− 15.48	− 5.90	785.69
1967	64.20	− 10.52	26.61	31.07	− 44.49	7.70	43.98	− 2.95	25.37	− 46.92	− 3.93	29.30	905.11
1968	− 49.64	− 14.97	0.17	71.55	− 13.22	− 1.20	− 14.80	13.01	39.78	16.60	32.69	−41.33	943.75
1969	2.30	− 40.84	30.27	14.70	− 12.62	− 64.37	− 57.72	21.25	− 23.63	42.90	− 43.69	−11.94	800.36
1970	− 56.30	33.53	7.98	− 49.50	− 35.63	− 16.91	50.59	30.46	− 3.90	− 5.07	38.48	44.83	838.92
1971	29.58	10.33	25.54	37.38	− 33.94	− 16.67	− 32.71	39.64	− 10.88	− 48.19	− 7.66	58.86	890.20
1972	11.97	25.96	12.57	13.47	6.55	− 31.69	− 4.29	38.99	− 10.46	2.25	62.69	1.81	1020.02
1973	− 21.00	− 43.95	− 4.06	− 29.58	− 20.02	− 9.70	34.69	− 38.83	59.53	9.48	−134.33	28.61	850.86
1974	4.69	4.98	− 13.85	− 9.93	− 34.58	0.24	− 44.98	− 78.85	− 70.71	57.65	− 46.86	− 2.42	616.24
1975	07.45	35.36	29.10	53.19	10.95	46.70	− 47.48	3.83	− 41.46	42.16	24.63	− 8.26	852.41
1976	122.87	− 2.67	26.84	− 2.60	− 21.62	27.55	− 18.14	− 10.90	16.45	− 25.26	− 17.71	57.43	1004.65
1977	− 50.28	− 17.95	− 17.29	7.77	− 28.24	17.64	− 26.23	− 28.58	− 14.38	− 28.76	11.35	1.47	831.17
1978	− 61.25	− 27.80	15.24	79.96	3.29	− 21.66	43.32	14.55	− 11.00	− 73.37	6.58	5.98	805.01
1979	34.21	− 30.40	53.36	− 7.28	− 32.57	19.65	4.44	41.21	− 9.05	− 62.88	6.65	16.39	838.74
1980	37.11	− 12.71	− 77.39	31.31	33.79	17.07	67.40	− 2.73	− 0.17	− 7.93	68.85	−29.35	963.99
1981	− 16.72	27.31	29.29	− 6.12	− 6.00	− 14.87	− 24.54	− 70.87	− 31.49	2.57	36.43	−13.98	875.00
1982	− 3.90	− 46.71	− 1.62	25.59	− 28.82	− 7.61	− 3.33	92.71	− 5.06	95.47	47.56	7.26	1046.54
1983	29.16	36.92	17.41	96.17	− 26.22	21.98	− 22.74	16.94	16.97	− 7.93	50.82	−17.38	1258.64
1984	− 38.06	− 65.95	10.26	5.86	− 65.90	27.55	− 17.12	109.10	− 17.67	0.67	− 18.44	22.63	1211.57
1985	75.20	− 2.76	− 17.23	− 8.72	57.35	20.05	11.99	− 13.44	− 5.38	45.68	97.82	74.54	1546.67
1986	24.32	138.07	109.55	− 34.63	92.73	16.01	−117.41	123.03	−130.76	110.23	36.42	−18.28	1895.95
1987	262.09	65.95	80.70	− 18.33	5.21	126.96	153.54	90.88	− 66.67	−602.75	−159.98	105.28	1938.83
1988	19.39	113.40	− 83.56	44.27	− 1.21	110.59	− 12.98	− 97.08	81.26	35.74	− 34.14	54.06	2168.57
1989	173.75	− 83.93	35.23	125.18	61.35	− 40.09	220.60	76.61	− 44.45	− 47.74	61.19	46.93	2753.20
1990	−162.66	36.71	79.96	− 50.45	219.90	4.03	24.51	−290.84	−161.88	− 10.15	117.32	74.01	2633.66
1991	102.73	145.79	31.68	− 25.99	139.63	−120.75	118.07	18.78	− 26.83	52.33	−174.42	274.15	3168.83
1992	54.56	44.28	− 32.20	123.65	37.76	− 78.36	75.26	−136.43	14.31	− 45.38	78.88	− 4.05	3301.11
1993	8.92	60.78	64.30	− 7.56	00.88	− 11.35	23.39	111.78	− 96.13	125.47	3.36	70.14	3754.09
1994	224.27	−146.34	−196.06	45.73	76.68	−133.41	139.54	148.92	− 70.23	64.93	−168.89	95.21	3834.44
1995	9.42	167.19	146.64	163.58	143.87	90.96	152.37	− 97.91	178.52	− 33.60	319.01	42.63	5117.12
1996	278.18	90.32	101.52	− 18.06	74.10	11.45	−125.72	87.30	265.96	147.21	492.32	−73.43	6448.27
1997	364.82	64.65	−294.26	425.51	322.05	341.75	549.82	−600.19	322.84	−503.18	381.05	85.12	7908.25
1998	− 1.75	639.22	254.09	263.56	−163.42	52.07	− 68.73	−1344.22	303.55	749.48	524.45	64.88	9181.43
1999	177.40	− 52.25	479.58	1002.88	−229.30	411.06	−315.65	174.13	−492.33	392.91	147.95	619.31	11497.12
2000	−556.59	−812.22	793.61	−188.01	−211.58	− 74.44	74.09	693.12	−564.18	320.22	−556.65	372.36	10786.85
2001	100.51	−392.08	−616.50	856.19	176.97	−409.54	20.41	−573.06	−1102.19	227.58	776.42	169.94	10021.50
2002	−101.50	186.13	297.81	−457.72	− 20.97	−681.99	−506.67	− 73.09	−1071.57	805.10	499.06	−554.46	8341.63
2003	−287.82	−162.73	101.05	487.96	370.17	135.18	248.36	182.02	−140.76	526.06	− 18.66	671.46	10453.92
2004	34.15	95.85	−226.22	−132.13	− 37.12	247.03	−295.77	34.21	− 93.65	− 52.80	400.55	354.99	10783.01
2005	−293.07	276.29	−262.47	−311.25	274.97	− 92.51	365.94	−159.31	87.10	−128.63	365.80	−88.37	10717.50
2006	147.36	128.55	115.91	257.82	−198.83	− 18.09	35.46	195.47	297.92	401.66	141.20	241.22	12463.15
2007	158.54	−353.06	85.72	708.56	564.73	− 219.02	− 196.63	145.75	537.89	34.38	− 558.29	− 106.90	13264.82
2008	− 614.46	− 383.97	− 3.50	557.24	− 181.81	− 1288.31	28.01	165.53	− 692.89	− 1525.65	− 495.97	− 52.65	8776.39
2009	− 775.53	− 937.93	545.99	559.20	332.21	− 53.33	724.61	324.67	216.00	0.45	632.11	83.21	10428.05
2010	− 360.72	257.93	531.37	151.98									
TOTALS	− 754.54	− 971.16	2337.90	4993.18	1620.24	− 1828.57	1423.20	− 660.03	− 2609.66	1145.50	3197.24	2915.18	
# Up	39	34	39	39	31	28	37	35	23	35	40	42	
# Down	22	27	22	22	29	32	23	25	37	25	20	18	

153

DOW JONES INDUSTRIALS MONTHLY CLOSING PRICES SINCE 1950

	Jan	Feb	Mar	Apr	May	Jun	Jul	Aug	Sep	Oct	Nov	Dec
1950	201.79	203.44	206.05	214.33	223.42	209.11	209.40	216.87	226.36	225.01	227.60	235.41
1951	248.83	252.05	247.94	259.13	249.65	242.64	257.86	270.25	271.16	262.35	261.27	269.23
1952	270.69	260.08	269.46	257.63	262.94	274.26	279.56	275.04	270.61	269.23	283.66	291.90
1953	289.77	284.27	279.87	274.75	272.28	268.26	275.38	261.22	264.04	275.81	281.37	280.90
1954	292.39	294.54	303.51	319.33	327.49	333.53	347.92	335.80	360.46	352.14	386.77	404.39
1955	408.83	411.87	409.70	425.65	424.86	451.38	465.85	468.18	466.62	454.87	483.26	488.40
1956	470.74	483.65	511.79	516.12	478.05	492.78	517.81	502.04	475.25	479.85	472.78	499.47
1957	479.16	464.62	474.81	494.36	504.93	503.29	508.52	484.35	456.30	441.04	449.87	435.69
1958	450.02	439.92	446.76	455.86	462.70	478.18	502.99	508.63	532.09	543.22	557.46	583.65
1959	593.96	603.50	601.71	623.75	643.79	643.60	674.88	664.41	631.68	646.60	659.18	679.36
1960	622.62	630.12	616.59	601.70	625.50	640.62	616.73	625.99	580.14	580.36	597.22	615.89
1961	648.20	662.08	676.63	678.71	696.72	683.96	705.37	719.94	701.21	703.92	721.60	731.14
1962	700.00	708.05	706.95	665.33	613.36	561.28	597.93	609.18	578.98	589.77	649.30	652.10
1963	682.85	662.94	682.52	717.70	726.96	706.88	695.43	729.32	732.79	755.23	750.52	762.95
1964	785.34	800.14	813.29	810.77	820.56	831.50	841.10	838.48	875.37	873.08	875.43	874.13
1965	902.86	903.48	889.05	922.31	918.04	868.03	881.74	893.10	930.58	960.82	946.71	969.26
1966	983.51	951.89	924.77	933.68	884.07	870.10	847.38	788.41	774.22	807.07	791.59	785.69
1967	849.89	839.37	865.98	897.05	852.56	860.26	904.24	901.29	926.66	879.74	875.81	905.11
1968	855.47	840.50	840.67	912.22	899.00	897.80	883.00	896.01	935.79	952.39	985.08	943.75
1969	946.05	905.21	935.48	950.18	937.56	873.19	815.47	836.72	813.09	855.99	812.30	800.36
1970	744.06	777.59	785.57	736.07	700.44	683.53	734.12	764.58	760.68	755.61	794.09	838.92
1971	868.50	878.83	904.37	941.75	907.81	891.14	858.43	898.07	887.19	839.00	831.34	890.20
1972	902.17	928.13	940.70	954.17	960.72	929.03	924.74	963.73	953.27	955.52	1018.21	1020.02
1973	999.02	955.07	951.01	921.43	901.41	891.71	926.40	887.57	947.10	956.58	822.25	850.86
1974	855.55	860.53	846.68	836.75	802.17	802.41	757.43	678.58	607.87	665.52	618.66	616.24
1975	703.69	739.05	768.15	821.34	832.29	878.99	831.51	835.34	793.88	836.04	860.67	852.41
1976	975.28	972.61	999.45	996.85	975.23	1002.78	984.64	973.74	990.19	964.93	947.22	1004.65
1977	954.37	936.42	919.13	926.90	898.66	916.30	890.07	861.49	847.11	818.35	829.70	831.17
1978	769.92	742.12	757.36	837.32	840.61	818.95	862.27	876.82	865.82	792.45	799.03	805.01
1979	839.22	808.82	862.18	854.90	822.33	841.98	846.42	887.63	878.58	815.70	822.35	838.74
1980	875.85	863.14	785.75	817.06	850.85	867.92	935.32	932.59	932.42	924.49	993.34	963.99
1981	947.27	974.58	1003.87	997.75	991.75	976.88	952.34	881.47	849.98	852.55	888.98	875.00
1982	871.10	824.39	822.77	848.36	819.54	811.93	808.60	901.31	896.25	991.72	1039.28	1046.54
1983	1075.70	1112.62	1130.03	1226.20	1199.98	1221.96	1199.22	1216.16	1233.13	1225.20	1276.02	1258.64
1984	1220.58	1154.63	1164.89	1170.75	1104.85	1132.40	1115.28	1224.38	1206.71	1207.38	1188.94	1211.57
1985	1286.77	1284.01	1266.78	1258.06	1315.41	1335.46	1347.45	1334.01	1328.63	1374.31	1472.13	1546.67
1986	1570.99	1709.06	1818.61	1783.98	1876.71	1892.72	1775.31	1898.34	1767.58	1877.81	1914.23	1895.95
1987	2158.04	2223.99	2304.69	2286.36	2291.57	2418.53	2572.07	2662.95	2596.28	1993.53	1833.55	1938.83
1988	1958.22	2071.62	1988.06	2032.33	2031.12	2141.71	2128.73	2031.65	2112.91	2148.65	2114.51	2168.57
1989	2342.32	2258.39	2293.62	2418.80	2480.15	2440.06	2660.66	2737.27	2692.82	2645.08	2706.27	2753.20
1990	2590.54	2627.25	2707.21	2656.76	2876.66	2880.69	2905.20	2614.36	2452.48	2442.33	2559.65	2633.66
1991	2736.39	2882.18	2913.86	2887.87	3027.50	2906.75	3024.82	3043.60	3016.77	3069.10	2894.68	3168.83
1992	3223.39	3267.67	3235.47	3359.12	3396.88	3318.52	3393.78	3257.35	3271.66	3226.28	3305.16	3301.11
1993	3310.03	3370.81	3435.11	3427.55	3527.43	3516.08	3539.47	3651.25	3555.12	3680.59	3683.95	3754.09
1994	3978.36	3832.02	3635.96	3681.69	3758.37	3624.96	3764.50	3913.42	3843.19	3908.12	3739.23	3834.44
1995	3843.86	4011.05	4157.69	4321.27	4465.14	4556.10	4708.47	4610.56	4789.08	4755.48	5074.49	5117.12
1996	5395.30	5485.62	5587.14	5569.08	5643.18	5654.63	5528.91	5616.21	5882.17	6029.38	6521.70	6448.27
1997	6813.09	6877.74	6583.48	7008.99	7331.04	7672.79	8222.61	7622.42	7945.26	7442.08	7823.13	7908.25
1998	7906.50	8545.72	8799.81	9063.37	8899.95	8952.02	8883.29	7539.07	7842.62	8592.10	9116.55	9181.43
1999	9358.83	9306.58	9786.16	10789.04	10559.74	10970.80	10655.15	10829.28	10336.95	10729.86	10877.81	11497.12
2000	10940.53	10128.31	10921.92	10733.91	10522.33	10447.89	10521.98	11215.10	10650.92	10971.14	10414.49	10786.85
2001	10887.36	10495.28	9878.78	10734.97	10911.94	10502.40	10522.81	9949.75	8847.56	9075.14	9851.56	10021.50
2002	9920.00	10106.13	10403.94	9946.22	9925.25	9243.26	8736.59	8663.50	7591.93	8397.03	8896.09	8341.63
2003	8053.81	7891.08	7992.13	8480.09	8850.26	8985.44	9233.80	9415.82	9275.06	9801.12	9782.46	10453.92
2004	10488.07	10583.92	10357.70	10225.57	10188.45	10435.48	10139.71	10173.92	10080.27	10027.47	10428.02	10783.01
2005	10489.94	10766.23	10503.76	10192.51	10467.48	10274.97	10640.91	10481.60	10568.70	10440.07	10805.87	10717.50
2006	10864.86	10993.41	11109.32	11367.14	11168.31	11150.22	11185.68	11381.15	11679.07	12080.73	12221.93	12463.15
2007	12621.69	12268.63	12354.35	13062.91	13627.64	13408.62	13211.99	13357.74	13895.63	13930.01	13371.72	13264.82
2008	12650.36	12266.39	12262.89	12820.13	12638.32	11350.01	11378.02	11543.55	10850.66	9325.01	8829.04	8776.39
2009	8000.86	7062.93	7608.92	8168.12	8500.33	8447.00	9171.61	9496.28	9712.28	9712.73	10344.84	10428.05
2010	10067.33	10325.26	10856.63	11008.61								

	Jan	Feb	Mar	Apr	May	Jun	Jul	Aug	Sep	Oct	Nov	Dec	Year's Change
1950	1.7	1.0	0.4	4.5	3.9	- 5.8	0.8	3.3	5.6	0.4	- 0.1	4.6	21.8
1951	6.1	0.6	- 1.8	4.8	- 4.1	- 2.6	6.9	3.9	- 0.1	- 1.4	- 0.3	3.9	16.5
1952	1.6	- 3.6	4.8	- 4.3	2.3	4.6	1.8	- 1.5	- 2.0	- 0.1	4.6	3.5	11.8
1953	- 0.7	- 1.8	- 2.4	- 2.6	- 0.3	- 1.6	2.5	- 5.8	0.1	5.1	0.9	0.2	- 6.6
1954	5.1	0.3	3.0	4.9	3.3	0.1	5.7	- 3.4	8.3	- 1.9	8.1	5.1	45.0
1955	1.8	0.4	- 0.5	3.8	- 0.1	8.2	6.1	- 0.8	1.1	- 3.0	7.5	- 0.1	26.4
1956	- 3.6	3.5	6.9	- 0.2	- 6.6	3.9	5.2	- 3.8	- 4.5	0.5	- 1.1	3.5	2.6
1957	- 4.2	- 3.3	2.0	3.7	3.7	- 0.1	1.1	- 5.6	- 6.2	- 3.2	1.6	- 4.1	- 14.3
1958	4.3	- 2.1	3.1	3.2	1.5	2.6	4.3	1.2	4.8	2.5	2.2	5.2	38.1
1959	0.4	- 0.02	0.1	3.9	1.9	- 0.4	3.5	- 1.5	- 4.6	1.1	1.3	2.8	8.5
1960	- 7.1	0.9	- 1.4	- 1.8	2.7	2.0	- 2.5	2.6	- 6.0	- 0.2	4.0	4.6	- 3.0
1961	6.3	2.7	2.6	0.4	1.9	- 2.9	3.3	2.0	- 2.0	2.8	3.9	0.3	23.1
1962	- 3.8	1.6	- 0.6	- 6.2	- 8.6	- 8.2	6.4	1.5	- 4.8	0.4	10.2	1.3	- 11.8
1963	4.9	- 2.9	3.5	4.9	1.4	- 2.0	- 0.3	4.9	- 1.1	3.2	- 1.1	2.4	18.9
1964	2.7	1.0	1.5	0.6	1.1	1.6	1.8	- 1.6	2.9	0.8	- 0.5	0.4	13.0
1965	3.3	- 0.1	- 1.5	3.4	- 0.8	- 4.9	1.3	2.3	3.2	2.7	- 0.9	0.9	9.1
1966	0.5	- 1.8	- 2.2	2.1	- 5.4	- 1.6	- 1.3	- 7.8	- 0.7	4.8	0.3	- 0.1	- 13.1
1967	7.8	0.2	3.9	4.2	- 5.2	1.8	4.5	- 1.2	3.3	- 2.9	0.1	2.6	20.1
1968	- 4.4	- 3.1	0.9	8.2	1.1	0.9	- 1.8	1.1	3.9	0.7	4.8	- 4.2	7.7
1969	- 0.8	- 4.7	3.4	2.1	- 0.2	- 5.6	- 6.0	4.0	- 2.5	4.4	- 3.5	- 1.9	- 11.4
1970	- 7.6	5.3	0.1	- 9.0	- 6.1	- 5.0	7.3	4.4	3.3	- 1.1	4.7	5.7	0.1
1971	4.0	0.9	3.7	3.6	- 4.2	0.1	- 4.1	3.6	- 0.7	- 4.2	- 0.3	8.6	10.8
1972	1.8	2.5	0.6	0.4	1.7	- 2.2	0.2	3.4	- 0.5	0.9	4.6	1.2	15.6
1973	- 1.7	- 3.7	- 0.1	- 4.1	- 1.9	- 0.7	3.8	- 3.7	4.0	- 0.1	- 11.4	1.7	- 17.4
1974	- 1.0	- 0.4	- 2.3	- 3.9	- 3.4	- 1.5	- 7.8	- 9.0	- 11.9	16.3	- 5.3	- 2.0	- 29.7
1975	12.3	6.0	2.2	4.7	4.4	4.4	- 6.8	- 2.1	- 3.5	6.2	2.5	- 1.2	31.5
1976	11.8	- 1.1	3.1	- 1.1	- 1.4	4.1	- 0.8	- 0.5	2.3	- 2.2	- 0.8	5.2	19.1
1977	- 5.1	- 2.2	- 1.4	0.02	- 2.4	4.5	- 1.6	- 2.1	- 0.2	- 4.3	2.7	0.3	- 11.5
1978	- 6.2	- 2.5	2.5	8.5	0.4	- 1.8	5.4	2.6	- 0.7	- 9.2	1.7	1.5	1.1
1979	4.0	- 3.7	5.5	0.2	- 2.6	3.9	0.9	5.3	NC	- 6.9	4.3	1.7	12.3
1980	5.8	- 0.4	-10.2	4.1	4.7	2.7	6.5	0.6	2.5	1.6	10.2	- 3.4	25.8
1981	- 4.6	1.3	3.6	- 2.3	- 0.2	- 1.0	- 0.2	- 6.2	- 5.4	4.9	3.7	- 3.0	- 9.7
1982	- 1.8	- 6.1	- 1.0	4.0	- 3.9	- 2.0	- 2.3	11.6	0.8	11.0	3.6	1.5	14.8
1983	3.3	1.9	3.3	7.5	- 1.2	3.5	- 3.3	1.1	1.0	- 1.5	1.7	- 0.9	17.3
1984	- 0.9	- 3.9	1.3	0.5	- 5.9	1.7	- 1.6	10.6	- 0.3	- 0.01	- 1.5	2.2	1.4
1985	7.4	0.9	- 0.3	- 0.5	5.4	1.2	- 0.5	- 1.2	- 3.5	4.3	6.5	4.5	26.3
1986	0.2	7.1	5.3	- 1.4	5.0	1.4	- 5.9	7.1	- 8.5	5.5	2.1	- 2.8	14.6
1987	13.2	3.7	2.6	- 1.1	0.6	4.8	4.8	3.5	- 2.4	-21.8	- 8.5	7.3	2.0
1988	4.0	4.2	- 3.3	0.9	0.3	4.3	- 0.5	- 3.9	4.0	2.6	- 1.9	1.5	12.4
1989	7.1	- 2.9	2.1	5.0	3.5	- 0.8	8.8	1.6	- 0.7	- 2.5	1.7	2.1	27.3
1990	- 6.9	0.9	2.4	- 2.7	9.2	- 0.9	- 0.5	- 9.4	- 5.1	- 0.7	6.0	2.5	- 6.6
1991	4.2	6.7	2.2	0.03	3.9	- 4.8	4.5	2.0	- 1.9	1.2	- 4.4	11.2	26.3
1992	- 2.0	1.0	- 2.2	2.8	0.1	- 1.7	3.9	- 2.4	0.9	0.2	3.0	1.0	4.5
1993	0.7	1.0	1.0	- 2.5	2.3	0.1	- 0.5	3.4	- 1.0	1.9	- 1.3	1.0	7.1
1994	3.3	- 3.0	- 4.6	1.2	1.2	- 2.7	3.1	3.8	- 2.7	2.1	- 4.0	1.2	- 1.5
1995	2.4	3.6	2.7	2.8	3.6	2.1	3.2	- 0.03	4.0	- 0.5	4.1	1.7	34.1
1996	3.3	0.7	0.8	1.3	2.3	0.2	- 4.6	1.9	5.4	2.6	7.3	- 2.2	20.3
1997	6.1	0.6	- 4.3	5.8	5.9	4.3	7.8	- 5.7	5.3	- 3.4	4.5	1.6	31.0
1998	1.0	7.0	5.0	0.9	- 1.9	3.9	- 1.2	-14.6	6.2	8.0	5.9	5.6	26.7
1999	4.1	- 3.2	3.9	3.8	- 2.5	5.4	- 3.2	- 0.6	- 2.9	6.3	1.9	5.8	19.5
2000	- 5.1	- 2.0	9.7	- 3.1	- 2.2	2.4	- 1.6	6.1	- 5.3	- 0.5	- 8.0	0.4	- 10.1
2001	3.5	- 9.2	- 6.4	7.7	0.5	- 2.5	- 1.1	- 6.4	- 8.2	1.8	7.5	0.8	- 13.0
2002	- 1.6	- 2.1	3.7	- 6.1	- 0.9	- 7.2	- 7.9	0.5	-11.0	8.6	5.7	- 6.0	- 23.4
2003	- 2.7	- 1.7	1.0	8.0	5.1	1.1	1.6	1.8	- 1.2	5.5	0.7	5.1	26.4
2004	1.7	1.2	- 1.6	- 1.7	1.2	1.8	- 3.4	0.2	0.9	1.4	3.9	3.2	9.0
2005	- 2.5	1.9	- 1.9	- 2.0	3.0	- 0.01	3.6	- 1.1	0.7	- 1.8	3.5	- 0.1	3.0
2006	2.5	0.1	1.1	1.2	- 3.1	0.01	0.5	2.1	2.5	3.2	1.6	1.3	13.6
2007	1.4	- 2.2	1.0	4.3	3.3	- 1.8	- 3.2	1.3	3.6	1.5	- 4.4	- 0.9	3.5
2008	- 6.1	- 3.5	- 0.6	4.8	1.1	- 8.6	- 1.0	1.2	- 9.1	- 16.9	- 7.5	0.8	- 38.5
2009	- 8.6	- 11.0	8.5	9.4	5.3	0.02	7.4	3.4	3.6	- 2.0	5.7	1.8	23.5
2010	- 3.7	2.9	5.9	1.5									
TOTALS	62.9	- 14.7	71.2	93.1	23.7	2.7	53.0	8.0	- 37.0	34.7	94.0	98.4	
AVG.	1.0	- 0.2	1.2	1.5	0.4	0.1	0.9	0.1	- 0.6	0.6	1.6	1.6	
# Up	37	32	40	42	35	32	32	34	26	35	40	45	
# Down	24	29	21	19	25	28	28	26	33	25	20	15	

	Jan	Feb	Mar	Apr	May	Jun	Jul	Aug	Sep	Oct	Nov	Dec
1950	17.05	17.22	17.29	18.07	18.78	17.69	17.84	18.42	19.45	19.53	19.51	20.41
1951	21.66	21.80	21.40	22.43	21.52	20.96	22.40	23.28	23.26	22.94	22.88	23.77
1952	24.14	23.26	24.37	23.32	23.86	24.96	25.40	25.03	24.54	24.52	25.66	26.57
1953	26.38	25.90	25.29	24.62	24.54	24.14	24.75	23.32	23.35	24.54	24.76	24.81
1954	26.08	26.15	26.94	28.26	29.19	29.21	30.88	29.83	32.31	31.68	34.24	35.98
1955	36.63	36.76	36.58	37.96	37.91	41.03	43.52	43.18	43.67	42.34	45.51	45.48
1956	43.82	45.34	48.48	48.38	45.20	46.97	49.39	47.51	45.35	45.58	45.08	46.67
1957	44.72	43.26	44.11	45.74	47.43	47.37	47.91	45.22	42.42	41.06	41.72	39.99
1958	41.70	40.84	42.10	43.44	44.09	45.24	47.19	47.75	50.06	51.33	52.48	55.21
1959	55.42	55.41	55.44	57.59	58.68	58.47	60.51	59.60	56.88	57.52	58.28	59.89
1960	55.61	56.12	55.34	54.37	55.83	56.92	55.51	56.96	53.52	53.39	55.54	58.11
1961	61.78	63.44	65.06	65.31	66.56	64.64	66.76	68.07	66.73	68.62	71.32	71.55
1962	68.84	69.96	69.55	65.24	59.63	54.75	58.23	59.12	56.27	56.52	62.26	63.10
1963	66.20	64.29	66.57	69.80	70.80	69.37	69.13	72.50	71.70	74.01	73.23	75.02
1964	77.04	77.80	78.98	79.46	80.37	81.69	83.18	81.83	84.18	84.86	84.42	84.75
1965	87.56	87.43	86.16	89.11	88.42	84.12	85.25	87.17	89.96	92.42	91.61	92.43
1966	92.88	91.22	89.23	91.06	86.13	84.74	83.60	77.10	76.56	80.20	80.45	80.33
1967	86.61	86.78	90.20	94.01	89.08	90.64	94.75	93.64	96.71	93.90	94.00	96.47
1968	92.24	89.36	90.20	97.59	98.68	99.58	97.74	98.86	102.67	103.41	108.37	103.86
1969	103.01	98.13	101.51	103.69	103.46	97.71	91.83	95.51	93.12	97.24	93.81	92.06
1970	85.02	89.50	89.63	81.52	76.55	72.72	78.05	81.52	84.21	83.25	87.20	92.15
1971	95.88	96.75	100.31	103.95	99.63	99.70	95.58	99.03	98.34	94.23	93.99	102.09
1972	103.94	106.57	107.20	107.67	109.53	107.14	107.39	111.09	110.55	111.58	116.67	118.05
1973	116.03	111.68	111.52	106.97	104.95	104.26	108.22	104.25	108.43	108.29	95.96	97.55
1974	96.57	96.22	93.98	90.31	87.28	86.00	79.31	72.15	63.54	73.90	69.97	68.56
1975	76.98	81.59	83.36	87.30	91.15	95.19	88.75	86.88	83.87	89.04	91.24	90.19
1976	100.86	99.71	102.77	101.64	100.18	104.28	103.44	102.91	105.24	102.90	102.10	107.46
1977	102.03	99.82	98.42	98.44	96.12	100.48	98.85	96.77	96.53	92.34	94.83	95.10
1978	89.25	87.04	89.21	96.83	97.24	95.53	100.68	103.29	102.54	93.15	94.70	96.11
1979	99.93	96.28	101.59	101.76	99.08	102.91	103.81	109.32	109.32	101.82	106.16	107.94
1980	114.16	113.66	102.09	106.29	111.24	114.24	121.67	122.38	125.46	127.47	140.52	135.76
1981	129.55	131.27	136.00	132.81	132.59	131.21	130.92	122.79	116.18	121.89	126.35	122.55
1982	120.40	113.11	111.96	116.44	111.88	109.61	107.09	119.51	120.42	133.71	138.54	140.64
1983	145.30	148.06	152.96	164.42	162.39	168.11	162.56	164.40	166.07	163.55	166.40	164.93
1984	163.41	157.06	159.18	160.05	150.55	153.18	150.66	166.68	166.10	166.09	163.58	167.24
1985	179.63	181.18	180.66	179.83	189.55	191.85	190.92	188.63	182.08	189.82	202.17	211.28
1986	211.78	226.92	238.90	235.52	247.35	250.84	236.12	252.93	231.32	243.98	249.22	242.17
1987	274.08	284.20	291.70	288.36	290.10	304.00	318.66	329.80	321.83	251.79	230.30	247.08
1988	257.07	267.82	258.89	261.33	262.16	273.50	272.02	261.52	271.91	278.97	273.70	277.72
1989	297.47	288.86	294.87	309.64	320.52	317.98	346.08	351.45	349.15	340.36	345.99	353.40
1990	329.08	331.89	339.94	330.80	361.23	358.02	356.15	322.56	306.05	304.00	322.22	330.22
1991	343.93	367.07	375.22	375.35	389.83	371.16	387.81	395.43	387.86	392.46	375.22	417.09
1992	408.79	412.70	403.69	414.95	415.35	408.14	424.21	414.03	417.80	418.68	431.35	435.71
1993	438.78	443.38	451.67	440.19	450.19	450.53	448.13	463.56	458.93	467.83	461.79	466.45
1994	481.61	467.14	445.77	450.91	456.50	444.27	458.26	475.49	462.69	472.35	453.69	459.27
1995	470.42	487.39	500.71	514.71	533.40	544.75	562.06	561.88	584.41	581.50	605.37	615.93
1996	636.02	640.43	645.50	654.17	669.12	670.63	639.95	651.99	687.31	705.27	757.02	740.74
1997	786.16	790.82	757.12	801.34	848.28	885.14	954.29	899.47	947.28	914.62	955.40	970.43
1998	980.28	1049.34	1101.75	1111.75	1090.82	1133.84	1120.67	957.28	1017.01	1098.67	1163.63	1229.23
1999	1279.64	1238.33	1286.37	1335.18	1301.84	1372.71	1328.72	1320.41	1282.71	1362.93	1388.91	1469.25
2000	1394.46	1366.42	1498.58	1452.43	1420.60	1454.60	1430.83	1517.68	1436.51	1429.40	1314.95	1320.28
2001	1366.01	1239.94	1160.33	1249.46	1255.82	1224.42	1211.23	1133.58	1040.94	1059.78	1139.45	1148.08
2002	1130.20	1106.73	1147.39	1076.92	1067.14	989.82	911.62	916.07	815.28	885.76	936.31	879.82
2003	855.70	841.15	849.18	916.92	963.59	974.50	990.31	1008.01	995.97	1050.71	1058.20	1111.92
2004	1131.13	1144.94	1126.21	1107.30	1120.68	1140.84	1101.72	1104.24	1114.58	1130.20	1173.82	1211.92
2005	1181.27	1203.60	1180.59	1156.85	1191.50	1191.33	1234.18	1220.33	1228.81	1207.01	1249.48	1248.29
2006	1280.08	1280.66	1294.83	1310.61	1270.09	1270.20	1276.66	1303.82	1335.85	1377.94	1400.63	1418.30
2007	1438.24	1406.82	1420.86	1482.37	1530.62	1503.35	1455.27	1473.99	1526.75	1549.38	1481.14	1468.36
2008	1378.55	1330.63	1322.70	1385.59	1400.38	1280.00	1267.38	1282.83	1166.36	968.75	896.24	903.25
2009	825.88	735.09	797.87	872.81	919.14	919.32	987.48	1020.62	1057.08	1036.19	1095.63	1115.10
2010	1073.87	1104.49	1169.43	1186.69								

NASDAQ COMPOSITE MONTHLY PERCENT CHANGES SINCE 1971

	Jan	Feb	Mar	Apr	May	Jun	Jul	Aug	Sep	Oct	Nov	Dec	Year's Change
1971	10.2	2.6	4.6	6.0	−3.6	−0.4	−2.3	3.0	0.6	−3.6	−1.1	9.8	27.4
1972	4.2	5.5	2.2	2.5	0.9	−1.8	−1.8	1.7	−0.3	0.5	2.1	0.6	17.2
1973	−4.0	−6.2	−2.4	−8.2	−4.8	−1.6	7.6	−3.5	6.0	−0.9	−15.1	−1.4	−31.1
1974	3.0	−0.6	−2.2	−5.9	−7.7	−5.3	−7.9	−10.9	−0.7	17.2	−3.5	−5.0	−35.1
1975	16.6	4.6	3.6	3.8	5.8	4.7	−4.4	−5.0	−5.9	3.6	2.4	−1.5	29.8
1976	12.1	3.7	0.4	−0.6	−2.3	2.6	1.1	−1.7	1.7	−1.0	0.9	7.4	26.1
1977	−2.4	−1.0	−0.5	1.4	0.1	4.3	0.9	−0.5	0.7	−3.3	5.8	1.8	7.3
1978	−4.0	0.6	4.7	8.5	4.4	0.05	5.0	6.9	−1.6	−16.4	3.2	2.9	12.3
1979	6.6	−2.6	7.5	1.6	−1.8	5.1	2.3	6.4	−0.3	−9.6	6.4	4.8	28.1
1980	7.0	−2.3	−17.1	6.9	7.5	4.9	8.9	5.7	3.4	2.7	8.0	−2.8	33.9
1981	−2.2	0.1	6.1	3.1	3.1	−3.5	−1.9	−7.5	−8.0	8.4	3.1	−2.7	−3.2
1982	−3.8	−4.8	−2.1	5.2	−3.3	−4.1	−2.3	6.2	5.6	13.3	9.3	0.04	18.7
1983	6.9	5.0	3.9	8.2	5.3	3.2	−4.6	−3.8	1.4	−7.4	4.1	−2.5	19.9
1984	−3.7	−5.9	−0.7	−1.3	−5.9	2.9	−4.2	10.9	−1.8	−1.2	−1.8	2.0	−11.2
1985	12.7	2.0	−1.7	0.5	3.6	1.9	1.7	−1.2	−5.8	4.4	7.3	3.5	31.4
1986	3.3	7.1	4.2	2.3	4.4	1.3	−8.4	3.1	−8.4	2.9	−0.3	−2.8	7.5
1987	12.2	8.4	1.2	−2.8	−0.3	2.0	2.4	4.6	−2.3	−27.2	−5.6	8.3	−5.4
1988	4.3	6.5	2.1	1.2	−2.3	6.6	−1.9	−2.8	3.0	−1.4	−2.9	2.7	15.4
1989	5.2	−0.4	1.8	5.1	4.4	−2.4	4.3	3.4	0.8	−3.7	0.1	−0.3	19.3
1990	−8.6	2.4	2.3	−3.6	9.3	0.7	−5.2	−13.0	−9.6	−4.3	8.9	4.1	−17.8
1991	10.8	9.4	6.5	0.5	4.4	−6.0	5.5	4.7	0.2	3.1	−3.5	11.9	56.8
1992	5.8	2.1	−4.7	−4.2	1.1	−3.7	3.1	−3.0	3.6	3.8	7.9	3.7	15.5
1993	2.9	−3.7	2.9	−4.2	5.9	0.5	0.1	5.4	2.7	2.2	−3.2	3.0	14.7
1994	3.0	−1.0	−6.2	−1.3	0.2	−4.0	2.3	6.0	−0.2	1.7	−3.5	0.2	−3.2
1995	0.4	5.1	3.0	3.3	2.4	8.0	7.3	1.9	2.3	−0.7	2.2	−0.7	39.9
1996	0.7	3.8	0.1	8.1	4.4	−4.7	−8.8	5.6	7.5	−0.4	5.8	−0.1	22.7
1997	6.9	−5.1	−6.7	3.2	11.1	3.0	10.5	−0.4	6.2	−5.5	0.4	−1.9	21.6
1998	3.1	9.3	3.7	1.8	−4.8	6.5	−1.2	−19.9	13.0	4.6	10.1	12.5	39.6
1999	14.3	−8.7	7.6	3.3	−2.8	8.7	−1.8	3.8	0.2	8.0	12.5	22.0	85.6
2000	−3.2	19.2	−2.6	−15.6	−11.9	16.6	−5.0	11.7	−12.7	−8.3	−22.9	−4.9	−39.3
2001	12.2	−22.4	−14.5	15.0	−0.3	2.4	−6.2	−10.9	−17.0	12.8	14.2	1.0	−21.1
2002	−0.8	−10.5	6.6	−8.5	−4.3	−9.4	−9.2	−1.0	−10.9	13.5	11.2	−9.7	−31.5
2003	−1.1	1.3	0.3	9.2	9.0	1.7	6.9	4.3	−1.3	8.1	1.5	2.2	50.0
2004	3.1	−1.8	−1.8	−3.7	3.5	3.1	−7.8	−2.6	3.2	4.1	6.2	3.7	8.6
2005	−5.2	−0.5	−2.6	−3.9	7.6	−0.5	6.2	−1.5	−0.02	−1.5	5.3	−1.2	1.4
2006	4.6	−1.1	2.6	−0.7	−6.2	−0.3	−3.7	4.4	3.4	4.8	2.7	−0.7	9.5
2007	2.0	−1.9	0.2	4.3	3.1	−0.05	−2.2	2.0	4.0	5.8	−6.9	−0.3	9.8
2008	−9.9	−5.0	0.3	5.9	4.6	−9.1	1.4	1.8	−11.6	−17.7	−10.8	2.7	−40.5
2009	−6.4	−6.7	10.9	12.3	3.3	3.4	7.8	1.5	5.6	−3.6	4.9	5.8	43.9
2010	−5.4	4.2	7.1	2.6									
TOTALS	113.4	10.7	30.6	61.3	47.1	37.3	−5.5	15.8	−33.3	7.8	65.4	78.1	
AVG.	2.8	0.3	0.8	1.5	1.2	1.0	−0.1	0.4	−0.9	0.2	1.7	2.0	
# Up	26	20	26	26	24	23	19	22	21	20	26	23	
# Down	14	20	14	14	15	16	20	17	18	19	13	16	

Based on NASDAQ composite, prior to February 5, 1971, based on National Quotation Bureau indices.

NASDAQ COMPOSITE MONTHLY CLOSING PRICES SINCE 1971

	Jan	Feb	Mar	Apr	May	Jun	Jul	Aug	Sep	Oct	Nov	Dec
1971	98.77	101.34	105.97	112.30	108.25	107.80	105.27	108.42	109.03	105.10	103.97	114.12
1972	118.87	125.38	128.14	131.33	132.53	130.08	127.75	129.95	129.61	130.24	132.96	133.73
1973	128.40	120.41	117.46	107.85	102.64	100.98	108.64	104.87	111.20	110.17	93.51	92.19
1974	94.93	94.35	92.27	86.86	80.20	75.96	69.99	62.37	55.67	65.23	62.95	59.82
1975	69.78	73.00	75.66	78.54	83.10	87.02	83.19	79.01	74.33	76.99	78.80	77.62
1976	87.05	90.26	90.62	90.08	88.04	90.32	91.29	89.70	91.26	90.35	91.12	97.88
1977	95.54	94.57	94.13	95.48	95.59	99.73	100.65	100.10	100.85	97.52	103.15	105.05
1978	100.84	101.47	106.20	115.18	120.24	120.30	126.32	135.01	132.89	111.12	114.69	117.98
1979	125.82	122.56	131.76	133.82	131.42	138.13	141.33	150.44	149.98	135.53	144.26	151.14
1980	161.75	158.03	131.00	139.99	150.45	157.78	171.81	181.52	187.76	192.78	208.15	202.34
1981	197.81	198.01	210.18	216.74	223.47	215.75	211.63	195.75	180.03	195.24	201.37	195.84
1982	188.39	179.43	175.65	184.70	178.54	171.30	167.35	177.71	187.65	212.63	232.31	232.41
1983	248.35	260.67	270.80	293.06	308.73	318.70	303.96	292.42	296.65	274.55	285.67	278.60
1984	268.43	252.57	250.78	247.44	232.82	239.65	229.70	254.64	249.94	247.03	242.53	247.35
1985	278.70	284.17	279.20	280.56	290.80	296.20	301.29	297.71	280.33	292.54	313.95	324.93
1986	335.77	359.53	374.72	383.24	400.16	405.51	371.37	382.86	350.67	360.77	359.57	349.33
1987	392.06	424.97	430.05	417.81	416.54	424.67	434.93	454.97	444.29	323.30	305.16	330.47
1988	344.66	366.95	374.64	379.23	370.34	394.66	387.33	376.55	387.71	382.46	371.45	381.38
1989	401.30	399.71	406.73	427.55	446.17	435.29	453.84	469.33	472.92	455.63	456.09	454.82
1990	415.81	425.83	435.54	420.07	458.97	462.29	438.24	381.21	344.51	329.84	359.06	373.84
1991	414.20	453.05	482.30	484.72	506.11	475.92	502.04	525.68	526.88	542.98	523.90	586.34
1992	620.21	633.47	603.77	578.68	585.31	563.60	580.83	563.12	583.27	605.17	652.73	676.95
1993	696.34	670.77	690.13	661.42	700.53	703.95	704.70	742.84	762.78	779.26	754.39	776.80
1994	800.47	792.50	743.46	733.84	735.19	705.96	722.16	765.62	764.29	777.49	750.32	751.96
1995	755.20	793.73	817.21	843.98	864.58	933.45	1001.21	1020.11	1043.54	1036.06	1059.20	1052.13
1996	1059.79	1100.05	1101.40	1190.52	1243.43	1185.02	1080.59	1141.50	1226.92	1221.51	1292.61	1291.03
1997	1379.85	1309.00	1221.70	1260.76	1400.32	1442.07	1593.81	1587.32	1685.69	1593.61	1600.55	1570.35
1998	1619.36	1770.51	1835.68	1868.41	1778.87	1894.74	1872.39	1499.25	1693.84	1771.39	1949.54	2192.69
1999	2505.89	2288.03	2461.40	2542.85	2470.52	2686.12	2638.49	2739.35	2746.16	2966.43	3336.16	4069.31
2000	3940.35	4696.69	4572.83	3860.66	3400.91	3966.11	3766.99	4206.35	3672.82	3369.63	2597.93	2470.52
2001	2772.73	2151.83	1840.26	2116.24	2110.49	2160.54	2027.13	1805.43	1498.80	1690.20	1930.58	1950.40
2002	1934.03	1731.49	1845.35	1688.23	1615.73	1463.21	1328.26	1314.85	1172.06	1329.75	1478.78	1335.51
2003	1320.91	1337.52	1341.17	1464.31	1595.91	1622.80	1735.02	1810.45	1786.94	1932.21	1960.26	2003.37
2004	2066.15	2029.82	1994.22	1920.15	1986.74	2047.79	1887.36	1838.10	1896.84	1974.99	2096.81	2175.44
2005	2062.41	2051.72	1999.23	1921.65	2068.22	2056.96	2184.83	2152.09	2151.69	2120.30	2232.82	2205.32
2006	2305.82	2281.39	2339.79	2322.57	2178.88	2172.09	2091.47	2183.75	2258.43	2366.71	2431.77	2415.29
2007	2463.93	2416.15	2421.64	2525.09	2604.52	2603.23	2545.57	2596.36	2701.50	2859.12	2660.96	2652.28
2008	2389.86	2271.48	2279.10	2412.80	2522.66	2292.98	2325.55	2367.52	2091.88	1720.95	1535.57	1577.03
2009	1476.42	1377.84	1528.59	1717.30	1774.33	1835.04	1978.50	2009.06	2122.42	2045.11	2144.60	2269.15
2010	2147.35	2238.26	2397.96	2461.19								

158 *Based on NASDAQ composite, prior to February 5, 1971, based on National Quotation Bureau indices.*

	Jan	Feb	Mar	Apr	May	Jun	Jul	Aug	Sep	Oct	Nov	Dec	Year's Change
1979	4.2	-3.5	6.0	0.3	-2.2	4.3	1.1	5.6	0.02	-7.1	5.1	2.1	16.1
1980	5.9	-0.5	-11.5	4.6	5.0	3.2	6.4	1.1	2.6	1.8	10.1	-3.9	25.6
1981	-4.6	1.0	3.8	-1.9	0.2	-1.2	-0.1	-6.2	-6.4	5.4	4.0	-3.3	-9.7
1982	-2.7	-5.9	-1.3	3.9	-3.6	-2.6	-2.3	11.3	1.2	11.3	4.0	1.3	13.7
1983	3.2	2.1	3.2	7.1	-0.2	3.7	-3.2	0.5	1.3	-2.4	2.0	-1.2	17.0
1984	-1.9	-4.4	1.1	0.3	-5.9	2.1	-1.8	10.8	-0.2	-0.1	-1.4	2.2	-0.1
1985	7.8	1.1	-0.4	-0.3	5.4	1.6	-0.8	-1.0	-3.9	4.5	6.5	4.1	26.7
1986	0.9	7.2	5.1	-1.3	5.0	1.4	-5.9	6.8	-8.5	5.1	1.4	-3.0	13.6
1987	12.7	4.0	1.9	-1.8	0.4	4.5	4.2	3.8	-2.4	-21.9	-8.0	7.2	0.02
1988	4.3	4.4	-2.9	0.7	0.2	4.8	-0.9	-3.3	3.9	2.0	-2.0	1.7	13.1
1989	6.8	-2.5	2.0	4.9	3.8	-0.8	8.2	1.7	-0.5	-2.8	1.5	1.8	25.9
1990	-7.4	1.2	2.2	-2.8	8.9	-0.7	-1.1	-9.6	-5.3	-0.8	6.4	2.7	-7.5
1991	4.5	6.9	2.5	-0.1	3.8	-4.7	4.6	2.2	-1.5	1.4	-4.1	11.2	28.8
1992	-1.4	0.9	-2.4	2.3	0.3	-1.9	4.1	-2.5	1.0	0.7	3.5	1.4	5.9
1993	0.7	0.6	2.2	-2.8	2.4	0.4	-0.4	3.5	-0.5	1.2	-1.7	1.6	7.3
1994	2.9	-2.9	-4.5	1.1	1.0	-2.9	3.1	3.9	-2.6	1.7	-3.9	1.2	-2.4
1995	2.4	3.8	2.3	2.5	3.5	2.4	3.7	0.5	3.9	-0.6	4.2	1.4	34.4
1996	3.1	1.1	0.7	1.4	2.1	-0.1	-4.9	2.5	5.5	2.1	7.1	-1.8	19.7
1997	5.8	0.2	-4.6	5.3	6.2	4.0	8.0	-4.9	5.4	-3.4	4.2	1.9	30.5
1998	0.6	7.0	4.9	0.9	-2.3	3.6	-1.3	-15.1	6.5	7.8	6.1	6.2	25.1
1999	3.5	-3.3	3.7	4.2	-2.3	5.1	-3.2	-1.0	-2.8	6.5	2.5	6.0	19.5
2000	-4.2	-0.4	8.9	-3.3	-2.7	2.5	-1.8	7.4	-4.8	-1.2	-9.3	1.1	-8.8
2001	3.2	-9.5	-6.7	8.0	0.5	-2.4	-1.4	-6.2	-8.6	2.0	7.5	0.9	-13.6
2002	-1.4	-2.1	4.0	-5.8	-1.0	-7.5	-7.5	0.3	-10.9	8.1	5.7	-5.8	-22.9
2003	-2.5	-1.7	0.9	7.9	5.5	1.2	1.8	1.9	-1.2	5.7	1.0	4.6	27.5
2004	1.8	1.2	-1.5	-1.9	1.3	1.7	-3.6	0.3	1.1	1.5	4.1	3.5	9.5
2005	-2.6	2.0	-1.7	-2.0	3.4	0.3	3.8	-1.1	0.8	-1.9	3.5	0.01	4.4
2006	2.7	0.01	1.3	1.1	-3.2	0.003	0.1	2.2	2.3	3.3	1.9	1.1	13.3
2007	1.8	-1.9	0.9	4.1	3.4	-2.0	-3.2	1.2	3.7	1.6	-4.5	-0.8	3.9
2008	-6.1	-3.3	-0.8	5.0	1.6	-8.5	-1.3	1.2	-9.7	-17.6	-7.9	1.3	-39.0
2009	-8.3	-10.7	8.5	10.0	5.3	0.1	7.5	3.4	3.9	-2.3	5.6	2.3	25.5
2010	-3.7	3.1	6.0	1.8									
TOTALS	32.0	-4.8	33.8	53.4	45.8	11.6	11.9	21.2	-26.7	11.6	55.1	49.0	
AVG.	1.0	-0.1	1.1	1.7	1.5	0.4	0.4	0.7	-0.9	0.4	1.8	1.6	
# Up	20	18	21	21	22	19	13	21	15	19	22	24	
# Down	12	14	11	11	9	12	18	10	16	12	9	7	

	Jan	Feb	Mar	Apr	May	Jun	Jul	Aug	Sep	Oct	Nov	Dec
1979	53.76	51.88	54.97	55.15	53.92	56.25	56.86	60.04	60.05	55.78	58.65	59.87
1980	63.40	63.07	55.79	58.38	61.31	63.27	67.30	68.05	69.84	71.08	78.26	75.20
1981	71.75	72.49	75.21	73.77	73.90	73.01	72.92	68.42	64.06	67.54	70.23	67.93
1982	66.12	62.21	61.43	63.85	61.53	59.92	58.54	65.14	65.89	73.34	76.28	77.24
1983	79.75	81.45	84.06	90.04	89.89	93.18	90.18	90.65	91.85	89.69	91.50	90.38
1984	88.69	84.76	85.73	86.00	80.94	82.61	81.13	89.87	89.67	89.62	88.36	90.31
1985	97.31	98.38	98.03	97.72	103.02	104.65	103.78	102.76	98.75	103.16	109.91	114.39
1986	115.39	123.71	130.07	128.44	134.82	136.75	128.74	137.43	125.70	132.11	133.97	130.00
1987	146.48	152.29	155.20	152.39	152.94	159.04	166.57	172.95	168.83	131.89	121.28	130.02
1988	135.55	141.54	137.45	138.37	138.66	145.31	143.99	139.26	144.68	147.55	144.59	146.99
1989	156.93	152.98	155.99	163.63	169.85	168.49	182.27	185.33	184.40	179.17	181.85	185.11
1990	171.44	173.43	177.28	172.32	187.66	186.29	184.32	166.69	157.83	156.62	166.69	171.22
1991	179.00	191.34	196.15	195.94	203.32	193.78	202.67	207.18	204.02	206.96	198.46	220.61
1992	217.52	219.50	214.29	219.13	219.71	215.60	224.37	218.86	221.15	222.65	230.44	233.59
1993	235.25	236.67	241.80	235.13	240.80	241.78	240.78	249.20	247.95	250.97	246.70	250.71
1994	258.08	250.52	239.19	241.71	244.13	237.11	244.44	254.04	247.49	251.62	241.82	244.65
1995	250.52	260.08	266.11	272.81	282.48	289.29	299.98	301.40	313.28	311.37	324.36	328.89
1996	338.97	342.56	345.01	349.84	357.35	357.10	339.44	347.79	366.77	374.38	401.05	393.75
1997	416.77	417.46	398.19	419.15	445.06	462.95	499.89	475.33	500.78	483.86	504.25	513.79
1998	517.02	553.14	580.31	585.46	572.16	592.57	584.97	496.66	529.11	570.63	605.31	642.87
1999	665.64	643.67	667.49	695.25	679.10	713.61	690.51	683.27	663.83	707.19	724.66	767.97
2000	736.08	733.04	797.99	771.58	750.98	769.68	755.57	811.17	772.60	763.06	692.40	700.09
2001	722.55	654.25	610.36	658.90	662.39	646.64	637.43	597.67	546.46	557.29	599.32	604.94
2002	596.66	583.88	607.35	572.04	566.18	523.72	484.39	486.08	433.22	468.51	495.00	466.18
2003	454.30	446.37	450.35	486.09	512.92	518.94	528.53	538.40	532.15	562.51	568.32	594.56
2004	605.21	612.58	603.42	591.83	599.40	609.31	587.21	589.09	595.66	604.51	629.26	650.99
2005	633.99	646.93	635.78	623.32	644.28	645.92	670.26	663.13	668.53	656.09	679.35	679.42
2006	697.79	697.83	706.74	714.37	691.78	691.80	692.59	707.55	723.48	747.30	761.43	770.08
2007	784.11	768.92	775.97	807.82	835.14	818.17	792.11	801.22	830.59	844.20	806.44	799.82
2008	750.97	726.42	720.32	756.03	768.28	703.22	694.07	702.17	634.08	522.47	481.43	487.77
2009	447.32	399.61	433.67	476.84	501.95	502.27	539.88	558.21	579.97	566.50	598.41	612.01
2010	589.41	607.45	643.79	655.06								

RUSSELL 2000 INDEX MONTHLY PERCENT CHANGES SINCE 1979

	Jan	Feb	Mar	Apr	May	Jun	Jul	Aug	Sep	Oct	Nov	Dec	Year's Change
1979	9.0	-3.2	9.7	2.3	-1.8	5.3	2.9	7.8	-0.7	-11.3	8.1	6.6	38.0
1980	8.2	-2.1	-18.5	6.0	8.0	4.0	11.0	6.5	2.9	3.9	7.0	-3.7	33.8
1981	-0.6	0.3	7.7	2.5	3.0	-2.5	-2.6	-8.0	-8.6	8.2	2.8	-2.0	-1.5
1982	-3.7	-5.3	-1.5	5.1	-3.2	-4.0	-1.7	7.5	3.6	14.1	8.8	1.1	20.7
1983	7.5	6.0	2.5	7.2	7.0	4.4	-3.0	-4.0	1.6	-7.0	5.0	-2.1	26.3
1984	-1.8	-5.9	0.4	-0.7	-5.4	2.6	-5.0	11.5	-1.0	-2.0	-2.9	1.4	-9.6
1985	13.1	2.4	-2.2	-1.4	3.4	1.0	2.7	-1.2	-6.2	3.6	6.8	4.2	28.0
1986	1.5	7.0	4.7	1.4	3.3	-0.2	-9.5	3.0	-6.3	3.9	-0.5	-3.1	4.0
1987	11.5	8.2	2.4	-3.0	-0.5	2.3	2.8	2.9	-2.0	-30.8	-5.5	7.8	-10.8
1988	4.0	8.7	4.4	2.0	-2.5	7.0	-0.9	-2.8	2.3	-1.2	-3.6	3.8	22.4
1989	4.4	0.5	2.2	4.3	4.2	-2.4	4.2	2.1	0.01	-6.0	0.4	0.1	14.2
1990	-8.9	2.9	3.7	-3.4	6.8	0.1	-4.5	-13.6	-9.2	-6.2	7.3	3.7	-21.5
1991	9.1	11.0	6.9	-0.2	4.5	-6.0	3.1	3.7	0.6	2.7	-4.7	7.7	43.7
1992	8.0	2.9	-3.5	-3.7	1.2	-5.0	3.2	-3.1	2.2	3.1	7.5	3.4	16.4
1993	3.2	-2.5	3.1	-2.8	4.3	0.5	1.3	4.1	2.7	2.5	-3.4	3.3	17.0
1994	3.1	-0.4	-5.4	0.6	-1.3	-3.6	1.6	5.4	-0.5	-0.4	-4.2	2.5	-3.2
1995	-1.4	3.9	1.6	2.1	1.5	5.0	5.7	1.9	1.7	-4.6	4.2	2.4	26.2
1996	-0.2	3.0	1.8	5.3	3.9	-4.2	-8.8	5.7	3.7	-1.7	4.0	2.4	14.8
1997	1.9	-2.5	-4.9	0.1	11.0	4.1	4.6	2.2	7.2	-4.5	-0.8	1.7	20.5
1998	-1.6	7.4	4.1	0.5	-5.4	0.2	-8.2	-19.5	7.6	4.0	5.2	6.1	-3.4
1999	1.2	-8.2	1.4	8.8	1.4	4.3	-2.8	-3.8	-0.1	0.3	5.9	11.2	19.6
2000	-1.7	16.4	-6.7	-6.1	-5.9	8.6	-3.2	7.4	-3.1	-4.5	-10.4	8.4	-4.2
2001	5.1	-6.7	-5.0	7.7	2.3	3.3	-5.4	-3.3	-13.6	5.8	7.6	6.0	1.0
2002	-1.1	-2.8	7.9	0.8	-4.5	-5.1	-15.2	-0.4	-7.3	3.1	8.8	-5.7	-21.6
2003	-2.9	-3.1	1.1	9.4	10.6	1.7	6.2	4.5	-2.0	8.3	3.5	1.9	45.4
2004	4.3	0.8	0.8	-5.2	1.5	4.1	-6.8	-0.6	4.6	1.9	8.6	2.8	17.0
2005	-4.2	1.6	-3.0	-5.8	6.4	3.7	6.3	-1.9	0.2	-3.2	4.7	-0.6	3.3
2006	8.9	-0.3	4.7	-0.1	-5.7	0.5	-3.3	2.9	0.7	5.7	2.5	0.2	17.0
2007	1.6	-0.9	0.9	1.7	4.0	-1.6	-6.9	2.2	1.6	2.8	-7.3	-0.2	-2.7
2008	-6.9	-3.8	0.3	4.1	4.5	-7.8	3.6	3.5	-8.1	-20.9	-12.0	5.6	-34.8
2009	-11.2	-12.3	8.7	15.3	2.9	1.3	9.5	2.8	5.6	-6.9	3.0	7.9	25.2
2010	-3.7	4.4	8.0	5.6									
TOTALS	55.7	27.4	38.3	60.4	59.5	21.6	-19.1	25.4	-19.9	-37.3	56.4	84.8	
AVG.	1.7	0.9	1.2	1.9	1.9	0.7	-0.6	0.8	-0.6	-1.2	1.8	2.7	
# Up	18	17	23	21	21	20	15	19	17	16	20	24	
# Down	14	15	9	11	10	11	16	12	14	15	11	7	

RUSSELL 2000 INDEX MONTHLY CLOSING PRICES SINCE 1979

	Jan	Feb	Mar	Apr	May	Jun	Jul	Aug	Sep	Oct	Nov	Dec
1979	44.18	42.78	46.94	48.00	47.13	49.62	51.08	55.05	54.68	48.51	52.43	55.91
1980	60.50	59.22	48.27	51.18	55.26	57.47	63.81	67.97	69.94	72.64	77.70	74.80
1981	74.33	74.52	80.25	82.25	84.72	82.56	80.41	73.94	67.55	73.06	75.14	73.67
1982	70.96	67.21	66.21	69.59	67.39	64.67	63.59	68.38	70.84	80.86	87.96	88.90
1983	95.53	101.23	103.77	111.20	118.94	124.17	120.43	115.60	117.43	109.17	114.66	112.27
1984	110.21	103.72	104.10	103.34	97.75	100.30	95.25	106.21	105.17	103.07	100.11	101.49
1985	114.77	117.54	114.92	113.35	117.26	118.38	121.56	120.10	112.65	116.73	124.62	129.87
1986	131.78	141.00	147.63	149.66	154.61	154.23	139.65	143.83	134.73	139.95	139.26	135.00
1987	150.48	162.84	166.79	161.82	161.02	164.75	169.42	174.25	170.81	118.26	111.70	120.42
1988	125.24	136.10	142.15	145.01	141.37	151.30	149.89	145.74	149.08	147.25	142.01	147.37
1989	153.84	154.56	157.89	164.68	171.53	167.42	174.50	178.20	178.21	167.47	168.17	168.30
1990	153.27	157.72	163.63	158.09	168.91	169.04	161.51	139.52	126.70	118.83	127.50	132.16
1991	144.17	160.00	171.01	170.61	178.34	167.61	172.76	179.11	180.16	185.00	176.37	189.94
1992	205.16	211.15	203.69	196.25	198.52	188.64	194.74	188.79	192.92	198.90	213.81	221.01
1993	228.10	222.41	229.21	222.68	232.19	233.35	236.46	246.19	252.95	259.18	250.41	258.59
1994	266.52	265.53	251.06	252.55	249.28	240.29	244.06	257.32	256.12	255.02	244.25	250.36
1995	246.85	256.57	260.77	266.17	270.25	283.63	299.72	305.31	310.38	296.25	308.58	315.97
1996	315.38	324.93	330.77	348.28	361.85	346.61	316.00	333.88	346.39	340.57	354.11	362.61
1997	369.45	360.05	342.56	343.00	380.76	396.37	414.48	423.43	453.82	433.26	429.92	437.02
1998	430.05	461.83	480.68	482.89	456.62	457.39	419.75	337.95	363.59	378.16	397.75	421.96
1999	427.22	392.26	397.63	432.81	438.68	457.68	444.77	427.83	427.30	428.64	454.08	504.75
2000	496.23	577.71	539.09	506.25	476.18	517.23	500.64	537.89	521.37	497.68	445.94	483.53
2001	508.34	474.37	450.53	485.32	496.50	512.64	484.78	468.56	404.87	428.17	460.78	488.50
2002	483.10	469.36	506.46	510.67	487.47	462.64	392.42	390.96	362.27	373.50	406.35	383.09
2003	372.17	360.52	364.54	398.68	441.00	448.37	476.02	497.42	487.68	528.22	546.51	556.91
2004	580.76	585.56	590.31	559.80	568.28	591.52	551.29	547.93	572.94	583.79	633.77	651.57
2005	624.02	634.06	615.07	579.38	616.71	639.66	679.75	666.51	667.80	646.61	677.29	673.22
2006	733.20	730.64	765.14	764.54	721.01	724.67	700.56	720.53	725.59	766.84	786.12	787.66
2007	800.34	793.30	800.71	814.57	847.19	833.69	776.13	792.86	805.45	828.02	767.77	766.03
2008	713.30	686.18	687.97	716.18	748.28	689.66	714.52	739.50	679.58	537.52	473.14	499.45
2009	443.53	389.02	422.75	487.56	501.58	508.28	556.71	572.07	604.28	562.77	579.73	625.39
2010	602.04	628.56	678.64	716.60								

10 BEST DAYS BY PERCENT AND POINT

	BY PERCENT CHANGE				BY POINT CHANGE		
DAY	CLOSE	PNT CHANGE	% CHANGE	DAY	CLOSE	PNT CHANGE	% CHANGE
DJIA 1901 to 1949							
3/15/33	62.10	8.26	15.3	10/30/29	258.47	28.40	12.3
10/6/31	99.34	12.86	14.9	11/14/29	217.28	18.59	9.4
10/30/29	258.47	28.40	12.3	10/5/29	341.36	16.19	5.0
9/21/32	75.16	7.67	11.4	10/31/29	273.51	15.04	5.8
8/3/32	58.22	5.06	9.5	10/6/31	99.34	12.86	14.9
2/11/32	78.60	6.80	9.5	11/15/29	228.73	11.45	5.3
11/14/29	217.28	18.59	9.4	6/19/30	228.97	10.13	4.6
12/18/31	80.69	6.90	9.4	9/5/39	148.12	10.03	7.3
2/13/32	85.82	7.22	9.2	11/22/28	290.34	9.81	3.5
5/6/32	59.01	4.91	9.1	10/1/30	214.14	9.24	4.5
DJIA 1950 to APRIL 2010							
10/13/08	9387.61	936.42	11.1	10/13/08	9387.61	936.42	11.1
10/28/08	9065.12	889.35	10.9	10/28/08	9065.12	889.35	10.9
10/21/87	2027.85	186.84	10.2	11/13/08	8835.25	552.59	6.7
3/23/09	7775.86	497.48	6.8	3/16/00	10630.60	499.19	4.9
11/13/08	8835.25	552.59	6.7	3/23/09	7775.86	497.48	6.8
11/21/08	8046.42	494.13	6.5	11/21/08	8046.42	494.13	6.5
7/24/02	8191.29	488.95	6.4	7/24/02	8191.29	488.95	6.4
10/20/87	1841.01	102.27	5.9	9/30/08	10850.66	485.21	4.7
3/10/09	6926.49	379.44	5.8	7/29/02	8711.88	447.49	5.4
7/29/02	8711.88	447.49	5.4	3/18/08	12392.66	420.41	3.0
S&P 500 1930 to APRIL 2010							
3/15/33	6.81	0.97	16.6	10/13/08	1003.35	104.13	11.6
10/6/31	9.91	1.09	12.4	10/28/08	940.51	91.59	10.8
9/21/32	8.52	0.90	11.8	3/16/00	1458.47	66.32	4.8
10/13/08	1003.35	104.13	11.6	1/3/01	1347.56	64.29	5.0
10/28/08	940.51	91.59	10.8	9/30/08	1166.36	59.97	5.4
2/16/35	10.00	0.94	10.4	11/13/08	911.29	58.99	6.9
8/17/35	11.70	1.08	10.2	3/23/09	822.92	54.38	7.1
3/16/35	9.05	0.82	10.0	3/18/08	1330.74	54.14	4.2
9/12/38	12.06	1.06	9.6	11/24/08	851.81	51.78	6.5
9/5/39	12.64	1.11	9.6	12/5/00	1376.54	51.57	3.9
NASDAQ 1971 to APRIL 2010							
1/3/01	2616.69	324.83	14.2	1/3/01	2616.69	324.83	14.2
10/13/08	1844.25	194.74	11.8	12/5/00	2889.80	274.05	10.5
12/5/00	2889.80	274.05	10.5	4/18/00	3793.57	254.41	7.2
10/28/08	1649.47	143.57	9.5	5/30/00	3459.48	254.37	7.9
4/5/01	1785.00	146.20	8.9	10/19/00	3418.60	247.04	7.8
4/18/01	2079.44	156.22	8.1	10/13/00	3316.77	242.09	7.9
5/30/00	3459.48	254.37	7.9	6/2/00	3813.38	230.88	6.4
10/13/00	3316.77	242.09	7.9	4/25/00	3711.23	228.75	6.6
10/19/00	3418.60	247.04	7.8	4/17/00	3539.16	217.87	6.6
5/8/02	1696.29	122.47	7.8	10/13/08	1844.25	194.74	11.8
RUSSELL 1000 1979 to APRIL 2010							
10/13/08	542.98	56.75	11.7	10/13/08	542.98	56.75	11.7
10/28/08	503.74	47.68	10.5	10/28/08	503.74	47.68	10.5
10/21/87	135.85	11.15	8.9	3/16/00	777.86	36.60	4.9
3/23/09	446.90	29.36	7.0	1/3/01	712.63	35.74	5.3
11/13/08	489.83	31.99	7.0	11/13/08	489.83	31.99	7.0
11/24/08	456.14	28.26	6.6	9/30/08	634.08	31.74	5.3
3/10/09	391.01	23.46	6.4	12/5/00	728.44	30.36	4.4
11/21/08	427.88	24.97	6.2	3/23/09	446.90	29.36	7.0
7/24/02	448.05	23.87	5.6	3/18/08	723.59	29.05	4.2
7/29/02	477.61	24.69	5.5	11/24/08	456.14	28.26	6.6
RUSSELL 2000 1979 to APRIL 2010							
10/13/08	570.89	48.41	9.3	10/13/08	570.89	48.41	9.3
11/13/08	491.23	38.43	8.5	9/18/08	723.68	47.30	7.0
3/23/09	433.72	33.61	8.4	11/13/08	491.23	38.43	8.5
10/21/87	130.65	9.26	7.6	10/16/08	536.57	34.46	6.9
10/28/08	482.55	34.15	7.6	10/28/08	482.55	34.15	7.6
11/24/08	436.80	30.26	7.4	3/23/09	433.72	33.61	8.4
3/10/09	367.75	24.49	7.1	3/18/08	681.93	31.45	4.8
9/18/08	723.68	47.30	7.0	9/18/07	806.63	30.82	4.0
10/16/08	536.57	34.46	6.9	12/16/08	482.85	30.28	6.7
10/30/87	118.26	7.46	6.7	11/24/08	436.80	30.26	7.4

10 <u>WORST</u> DAYS BY PERCENT AND POINT

	BY PERCENT CHANGE				BY POINT CHANGE		
DAY	CLOSE	PNT CHANGE	% CHANGE	DAY	CLOSE	PNT CHANGE	% CHANGE
DJIA 1901 to 1949							
10/28/29	260.64	−38.33	−12.8	10/28/29	260.64	−38.33	−12.8
10/29/29	230.07	−30.57	−11.7	10/29/29	230.07	−30.57	−11.7
11/6/29	232.13	−25.55	−9.9	11/6/29	232.13	−25.55	−9.9
8/12/32	63.11	−5.79	−8.4	10/23/29	305.85	−20.66	−6.3
3/14/07	55.84	−5.05	−8.3	11/11/29	220.39	−16.14	−6.8
7/21/33	88.71	−7.55	−7.8	11/4/29	257.68	−15.83	−5.8
10/18/37	125.73	−10.57	−7.8	12/12/29	243.14	−15.30	−5.9
2/1/17	88.52	−6.91	−7.2	10/3/29	329.95	−14.55	−4.2
10/5/32	66.07	−5.09	−7.2	6/16/30	230.05	−14.20	−5.8
9/24/31	107.79	−8.20	−7.1	8/9/29	337.99	−14.11	−4.0
DJIA 1950 to APRIL 2010							
10/19/87	1738.74	−508.00	−22.6	9/29/08	10365.45	−777.68	−7.0
10/26/87	1793.93	−156.83	−8.0	10/15/08	8577.91	−733.08	−7.9
10/15/08	8577.91	−733.08	−7.9	9/17/01	8920.70	−684.81	−7.1
12/1/08	8149.09	−679.95	−7.7	12/1/08	8149.09	−679.95	−7.7
10/9/08	8579.19	−678.91	−7.3	10/9/08	8579.19	−678.91	−7.3
10/27/97	7161.15	−554.26	−7.2	4/14/00	10305.77	−617.78	−5.7
9/17/01	8920.70	−684.81	−7.1	10/27/97	7161.15	−554.26	−7.2
9/29/08	10365.45	−777.68	−7.0	10/22/08	8519.21	−514.45	−5.7
10/13/89	2569.26	−190.58	−6.9	8/31/98	7539.07	−512.61	−6.4
1/8/88	1911.31	−140.58	−6.9	10/7/08	9447.11	−508.39	−5.1
S&P 500 1930 to APRIL 2010							
10/19/87	224.84	−57.86	−20.5	9/29/08	1106.39	−106.62	−8.8
3/18/35	8.14	−0.91	−10.1	10/15/08	907.84	−90.17	−9.0
4/16/35	8.22	−0.91	−10.0	4/14/00	1356.56	−83.95	−5.8
9/3/46	15.00	−1.65	−9.9	12/1/08	816.21	−80.03	−8.9
10/18/37	10.76	−1.10	−9.3	10/9/08	909.92	−75.02	−7.6
10/15/08	907.84	−90.17	−9.0	8/31/98	957.28	−69.86	−6.8
12/1/08	816.21	−80.03	−8.9	10/27/97	876.99	−64.65	−6.9
7/20/33	10.57	−1.03	−8.9	10/7/08	996.23	−60.66	−5.7
9/29/08	1106.39	−106.62	−8.8	9/15/08	1192.70	−59.00	−4.7
7/21/33	9.65	−0.92	−8.7	10/22/08	896.78	−58.27	−6.1
NASDAQ 1971 to APRIL 2010							
10/19/87	360.21	−46.12	−11.4	4/14/00	3321.29	−355.49	−9.7
4/14/00	3321.29	−355.49	−9.7	4/3/00	4223.68	−349.15	−7.6
9/29/08	1983.73	−199.61	−9.1	4/12/00	3769.63	−286.27	−7.1
10/26/87	298.90	−29.55	−9.0	4/10/00	4188.20	−258.25	−5.8
10/20/87	327.79	−32.42	−9.0	1/4/00	3901.69	−229.46	5.6
12/1/08	1398.07	−137.50	−9.0	3/14/00	4706.63	−200.61	−4.1
8/31/98	1499.25	−140.43	−8.6	5/10/00	3384.73	−200.28	−5.6
10/15/08	1628.33	−150.68	−8.5	5/23/00	3164.55	−199.66	−5.9
4/3/00	4223.68	−349.15	−7.6	9/29/08	1983.73	−199.61	−9.1
1/2/01	2291.86	−178.66	−7.2	10/25/00	3229.57	−190.22	−5.6
RUSSELL 1000 1979 to APRIL 2010							
10/19/87	121.04	−28.40	−19.0	9/29/08	602.34	−57.35	−8.7
10/15/08	489.71	−49.11	−9.1	10/15/08	489.71	−49.11	−9.1
12/1/08	437.75	−43.68	−9.1	4/14/00	715.20	−45.74	−6.0
9/29/08	602.34	−57.35	−8.7	12/1/08	437.75	−43.68	−9.1
10/26/87	119.45	−10.74	−8.3	10/9/08	492.13	−40.05	−7.5
10/9/08	492.13	−40.05	−7.5	8/31/98	496.66	−35.77	−6.7
11/20/08	402.91	−29.62	−6.9	10/27/97	465.44	−32.96	−6.6
8/31/98	496.66	−35.77	−6.7	10/7/08	538.15	−32.64	−5.7
10/27/97	465.44	−32.96	−6.6	9/15/08	650.57	−32.15	−4.7
11/19/08	432.53	−28.80	−6.2	10/22/08	484.08	−31.56	−6.1
RUSSELL 2000 1979 to APRIL 2010							
10/19/87	133.60	−19.14	−12.5	12/1/08	417.07	−56.07	−11.9
12/1/08	417.07	−56.07	−11.9	10/15/08	502.11	−52.54	−9.5
10/15/08	502.11	−52.54	−9.5	10/9/08	499.20	−47.37	−8.7
10/26/87	110.33	−11.26	−9.3	9/29/08	657.72	−47.07	−6.7
10/20/87	121.39	−12.21	−9.1	10/7/08	558.95	−36.96	−6.2
10/9/08	499.20	−47.37	−8.7	4/14/00	453.72	−35.50	−7.3
11/19/08	412.38	−35.13	−7.9	11/19/08	412.38	−35.13	−7.9
4/14/00	453.72	−35.50	−7.3	11/14/08	456.52	−34.71	−7.1
11/14/08	456.52	−34.71	−7.1	9/17/08	676.38	−34.27	−4.8
1/20/09	433.65	−32.80	−7.0	10/2/08	637.67	−33.92	−5.1

10 <u>BEST</u> WEEKS BY PERCENT AND POINT

WEEK ENDS	BY PERCENT CHANGE CLOSE	PNT CHANGE	% CHANGE	WEEK ENDS	BY POINT CHANGE CLOSE	PNT CHANGE	% CHANGE
			DJIA 1901 to 1949				
8/6/32	66.56	12.30	22.7	12/7/29	263.46	24.51	10.3
6/25/38	131.94	18.71	16.5	6/25/38	131.94	18.71	16.5
2/13/32	85.82	11.37	15.3	6/27/31	156.93	17.97	12.9
4/22/33	72.24	9.36	14.9	11/22/29	245.74	17.01	7.4
10/10/31	105.61	12.84	13.8	8/17/29	360.70	15.86	4.6
7/30/32	54.26	6.42	13.4	12/22/28	285.94	15.22	5.6
6/27/31	156.93	17.97	12.9	8/24/29	375.44	14.74	4.1
9/24/32	74.83	8.39	12.6	2/21/29	310.06	14.21	4.8
8/27/32	75.61	8.43	12.6	5/10/30	272.01	13.70	5.3
3/18/33	60.56	6.72	12.5	11/15/30	186.68	13.54	7.8
			DJIA 1950 to APRIL 2010				
10/11/74	658.17	73.61	12.6	10/31/08	9325.01	946.06	11.3
10/31/08	9325.01	946.06	11.3	11/28/08	8829.04	782.62	9.7
8/20/82	869.29	81.24	10.3	3/17/00	10595.23	666.41	6.7
11/28/08	8829.04	782.62	9.7	3/21/03	8521.97	662.26	8.4
3/13/09	7223.98	597.04	9.0	9/28/01	8847.56	611.75	7.4
10/8/82	986.85	79.11	8.7	7/17/09	8743.94	597.42	7.3
3/21/03	8521.97	662.26	8.4	3/13/09	7223.98	597.04	9.0
8/3/84	1202.08	87.46	7.9	7/2/99	11139.24	586.68	5.6
9/28/01	8847.56	611.75	7.4	4/20/00	10844.05	538.28	5.2
7/17/09	8743.94	597.42	7.3	2/1/08	12743.19	536.02	4.4
			S&P 500 1930 to APRIL 2010				
8/6/32	7.22	1.12	18.4	6/2/00	1477.26	99.24	7.2
6/25/38	11.39	1.72	17.8	11/28/08	896.24	96.21	12.0
7/30/32	6.10	0.89	17.1	10/31/08	968.75	91.98	10.5
4/22/33	7.75	1.09	16.4	4/20/00	1434.54	77.98	5.8
10/11/74	71.14	8.80	14.1	7/2/99	1391.22	75.91	5.8
2/13/32	8.80	1.08	14.0	3/3/00	1409.17	75.81	5.7
9/24/32	8.52	1.02	13.6	9/28/01	1040.94	75.14	7.8
10/10/31	10.64	1.27	13.6	3/13/09	756.55	73.17	10.7
8/27/32	8.57	1.01	13.4	10/16/98	1056.42	72.10	7.3
3/18/33	6.61	0.77	13.2	3/17/00	1464.47	69.40	5.0
			NASDAQ 1971 to APRIL 2010				
6/2/00	3813.38	608.27	19.0	6/2/00	3813.38	608.27	19.0
4/12/01	1961.43	241.07	14.0	2/4/00	4244.14	357.07	9.2
11/28/08	1535.57	151.22	10.9	3/3/00	4914.79	324.29	7.1
10/31/08	1720.95	168.92	10.9	4/20/00	3643.88	322.59	9.7
3/13/09	1431.50	137.65	10.6	12/8/00	2917.43	272.14	10.3
4/20/01	2163.41	201.98	10.3	4/12/01	1961.43	241.07	14.0
12/8/00	2917.43	272.14	10.3	7/14/00	4246.18	222.98	5.5
4/20/00	3643.88	322.59	9.7	1/12/01	2626.50	218.85	9.1
10/11/74	60.42	5.26	9.5	4/28/00	3860.66	216.78	6.0
2/4/00	4244.14	357.07	9.0	12/23/99	3969.44	216.38	5.8
			RUSSELL 1000 1979 to APRIL 2010				
11/28/08	481.43	53.55	12.5	6/2/00	786.02	57.93	8.0
10/31/08	522.47	50.94	10.8	11/28/08	481.43	53.55	12.5
3/13/09	411.10	39.88	10.7	10/31/08	522.47	50.94	10.8
8/20/82	61.51	4.83	8.5	4/20/00	757.32	42.12	5.9
6/2/00	785.02	57.93	8.0	3/3/00	756.41	41.55	5.8
9/28/01	546.46	38.48	7.6	3/13/09	411.10	39.88	10.7
10/16/98	546.09	38.45	7.6	7/2/99	723.25	38.80	5.7
8/3/84	87.43	6.13	7.5	9/28/01	546.46	38.48	7.6
3/21/03	474.58	32.69	7.4	10/16/98	546.09	38.45	7.6
10/8/82	71.55	4.90	7.4	2/1/08	761.15	36.97	5.1
			RUSSELL 2000 1979 to APRIL 2010				
11/28/08	473.14	66.60	16.4	11/28/08	473.14	66.60	16.4
10/31/08	537.52	66.40	14.1	10/31/08	537.52	66.40	14.1
6/2/00	513.03	55.66	12.2	6/2/00	513.03	55.66	12.2
3/13/09	393.09	42.04	12.0	3/13/09	393.09	42.04	12.0
7/17/09	519.22	38.24	8.0	2/1/08	730.50	41.90	6.1
10/16/98	342.87	24.47	7.7	3/3/00	597.88	41.14	7.4
12/18/87	116.94	8.31	7.7	10/5/07	844.87	39.42	4.9
3/3/00	597.88	41.14	7.4	7/17/09	519.22	38.24	8.0
3/27/09	429.00	28.89	7.2	3/5/10	666.02	37.46	6.0
10/23/98	367.05	24.18	7.1	10/9/09	614.92	34.72	6.0

10 <u>WORST</u> WEEKS BY PERCENT AND POINT

	BY PERCENT CHANGE					BY POINT CHANGE		
WEEK ENDS	CLOSE	PNT CHANGE	% CHANGE		WEEK ENDS	CLOSE	PNT CHANGE	% CHANGE
DJIA 1901 to 1949								
7/22/33	88.42	−17.68	−16.7		11/8/29	236.53	−36.98	−13.5
5/18/40	122.43	−22.42	−15.5		12/8/28	257.33	−33.47	−11.5
10/8/32	61.17	−10.92	−15.2		6/21/30	215.30	−28.95	−11.9
10/3/31	92.77	−14.59	−13.6		10/19/29	323.87	−28.82	−8.2
11/8/29	236.53	−36.98	−13.5		5/3/30	258.31	−27.15	−9.5
9/17/32	66.44	−10.10	−13.2		10/31/29	273.51	−25.46	−8.5
10/21/33	83.64	−11.95	−12.5		10/26/29	298.97	−24.90	−7.7
12/12/31	78.93	−11.21	−12.4		5/18/40	122.43	−22.42	−15.5
5/8/15	62.77	−8.74	−12.2		2/8/29	301.53	−18.23	−5.7
6/21/30	215.30	−28.95	−11.9		10/11/30	193.05	−18.05	−8.6
DJIA 1950 to APRIL 2010								
10/10/08	8451.19	−1874.19	−18.2		10/10/08	8451.19	−1874.19	−18.2
9/21/01	8235.81	−1369.70	−14.3		9/21/01	8235.81	−1369.70	−14.3
10/23/87	1950.76	−295.98	−13.2		3/16/01	9823.41	−821.21	−7.7
10/16/87	2246.74	−235.47	−9.5		10/3/08	10325.38	−817.75	−7.3
10/13/89	2569.26	−216.26	−7.8		4/14/00	10305.77	−805.71	−7.3
3/16/01	9823.41	−821.21	−7.7		7/12/02	8684.53	−694.97	−7.4
7/19/02	8019.26	−665.27	−7.7		7/19/02	8019.26	−665.27	−7.7
12/4/87	1766.74	−143.74	−7.5		10/15/99	10019.71	−630.05	−5.9
9/13/74	627.19	−50.69	−7.5		7/27/07	13265.47	−585.61	−4.2
9/12/86	1758.72	−141.03	−7.4		10/19/07	13522.02	−571.06	−4.1
S&P 500 1930 to APRIL 2010								
7/22/33	9.71	−2.20	−18.5		10/10/08	899.22	−200.01	−18.2
10/10/08	899.22	−200.01	−18.2		4/14/00	1356.56	−159.79	−10.5
5/18/40	9.75	−2.05	−17.4		9/21/01	965.80	−126.74	−11.6
10/8/32	6.77	−1.38	−16.9		10/3/08	1099.23	−113.78	−9.4
9/17/32	7.50	−1.28	−14.6		10/15/99	1247.41	−88.61	−6.6
10/21/33	8.57	−1.31	−13.3		3/16/01	1150.53	−82.89	−6.7
10/3/31	9.37	−1.36	−12.7		1/28/00	1360.16	−81.20	−5.6
10/23/87	248.22	−34.48	−12.2		1/18/08	1325.19	−75.83	−5.4
12/12/31	8.20	−1.13	−12.1		7/27/07	1458.95	−75.15	−4.9
3/26/38	9.20	−1.21	−11.6		7/19/02	847.76	−73.63	−8.0
NASDAQ 1971 to APRIL 2010								
4/14/00	3321.29	−1125.16	−25.3		4/14/00	3321.29	−1125.16	−25.3
10/23/87	328.45	−77.88	−19.2		7/28/00	3663.00	−431.45	−10.5
9/21/01	1423.19	−272.19	−16.1		11/10/00	3028.99	−422.59	−12.2
10/10/08	1649.51	−297.88	−15.3		3/31/00	4572.83	−390.20	−7.9
11/10/00	3028.99	−422.59	−12.2		1/28/00	3887.07	−348.33	−8.2
10/3/08	1947.39	−235.95	−10.8		10/6/00	3361.01	−311.81	−8.5
7/28/00	3663.00	−431.45	−10.5		10/10/08	1649.51	−297.88	−15.3
10/24/08	1552.03	−159.26	−9.3		5/12/00	3529.06	−287.76	−7.5
12/15/00	2653.27	−264.16	−9.1		9/21/01	1423.19	−272.19	−16.1
12/1/00	2645.29	−259.09	−8.9		12/15/00	2653.27	−264.16	−9.1
RUSSELL 1000 1979 to APRIL 2010								
10/10/08	486.23	−108.31	−18.2		10/10/08	486.23	−108.31	−18.2
10/23/87	130.19	−19.25	−12.9		4/14/00	715.20	−90.39	−11.2
9/21/01	507.98	−67.59	−11.7		9/21/01	507.98	−67.59	−11.7
4/14/00	715.20	−90.39	−11.2		10/3/08	594.54	−65.15	−9.9
10/3/08	594.54	−65.15	−9.9		10/15/99	646.79	−43.89	−6.4
10/16/87	149.44	−14.42	−8.8		3/16/01	605.71	−43.88	−6.8
11/21/08	427.88	−41.15	−8.8		7/27/07	793.72	−41.97	−5.0
9/12/86	124.95	−10.87	−8.0		1/28/00	719.67	−41.85	−5.5
7/19/02	450.64	−36.13	−7.4		11/21/08	427.88	−41.15	−8.8
10/24/08	471.53	−36.29	−7.2		1/18/08	719.58	−41.12	−5.4
RUSSELL 2000 1979 to APRIL 2010								
10/23/87	121.59	−31.15	−20.4		10/10/08	522.48	−96.92	−15.7
4/14/00	453.72	−89.27	−16.4		4/14/00	453.72	−89.27	−16.4
10/10/08	522.48	−96.92	−15.7		10/3/08	619.40	−85.39	−12.1
9/21/01	378.89	−61.84	−14.0		9/21/01	378.89	−61.84	−14.0
10/3/08	619.40	−85.39	−12.1		7/27/07	777.83	−58.61	−7.0
11/21/08	406.54	−49.98	−11.0		10/24/08	471.12	−55.31	−10.5
10/24/08	471.12	−55.31	−10.5		3/2/07	775.44	−51.20	−6.2
3/6/09	351.05	−37.97	−9.8		1/4/08	721.60	−50.16	−6.5
11/14/08	456.52	−49.27	−9.7		11/21/08	406.54	−49.98	−11.0
8/28/98	358.54	−37.10	−9.4		11/14/08	456.52	−49.27	−9.7

10 <u>BEST</u> MONTHS BY PERCENT AND POINT

	BY PERCENT CHANGE				BY POINT CHANGE		
MONTH	CLOSE	PNT CHANGE	% CHANGE	MONTH	CLOSE	PNT CHANGE	% CHANGE
DJIA 1901 to 1949							
APR-1933	77.66	22.26	40.2	NOV-1928	293.38	41.22	16.3
AUG-1932	73.16	18.90	34.8	JUN-1929	333.79	36.38	12.2
JUL-1932	54.26	11.42	26.7	AUG-1929	380.33	32.63	9.4
JUN-1938	133.88	26.14	24.3	JUN-1938	133.88	26.14	24.3
APR-1915	71.78	10.95	18.0	AUG-1928	240.41	24.41	11.3
JUN-1931	150.18	21.72	16.9	APR-1933	77.66	22.26	40.2
NOV-1928	293.38	41.22	16.3	FEB-1931	189.66	22.11	13.2
NOV-1904	52.76	6.59	14.3	JUN-1931	150.18	21.72	16.9
MAY-1919	105.50	12.62	13.6	AUG-1932	73.16	18.90	34.8
SEP-1939	152.54	18.13	13.5	JAN-1930	267.14	18.66	7.5
DJIA 1950 to APRIL 2010							
JAN-1976	975.28	122.87	14.4	APR-1999	10789.04	1002.88	10.2
JAN-1975	703.69	87.45	14.2	APR-2001	10734.97	856.19	8.7
JAN-1987	2158.04	262.09	13.8	OCT-2002	8397.03	805.10	10.6
AUG-1982	901.31	92.71	11.5	MAR-2000	10921.92	793.61	7.8
OCT-1982	991.72	95.47	10.7	NOV-2001	9851.56	776.42	8.6
OCT-2002	8397.03	805.10	10.6	OCT-1998	8592.10	749.48	9.6
APR-1978	837.32	79.96	10.6	JUL-2009	9171.61	724.61	8.6
APR-1999	10789.04	1002.88	10.2	APR-2007	13062.91	708.56	5.7
NOV-1962	649.30	59.53	10.1	AUG-2000	11215.10	693.12	6.6
NOV-1954	386.77	34.63	9.8	DEC-2003	10453.92	671.46	6.9
S&P 500 1930 to APRIL 2010							
APR-1933	8.32	2.47	42.2	MAR-2000	1498.58	132.16	9.7
JUL-1932	6.10	1.67	37.7	APR-2001	1249.46	89.13	7.7
AUG-1932	8.39	2.29	37.5	AUG-2000	1517.68	86.85	6.1
JUN-1938	11.56	2.29	24.7	OCT-1998	1098.67	81.66	8.0
SEP-1939	13.02	1.84	16.5	DEC-1999	1469.25	80.34	5.8
OCT-1974	73.90	10.36	16.3	OCT-1999	1362.93	80.22	6.3
MAY-1933	9.64	1.32	15.9	NOV-2001	1139.45	79.67	7.5
APR-1938	9.70	1.20	14.1	APR-2009	872.81	74.94	9.4
JUN-1931	14.83	1.81	13.9	JUN-1999	1372.71	70.87	5.4
JAN-1987	274.08	31.91	13.2	OCT-2002	885.76	70.48	8.6
NASDAQ 1971 to APRIL 2010							
DEC-1999	4069.31	733.15	22.0	FEB-2000	4696.69	756.34	19.2
FEB-2000	4696.69	756.34	19.2	DEC-1999	4069.31	733.15	22.0
OCT-1974	65.23	9.56	17.2	JUN-2000	3966.11	565.20	16.6
JAN-1975	69.78	9.96	16.6	AUG-2000	4206.35	439.36	11.7
JUN-2000	3966.11	565.20	16.6	NOV-1999	3336.16	369.73	12.5
APR-2001	2116.24	275.98	15.0	JAN-1999	2505.89	313.20	14.3
JAN-1999	2505.89	313.20	14.3	JAN-2001	2772.73	302.21	12.2
NOV-2001	1930.58	240.38	14.2	APR-2001	2116.24	275.98	15.0
OCT-2002	1329.75	157.69	13.5	DEC-1998	2192.69	243.15	12.5
OCT-1982	212.63	24.98	13.3	NOV-2001	1930.58	240.38	14.2
RUSSELL 1000 1979 to APRIL 2010							
JAN-1987	146.48	16.48	12.7	MAR-2000	797.99	64.95	8.9
OCT-1982	73.34	7.45	11.3	AUG-2000	811.17	55.60	7.4
AUG-1982	65.14	6.60	11.3	APR-2001	658.90	48.54	8.0
DEC-1991	220.61	22.15	11.2	OCT-1999	707.19	43.36	6.5
AUG-1984	89.87	8.74	10.8	DEC-1999	767.97	43.31	6.0
NOV-1980	78.26	7.18	10.1	APR-2009	476.84	43.17	10.0
APR-2009	476.84	43.17	10.0	NOV-2001	599.32	42.03	7.5
MAY-1990	187.66	15.34	8.9	OCT-1998	570.63	41.52	7.8
MAR-2000	797.99	64.95	8.9	JUL-2009	539.88	37.61	7.5
MAR-2009	433.67	34.06	8.5	DEC-1998	642.87	37.56	6.2
RUSSELL 2000 1979 to APRIL 2010							
FEB-2000	577.71	81.48	16.4	FEB-2000	577.71	81.48	16.4
APR-2009	487.56	64.81	15.3	APR-2009	487.56	64.81	15.3
OCT-1982	80.86	10.02	14.1	JAN-2006	733.20	59.98	8.9
JAN-1985	114.77	13.28	13.1	DEC-1999	504.75	50.67	11.2
AUG-1984	106.21	10.96	11.5	MAR-2010	678.64	50.08	8.0
JAN-1987	150.48	15.48	11.5	NOV-2004	633.77	49.98	8.6
DEC-1999	504.75	50.67	11.2	JUL-2009	556.71	48.43	9.5
JUL-1980	63.81	6.34	11.0	DEC-2009	625.39	45.66	7.9
MAY-1997	380.76	37.76	11.0	MAY-2003	441.00	42.32	10.6
FEB-1991	160.00	15.83	11.0	OCT-2006	766.84	41.25	5.7

10 <u>WORST</u> MONTHS BY PERCENT AND POINT

	BY PERCENT CHANGE				BY POINT CHANGE		
MONTH	CLOSE	PNT CHANGE	% CHANGE	MONTH	CLOSE	PNT CHANGE	% CHANGE
DJIA 1901 to 1949							
SEP-1931	96.61	−42.80	−30.7	OCT-1929	273.51	−69.94	−20.4
MAR-1938	98.95	−30.69	−23.7	JUN-1930	226.34	−48.73	−17.7
APR-1932	56.11	−17.17	−23.4	SEP-1931	96.61	−42.80	−30.7
MAY-1940	116.22	−32.21	−21.7	SEP-1929	343.45	−36.88	−9.7
OCT-1929	273.51	−69.94	−20.4	SEP-1930	204.90	−35.52	−14.8
MAY-1932	44.74	−11.37	−20.3	NOV-1929	238.95	−34.56	−12.6
JUN-1930	226.34	−48.73	−17.7	MAY-1940	116.22	−32.21	−21.7
DEC-1931	77.90	−15.97	−17.0	MAR-1938	98.95	−30.69	−23.7
FEB-1933	51.39	−9.51	−15.6	SEP-1937	154.57	−22.84	−12.9
MAY-1931	128.46	−22.73	−15.0	MAY-1931	128.46	−22.73	−15.0
DJIA 1950 to APRIL 2010							
OCT-1987	1993.53	−602.75	−23.2	OCT-2008	9325.01	−1525.65	−14.1
AUG-1998	7539.07	−1344.22	−15.1	AUG-1998	7539.07	−1344.22	−15.1
OCT-2008	9325.01	−1525.65	−14.1	JUN-2008	11350.01	−1288.31	−10.2
NOV-1973	822.25	−134.33	−14.0	SEP-2001	8847.56	−1102.19	−11.1
SEP-2002	7591.93	−1071.57	−12.4	SEP-2002	7591.93	−1071.57	−12.4
FEB-2009	7062.93	−937.93	−11.7	FEB-2009	7062.93	−937.93	−11.7
SEP-2001	8847.56	−1102.19	−11.1	FEB-2000	10128.31	−812.22	−7.4
SEP-1974	607.87	−70.71	−10.4	JAN-2009	8000.86	−775.53	−8.8
AUG-1974	678.58	−78.85	−10.4	SEP-2008	10850.66	−692.89	−6.0
JUN-2008	11350.01	−1288.31	−10.2	JUN-2002	9243.26	−681.99	−6.9
S&P 500 1930 to APRIL 2010							
SEP-1931	9.71	−4.15	−29.9	OCT-2008	968.75	−197.61	−16.9
MAR-1938	8.50	−2.84	−25.0	AUG-1998	957.28	−163.39	−14.6
MAY-1940	9.27	−2.92	−24.0	FEB-2001	1239.94	−126.07	−9.2
MAY-1932	4.47	−1.36	−23.3	JUN-2008	1280.00	−120.38	−8.6
OCT-1987	251.79	−70.04	−21.8	SEP-2008	1166.36	−116.47	−9.1
APR-1932	5.83	−1.48	−20.2	NOV-2000	1314.95	−114.45	−8.0
FEB-1933	5.66	−1.28	−18.4	SEP-2002	815.28	−100.79	−11.0
OCT-2008	968.75	−197.61	−16.9	SEP-2001	1040.94	−92.64	−8.2
JUN-1930	20.46	−4.03	−16.5	FEB-2009	735.09	−90.79	−11.0
AUG-1998	957.28	−163.39	−14.6	JAN-2008	1378.55	−89.81	−6.1
NASDAQ 1971 to APRIL 2010							
OCT-1987	323.30	−120.99	−27.2	NOV-2000	2597.93	−771.70	−22.9
NOV-2000	2597.93	−771.70	−22.9	APR-2000	3860.66	−712.17	−15.6
FEB-2001	2151.83	−620.90	−22.4	FEB-2001	2151.83	−620.90	−22.4
AUG-1998	1499.25	−373.14	−19.9	SEP-2000	3672.82	−533.53	−12.7
OCT-2008	1720.95	−370.93	−17.7	MAY-2000	3400.91	459.75	−11.9
MAR-1980	131.00	−27.03	−17.1	AUG-1998	1499.25	−373.14	−19.9
SEP-2001	1498.80	−306.63	−17.0	OCT-2008	1720.95	−370.93	−17.7
OCT-1978	111.12	−21.77	−16.4	MAR-2001	1840.26	−311.57	−14.5
APR-2000	3860.66	−712.17	−15.6	SEP-2001	1498.80	−306.63	−17.0
NOV-1973	93.51	−16.66	−15.1	OCT-2000	3369.63	−303.19	−8.3
RUSSELL 1000 1979 to APRIL 2010							
OCT-1987	131.89	−36.94	−21.9	OCT-2008	522.47	−111.61	−17.6
OCT-2008	522.47	−111.61	−17.6	AUG-1998	496.66	−88.31	−15.1
AUG-1998	496.66	−88.31	−15.1	NOV-2000	692.40	−70.66	−9.3
MAR-1980	55.79	−7.28	−11.5	FEB-2001	654.25	−68.30	−9.5
SEP-2002	433.22	−52.86	−10.9	SEP-2008	634.08	−68.09	−9.7
FEB-2009	399.61	−47.71	−10.7	JUN-2008	703.22	−65.06	−8.5
SEP-2008	634.08	−68.09	−9.7	SEP-2002	433.22	−52.86	−10.9
AUG-1990	166.69	−17.63	−9.6	SEP-2001	546.46	−51.21	−8.6
FEB-2001	654.25	−68.30	−9.5	JAN-2008	750.97	−48.85	−6.1
NOV-2000	692.40	−70.66	−9.3	FEB-2009	399.61	−47.71	−10.7
RUSSELL 2000 1979 to APRIL 2010							
OCT-1987	118.26	−52.55	−30.8	OCT-2008	537.52	−142.06	−20.9
OCT-2008	537.52	−142.06	−20.9	AUG-1998	337.95	−81.80	−19.5
AUG-1998	337.95	−81.80	−19.5	JUL-2002	392.42	−70.22	−15.2
MAR-1980	48.27	−10.95	−18.5	NOV-2008	473.14	−64.38	−12.0
JUL-2002	392.42	−70.22	−15.2	SEP-2001	404.87	−63.69	−13.6
AUG-1990	139.52	−21.99	−13.6	NOV-2007	767.77	−60.25	−7.3
SEP-2001	404.87	−63.69	−13.6	SEP-2008	679.58	−59.92	−8.1
FEB-2009	389.02	−54.51	−12.3	JUN-2008	689.66	−58.62	−7.8
NOV-2008	473.14	−64.38	−12.0	JUL-2007	776.13	−57.56	−6.9
OCT-1979	48.51	−6.17	−11.3	JAN-2009	443.53	−55.92	−11.2

10 <u>BEST</u> QUARTERS BY PERCENT AND POINT

	BY PERCENT CHANGE				BY POINT CHANGE		
QUARTER	CLOSE	PNT CHANGE	% CHANGE	QUARTER	CLOSE	PNT CHANGE	% CHANGE
DJIA 1901 to 1949							
JUN-1933	98.14	42.74	77.1	DEC-1928	300.00	60.57	25.3
SEP-1932	71.56	28.72	67.0	JUN-1933	98.14	42.74	77.1
JUN-1938	133.88	34.93	35.3	MAR-1930	286.10	37.62	15.1
SEP-1915	90.58	20.52	29.3	JUN-1938	133.88	34.93	35.3
DEC-1928	300.00	60.57	25.3	SEP-1927	197.59	31.36	18.9
DEC-1904	50.99	8.80	20.9	SEP-1928	239.43	28.88	13.7
JUN-1919	106.98	18.13	20.4	SEP-1932	71.56	28.72	67.0
SEP-1927	197.59	31.36	18.9	JUN-1929	333.79	24.94	8.1
DEC-1905	70.47	10.47	17.4	SEP-1939	152.54	21.91	16.8
JUN-1935	118.21	17.40	17.3	SEP-1915	90.58	20.52	29.3
DJIA 1950 to APRIL 2010							
MAR-1975	768.15	151.91	24.7	DEC-1998	9181.43	1338.81	17.1
MAR-1987	2304.69	408.74	21.6	SEP-2009	9712.28	1265.28	15.0
MAR-1986	1818.61	271.94	17.6	JUN-1999	10970.80	1184.64	12.1
MAR-1976	999.45	147.04	17.2	DEC-2003	10453.92	1178.86	12.7
DEC-1998	9181.43	1338.81	17.1	DEC-2001	10021.50	1173.94	13.3
DEC-1982	1046.54	150.29	16.8	DEC-1999	11497.12	1160.17	11.2
JUN-1997	7672.79	1089.31	16.5	JUN-1997	7672.79	1089.31	16.5
DEC-1985	1546.67	218.04	16.4	JUN-2007	13408.62	1054.27	8.5
SEP-2009	9712.28	1265.28	15.0	JUN-2003	8985.44	993.31	12.4
JUN-1975	878.99	110.84	14.4	MAR-1998	8799.81	891.56	11.3
S&P 500 1930 to APRIL 2010							
JUN-1933	10.91	5.06	86.5	DEC-1998	1229.23	212.22	20.9
SEP-1932	8.08	3.65	82.4	DEC-1999	1469.25	186.54	14.5
JUN-1938	11.56	3.06	36.0	SEP-2009	1057.08	137.76	15.0
MAR-1975	83.36	14.80	21.6	MAR-1998	1101.75	131.32	13.5
DEC-1998	1229.23	212.22	20.9	JUN-1997	885.14	128.02	16.9
JUN-1935	10.23	1.76	20.8	JUN-2003	974.50	125.32	14.8
MAR-1987	291.70	49.53	20.5	JUN-2009	919.32	121.45	15.2
SEP-1939	13.02	2.16	19.9	DEC-2003	1111.92	115.95	11.6
MAR-1943	11.58	1.81	18.5	DEC-2001	1148.08	107.14	10.3
MAR-1930	25.14	3.69	17.2	DEC-2004	1211.92	97.34	8.7
NASDAQ 1971 to APRIL 2010							
DEC-1999	4069.31	1323.15	48.2	DEC-1999	4069.31	1323.15	48.2
DEC-2001	1950.40	451.60	30.1	MAR-2000	4572.83	503.52	12.4
DEC-1998	2192.69	498.85	29.5	DEC-1998	2192.69	498.85	29.5
MAR-1991	482.30	108.46	29.0	DEC-2001	1950.40	451.60	30.1
MAR-1975	75.66	15.84	26.5	JUN-2001	2160.54	320.28	17.4
DEC-1982	232.41	44.76	23.9	JUN-2009	1835.04	306.45	20.0
MAR-1987	430.05	80.72	23.1	SEP-2009	2122.42	287.38	15.7
JUN-2003	1622.80	281.63	21.0	JUN-2003	1622.80	281.63	21.0
JUN-1980	157.78	26.78	20.4	DEC-2004	2175.44	278.60	14.7
JUN-2009	1835.04	306.45	20.0	MAR-1999	2461.40	268.71	12.3
RUSSELL 1000 1979 to APRIL 2010							
DEC-1998	642.87	113.76	21.5	DEC-1998	642.87	113.76	21.5
MAR-1987	155.20	25.20	19.4	DEC-1999	767.97	104.14	15.7
DEC-1982	77.24	11.35	17.2	SEP-2009	579.97	77.70	15.5
JUN-1997	462.95	64.76	16.3	JUN-2009	502.27	68.60	15.8
DEC-1985	114.39	15.64	15.8	JUN-2003	518.94	68.59	15.2
JUN-2009	502.27	68.60	15.8	MAR-1998	580.31	66.52	12.9
DEC-1999	767.97	104.14	15.7	JUN-1997	462.95	64.76	16.3
SEP-2009	579.97	77.70	15.5	DEC-2003	594.56	62.41	11.7
JUN-2003	518.94	68.59	15.2	DEC-2001	604.94	58.48	10.7
MAR-1991	196.15	24.93	14.6	DEC-2004	650.99	55.33	9.3
RUSSELL 2000 1979 to APRIL 2010							
MAR-1991	171.01	38.85	29.4	SEP-2009	604.28	96.00	18.9
DEC-1982	88.90	18.06	25.5	MAR-2006	765.14	91.92	13.7
MAR-1987	166.79	31.79	23.5	JUN-2009	508.28	85.53	20.2
JUN-2003	448.37	83.83	23.0	JUN-2003	448.37	83.83	23.0
SEP-1980	69.94	12.47	21.7	DEC-2001	488.50	83.63	20.7
DEC-2001	488.50	83.63	20.7	DEC-2004	651.57	78.63	13.7
JUN-1983	124.17	20.40	19.7	DEC-1999	504.75	77.45	18.1
JUN-1980	57.47	9.20	19.1	DEC-2003	556.91	69.23	14.2
DEC-1999	504.75	77.45	18.1	JUN-2001	512.64	62.11	13.8
SEP-2009	604.28	96.00	18.9	DEC-2006	787.66	62.07	8.6

10 <u>WORST</u> QUARTERS BY PERCENT AND POINT

	BY PERCENT CHANGE			BY POINT CHANGE			
QUARTER	CLOSE	PNT CHANGE	% CHANGE	QUARTER	CLOSE	PNT CHANGE	% CHANGE
DJIA 1901 to 1949							
JUN-1932	42.84	–30.44	–41.5	DEC-1929	248.48	–94.97	–27.7
SEP-1931	96.61	–53.57	–35.7	JUN-1930	226.34	–59.76	–20.9
DEC-1929	248.48	–94.97	–27.7	SEP-1931	96.61	–53.57	–35.7
SEP-1903	33.55	–9.73	–22.5	DEC-1930	164.58	–40.32	–19.7
DEC-1937	120.85	–33.72	–21.8	DEC-1937	120.85	–33.72	–21.8
JUN-1930	226.34	–59.76	–20.9	SEP-1946	172.42	–33.20	–16.1
DEC-1930	164.58	–40.32	–19.7	JUN-1932	42.84	–30.44	–41.5
DEC-1931	77.90	–18.71	–19.4	JUN-1940	121.87	–26.08	–17.6
MAR-1938	98.95	–21.90	–18.1	MAR-1939	131.84	–22.92	–14.8
JUN-1940	121.87	–26.08	–17.6	JUN-1931	150.18	–22.18	–12.9
DJIA 1950 to APRIL 2010							
DEC-1987	1938.83	–657.45	–25.3	DEC-2008	8776.39	–2074.27	–19.1
SEP-1974	607.87	–194.54	–24.2	SEP-2001	8847.56	–1654.84	–15.8
JUN-1962	561.28	–145.67	–20.6	SEP-2002	7591.93	–1651.33	–17.9
DEC-2008	8776.39	–2074.27	–19.1	MAR-2009	7608.92	–1167.47	–13.3
SEP-2002	7591.93	–1651.33	–17.9	JUN-2002	9243.26	–1160.68	–11.2
SEP-2001	8847.56	–1654.84	–15.8	SEP-1998	7842.62	–1109.40	–12.4
SEP-1990	2452.48	–428.21	–14.9	MAR-2008	12262.89	–1001.93	–7.6
MAR-2009	7608.92	–1167.47	–13.3	JUN-2008	11350.01	–912.88	–7.4
SEP-1981	849.98	–126.90	–13.0	MAR-2001	9878.78	–908.07	–8.4
JUN-1970	683.53	–102.04	–13.0	DEC-1987	1938.83	–657.45	–25.3
S&P 500 1930 to APRIL 2010							
JUN-1932	4.43	–2.88	–39.4	DEC-2008	903.25	–263.11	–22.6
SEP-1931	9.71	–5.12	–34.5	SEP-2001	1040.94	–183.48	–15.0
SEP-1974	63.54	–22.46	–26.1	SEP-2002	815.28	–174.54	–17.6
DEC-1937	10.55	–3.21	–23.3	MAR-2001	1160.33	–159.95	–12.1
DEC-1987	247.08	–74.75	–23.2	JUN-2002	989.82	–157.57	–13.7
DEC-2008	903.25	–263.11	–22.6	MAR-2008	1322.70	–145.66	–9.9
JUN-1962	54.75	–14.80	–21.3	SEP-1998	1017.01	–116.83	–10.3
MAR-1938	8.50	–2.05	–19.4	DEC-2000	1320.28	–116.23	–8.1
JUN-1970	72.72	–16.91	–18.9	SEP-2008	1166.36	–113.64	–8.9
SEP-1946	14.96	–3.47	–18.8	MAR-2009	797.87	–105.38	–11.0
NASDAQ 1971 to APRIL 2010							
DEC-2000	2470.52	–1202.30	–32.7	DEC-2000	2470.52	–1202.30	–32.7
SEP-2001	1498.80	–661.74	–30.6	SEP-2001	1498.80	–661.74	–30.6
SEP-1974	55.67	–20.29	–26.7	MAR-2001	1840.26	–630.26	–25.5
DEC-1987	330.47	–113.82	–25.6	JUN-2000	3966.11	–606.72	–13.3
MAR-2001	1840.26	–630.26	–25.5	DEC-2008	1577.03	–514.85	–24.6
SEP-1990	344.51	–117.78	–25.5	JUN-2002	1463.21	–382.14	–20.7
DEC-2008	1577.03	–514.85	–24.6	MAR-2008	2279.10	–373.18	–14.1
JUN-2002	1463.21	–382.14	–20.7	SEP-2000	3672.82	–293.29	–7.4
SEP-2002	1172.06	–291.15	–19.9	SEP-2002	1172.06	–291.15	–19.9
JUN-1974	75.96	–16.31	–17.7	SEP-2008	2091.88	–201.10	–8.8
RUSSELL 1000 1979 to APRIL 2010							
DEC-2008	487.77	–146.31	–23.1	DEC-2008	487.77	–146.31	–23.1
DEC-1987	130.02	–38.81	–23.0	SEP-2001	546.46	–100.18	–15.5
SEP-2002	433.22	–90.50	–17.3	SEP-2002	433.22	–90.50	–17.3
SEP-2001	546.46	–100.18	–15.5	MAR-2001	610.36	–89.73	–12.8
SEP-1990	157.83	–28.46	–15.3	JUN-2002	523.72	–83.63	–13.8
JUN-2002	523.72	–83.63	–13.8	MAR-2008	720.32	–79.50	–9.9
MAR-2001	610.36	–89.73	–12.8	DEC-2000	700.09	–72.51	–9.4
SEP-1981	64.06	–8.95	–12.3	SEP-2008	634.08	–69.14	–9.8
MAR-2009	433.67	–54.10	–11.1	SEP-1998	529.11	–63.46	–10.7
SEP-1998	529.11	–63.46	–10.7	MAR-2009	433.67	–54.10	–11.0
RUSSELL 2000 1979 to APRIL 2010							
DEC-1987	120.42	–50.39	–29.5	DEC-2008	499.45	–180.13	–26.5
DEC-2008	499.45	–180.13	–26.5	SEP-2001	404.87	–107.77	–21.0
SEP-1990	126.70	–42.34	–25.0	SEP-2002	362.27	–100.37	–21.7
SEP-2002	362.27	–100.37	–21.7	SEP-1998	363.59	–93.80	–20.5
SEP-2001	404.87	–107.77	–21.0	MAR-2008	687.97	–78.06	–10.2
SEP-1998	363.59	–93.80	–20.5	MAR-2009	422.75	–76.70	–15.4
SEP-1981	67.55	–15.01	–18.2	DEC-1987	120.42	–50.39	–29.5
MAR-2009	422.75	–76.70	–15.4	JUN-2002	462.64	–43.82	–8.7
MAR-1980	48.27	–7.64	–13.7	SEP-1990	126.70	–42.34	–25.0
SEP-1986	134.73	–19.50	–12.6	JUN-2006	724.67	–40.47	–5.3

10 <u>BEST</u> YEARS BY PERCENT AND POINT

	BY PERCENT CHANGE				BY POINT CHANGE		
YEAR	CLOSE	PNT CHANGE	% CHANGE	YEAR	CLOSE	PNT CHANGE	% CHANGE
DJIA 1901 to 1949							
1915	99.15	44.57	81.7	1928	300.00	97.60	48.2
1933	99.90	39.97	66.7	1927	202.40	45.20	28.8
1928	300.00	97.60	48.2	1915	99.15	44.57	81.7
1908	63.11	20.07	46.6	1945	192.91	40.59	26.6
1904	50.99	15.01	41.7	1935	144.13	40.09	38.5
1935	144.13	40.09	38.5	1933	99.90	39.97	66.7
1905	70.47	19.48	38.2	1925	156.66	36.15	30.0
1919	107.23	25.03	30.5	1936	179.90	35.77	24.8
1925	156.66	36.15	30.0	1938	154.76	33.91	28.1
1927	202.40	45.20	28.8	1919	107.23	25.03	30.5
DJIA 1950 to APRIL 2010							
1954	404.39	123.49	44.0	1999	11497.12	2315.69	25.2
1975	852.41	236.17	38.3	2003	10453.92	2112.29	25.3
1958	583.65	147.96	34.0	2006	12463.15	1745.65	16.3
1995	5117.12	1282.68	33.5	2009	10428.05	1651.66	18.8
1985	1546.67	335.10	27.7	1997	7908.25	1459.98	22.6
1989	2753.20	584.63	27.0	1996	6448.27	1331.15	26.0
1996	6448.27	1331.15	26.0	1995	5117.12	1282.68	33.5
2003	10453.92	2112.29	25.3	1998	9181.43	1273.18	16.1
1999	11497.12	2315.69	25.2	2007	13264.82	801.67	6.4
1997	7908.25	1459.98	22.6	1989	2753.20	584.63	27.0
S&P 500 1930 to APRIL 2010							
1933	10.10	3.21	46.6	1998	1229.23	258.80	26.7
1954	35.98	11.17	45.0	1999	1469.25	240.02	19.5
1935	13.43	3.93	41.4	2003	1111.92	232.10	26.4
1958	55.21	15.22	38.1	1997	970.43	229.69	31.0
1995	615.93	156.66	34.1	2009	1115.10	211.85	23.5
1975	90.19	21.63	31.5	2006	1418.30	170.01	13.6
1997	970.43	229.69	31.0	1995	615.93	156.66	34.1
1945	17.36	4.08	30.7	1996	740.74	124.81	20.3
1936	17.18	3.75	27.9	2004	1211.92	100.00	9.0
1989	353.40	75.68	27.3	1991	417.09	86.87	26.3
NASDAQ 1971 to APRIL 2010							
1999	4069.31	1876.62	85.6	1999	4069.31	1876.62	85.6
1991	586.34	212.50	56.8	2009	2269.15	692.12	43.9
2003	2003.37	667.86	50.0	2003	2003.37	667.86	50.0
2009	2269.15	692.12	43.9	1998	2192.69	622.34	39.6
1995	1052.13	300.17	39.9	1995	1052.13	300.17	39.9
1998	2192.69	622.34	39.6	1997	1570.35	279.32	21.6
1980	202.34	51.20	33.9	1996	1291.03	238.90	22.7
1985	324.93	77.58	31.4	2007	2652.28	236.99	9.8
1975	77.62	17.80	29.8	1991	586.34	212.50	56.8
1979	151.14	33.16	28.1	2006	2415.29	209.97	9.5
RUSSELL 1000 1979 to APRIL 2010							
1995	328.89	84.24	34.4	1008	642.87	129.08	25.1
1997	513.79	120.04	30.5	2003	594.56	128.38	27.5
1991	220.61	49.39	28.8	1999	767.97	125.10	19.5
2003	594.56	128.38	27.5	2009	612.01	124.24	25.5
1985	114.39	24.08	26.7	1997	513.79	120.04	30.5
1989	185.11	38.12	25.9	2006	770.08	90.66	13.3
1980	75.20	15.33	25.6	1995	328.89	84.24	34.4
2009	612.01	124.24	25.5	1996	393.75	64.86	19.7
1998	642.87	129.08	25.1	2004	650.99	56.43	9.5
1996	393.75	64.86	19.7	1991	220.61	49.39	28.8
RUSSELL 2000 1979 to APRIL 2010							
2003	556.91	173.82	45.4	2003	556.91	173.82	45.4
1991	189.94	57.78	43.7	2009	625.39	125.94	25.2
1979	55.91	15.39	38.0	2006	787.66	114.44	17.0
1980	74.80	18.89	33.8	2004	651.57	94.66	17.0
1985	129.87	28.38	28.0	1999	504.75	82.79	19.6
1983	112.27	23.37	26.3	1997	437.02	74.41	20.5
1995	315.97	65.61	26.2	1995	315.97	65.61	26.2
2009	625.39	125.94	25.2	1991	189.94	57.78	43.7
1988	147.37	26.95	22.4	1996	362.61	46.64	14.8
1982	88.90	15.23	20.0	1993	258.59	37.58	17.0

10 <u>WORST</u> YEARS BY PERCENT AND POINT

	BY PERCENT CHANGE				BY POINT CHANGE		
YEAR	CLOSE	PNT CHANGE	% CHANGE	YEAR	CLOSE	PNT CHANGE	% CHANGE
DJIA 1901 to 1949							
1931	77.90	−86.68	−52.7	1931	77.90	−86.68	−52.7
1907	43.04	−26.08	−37.7	1930	164.58	−83.90	−33.8
1930	164.58	−83.90	−33.8	1937	120.85	−59.05	−32.8
1920	71.95	−35.28	−32.9	1929	248.48	−51.52	−17.2
1937	120.85	−59.05	−32.8	1920	71.95	−35.28	−32.9
1903	35.98	−11.12	−23.6	1907	43.04	−26.08	−37.7
1932	59.93	−17.97	−23.1	1917	74.38	−20.62	−21.7
1917	74.38	−20.62	−21.7	1941	110.96	−20.17	−15.4
1910	59.60	−12.96	−17.9	1940	131.13	−19.11	−12.7
1929	248.48	−51.52	−17.2	1932	59.93	−17.97	−23.1
DJIA 1950 to APRIL 2010							
2008	8776.39	−4488.43	−33.8	2008	8776.39	−4488.43	−33.8
1974	616.24	−234.62	−27.6	2002	8341.63	−1679.87	−16.8
1966	785.69	−183.57	−18.9	2001	10021.50	−765.35	−7.1
1977	831.17	−173.48	−17.3	2000	10786.85	−710.27	−6.2
2002	8341.63	−1679.87	−16.8	1974	616.24	−234.62	−27.6
1973	850.86	−169.16	−16.6	1966	785.69	−183.57	−18.9
1969	800.36	−143.39	−15.2	1977	831.17	−173.48	−17.3
1957	435.69	−63.78	−12.8	1973	850.86	−169.16	−16.6
1962	652.10	−79.04	−10.8	1969	800.36	−143.39	−15.2
1960	615.89	−63.47	−9.3	1990	2633.66	−119.54	−4.3
S&P 500 1930 to APRIL 2010							
1931	8.12	−7.22	−47.1	2008	903.25	−565.11	−38.5
1937	10.55	−6.63	−38.6	2002	879.82	−268.26	−23.4
2008	903.25	−565.11	−38.5	2001	1148.08	−172.20	−13.0
1974	68.56	−28.99	−29.7	2000	1320.28	−148.97	−10.1
1930	15.34	−6.11	−28.5	1974	68.56	−28.99	−29.7
2002	879.82	−268.26	−23.4	1990	330.22	−23.18	−6.6
1941	8.69	−1.89	−17.9	1973	97.55	−20.50	−17.4
1973	97.55	−20.50	−17.4	1981	122.55	−13.21	−9.7
1940	10.58	−1.91	−15.3	1977	95.10	−12.36	−11.5
1932	6.89	−1.23	−15.1	1966	80.33	−12.10	−13.1
NASDAQ 1971 to APRIL 2010							
2008	1577.03	−1075.25	−40.5	2000	2470.52	−1598.79	−39.3
2000	2470.52	−1598.79	−39.3	2008	1577.03	−1075.25	−40.5
1974	59.82	−32.37	−35.1	2002	1335.51	−614.89	−31.5
2002	1335.51	−614.89	−31.5	2001	1950.40	−520.12	−21.1
1973	92.19	−41.54	−31.1	1990	373.84	−80.98	−17.8
2001	1950.40	−520.12	−21.1	1973	92.19	−41.54	−31.1
1990	373.84	−80.98	−17.8	1974	59.82	−32.37	−35.1
1984	247.35	−31.25	−11.2	1984	247.35	−31.25	−11.2
1987	330.47	−18.86	−5.4	1994	751.96	−24.84	−3.2
1981	195.84	−6.50	−3.2	1987	330.47	−18.86	−5.4
RUSSELL 1000 1979 to APRIL 2010							
2008	487.77	−312.05	−39.0	2008	487.77	−312.05	−39.0
2002	466.18	−138.76	−22.9	2002	466.18	−138.76	−22.9
2001	604.94	−95.15	−13.6	2001	604.94	−95.15	−13.6
1981	67.93	−7.27	−9.7	2000	700.09	−67.88	−8.8
2000	700.09	−67.88	−8.8	1990	171.22	−13.89	−7.5
1990	171.22	−13.89	−7.5	1981	67.93	−7.27	−9.7
1994	244.65	−6.06	−2.4	1994	244.65	−6.06	−2.4
1984	90.31	−0.07	−0.1	1984	90.31	−0.07	−0.1
1987	130.02	0.02	0.02	1987	130.02	0.02	0.02
2007	799.82	29.74	3.9	1979	59.87	8.29	16.0
RUSSELL 2000 1979 to APRIL 2010							
2008	499.45	−266.58	−34.8	2008	499.45	−266.58	−34.8
2002	383.09	−105.41	−21.6	2002	383.09	−105.41	−21.6
1990	132.16	−36.14	−21.5	1990	132.16	−36.14	−21.5
1987	120.42	−14.58	−10.8	2007	766.03	−21.63	−2.7
1984	101.49	−10.78	−9.6	2000	483.53	−21.22	−4.2
2000	483.53	−21.22	−4.2	1998	421.96	−15.06	−3.4
1998	421.96	−15.06	−3.4	1987	120.42	−14.58	−10.8
1994	250.36	−8.23	−3.2	1984	101.49	−10.78	−9.6
2007	766.03	−21.63	−2.7	1994	250.36	−8.23	−3.2
1981	73.67	−1.13	−1.5	1981	73.67	−1.13	−1.5

STRATEGY PLANNING AND RECORD SECTION

CONTENTS

These forms are available at our website www.stocktradersalmanac.com.

PORTFOLIO AT START OF 2011

DATE ACQUIRED	NO. OF SHARES	SECURITY	PRICE	TOTAL COST	PAPER PROFITS	PAPER LOSSES

ADDITIONAL PURCHASES

DATE ACQUIRED	NO. OF SHARES	SECURITY	PRICE	TOTAL COST	REASON FOR PURCHASE PRIME OBJECTIVE, ETC.

ADDITIONAL PURCHASES

DATE ACQUIRED	NO. OF SHARES	SECURITY	PRICE	TOTAL COST	REASON FOR PURCHASE PRIME OBJECTIVE, ETC.

SHORT-TERM TRANSACTIONS

Pages 175–178 can accompany next year's income tax return (Schedule D). Enter transactions as completed to avoid last-minute pressures.

NO. OF SHARES	SECURITY	DATE ACQUIRED	DATE SOLD	SALE PRICE	COST	LOSS	GAIN

TOTALS: Carry over to next page

175

SHORT-TERM TRANSACTIONS *(continued)*

NO. OF SHARES	SECURITY	DATE ACQUIRED	DATE SOLD	SALE PRICE	COST	LOSS	GAIN

TOTALS:

LONG-TERM TRANSACTIONS

Pages 175–178 can accompany next year's income tax return (Schedule D). Enter transactions as completed to avoid last-minute pressures.

NO. OF SHARES	SECURITY	DATE ACQUIRED	DATE SOLD	SALE PRICE	COST	LOSS	GAIN

TOTALS: Carry over to next page

LONG-TERM TRANSACTIONS *(continued)*

NO. OF SHARES	SECURITY	DATE ACQUIRED	DATE SOLD	SALE PRICE	COST	LOSS	GAIN

TOTALS:

INTEREST/DIVIDENDS RECEIVED DURING 2011

SHARES	STOCK/BOND	FIRST QUARTER		SECOND QUARTER		THIRD QUARTER		FOURTH QUARTER	
		$		$		$		$	

BROKERAGE ACCOUNT DATA 2011

	MARGIN INTEREST	TRANSFER TAXES	CAPITAL ADDED	CAPITAL WITHDRAWN
JAN				
FEB				
MAR				
APR				
MAY				
JUN				
JUL				
AUG				
SEP				
OCT				
NOV				
DEC				

PORTFOLIO PRICE RECORD 2011 (FIRST HALF)

Place purchase price above stock name and weekly closes below.

STOCKS Week Ending	1	2	3	4	5	6	7	8	9	10
JANUARY 31										
7										
14										
21										
28										
FEBRUARY 4										
11										
18										
25										
MARCH 4										
11										
18										
25										
APRIL 1										
8										
15										
22										
29										
MAY 6										
13										
20										
27										
JUNE 3										
10										
17										
24										

PORTFOLIO PRICE RECORD 2011 (SECOND HALF)

Place purchase price above stock name and weekly closes below.

STOCKS										
Week Ending	1	2	3	4	5	6	7	8	9	10
JULY 1										
8										
15										
22										
29										
AUGUST 5										
12										
19										
26										
SEPTEMBER 2										
9										
16										
23										
30										
OCTOBER 7										
14										
21										
28										
NOVEMBER 4										
11										
18										
25										
DECEMBER 2										
9										
16										
23										
30										

WEEKLY INDICATOR DATA 2011 (FIRST HALF)

Week Ending	Dow Jones Industrial Average	Net Change for Week	Net Change on Friday	Net Change Next Monday	S&P or NASDAQ	NYSE Advances	NYSE Declines	New Highs	New Lows	CBOE Put/Call Ratio	90-Day Treas. Rate	Moody's AAA Rate
JANUARY 31												
7												
14												
21												
28												
FEBRUARY 4												
11												
18												
25												
MARCH 4												
11												
18												
25												
APRIL 1												
8												
15												
22												
29												
MAY 6												
13												
20												
27												
JUNE 3												
10												
17												
24												

WEEKLY INDICATOR DATA 2011 (SECOND HALF)

	Week Ending	Dow Jones Industrial Average	Net Change for Week	Net Change on Friday	Net Change Next Monday	S&P or NASDAQ	NYSE Advances	NYSE Declines	New Highs	New Lows	CBOE Put/Call Ratio	90-Day Treas. Rate	Moody's AAA Rate
JULY	1												
	8												
	15												
	22												
	29												
AUGUST	5												
	12												
	19												
	26												
SEPTEMBER	2												
	9												
	16												
	23												
	30												
OCTOBER	7												
	14												
	21												
	28												
NOVEMBER	4												
	11												
	18												
	25												
DECEMBER	2												
	9												
	16												
	23												
	30												

MONTHLY INDICATOR DATA 2011

	DJIA% Last 3 + 1st 2 Days	DJIA% 9th to 11th Trading Days	DJIA% Change Rest of Month	DJIA% Change Whole Month	% Change Your Stocks	Gross Domestic Product	Prime Rate	Trade Deficit $ Billion	CPI % Change	% Unem- ployment Rate
JAN										
FEB										
MAR										
APR										
MAY										
JUN										
JUL										
AUG										
SEP										
OCT										
NOV										
DEC										

INSTRUCTIONS:

Weekly Indicator Data (pages 182–183). Keeping data on several indicators may give you a better feel of the market. In addition to the closing DJIA and its net change for the week, post the net change for Friday's Dow and also the following Monday's. A series of "down Fridays" followed by "down Mondays" often precedes a downswing. Tracking either the S&P or NASDAQ composite, and advances and declines, will help prevent the Dow from misleading you. New highs and lows and put/call ratios (www.cboe.com) are also useful indicators. All these weekly figures appear in weekend papers or *Barron's*. Data for 90-day Treasury Rate and Moody's AAA Bond Rate are quite important for tracking short- and long-term interest rates. These figures are available from:

Weekly U.S. Financial Data
Federal Reserve Bank of St. Louis
P.O. Box 442
St. Louis MO 63166
http://research.stlouisfed.org

Monthly Indicator Data. The purpose of the first three columns is to enable you to track the market's bullish bias near the end, beginning, and middle of the month, which has been shifting lately (see pages 88, 145, and 146). Market direction, performance of your stocks, gross domestic product, prime rate, trade deficit, Consumer Price Index, and unemployment rate are worthwhile indicators to follow. Or, readers may wish to gauge other data.

PORTFOLIO AT END OF 2011

DATE ACQUIRED	NO. OF SHARES	SECURITY	PRICE	TOTAL COST	PAPER PROFITS	PAPER LOSSES

IF YOU DON'T PROFIT FROM YOUR INVESTMENT MISTAKES, SOMEONE ELSE WILL

No matter how much we may deny it, almost every successful person in Wall Street pays a great deal of attention to trading suggestions—especially when they come from "the right sources."

One of the hardest things to learn is to distinguish between good tips and bad ones. Usually, the best tips have a logical reason in back of them, which accompanies the tip. Poor tips usually have no reason to support them.

The important thing to remember is that the market discounts. It does not review, it does not reflect. The Street's real interest in "tips," inside information, buying and selling suggestions, and everything else of this kind emanates from a desire to find out just what the market has on hand to discount. The process of finding out involves separating the wheat from the chaff—and there is plenty of chaff.

HOW TO MAKE USE OF STOCK "TIPS"

- The source should be **reliable**. (By listing all "tips" and suggestions on a Performance Record of Recommendations, such as the form below, and then periodically evaluating the outcomes, you will soon know the "batting average" of your sources.)

- The story should make sense. Would the merger violate antitrust laws? Are there too many computers on the market already? How many years will it take to become profitable?

- The stock should not have had a recent sharp run-up. Otherwise, the story may already be discounted, and confirmation or denial in the press would most likely be accompanied by a sell-off in the stock.

PERFORMANCE RECORD OF RECOMMENDATIONS

STOCK RECOMMENDED	BY WHOM	DATE	PRICE	REASON FOR RECOMMENDATION	SUBSEQUENT ACTION OF STOCK

INDIVIDUAL RETIREMENT ACCOUNTS: MOST AWESOME INVESTMENT INCENTIVE EVER DEVISED

MAX IRA INVESTMENTS OF $5,000* A YEAR COMPOUNDED AT VARIOUS INTEREST RATES OF RETURN FOR DIFFERENT PERIODS

Annual Rate	5 Yrs	10 Yrs	15 Yrs	20 Yrs	25 Yrs	30 Yrs	35 Yrs	40 Yrs	45 Yrs	50 Yrs
1%	$25,760	$52,834	$81,289	$111,196	$142,628	$175,664	$210,384	$246,876	$285,229	$325,539
2%	26,541	55,844	88,196	123,917	163,355	206,897	254,972	308,050	366,653	431,355
3%	27,342	59,039	95,784	138,382	187,765	245,013	311,380	388,316	477,507	580,904
4%	28,165	62,432	104,123	154,846	216,559	291,642	382,992	494,133	629,353	793,869
5%	29,010	66,034	113,287	173,596	250,567	348,804	474,182	634,199	838,426	1,099,077
6%	29,877	69,858	123,363	194,964	290,782	419,008	590,604	820,238	1,127,541	1,538,780
7%	30,766	73,918	134,440	219,326	338,382	505,365	739,567	1,068,048	1,528,759	2,174,930
8%	31,680	78,227	146,621	247,115	394,772	611,729	930,511	1,398,905	2,087,130	3,098,359
9%	32,617	82,801	160,017	278,823	461,620	742,876	1,175,624	1,841,459	2,865,930	4,442,205
10%	33,578	87,656	174,749	315,012	540,909	904,717	1,490,634	2,434,259	3,953,977	6,401,497
11%	34,564	92,807	190,950	356,326	634,994	1,104,566	1,895,822	3,229,135	5,475,844	9,261,680
12%	35,576	98,273	208,766	403,494	746,670	1,351,463	2,417,316	4,295,712	7,606,088	13,440,102
13%	36,614	104,072	228,359	457,350	879,250	1,656,576	3,088,747	5,727,429	10,589,030	19,546,215
14%	37,678	110,223	249,902	518,842	1,036,664	2,033,685	3,953,364	7,649,543	14,766,219	28,468,772
15%	38,769	116,746	273,587	589,051	1,223,560	2,499,785	5,066,728	10,229,769	20,614,489	41,501,869
16%	39,887	123,665	299,625	669,203	1,445,441	3,075,808	6,500,135	13,692,392	28,798,589	60,526,763
17%	41,034	131,000	328,244	760,693	1,708,813	3,787,519	8,344,972	18,336,953	40,243,850	88,273,585
18%	42,210	138,776	359,695	865,105	2,021,361	4,666,593	10,718,245	24,562,957	56,236,305	128,697,253
19%	43,415	147,018	394,251	984,237	2,392,153	5,751,937	13,769,572	32,902,482	78,560,374	187,516,251
20%	44,650	155,752	432,211	1,120,128	2,831,886	7,091,289	17,690,047	44,063,147	109,687,860	272,983,145

* At press time, 2011 Contribution Limit will be indexed to inflation.

TOP 300 EXCHANGE TRADED FUNDS (As of 4/30/2010)

By Average Daily Volume. See pages 92, 94, and 96, Almanac Investor and stocktradersalmanac.com for more.

SPY	S&P 500 Spyder	ILF	iShares S&P Latin America 40
XLF	SPDR Financial	ERY	Direxion Energy Bear 3x
QQQQ	PowerShares QQQ	SCO	ProShares UltraShort DJ-AIG Crude Oil
EEM	iShares Emerging Market Income	EEV	ProShares UltraShort MSCI Emrgng Mrkts
FAZ	Direxion Financial Bear 3x	DBC	PowerShares DB Commodity
IWM	iShares Russell 2000	IWO	iShares Russell 2000 Growth
SDS	ProShares UltraShort S&P 500	SH	ProShares Short S&P 500
FAS	Direxion Financial Bull 3x	IYM	iShares DJ US Basic Materials
UNG	United States Natural Gas	VTI	Vanguard Total Market VIPERS
FXI	iShares FTSE/Xinhua China 25	IWD	iShares Russell 1000 Value
EWJ	iShares Japan	IYF	iShares DJ US Financial
TZA	Direxion Small Cap Bear 3x	JNK	SPDR Barclays High Yield Bond
XLE	SPDR Energy	DBA	PowerShares DB Agriculture
SSO	ProShares Ultra S&P 500	RTH	Retail HOLDRs
EWZ	iShares Brazil	IWB	iShares Russell 1000
EFA	iShares EAFE	IWN	iShares Russell 2000 Value
UYG	ProShares Ultra Financials	EWM	iShares Malaysia
GLD	SPDR Gold	GDXJ	Market Vectors Jr Gold Miners
QID	ProShares UltraShort QQQ	ZSL	ProShares UltraShort Silver
SMH	Semiconductor HOLDRs	EPP	iShares Pacific Ex-Japan
GDX	Market Vectors Gold Miners	IJR	iShares S&P Small Cap 600
XLB	SPDR Materials	EDZ	Direxion Emerging Markets Bear 3x
IYR	iShares DJ US Real Estate	UPRO	ProShares UltraPro S&P 500
EWT	iShares Taiwan	EWG	iShares Germany
SRS	ProShares UltraShort Rl Estate	IWS	iShares Russell Mid Cap Val
URE	ProShares Ultra Real Estate	EWU	iShares United Kingdom
SKF	ProShares UltraShort Financial	ICF	iShares Cohen & Steers Realty
XLI	SPDR Industrial	TIP	iShares Barclays TIPS Bond
XRT	SPDR Retail	VEA	Vanguard Europe Pacific
VWO	Emerging Markets VIPERS	EPI	WisdomTree India Earnings Fund
USO	United States Oil Fund	IVW	iShares S&P 500 BARRA Growth
SLV	iShares Silver Trust	EDC	Direxion Emerging Markets Bull 3x
XLK	SPDR Tech	PFF	iShares S&P US Preferred
DIA	Diamonds	VEU	Vanguard FTSE All-World ex-US
TNA	Direxion Small Cap Bull 3x	LQD	iShares GS Corporate Bond
QLD	ProShares Ultra QQQ	HYG	iShares iBoxx $ HY Corp Bond
XLV	SPDR Healthcare	RSP	Rydex S&P Equal Weight
BGZ	Direxion Large Cap Bear 3x	TYP	Direxion Technology Bear 3x
XLU	SPDR Utilities	IJH	iShares S&P Mid Cap 400
XLP	SPDR Consumer Staples	RKH	Regional Bank HOLDRs
EWH	iShares Hong Kong	SHY	iShares Barclays 1-3Yr Trsry Bnd
XME	SPDR Metals & Mining	IWP	iShares Russell Mid Cap Gr
OIH	Oil Service HOLDRs	IYT	iShares DJ Transports
TBT	ProShares UltraShort Barclays 20+ Yr	PGF	PowerShares Fin Preferred
TWM	ProShares UltraShort R2K	IWR	iShares Russell Mid Cap
XHB	SPDR Homebuilders	VGK	European VIPERS
XLY	SPDR Consumer Discretionary	KIE	KBW Insurance
UUP	PowerShares DB US Dollar-Bull	FCG	First Trust ISE-Revere Natural Gas
KBE	KBW Bank	MOO	Market Vectors Agribusiness
UYM	ProShares Ultra Materials	EUO	ProShares UltraShort Euro
EWA	iShares Australia	AGG	iShares Barclays Aggregate Bond
DXD	ProShares UltraShort Dow 30	IBB	iShares NASDAQ Biotech
BGU	Direxion Large Cap Bull 3x	OEF	iShares S&P 100
UCO	ProShares Ultra DJ-AIG Crude Oil	BND	Vanguard Total Bond Market
FXP	ProShares UltraShort FTSE/Xinhua China 25	FXE	CurrencyShares Euro
KRE	KBW Regional Bank	KOL	Market Vectors Coal
SPXU	ProShares UltraPro Short S&P 500	IWV	iShares Russell 3000
SMN	ProShares UltraShort Materials	PBW	PowerShares Wilder Hill Energy
IVV	iShares S&P 500	DBB	PowerShares DB Base Metals
DIG	ProShares Ultra Oil & Gas	DRN	Direxion Daily Real Estate Bull 3X
XOP	SPDR Oil & Gas Explore & Prod	IYZ	iShares DJ US Telecom
EWY	iShares South Korea	AGQ	ProShares Ultra Silver
TLT	iShares Barclays 20+yr Bond	BRF	Market Vectors Brazil Small-Cap
RSX	Market Vectors Russia Trust	SHV	iShares Barclays Shrt-Term Trsry
ERX	Direxion Energy Bull 3x	GLL	ProShares UltraShort Gold
EWC	iShares Canada	RWR	SPDR DJ REIT
EWS	iShares Singapore	TYH	Direxion Technology Bull 3x
UWM	ProShares Ultra Russell 2000	BSV	Vanguard Short-Term Bond
VNQ	REIT VIPERS	TAN	Claymore/MAC Global Solar
DDM	ProShares Ultra Dow 30	PGX	PowerShares Preferred
EWW	iShares Mexico	PPH	Pharmaceutical HOLDRs
IWF	iShares Russell 1000 Growth	DVY	iShares DJ Select Dvdnd Index
MDY	S&P Mid Cap 400 SPDR	CSJ	iShares Barclays 1-3Yr Crdt Bond
DRV	Direxion Daily Real Estate Bear 3X	VB	Small Cap VIPERS
DUG	ProShares UltraShort Oil&Gas	ITB	iShares DJ US Home Const

TOP 300 EXCHANGE TRADED FUNDS (As of 4/30/2010)

By Average Daily Volume. See pages 92, 94, and 96, Almanac Investor and stocktradersalmanac.com for more.

GSG	iShares GSCI Commodity	VV	Vanguard Large Cap VIPERS
SHM	SPDR Barclays Short Term Muni Bond	PGJ	PowerShares Golden Dragon
IEF	iShares Barclays 7-10 Year	PZA	PowerShares Insrd Ntnl Muni Bond
VIG	Vanguard Dividend Appreciation	SCHX	Schwab U.S. Large-Cap
IYW	iShares DJ US Tech	EMB	iShares JPMorgan USD Emrgng Mrkts Bond
VUG	Vanguard Growth VIPERS	IXC	iShares S&P Global Energy
IVE	iShares S&P 500/BARRA Value	FXA	CurrencyShares Aussie Dollar
PVI	PowerShares VRDO Tax-Free	IJT	iShares S&P Sm Cp 600 BARRA Gr
EEB	Claymore/BNY BRIC	EPV	ProShares UltraShort MSCI Europe
IGE	iShares Natural Resources	IGW	iShares Semiconductor
IEO	iShares DJ US Oil&Gas Exp&Prod	VPL	Pacific VIPERS
BIL	SPDR Barclays 1-3 Month T-Bill	QTEC	First Trust NASDAQ-100-Tech
SLX	Market Vectors Steel	EWP	iShares Spain
USD	ProShares Ultra Semiconductors	BIK	SPDR S&P BRIC 40
PIN	PowerShares India	SCHA	Schwab U.S. Small-Cap
DOG	ProShares Short Dow 30	VDE	Energy VIPERS
IEV	iShares S&P Europe 350	SCHF	Schwab International Equity
VTV	Vanguard Value VIPERS	IAT	iShares DJ US Regional Banks
SDY	SPDR Dividend	EFG	iShares MSCI EAFE Growth
HAO	Claymore/AlphaShares China Sm Cp	MXI	iShares S&P Global Materials
IJS	iShares S&P Sm Cp 600/BARRA Va	DBV	PowerShares DB G10 Currency
CYB	WisdomTree Dreyfus Chinese Yuan	ADRE	BLDRS Emerging Market 50
RWM	ProShares Short Russell 2000	MVV	ProShares Ultra Mid Cap 400
AAXJ	iShares MSCI Asia ex Japan	PID	PowerShares Int' Dvdnd
IAI	iShares DJ US Broker-Dealers	VBK	Small Cap Growth VIPERS
BKF	iShares MSCI BRIC	WIP	SPDR DB Int Govt Inflation-Protected
PHO	PowerShares Water Resource	VAW	Materials VIPERS
PCY	PowerShares Emrgng Mrkts Svrgn Debt	FXY	CurrencyShares Japanese Yen
EZU	iShares EMU	PWV	PowerShares Dynamic Lg Cap Val
EWK	iShares Belgium	FXZ	First Trust Materials
IYG	iShares DJ US Financial Serv	EWL	iShares Switzerland
PSQ	ProShares Short QQQ	ROM	ProShares Ultra Technology
SSG	ProShares UltraShort Semi	DGS	WisdomTree Emrgng Mrkts Sm Cp Dvdnd
EZA	iShares S Africa Index	PPLT	ETFS Physical Platinum
ACWI	iShares MSCI ACWI	SIVR	ETFS Silver
EWQ	iShares France	FXO	First Trust Financials
XBI	SPDR Biotech	REW	ProShares UltraShort Tech
UDN	PowerShares DB US Dollar-Bear	VO	Mid Cap VIPERS
IJK	iShares S&P Md Cp 400/BARRA Gr	PEY	PowerShares High Yield
TUR	iShares MSCI Turkey Investable	GWX	SPDR S&P International SmCp
BWX	SPDR Barclays Intl Treasury Bond	VBR	Vanguard Small Cap Val VIPERS
DBO	PowerShares DB Oil	STPZ	PIMCO 1-5 Year US TIPS
PHYS	Sprott Physical Gold	GMF	SPDR S&P Emerging Asia Pacific
TFI	SPDR Barclays Municipal Bond	ACWX	iShares MSCI ACWI ex US
XES	SPDR Oil & Gas Equip & Service	FXD	First Trust Consumer Discr
IYE	iShares DJ US Energy	EWN	iShares Netherlands
VT	Vanguard Total World	DEM	WisdomTree Emerging Markets HY
MZZ	ProShares UltraShrt Md Cp 400	EWO	iShares Austria
IAU	iShares Comex Gold	IGF	iShares S&P Global Infrastructure
IJJ	iShares S&P Md Cp 400/BARRA Va	KCE	KBW Capital Mkts
CEW	WisdomTree Dreyfus Emerging Currency	MBB	iShares Barclays MBS Fixed-Rate
YCS	ProShares UltraShort Yen	BIV	Vanguard Intermed-Term Bond
RWX	SPDR DJ Wilshire Int Real Estate	PST	ProShares UltraShort Barclays 7-10 Yr
UGL	ProShares Ultra Gold	DBP	PowerShares DB Precious Metals
SCZ	iShares MSCI EAFE Small Cap	RSW	Rydex Inverse 2x S&P 500
SEA	Claymore/Delta Global Shipping	IGN	iShares Multimedia Networking
IEZ	iShares DJ US Oil Equip & Serv	EWI	iShares Italy
VGT	IT VIPERS	RSU	Rydex 2x S&P 500
IWC	iShares Russell Microcap	FDN	First Trust DJ Internet
EWD	iShares Sweden	SCHE	Schwab Emerging Markets
PIO	PowerShares Global Water	TAO	Claymore/AlphaShares China RE
ECH	iShares MSCI Chile	EUM	ProShares Short MSCI Emrgng Mrkts
XSD	SPDR Semiconductors	IYH	iShares DJ US Healthcare
CIU	iShares Barclays Intrm Crdt Bond	IOO	iShares S&P Global 100
THD	iShares MSCI Thailand Investable	CUT	Claymore/Clear Global Timber
EFV	iShares MSCI EAFE Value	VNM	Market Vectors Vietnam
GUR	SPDR S&P Emerging Europe	IHF	iShares DJ US Healthcare Prov
PXH	PowerShares FTSE RAFI Emrgng Mrkt	PWB	PowerShares Large Cap Growth
PALL	ETFS Physical Palladium	FBT	First Trust Amex Biotech
FXC	CurrencyShares Canadian Dollar	PHB	PowerShares Hgh Yld Corp Bond
TBF	ProShares Short 20+ Year Treasury	BZQ	ProShares UltraShort MSCI Brazil
CVY	Claymore/Zacks Yield Hog	GCC	GreenHaven Cont Commodity
SCHB	Schwab U.S. Broad Market	RPV	Rydex S&P 500 Va
VFH	Financial VIPERS	PBS	PowerShares Dyn Media
PSP	PowerShares Listed Private Eq	CGW	Claymore S&P Global Water

NEW OPTION TRADING CODES

Expanding equity, exchange traded fund (ETF), and derivative markets have mushroomed in recent years, creating problems for single letter strike price and expiration codes, underlying option symbols, and the entire option contract coding system. With the proliferation of Long-term Equity AnticiPation Securities (LEAPS®), flexible (FLEX) options contracts, and other non-standard options, the old three- to five-letter option coding convention has been rendered obsolete. Letters will no longer be used to indicate strike (exercise) prices and expiration dates.

To ensure we covered all the essential information as we distilled these sweeping changes onto one page, we consulted with two of our most trusted colleagues in this arena: options guru, Larry McMillan at *www.optionstrategist.com* and professional trader, John Person, our *Commodity Trader's Almanac* coauthor, at *www.nationalfutures.com*.

On May 14, 2010, the total overhaul of option trading codes was completed. This process began in July 2005 when the Options Clearing Corporation (OCC) put together an industry consortium to address the inherent and growing problem with option trading codes. Over the next several years, the Symbology Committee of broker dealers, exchanges, vendors, and the OCC developed the Options Symbology Initiative (OSI).

Options Symbology Initiative (OSI)

OSI was a comprehensive, industry-wide conversion to the new method of identifying exchange-listed options. New option trading codes are more transparent, easy to understand and can accommodate newer types of options. New option root symbols match underlying security symbols, eliminate the need for wrap, LEAP, and the plethora of other symbols created by the 5-letter code limitations, and reduce corporate action symbol conversions and back-office errors. For the most part, each security will have one root symbol instead of the myriad of root symbols the old system created. Thousands of symbols have been freed up, and all symbols have become much more intuitive.

The new coding method is robust though long, up to 21 characters: six characters for option symbols; two each for expiration year, month, and day; one for call or put ("C" or "P"), five characters for strike dollar amount, and 3 characters for strike decimal amount. Fractions have also been eliminated, and all options have been converted to 3 decimals. For example, the old symbol for the Microsoft May 2010 25 Call was MSQEE. It is now MSFT100522C00025000.

OLD OPTION CODES

Option Root Symbol	Expiration Date Code	Strike Price Code
XXX	X	X
3 Characters	1 Characters	1 Characters

NEW OPTION CODES

Symbol	Year	Month	Day	Call/Put (C/P)	Strike Dollar	Strike Decimal
XXXXXX	XX	XX	XX	X	XXXXX	XXX
6 Characters	2 Characters	2 Characters	2 Characters	1 Characters	5 Characters	3 Characters

In some instances, the option trading code could be as long as 24 characters. FLEX option symbols begin with a numeric value. Adjusted symbols will be appended with a numeric value as the last character of the symbol. But a few exceptions will remain. Non-standard symbols that do not equal the primary underlying security will consolidate to a unique root symbol. We need to be familiar with this new symbology that the OCC, Chicago Board Options Exchange (CBOE), and other exchanges use. But many data vendors, brokerage firms, and other data providers have made minor adjustments, creating their own version. However, in addition to the symbol, the full name of the option is usually displayed: MSFT May 2010 25.000 call (MSFT100522C00025000).

Details of the "old way" can be found on page 190 of the *2010 Stock Trader's Almanac*.

Sources: Larry McMillan, John Person, cboe.com, and theocc.com

G. M. LOEB'S "BATTLE PLAN" FOR INVESTMENT SURVIVAL

LIFE IS CHANGE: Nothing can ever be the same a minute from now as it was a minute ago. Everything you own is changing in price and value. You can find that last price of an active security on the stock ticker, but you cannot find the next price anywhere. The value of your money is changing. Even the value of your home is changing, though no one walks in front of it with a sandwich board consistently posting the changes.

RECOGNIZE CHANGE: Your basic objective should be to profit from change. The art of investing is being able to recognize change and to adjust investment goals accordingly.

WRITE THINGS DOWN: You will score more investment success and avoid more investment failures if you write things down. Very few investors have the drive and inclination to do this.

KEEP A CHECKLIST: If you aim to improve your investment results, get into the habit of keeping a checklist on every issue you consider buying. Before making a commitment, it will pay you to write down the answers to at least some of the basic questions—How much am I investing in this company? How much do I think I can make? How much do I have to risk? How long do I expect to take to reach my goal?

HAVE A SINGLE RULING REASON: Above all, writing things down is the best way to find "the ruling reason." When all is said and done, there is invariably a single reason that stands out above all others, why a particular security transaction can be expected to show a profit. All too often, many relatively unimportant statistics are allowed to obscure this single important point.

Any one of a dozen factors may be the point of a particular purchase or sale. It could be a technical reason—an increase in earnings or dividend not yet discounted in the market price—a change of management—a promising new product—an expected improvement in the market's valuation of earnings—or many others. But, in any given case, one of these factors will almost certainly be more important than all the rest put together.

CLOSING OUT A COMMITMENT: If you have a loss, the solution is automatic, provided you decide what to do at the time you buy. Otherwise, the question divides itself into two parts. Are we in a bull or bear market? Few of us really know until it is too late. For the sake of the record, if you think it is a bear market, just put that consideration first and sell as much as your conviction suggests and your nature allows.

If you think it is a bull market, or at least a market where some stocks move up, some mark time, and only a few decline, do not sell unless:

- ✓ You see a bear market ahead.
- ✓ You see trouble for a particular company in which you own shares.
- ✓ Time and circumstances have turned up a new and seemingly far better buy than the issue you like least in your list.
- ✓ Your shares stop going up and start going down.

A subsidiary question is, which stock to sell first? Two further observations may help:

- ✓ Do not sell solely because you think a stock is "overvalued."
- ✓ If you want to sell some of your stocks and not all, in most cases it is better to go against your emotional inclinations and sell first the issues with losses, small profits, or none at all, the weakest, the most disappointing, etc.

Mr. Loeb is the author of *The Battle for Investment Survival*, John Wiley & Sons.

G. M. LOEB'S INVESTMENT SURVIVAL CHECKLIST

OBJECTIVES AND RISKS

Security		Price	Shares	Date

"Ruling reason" for commitment	Amount of commitment $ _____
	% of my investment capital _____ %

Price objective	Est. time to achieve it	I will risk _____ points	Which would be $ _____

TECHNICAL POSITION

Price action of stock:

❏ Hitting new highs   ❏ In a trading range

❏ Pausing in an uptrend   ❏ Moving up from low ground

❏ Acting stronger than market   ❏ _____

Dow Jones Industrial Average

Trend of market

SELECTED YARDSTICKS

	Price Range		Earnings Per Share Actual or Projected	Price/Earnings Ratio Actual or Projected
	High	Low		
Current year				
Previous year				

Merger possibilities	Years for earnings to double in past
Comment on future	Years for market price to double in past

PERIODIC RE-CHECKS

Date	Stock Price	DJIA	Comment	Action taken, if any

COMPLETED TRANSACTIONS

Date closed	Period of time held	Profit or loss

Reason for profit or loss

192